D0048399

REFIGURING WOMAN

Refiguring Woman

*Perspectives on Gender and
the Italian Renaissance*

EDITED WITH AN INTRODUCTION BY
Marilyn Migiel and
Juliana Schiesari

Cornell University Press

ITHACA AND LONDON

Copyright © 1991 by Cornell University

All rights reserved. Except for brief quotations in a review, this book, or parts thereof, must not be reproduced in any form without permission in writing from the publisher. For information, address Cornell University Press, 124 Roberts Place, Ithaca, New York 14850.

First published 1991 by Cornell University Press.

International Standard Book Number 0-8014-2538-7 (cloth)
International Standard Book Number 0-8014-9771-X (paper)
Library of Congress Catalog Card Number 90-55736
Printed in the United States of America
Librarians: Library of Congress cataloging information
appears on the last page of the book.

⊗ The paper in this book meets the minimum requirements
of the American National Standard for Information Sciences—
Permanence of Paper for Printed Library Materials, ANSI Z39.48-1984.

CONTENTS

ACKNOWLEDGMENTS

This book grew out of a symposium held at Cornell University in April 1988. The Istituto Italiano di Cultura (New York) was the major sponsor of the symposium, and we welcome this chance to thank the Istituto in print for its very generous support. Many departments and programs at Cornell University were instrumental in bringing about the symposium, including the Department of Romance Studies, the Western Societies Program, the Society for the Humanities, the Dean of the College of Arts and Sciences, the Renaissance Colloquium, and the Women's Studies Program. In addition, the Dean of Arts and Sciences and the Department of French and Italian at Miami University were forthcoming with aid. We are most grateful to all of these institutions and offices both for their financial contributions and for their encouragement of our project.

We are happy to acknowledge the indirect role that the Mellon Foundation and the Cornell University Humanities Council played when they offered Juliana Schiesari a Mellon Fellowship in the Humanities which brought her to Cornell for 1989–90. This grant, which gave her the opportunity to work on her own book manuscript, permitted the two editors to be at the same institution during a crucial period in the editing of this book.

We acknowledge gratefully permission to print the revised English version of Elizabeth S. Cohen's "No Longer Virgins," which originally appeared in Italian as "La verginità perduta: Autorappresentazione di giovani donne nella Roma barocca," *Quaderni storici* 67:1 (1989): 169–91, and permission to print in Stephanie Jed's "Chastity on the Page" material that also appeared in her *Chaste Thinking: The Rape of Lucretia and the Birth of Humanism* (Bloomington: Indiana University Press, 1989).

Our most pleasurable task is to thank those colleagues who were especially important to this project at its various stages. Anita Grossvogel and William J. Kennedy were supportive presences throughout the symposium. We especially appreciated the contributions of Nelly Furman, who was the most intellectually energetic member of our symposium audience and offered many beneficial insights. Dolora Wojciehowski read a portion of the manuscript with her seminar "Did Women Have a Renaissance?" and sent us many valuable comments and observations. Albert Ascoli was a highly astute reader of the manuscript in its final stages and made especially constructive comments and queries. Winthrop Wetherbee's insightful comments brought us to define the project more clearly. Myra Best, Lauren Lee, Matthew Munich, Patrice Proulx, and Alan Smith provided research and editorial assistance as we were preparing the manuscript. Dianne Ferriss was a wonderfully patient and careful proofreader. Bernhard Kendler, our editor at Cornell University Press, has been supportive of the project throughout.

Finally, Barbara Spackman, Andrzej Warminski, and Georges Van den Abbeele have participated in countless conversations and debates in Ithaca, Slaterville Springs, Chicago, and Oxford, Ohio; and they have maintained a steady exchange of electronic mail with us. They have provided invaluable readings and suggestions; they have offered advice about the perils that awaited us; and their wit has kept us sane. Traces of their recommendations appear throughout this manuscript, and we therefore owe the greatest debt to them as our friends.

MARILYN MIGIEL AND JULIANA SCHIESARI

Ithaca, New York

REFIGURING WOMAN

Marilyn Migiel and Juliana Schiesari

Introduction

In recent years feminism has unmasked the patriarchal basis of Western culture and has challenged that culture to rethink its social hierarchies and to be sensitive to the role gender has played in their production. While numerous critical and historical studies of women's roles have appeared, little has been done to reconsider the figure of woman in what is all too readily understood as the bastion of humanist thought. This volume of essays reconsiders gender in the specific context of the Italian Renaissance.

This reassessment of the Renaissance reflects the profound changes that have taken place in the conceptions of the self and the conditions of social and cultural existence. Modern critical approaches such as Marxism, feminism, psychoanalysis, deconstruction, and neohistoricism have drawn our attention to problematic and divisive differences (of meaning, language, gender, race, class, and nationality) that have been ignored in the past. As a result, contemporary readers influenced by these discourses have become more attentive to the ways in which the selection and interpretation of texts have contributed to the formation of ideologies that have long resisted interrogation.

Once idealized and romanticized as a being whose multiple talents and capacity for transformation revealed his infinite freedom and power, "Renaissance man" is losing ground as contemporary studies in the humanities begin to question their own humanist roots and their investment in telling a story of man which is but a single possible representation of humanity. In the wake of critiques of idealist thought and its paradigms, the historical origin of selfhood and of social and political structures has become a field of critical investigation. A sense of the historical and sociocultural conditioning of the individual has

I

replaced earlier presuppositions about the self as a kind of timeless and ungendered essence. If the Renaissance once meant the flowering of great works by great men in the expression of a *Geistesgeschichte,* Marxism and feminism have taught us that individual freedom and self-expression were not available to all subjects at the time. And while the Renaissance once meant the advent of the "individual," feminism and psychoanalysis now require that we question how individuality has been predicated on an unspoken hierarchy of differences. Such theoretical and political discourses have recast our understanding of Renaissance culture and civilization in ways that are as irrevocable as they are provocative of further debate.[1]

Indeed, we are now more aware that the term *Renaissance,* as applied to various historical periods and cultural institutions between the mid-fourteenth and mid-seventeenth centuries, is a function of the romanticist idealism espoused by scholars such as Jules Michelet and Jacob Burckhardt in their monumental histories.[2] Many scholars now prefer the more neutral term *early modern,* but both remain in current usage.

---

[1]Peter Burke, *The Italian Renaissance: Culture and Society in Italy* (Princeton: Princeton University Press, 1986), reflects on the way in which our conception of the Renaissance has changed in this century, and even in the last quarter-century. *Literary Theory / Renaissance Texts,* ed. Patricia Parker and David Quint (Baltimore: Johns Hopkins University Press, 1986) includes a selection of essays written since 1975 which implicitly testify to the ideological changes in the conceptions of the individual, of history, and of humanist theoretical and pedagogical endeavors; Anthony Grafton and Lisa Jardine, *From Humanism to the Humanities* (Cambridge, Mass.: Harvard University Press, 1986), focus on the humanist program of education in order to demonstrate the consequences it has had for contemporary studies in the humanities.

Developments in Shakespearean criticism have been particularly instrumental in defining new directions in Renaissance studies. On this front, see especially *Shakespeare and the Question of Theory,* ed. Geoffrey Hartman and Patricia Parker (New York: Methuen, 1985); *Representing Shakespeare: New Psychoanalytic Essays,* ed. Murray Schwartz and Coppélia Kahn (Baltimore: Johns Hopkins University Press, 1980); Coppélia Kahn, *Man's Estate: Masculine Identity in Shakespeare* (Berkeley: University of California Press, 1981); Joel Fineman, *Shakespeare's Perjured Eye* (Berkeley: University of California Press, 1986). New-historicist studies of the Renaissance were inaugurated by Stephen Greenblatt, *Renaissance Self-Fashioning: From More to Shakespeare* (Chicago: University of Chicago Press, 1980); see also his more recent *Shakespearean Negotiations* (Berkeley: University of California Press, 1988). For a very insightful discussion of the ideological differences among Shakespearean critics, see Lynda E. Boose, "The Family in Shakespeare Studies; or—Studies in the Family of Shakespeareans; or—The Politics of Politics," *Renaissance Quarterly* 40:4 (Winter 1987): 707–42.

[2]See Jules Michelet, *Histoire de France au seizième siècle: Renaissance, réforme* (1855), ed. Robert Casanova, in *Oeuvres complètes,* ed. Paul Viallaneix (Paris: Flammarion, 1971–82); Jacob Burckhardt, *The Civilization of the Renaissance in Italy* (1860), trans. S. G. C. Middlemore (New York: Harper Torchbooks, 1958).

The uncertainty regarding the naming of this period is indicative of its privileged position in current historical reflections and our investment in questioning the boundaries and ideologies of the "Renaissance."[3]

Reading the Renaissance with a sensitivity to the exclusion of women's accomplishments leads to the overturning of a host of assumptions about that period, revealing the implicit and explicit misogyny of many Renaissance discursive and social practices.[4] The discovery of previously undisclosed archival material by and about women has forced a radical reconceptualization of the early modern world of women, whose realities were for so long suppressed or forgotten. In the field of Renaissance studies this tendency has expressed itself in publications on the *querelle des femmes,* on women's work and everyday life, and on the women who were humanists, writers, mystics, courtesans, and patrons of the arts; in addition, there have been innumerable studies of female characters in literary texts.[5]

This plethora of new information, in turn, demands more sophisticated modes of interpretation which are as cognizant of the social, cultural, and discursive construction of gender as they are aware of the oppressive conditions that buried that information in libraries and archives. Gender studies offer a locus from which to discern the historic complicities, compromises, and divergences between selfhood and artistic expression, between the rise of cultural institutions and the forces of patriarchy and early capitalism. We see in gender studies a promising terrain for the study of textual and political systems, precisely because woman typically occupies a conflicted position within systems that depend on difference for their articulation, and she is easily encoded as a displaced figure for the repressed contradictions within the system itself. Inquiry into gender representations shows how authoritative cultural

[3]Leah Marcus sets out the issues in her "Disestablishing the Renaissance (?): New Directions in Early Modern Studies," forthcoming in a publication tentatively entitled *Redrawing the Boundaries of Literary Study in English,* ed. Stephen Greenblatt and Giles Gunn (New York: MLA Publications, 1991). We thank Dolora Wojciehowski for bringing this article to our attention, and Leah Marcus for allowing us to read it in manuscript.

[4]Joan Kelly's article "Did Women Have a Renaissance?" in *Women, History, and Theory: The Essays of Joan Kelly* (Chicago: University of Chicago Press, 1984), pp. 19–50, is the main point of reference for studies that rethink "progressive" movements in history from the point of view of their effects on marginalized subjects.

[5]It is beyond the scope of this volume to reproduce or add systematically to the vast bibliography on these subjects, which would run to many pages. We refer the interested bibliographer to the information provided in *Rewriting the Renaissance: The Discourses of Sexual Difference in Early Modern Europe,* ed. Margaret W. Ferguson, Maureen Quilligan, and Nancy J. Vickers (Chicago: University of Chicago Press, 1986).

discourses rely on a structured elision of (gender) difference and continue to speak their muted (and gendered) secret. This perspective exposes the governing assumptions about gender roles; it reveals both the interstructuring relations between those roles and the degree to which gender identity is embedded in forms of authority (textual, sexual, familial, political). In the course of demystifying traditional models, it is then possible to rewrite those models and myths for women as well as for men, and to resist appropriation by potentially oppressive institutions.

Nevertheless, interest in gender has been more prominent in certain areas of study and disciplines than in others. As one considers the flurry of scholarly activity in gender studies and the Renaissance in recent years, one is bound also to notice Italy's still very marginal presence in this debate, which has come to be dominated above all by England. The reasons are undoubtedly political, institutional, and historical; they have to do not only with the development of Renaissance studies in the United States and with the development of Italian studies both in Italy and abroad, but also with the relation of Italian studies to current theoretical endeavors in the humanities. This volume, and the symposium that preceded it, is a response to the partial view of Italian discourse in current theoretical debates and to the evasion of those theoretical debates in Italian studies.[6]

In choosing the essays for this volume, we were not inspired by "nationalist" fervor; nor do we perceive the Renaissance as a privileged field of critical investigation. The Italian Renaissance raises theoretical and interpretive issues which are, however, different from those raised by other national literatures and cultures of the Renaissance. Consequently, the essays that follow, taken together, reveal some interesting points about the ideological bias of current "comparatist" investigations of gender in the Renaissance.[7] The excellent and influential *Rewriting the Renaissance: The Discourses of Sexual Difference in Early*

---

[6]Several Italian journals recognized this problem at about the same time that the symposium "Refiguring Woman" was being planned and have since published issues dealing with feminist and gender issues. See "Woman and Italy," *The Italianist* 7 (1987); "Women's Voices," *Italica* 65:4 (1988); and "Women's Voices in Italian Literature," *Annali d'italianistica* 7 (1989). As Rebecca West notes in her "'A voce piena': An Introduction to Women's Voices in Italian Literature," in *Annali d'italianistica* 7 (1989): 4–5, the issues published by *The Italianist* and *Italica* were the result of their editorial boards' response to contributors' submissions.

[7]We have in mind the volumes *Beyond Their Sex: Learned Women of the European Past*, ed. Patricia H. Labalme (New York: New York University Press, 1980), and *Women in the Middle Ages and the Renaissance: Literary and Historical Perspectives*, ed. Mary Beth

Modern Europe, edited by Margaret Ferguson, Maureen Quilligan, and Nancy Vickers, is particularly illuminating because the editors present a well-articulated theoretical position. There are at least two developments in addition to capitalism, they point out, which merit our attention as we study the social relations between the sexes in this period: "One is the emergence of those centrally administered nation-states to which we owe the existence of powerful female queens within the royal dynasties of Spain, France, and England; the other is the significant set of changes that occurred in the structure of the family and therefore in women's roles during this era" (pp. xvii–xviii).

But the essays in *Rewriting the Renaissance* focus primarily on English (and especially Elizabethan) matters.[8] The editors explain, "Because England was ruled so long and successfully by a female prince during a period when the relations between men and women at all levels of society were undergoing significant changes—many of which affected women adversely—that country offers a particularly rich field of inquiry for feminist scholars" (p. xx).[9]

Of course, could not the same argument be used to justify the study of any culture or society in which gender identity is (or is not) the subject of lively debate, is (or is not) in flux? And does not an overemphasis on the figure of the truly "powerful woman" (such as Elizabeth I, who wielded absolute power, including the power of life and death over her subjects) limit the study of gender?[10] Can we not also

Rose (Syracuse: Syracuse University Press, 1985), as well as Ferguson, Quilligan, and Vickers, *Rewriting the Renaissance,* which we discuss in this essay.

[8]A relatively small number of essays discuss French, Italian, and German Renaissance materials, but none of them mentions Spain. For an analysis of the way in which *Rewriting the Renaissance* appears to map out a polarized relation with Italian Petrarchism and humanism in particular, see Marilyn Migiel, "Gender Studies and the Italian Renaissance," forthcoming in *Forum Italicum,* as the proceedings of the symposium "Interpreting the Italian Renaissance: Twentieth-Century Perspectives," SUNY–Stony Brook, March 1–3, 1990.

[9]Perceiving that this explanation will not be sufficient, they add somewhat later, "If the present volume contains what seems a disproportionate number of essays about English court culture, this may be a sign of the crucial twist given to the ideology of gender in both the Elizabethan and the Jacobean eras by Elizabeth's problematic presence on the throne. For this reason, and also because England underwent a uniquely swift transition from absolutist state to the limited monarchy ushered in by the bourgeois revolution of the mid-seventeenth century, the moment of England's initial imperial expansion is of special interest to scholars who are beginning to look at Renaissance culture from an interdisciplinary, feminist perspective" (p. xx).

[10]In other words, although in the Italian Renaissance, "the exercise of political power by women was far more rare than under feudalism," as Joan Kelly observed in "Did Women Have a Renaissance?" p. 31, we should not succumb to excessive fascination

profitably study gender in all discourses in which sexual and gender difference is elaborated or elided? Reappropriating the perspective offered by a Renaissance Italian culture and society can change our perception of gender studies.

In this book, therefore, what is asked first of all is how the terms that structure the discourse about woman (and thus the discourse about identity and difference) condition "truth" as it has been found in the Western tradition.

In his *Civilization of the Renaissance in Italy* (1860), Jacob Burckhardt could still minimize the extent of gender difference with such a sweeping statement as: "To understand the higher forms of social intercourse at this period we must keep before our minds the fact that women stood on a footing of perfect equality with men."[11] Barely masked inequalities emerge shortly thereafter, however, as Burckhardt shows that for him, as for traditional humanism, the mirror of perfection reflects the male ideal: "One [woman] indeed, Vittoria Colonna, may be called immortal. If any proof were needed of the assertion made above, it would be found in the *manly* tone of [her] poetry."[12] The category of "woman" is marked as noteworthy when woman removes all signs of her sex and best approximates "man"; the highest praise a woman could receive would be to pass unnoticed for a man—unnoticed, that is, were it not for telltale signs. Burckhardt notes of Colonna that "we should not hesitate to attribute [her poetry] to male authors, if we had not clear external evidence to prove the contrary."[13]

Citations of Burckhardt seem to be de rigueur in revisionist interpretations of the Renaissance, for he is a principal spokesman for the

---

with those forms of power (feudal, absolutist, and monarchical) that can give a small group of aristocratic women great prominence.

For a forceful critique of such a fascination with the mythology of Renaissance self-fashioning, see Marguerite Waller, "Academic Tootsie: The Denial of Difference and the Difference It Makes," *diacritics* 17:1 (Spring 1987): 2–20. In the course of an informed commentary on the status of gender in Shakespearean studies, Lynda E. Boose also criticizes the new historicists' erasure of gender difference and their fascination with the absolutist court; see "The Family in Shakespeare Studies," esp. pp. 728–32; Boose's argument relies in part on insights provided by Walter Cohen, "Political Criticism of Shakespeare," in *Shakespeare Reproduced: The Text in History and Ideology,* ed. Jean E. Howard and Marion F. O'Connor (New York: Methuen, 1987), pp. 18–46.

[11]Burckhardt, *The Civilization of the Renaissance in Italy,* 2:389.
[12]Ibid., 2:390; emphasis added.
[13]Ibid., 2:390.

once canonical dismissal of gender difference.[14] The use of these "demystifying" citations is part of our decision in this volume to concentrate on *textual*—and therefore epistemological and hermeneutic—issues.

The three essays in Part I, "The Hermeneutics of Gender," address just these issues. Assuming a metacritical perspective, the essays call attention to the production of and commentary on texts as the locus of well-entrenched ideologies that use the figure of woman (enchantress or hag, chaste or vulgar, pure or impure) to construct a hermeneutic model that opposes essence and appearance, pure origin and corrupted facsimile. At the same time, of course, those ideologies must maintain that truth is ungendered, lest it be possible to perceive and undo the logic in which they are rooted.

In *"Inter musam et ursam moritur:* Folengo and the Gaping 'Other' Mouth," Barbara Spackman calls our attention to the grotesque female body and the theme of female sexuality in macaronic poetry of the Italian Renaissance, notably Tifi Odasi's *Macaronea* and Teofilo Folengo's *Baldus.* Noting that scholars have preferred to use philological and anthropological investigation in order to avoid the theme of female sexuality, Spackman focuses on the *bocca sdentata* (the gaping, toothless mouth) as the displacement upwards of the *vagina dentata.* In a critique of the topos of the enchantress turned toothless hag, a topos central to the hermeneutics that would find essence beneath appearance, Spackman presents a deconstructionist argument: to side either with the enchantress (as do those who turn away from the "vulgar matter" of female sexuality in these texts) or with the hag (like others who would take the female grotesque body as a subversive moment) is to remain within that hermeneutic model. Instead, Spackman focuses on the figure of woman in the theories of literary and biological origin in Folengo's *Baldus.* There, in the fate of Leonardus (who is killed by "conjugal bears") and of the poet himself (who is almost—but not

[14]The polemic involving Burckhardt has served to mark scholars' particular critical approach and field of inquiry. See, for example, *The Paradise of Women: Writings by Englishwomen of the Renaissance,* ed. Betty Travitsky (Westport, Conn.: Greenwood Press, 1981). The introduction to Ferguson, Quilligan, and Vickers, *Rewriting the Renaissance,* puts Burckhardt's statement into question by calling on Arcangela Tarabotti, a seventeenth-century Venetian nun, to testify to the continued inequalities of social relations between the sexes; this particular strategy is crucial to the editors' continued emphasis on the power and powerlessness of real women (pp. xv–xvi). At the beginning of "In Praise of Virtuous Women?: For a Genealogy of Gender Morals in Renaissance Italy," *Annali d'italianistica* 7 (1989): 68–69, Juliana Schiesari discusses Burckhardt's reliance on a male standard of *virtù.*

quite—condemned to "toothlessness"), we see the conflicted result of the attempt to deny that truth is gendered. Spackman makes explicit the claim crucial to this volume: that to refigure woman is tantamount to refiguring truth.

Elena Ciletti, in "Patriarchal Ideology in the Renaissance Iconography of Judith," focuses on a figure whose image was reproduced countless times in the Renaissance. Through a historical analysis of biblical, patristic, and psychoanalytic texts, as well as an examination of the medieval and Renaissance images of Judith, Ciletti demonstrates how the fathers of culture "have periodically imposed on her image a complex overlay of 'correcting' distortions." Ciletti's historicization of the debate about Judith is crucial in that, by showing how artists and interpreters over the centuries have refigured Judith in order to reproduce the patriarchal categories of sexual restraint and sexual license, this analysis forces us as readers to reflect on the particular interpretive stance a twentieth-century audience assumes before Judith, making us aware of the specular function that the figure of Judith has had for various cultures.

Claudia Lazzaro's essay, "The Visual Language of Gender in Sixteenth-Century Garden Sculpture," explores the gendering of visual signs and their significance for understanding gender in the natural world. Modern scholarship, in presenting the garden as the result of man's domination of nature, offers only a partial perspective. This has encouraged an inability to see the way in which the garden was the representational site not only of art but also of nature as well as a "third nature" resulting from their combination. The relief at Fontana Papacqua (which has resisted definitive interpretation) provides an illuminating example of the necessity of recognizing how representations of nature differ from those of human culture. One can perceive and understand both sets of conventions only if one is willing to accept that man is not the measure of all things.

In "Chastity on the Page: A Feminist Use of Paleography," Stephanie Jed seeks to exhume certain deftly interred assumptions and contradictions in humanist thought. Jed draws attention to the logic of sexual violence and sexual restraints in Coluccio Salutati's *Declamatio Lucretiae,* a dialogue in which the rape of the Roman matron Lucretia is presented as the necessary prologue to republican freedom. By means of a materialist analysis of the manuscript reproduction of the dialogue and the cultural debates about scribal practices in humanist fifteenth-century Italy, she demonstrates that the categories used to describe graphic and editorial practices are gendered, and she asserts that if one were able to change the categories adopted to describe the material production of cultural discourses, one would also succeed in interrupting the logic of sexual violence that those discourses transmit. In order to expose the gendered and historical conditions that give rise to texts, feminist scholars must appropriate paleography for their own ends. Jed's essay demonstrates that earlier ways of understanding humanism (as well as liberty, virtue, chastity, and so on) represent only part of the picture, and that other aspects come to be included in the field of vision only because of the efforts of feminist scholars and theorists of gender who study humanism.

What directions do we take in speaking about women as historical subjects and agents? What relation is there between gender ideology and praxis? How do women internalize—how do they resist—gender roles? How does ideology mask the existence of the oppression of women? Such questions are addressed in Part II, "The Political Economy of Gender."

Three essays—Stanley Chojnacki's on "'The Most Serious Duty': Motherhood, Gender, and Patrician Culture in Renaissance Venice," Sharon Strocchia's "Funerals and the Politics of Gender in Early Renaissance Florence," and Elizabeth Cohen's "No Longer Virgins: Self-Presentation by Young Women in Late Renaissance Rome"—are particularly attentive to the study of gender within textual and social contexts. As they examine the shifting definitions and politics of gender roles in the Renaissance, these authors turn to archival evidence in order to judge the relation between societal and cultural norms governing gender on the one hand, and the gender identities of individual men and women on the other.

Chojnacki, examining evidence from patrician families in republican Venice, is able to put into perspective the more pessimistic view of the role of mothers in socioeconomic life.[15] He argues that married women, "owing to their distinctive placement overlapping two lineages and families . . . had greater flexibility in their family and kinship orientation than did men." In providing for their children in their wills,

---

[15]For a well-known example of this bleak view, see Christiane Klapisch-Zuber, *Women, Family, and Ritual in Renaissance Italy*, trans. Lydia G. Cochrane (Chicago: University of Chicago Press, 1985), esp. chap. 5, "The 'Cruel Mother': Maternity, Widowhood, and Dowry in Florence in the Fourteenth and Fifteenth Centuries," and chap. 10, "The Griselda Complex: Dowry and Marriage Gifts in the Quattrocento." In his foreword to the English translation, David Herlihy is careful to point out that we should not exaggerate Klapisch-Zuber's conclusions by assuming that the socioeconomic situation of these Tuscan women was the case in general.

mothers were able to work either with or against the wishes of fathers, with the effect of allowing a broader range of gender identities for their children. Chojnacki carefully assesses the modifications in male and female gender identities, as well as in patrilinear and bilateral kinship structures, which were brought about through the direct and indirect actions of patrician mothers.

Strocchia analyzes how funerary practices in Florence in the fourteenth and fifteenth centuries served to define gender roles. She argues that the rise of civic humanism brought with it new conventions in funerary practices, such as orations, consolatory letters, and a variety of models for the public expression of grief and mourning; these new practices intersected with the larger political changes in the structure of the Florentine oligarchy. Such innovations delineated a more marked gender difference in funerary rituals than had previously existed, and Strocchia notes that "the stylistic twists in these elite funerals positioned a select group of men more visibly in a context of authority, while the trappings of wealth adorning affluent women's funerals isolated them in a context of goods and property far removed from esteemed civic affairs."

Cohen studies the politics of identity and self-presentation in the court testimonies of young Roman women who had been deflowered prematurely and illicitly. She examines how these nonelite women sought some measure of self-determination in their rhetorical self-assertions, even within a social and cultural system that defined the acceptable forms of sexual expression, and within a judicial system that tended to make each young woman tell the same conventional tale.

Mobilizing a Marxian theoretical framework in "Economy, Woman, and Renaissance Discourse," Carla Freccero most forcefully expresses the concern that historical investigation is politically interested, especially when it begs the question of systemic oppression. Her response to the discussions of women's empowerment within the domestic sphere is to explore the gendering of economics and the economics of gender. According to Freccero, woman is a contradiction within the capitalist system on two points: (1) if woman is not "made," how can she be "owned"? and (2) does woman belong to someone, or is she exchangeable? Arguing that the entrenchment in patriarchy is most clearly delineated in writings on education and the family, Freccero shows that the renewed interest in writing about domestic life was a sign that patriarchal forces needed to redefine the limits of propriety, especially in the social configuration of urban Italy. Her analysis of the ideology of Leon Battista Alberti's *Della famiglia* (*On the Family*) depends on revealing how the text smooths over the way in which such mutually exclusive possibilities exist simultaneously within patriarchal capitalism. For Freccero, that hidden ideology informs the relation between political economy and woman in our own time as well as in the Renaissance. She calls on readers to consider their own political investment in a revisionist history that makes women "visible."

The final group of essays, Part III, "Woman and the Canon," focuses on literary texts that have been marginalized in scholarly discourse. Since feminist discourse so directly calls into question the canon of great works by great men, it has easily been identified as a prime adversary by advocates of the canon. The attacks launched against those who question the canon are frequently uninformed, however, and rely on a rather simplistic notion of what would be substituted for the "great books" under a different principle of selection. By proposing ways to interpret marginalized works as something other than a flawed figure of perfection, the four essays show us that the study of non-canonical writings is important not only because it helps us to understand the criteria by which certain cultural discourses and not others have come to be considered legitimate, even accepted as dominant, but also because it argues the changeability of the canon by revealing the historical mechanism of its construction through exclusion and de-valuation. The canon is not the *legacy* of the past but rather the present's *construction* of the past. As such, the canon can only be—and must be—continually redefined.

Marilyn Migiel addresses the question of how to read a "minor" work sometimes included in a tradition of humanist philosophical de-bate. In "The Dignity of Man: A Feminist Perspective," Migiel argues in favor of reading Giovan Battista Gelli's *Circe* as an ironic text. In its staging of dialogues among Ulysses, Circe, and a group of Ulysses' companions deciding between lives as animals or humans, this work makes clear the underlying ideological assumptions and implications of a certain position in the debate on the purpose and conditions of human life. Rather than being a marginal addition to the grand debate on the dignity of man, *La Circe* should be read as a work that shows how the valorization of difference (specifically sexual difference and the division of labor) is at the heart of the division between "high" and "low" cultural forms. The previously unperceived ironies of this text should make us ask how many other ironic discourses have also fallen on deaf ears.

Situating her "Gendering of Melancholia: Torquato Tasso and Isa-bella di Morra" in response to Stephen Greenblatt's dismissal of psychoanalysis from the field of Renaissance studies, Juliana Schiesari argues the pertinence of the psychoanalytic approach to the reading of premodern texts. Her historicization of a psychoanalytic category (the neurosis of melancholy) serves to reveal the gendered values that underpin its representation and therefore participates in a feminist revision of psychoanalysis from within the field of psychoanalysis itself. In exploring how melancholia appears as a cultural form for a privileged and legitimated male subjectivity, Schiesari compares two sixteenth-century autobiographical *canzoni* in which a poet mourns a loss: one by Torquato Tasso, melancholic par excellence, and the other by Isabella di Morra, an author who, until she was rediscovered by Benedetto Croce in 1929, had been lost to the reading public. The analysis of the poems shows how the male melancholic is able to capitalize on his loss and turn it into a cultural gain. By contrast, Isabella di Morra, in mourning the loss of a community in which she might participate as well as the loss her family members experience, provides us with another model for the subject's eros: one whose sense of intersubjectivity resists a narcissistic eros dependent on the negation of others. The essay poses pressing questions about the relation between the forms of aesthetic expression so highly valued by Western culture and the recognition of disempowered historical subjects.

Ann Rosalind Jones, in "New Songs for the Swallow: Ovid's Philomela in Tullia d'Aragona and Gaspara Stampa," discusses the ways in which male and female poets of the Italian Renaissance necessarily assumed a different relation to a fundamental source of poetic images, Ovid's *Metamorphoses*. Women poets had no female model for their poetic activity, but they did have Ovid's terrifying tales of women deprived of speech (Echo and Philomela). In a way that is somewhat reminiscent of the investigation of women's empowerment in Part II of this volume, Jones analyzes how women poets were able to turn Ovid's images of silenced female victims to their own advantage by assuming a less defensive attitude toward them. Aware of premodern and modern readings of the myths of Echo and Philomela, Jones situates her work in the context of modern feminists' search for myths that will permit political and social transformations.

This book draws on the perspectives of scholars who work within and across established disciplines and critical approaches. Hence, the topics treated herein have been determined not only by the authors' scholarly disciplines (literature, history, art history) but also by their theoretical orientations (psychoanalytic, Marxist, deconstructive, rhetorical, iconographic) and by their differing applications of the category of gender. Interdisciplinary study involves the crossing over of methodological boundaries *within* a discipline as well as the reconceptualization of relations among disciplines. In keeping with the aim of encouraging diverse, even conflicting critical perspectives, we have selected essays representative of the most provocative currents of thought in gender studies and the Italian Renaissance today.

This renewed attention to Renaissance Italian culture and society allows a somewhat different configuration of questions about gender to appear. Because the early Italian literary and philosophical tradition is much more concretely tied to the hermeneutics of gender than are other national traditions, Italy foregrounds the construction of the figure of woman in discursive practices and reaffirms that the figure is always a *textual* construct, a fact that may be overlooked in the empirical study of women.[16] Needless to say, this use of the term *textual* by no means excludes the visual text, nor does it privilege the literary over the historical. By entitling this volume *Refiguring Woman*—not *Women*—we aim to expand the analysis of gender beyond the empirical study of women. Women authors, women characters, and women as historical subjects have often been the primary focus of feminist and gender studies. While such research performs the necessary task of making available writings by and about women that have been suppressed, it also runs the risk of isolating women's studies in a ghettoized terrain that its opponents can conveniently disregard. Such archival research may also encourage an essentialist view of woman, which all too easily neglects the ways in which that view of woman is itself a socially and ideologically constructed figure.[17] Rewriting the ideal of (Renaissance) man so that it includes women should not mean reconstituting the figure of woman as the new object of traditional empirical and archeological scholarship. The figure of woman must be displaced—refigured—if empirical research on women is not to remain tributary to the paradigms and procedures of a patriarchal academy. The increasing acceptance of gender studies within the institution has been marked by the proliferation of conferences, lectures, and scholarly publications; but a radical view of gender studies can never

---

[16]Migiel advances this argument in "Gender Studies and the Italian Renaissance."

[17]Teresa de Lauretis has succinctly distinguished between the terms *woman* and *women*. See her *Alice doesn't: Feminism, Semiotics, Cinema* (Bloomington: Indiana University Press, 1984), p. 5: "By 'woman' I mean a fictional construct, a distillate from diverse but congruent discourses dominant in Western cultures. . . . By *women*, on the other hand, I will mean the real historical beings who cannot as yet be defined outside of those discursive formations, but whose material existence is nonetheless certain."

make of them something that fits neatly into mainstream, traditional modes of interpretation. Thus, while many of the essays in this volume continue the important work of analyzing the historical and social situation of Renaissance women, of explicating texts by women writers, and of deconstructing the role of female characters in male literary and pictorial representations, other essays, or parts of the same essays, seek to discuss and dislodge that "other" of Renaissance man, Renaissance woman, whose implicit *figura* subtends the very construction and allocation of gender roles in the early modern period.

Italy offers an interesting locus from which to discern how women responded to patriarchal dominance. A male-dominated society and culture determined the role of woman in both public and private domains; the powerful elite of the Italian Renaissance institutionalized these discourses about woman, the influences of which were felt throughout Europe. Some women in Italy accepted, and lived, with these norms; others resisted and reinterpreted the boundaries that their society and culture set for them. The essays of Part II, "The Political Economy of Gender," exhort us to refine the dialogue between literary critics and historians (particularly social historians) in order to bridge the gap between the study of gender relations in the past and contemporary resistance to oppressive ideologies.

Italian culture is crucial to the formation of the Renaissance canon of great works; and not enough has been done to study canon formation in Italy. This may be because the Petrarchan and humanist traditions loom so large, and because so many Renaissance Italian women writers chose to remain within these traditions. The three essays of Part III, "Woman and the Canon," question humanism and the Italian lyric tradition by examining their discursive strategies. What one discovers in the process of reading canonical and noncanonical authors together is not, as some supporters of the traditional canon might fear, that the canon should be abandoned, but that it cannot be read without an acute awareness of how it was formed.

Finally, Italy foregrounds (as some other much more centralized nation-states do not) how complex and unstable the question of gender is. Consider, for example, that Italy did not consolidate its existence as a nation-state until the decade after Burckhardt wrote his history of the culture of the Italian Renaissance. Any study of Renaissance Italy inevitably finds itself situated within the particularity of the city, court, or region. The culture of the Italic peninsula is not that of a nation-state: it is made up of the great epics of Ferrara, the philosophical schools of Padua, the women's poetry of Venice, the ducal palace of Mantua, the historical and political thought of Florence, and so forth. The diversity of Renaissance city-states within Italy does not allow them to be readily subsumed under the common measure of global categories. Italy—and in particular Renaissance Italy—resists the generalization of its culture into social, discursive, and aesthetic paradigms. Resistance to the total-izing view is of prime importance in confronting the complexity of gender relations.

Crucial to the pursuit of gender criticism and feminist criticism as we envision them is the critical practice of a double reading and a double writing. As pioneered by Joan Kelly-Gadol's concept of the "double vision,"[18] this practice entails reading the situation of woman from both inside and outside the patriarchal conventions that first engendered that situation. It should account for the voices that are silent as well as those that are heard; it should gauge the way in which social and discursive practices both exclude and empower; it is attentive to women's attempts at self-empowerment as well as to those social and discursive practices that have excluded women, or, at best, defined woman through a one-sided perspective. By reexamining the polariza-tions that have served to structure much of Renaissance discourse in the past and to define it unilaterally ("high" versus "low" discourse, cul-ture versus nature, great art versus nonart, power and strength versus virtue and beauty, masculine versus feminine), a double-visioned prac-tice does more than reverse the opposed terms; it requires a fundamen-tal dislodging of the opposition as such, which relinquishes valuing one term against another and instead promotes a questioning of the entire system of terms.[19] By acknowledging the structuring role of contradictions and conflicts, it refuses to precipitate interpretive clo-sure. A double reading and a double writing thus aim to maintain a perpetual critique that keeps relocating the site in which analysis takes place. In other words, resistance to male appropriation ought to arise not from peremptory dismissal, or from rewritings that remain merely a negative, reverse image of phallocentrism, but rather from a ceaseless displacement of patriarchy's forms, conventions, discourses, and prac-tices. The blind credence that is granted to certain forms of authority relies primarily on the refusal to read critically, and it is to be hoped that such credence can be impugned, at least in part, by *Refiguring Woman*.

[18]Kelly, "The Doubled Vision of Feminist Theory," in *Women, History, and Theory*, pp. 51–64.

[19]Joan Wallach Scott, in the introduction to her *Gender and the Politics of History* (New York: Columbia University Press, 1988), outlines some of the implications that de-construction has for the work of feminist historians.

I

THE HERMENEUTICS
OF GENDER

Barbara Spackman

Inter musam et ursam moritur:
Folengo and the Gaping "Other" Mouth

Although it is a commonplace that macaronic poetry shows the "underside" of the Renaissance, criticism of these texts has for the most part focused on the (certainly valuable) tasks of solving lexical puzzles, investigating the anthropological origins of certain culinary tidbits, and analyzing the highly sophisticated relation between the vulgate, Latin, and dialect.[1] These texts are about the *volgare* in more than the lin-

---

[1]Macaronic is a hybrid language that combines elements from classical Latin and Italian, predominantly dialects of the regions of Padua, Mantua, and Cremona. Its morphology remains Latin while its lexical and syntactic structures are derived from dialect; hence dialect and Italian stems are declined and conjugated as though they were Latin, and inserted into classical hexameters. Macaronic is thus to be distinguished from *mescidanza*, in which the vulgate is inserted into a Latin context (or vice versa) without altering the structure of either language. For linguistic analyses of macaronic, see Ugo Paoli, *Il latino maccheronico* (Florence: Le Monnier, 1959); Ivano Paccagnella, "Mescidanza e macaronismo: Dall'ibridismo delle prediche all'interferenza delle macaronee," in *Giornale storico della letteratura italiana* 150 (1973): 363–81; and Paccagnella, *Le macaronee padovane: Tradizione e lingua* (Padua: Antenore, 1979). Luigi Messedaglia's classic *Vita e costume della rinascenza in Merlin Cocai*, ed. Eugenio and Myriam Billanovich (Padua: Antenore, 1973), provides valuable anthropological and sociolinguistic information.

The texts to which I refer are Tifi Odasi's *Macaronea*, dated approximately 1490, and Teofilo Folengo's *Baldus*, an epic romance that saw four editions, beginning with the Paganini edition in 1517, continuing with the Toscolana edition of 1521 and the Cipadense edition of 1539, and ending with the posthumous Vigaso Cocaio edition of 1552. Unless otherwise noted, all quotations from *Baldus* are taken from Carlo Cordié, ed., *Folengo, Aretino, Doni: Opere di Teofilo Folengo* (Milan: Ricciardi, 1977). Cordié's edition provides a not always accurate Italian translation, and does not reprint the entire *Baldus*, which can be found in *Le maccheronee*, ed. Alessandro Luzio (Bari: Laterza, 1927–28) and in Teofilo Folengo, *Baldus*, ed. Emilio Faccioli (Turin: Einaudi, 1989). All translations are my own.

guistic sense, however; and while recent studies have examined one of these senses in focusing on the "realistic" representation of peasant life in macaronic poetry, they have left untouched what is perhaps most "vulgar."[2] Philology has thus served as a sort of prophylaxis, protecting critics from the "cunctivorans aperta vorago" ("the all-devouring open gorge" [*Il Baldus* 16.531]): the theme of female sexuality, central to pre-Folenghian macaronic texts, in which the muse is whore and the grotesque body female. Here the Bakhtinian-Rabelaisian "gaping mouth" is not that of Pantagruel but rather the gaping "other" mouth, the "potifarum potissima pota potaza" of Tifi Odasi's "massara dello speziale" (apothecary's wife):

> In mediis gambis apud foramina culi,
> quem tu magnificum poteris iurare busazum,
> ingens apparet variisque meatibus antrum
> extraque pendentes rubei marzique figati,
> nomine quo proprio vocatur potaza
> et circumcirca silvae longique pillazi.
> Dicite vos, nimphae, totum que cernitis orbem,
> que subter terram facitis ubicumque viazos,
> tu quoque, speluncas intrans, Neptune, per omnes,
> illi ego quam similem possim conferre cavernam:
> illic cum velis possent natare galiae,
> illic continuae cimices fecere niarum,
> hic gambareli, pulices habitantque peochi,
> et quas producit piatolas locis ille malignus,
> non sunt granceolis magnis, mihi crede, minores.
> Hinc fetor innumerus, hinc illa opaca mephitis
> exalat nasis multum fugienda fetorque.
> Multaque pretereo, quod si omnia dicere vellem
> possem de carta totam vacuare Bataiam.
> At cum purpureus venit dux ille Ferare
> nec panesellos nec tunc fruat ista fazollos:
> omnia per cossas, gambas pedesque colantur;
> sanguinis illius factum cum crusta ruborem,
> iam gambe et cossae videntur gambara cocta.

[2]See Luigi Messedaglia's "Aspetti della realtà storica in Merlin Cocai," in *Vita e costume della rinascenza;* Ettore Bonora, "Folengo e il mondo contadino," in *Retorica e invenzione: Studi sulla letteratura italiana del Rinascimento* (Milan: Rizzoli, 1970); Anna Fontes, "Mantoue et Cipada dans les quatres rédactions du *Baldus* de Teofilo Folengo," in *Ville et campagne dans la littérature italienne de la Renaissance,* vol. 1, *Le paysan travesti,* ed. André Rochon (Paris: Université de la Sorbonne Nouvelle, 1976); Giuseppe Tonna, "Il mondo contadino nel *Baldus:* Ideologia e struttura," in *Folengo e dintorni,* ed. Pietro Gibellini (Brescia: Grafo, 1980).

Semper habet ungues multo de sanguine plenas
cum quibus et cenam facit et disnare Cusino.[3]

[Between the legs near the aperture of the ass, which you will swear is a
great nasty hole, there appears an enormous cave with various openings
which, with red and repulsive livers hanging out and surrounded by
forests of long hairs, is everywhere called the *potaza*. Tell, you nymphs
who see the entire globe and journey everywhere beneath the earth, and
you, Neptune, who enter all the caves, I can compare it to a cavern: there
galleons with sails can swim, there bedbugs are always nesting, here live
crayfish and lice and fleas, and the crab lice that this malignant place
produces are not smaller than large crabs, believe me. Here there is
immense stench, here mephitic shadows exhale much stink to make the
nose flee. I omit many things, for if I wished to recount all, I would
empty the city of Battaglia of all its paper. And when that purple Duke of
Ferrara comes, this one uses neither rags nor hankies: it all flows down
the thighs and legs and feet. Her blood makes a red crust so her legs and
thighs look like cooked lobsters: her fingernails, with which she makes
supper and feeds Cusinus, are always full of lots of blood.]

Descriptions such as this are to be counted among the sources—if not
the glosses—of the Bakhtinian-Rabelaisian "gaping mouth," for macaronic texts, and Folengo's *Baldus* in particular, are among the acknowledged sources of *Gargantua et Pantagruel*. One wishes, however,
that Bakhtin had taken Rabelais's Italian sources more seriously, for
he might have discovered that the gaping, devouring mouth was already the product of an inversion and of a displacement upwards of the
"female mouth."[4] The grotesque body he describes as an ungendered—that is to say, male—body, equipped with phallus, anus, and
mouth, would then be grotesque precisely because it is already a
hybrid: a male body marked by a displaced female "mouth."[5] But
Bakhtin hastily dismisses the macaronic sources and, as several studies

[3]Tifi Odasi, *Macaronea* 523–48. The edition used is Paccagnella, *Le macaronee padovane*
pp. 114–33. There is, to my knowledge, no published English translation of Tifi's
work; the translation herein is mine.

[4]"A certain influence of Folengo on Rabelais cannot be denied, but it concerns
superficial elements and, generally speaking, is not essential." See Mikhail Bakhtin,
Rabelais and His World, trans. Hélène Iswolsky (Cambridge, Mass.: MIT Press, 1965), p.
299.

[5]Peter Stallybrass notes the "'ungendered'—i.e. implicitly male—body." See his
"Patriarchal Territories: The Body Enclosed," in *Rewriting the Renaissance: The Dis-
courses of Sexual Difference in Early Modern Europe*, ed. Margaret W. Ferguson, Maureen
Quilligan, and Nancy J. Vickers (Chicago: University of Chicago Press, 1986), p. 125.

have pointed out, has little to say about the female grotesque.[6] I would like to suggest here that the macaronic tradition has much to say both about the female grotesque and the ways in which it may or may not be subversive, and (to put it in Rabelaisian form) about "How Pantagruel Came to Have a Gaping Mouth."

The grotesque female body in Tifi Odasi is not a product of an inversion, not a "woman on top," but rather a bleeding, vermin-infested "pota potaza." This grotesque is not an isolated occurrence, nor does it appear only in the satirical "literature of the underside"; it belongs to the genealogy of the topos of the enchantress-turned-hag, a topos that opposes the beautiful enchantress (woman as lie) to the ugly, toothless old hag hidden beneath her artifice (woman as truth). From Dante's "femmina balba" in *Purgatorio* 19, to Ariosto's Alcina and Machiavelli's "lavandaia" in his letter to Luigi Guicciardini, this topos effects a transfer through displacement: the *bocca sdentata* of the hag stands for the "other mouth," the *vagina dentata*.[7] Indeed, this particular female grotesque stands as the hermeneutic figure par excellence, for it would reveal truth beneath falsehood, plain speech beneath cosmetic rhetoric, essence beneath appearance. As a figure of truth, the toothless mouth and the stench it exhales are so much a part of the Western tradition that Nietzsche must overturn such a figure in the preface to *The Gay Science* is order to critique the hermeneutic model that finds essence beneath

---

[6]Indeed, certain studies have suggested that the grotesque female body, the unruly woman or the "woman on top," might lead us out of simple *inversions* (which can always be reinverted) to true *subversion*. While in certain texts and contexts this does seem to be so (Stallybrass's essay on Othello and the "body enclosed" is a convincing case in point), the macaronic tradition presents a rather different configuration. See Stallybrass, "Patriarchal Territories," pp. 123–42; Peter Stallybrass and Allon White, *The Politics and Poetics of Transgression* (Ithaca: Cornell University Press, 1986); Mary Russo, "Female Grotesques: Carnival and Theory," in *Feminist Studies / Critical Studies,* ed. Teresa de Lauretis (Bloomington: Indiana University Press, 1986), pp. 213–29; and Natalie Zemon Davis, "Women on Top," in *Society and Culture in Early Modern France* (Stanford: Stanford University Press, 1965), pp. 124–52.

[7]See Dante Alighieri, *Purgatorio* 19, in particular lines 7–9, 16–21, and 31–33; Ludovico Ariosto, *Orlando Furioso* 7.73.1–74.4; and Niccolò Machiavelli, "Spectabili viro L. Guicciardini in Mantova tanquam fratri carissimo," in *Lettere,* ed. Giuseppe Lesca (Florence: Rinascimento del Libro, 1929), pp. 26–27. Machiavelli's letter is dated 1509. One might also cite the unveiling of Acratia in Book 5 of Giovanni Giorgio Trissino's *L'Italia liberata dai Goti,* or, to give a more recent example, Stanley Kubrick's film *The Shining,* in which the writer played by Jack Nicholson comes across an alluring woman who turns to face him and reveals herself to be a sickly hag. Here too, the enchantress-turned-hag can be read as a metaphor for the truth of the writer's work: later in the film his wife will discover that his text consists of nothing other than the sentence "All work and no play makes Jack a dull boy" repeated over and over again.

appearance.⁸ Refiguring woman is tantamount to refiguring truth, and to side with *either* the enchantress *or* the hag is to remain solidly within that tradition. The appearance of this topos in macaronic texts is thus a continuation and *amplificatio* of a founding figure of "high" literature. Insofar as macaronic poetry "lowers" high literature, we may see its elaboration of this topos as an example of what Peter Stallybrass and Allon White, in *The Politics and Poetics of Transgression,* have called "displaced abjection": "the process whereby 'low' social groups turn their figurative and actual power, *not* against those in authority but against those who are even 'lower' (women, Jews, animals, particularly cats and pigs)."⁹ But from this *amplificatio* and displaced abjection there emerges a "truth-about-truth": the truth revealed in the *bocca sdentata* is not only *the* truth but also "the-truth-about-woman," or, put another way, for the Western philosophical tradition, the truth-about-woman is *the* truth. Accepting *this* truth would mean accepting the notion that truth is gendered, that the mouth that speaks the "truth" is the gaping "other mouth."

Critics of macaronic from its nineteenth-century rediscovery to the

---

⁸See Friedrich Nietzsche, preface to the second edition of *The Gay Science,* trans. Walter Kaufmann (New York: Vintage, 1974), p. 38: "We no longer believe that truth remains truth when the veils are withdrawn. . . . Perhaps truth is a woman who has reasons for not letting us see her reasons? Perhaps her name is—to speak Greek—*Baubo?*" The Nietzschean critique of the hermeneutic model is both continued and itself critiqued by Jacques Derrida in *Éperons: Les styles de Nietzsche / Spurs: Nietzsche's Styles,* trans. Barbara Harlow (Chicago: University of Chicago Press, 1979). The topos of the enchantress-turned-hag and its implication in the hermeneutic model is the implicit "subject" of his discussion of woman as "twice castration: once as truth and once as untruth" (p. 97). Derrida recognizes the genderedness of the truth of philosophy: "Although there is no truth in itself of the sexual difference in itself, of either man or woman in itself, all of ontology nonetheless, with its inspection, appropriation, identification and verification of identity, has resulted in concealing, even as it presupposes it, this undecidability. Somewhere here, beyond the mythology of the signature, beyond the authorial theology, the biographical desire has been inscribed in the text" (pp. 103–5). The castrating woman, the hag, woman as nontruth, are still caught up in the phallogocentric, hermeneutic model; a "third, affirming woman" for whom castration "n'a pas lieu" (does not take place, has no place; p. 96) would instead undo that model. Like Nietzsche, however, Derrida continues to identify feminism with the castrating woman and, in what would seem to be another act of appropriation, reserves for himself the (non)position of the "third woman." See also his remarks in James Creech, Peggy Kamuf, and Jane Todd, "Deconstruction in America: An Interview with Jacques Derrida," *Critical Exchange* 17 (Winter 1985): 28–32.

⁹Stallybrass and White, *The Politics and Poetics of Transgression,* p. 53. Mary Russo also notes that the female grotesque is frequently a product of "displaced abjection"; "Female Grotesques," p. 221.

present have been loath to accept any such thing, and have concentrated instead on an inversion that is more traditionally carnivalesque: the hierarchy inverted in macaronic texts is in fact not that of man and woman, upper and lower classes, human and animal, but rather of languages and linguistic registers. In the hybridization of Latin, dialect, and the vulgate, macaronic can be said to be the carnival of the *questione della lingua*. Critics are particularly eager to participate in this carnival; the question was decided long ago, and titillation is created in the slippage between the "vulgarity" of what is represented and the "vulgate" adopted in its representation. Ettore Bonora's response to the passage cited from Tifi Odasi is typical.

> La cruda vena caricaturale dei maccheronici padovani e in particolare il compiacimento con il quale essi trattano una materia laida e ripugnante, fermano l'attenzione del lettore; ma persino in un brano di scoperta volgarità quale è nell'Odasi il ritratto della massara dello speziale torna a sconcertrarci questo contrasto fra dialetto e latino, che nel vivo di un così insolito grottesco può dar luogo a un verso di autentico colore classico: "Ingens apparet variisque meatibus antrum" subito seguito per di più da un'invocazione nella quale gli elementi linguistici volgari e le infrazioni alla sintassi normale sembrano il risultato non si sa bene se di una ricerca forzata o di gratuita sciatteria.[10]

> [The crude vein of caricature found in the Paduan macaronic writers, and in particular the delight with which they treat an ugly and repulsive matter, arrest the attention of the reader. Yet even in a passage of unabashed vulgarity such as that of Tifi Odasi's portrait of the apothecary's wife, the contrast between dialect and Latin returns to unsettle us. Even in the thick of such an unusual grotesque, this contrast can give rise to an authentically classical verse: "Ingens apparet variisque meatibus antrum," immediately followed by an invocation in which it is difficult to tell whether the linguistic elements of the vulgate and the infractions of normal syntax are the result of a deliberate attempt or of gratuitous slovenliness.]

Avoidance of the gaping "other" mouth produces a gaping hole in this critic's response: his attention is arrested by the vulgarity of the "materia laida" but quickly diverted to a different vulgarity: "questo contrasto fra dialetto e latino," "gli elementi linguistici volgari."[11] Bonora

[10]Ettore Bonora, *Le maccheronee di Teofilo Folengo* (Venice: Neri Pozza, 1956), p. 39.
[11]Ivano Paccagnella, *Le macaronee padovane,* p. 74, similarly avoids contact with the content of the description. Preceding his citation of lines 529–37, he writes: "Un

has "nothing to say" about the "ugly and repulsive matter." Critics of macaronic poetry are not alone in their fear and loathing; indeed, they trope Folengo himself, for his *Baldus,* too, represents a flight from the grotesque female body of his predecessor Tifi Odasi. In the *Baldus,* a text that insistently foregrounds its own literary origins, this flight is all the more striking since it aims to desexualize biological origins. Folengo flees to the kitchen, where the muses are no longer whores but "good mothers" and cooks, dispensing mountains of gnocchi and ravioli and dripping not menstrual blood but grease. Indeed, Folengo's *Baldus* seems to recount only half of the Ariostan chiasmus, only "l'arme, i cavallier" ("arms, knights"), and to exclude virulently "le donne, gli amori" ("ladies, love"); it is filled with rollicking good times, just-among-us-boys adventures, and is punctuated by several extensive invectives against women and one housewifely defense (the defense is excluded from Cordié's edition, but appears in both Luzio's and Faccioli's editions). Avoidance of the gaping "other" mouth and the desexualization of the muse-as-mother go hand in hand with the appearance of the topos of *inter faeces et urinam nascimur:* like Freud's infantile theorists of sexuality, Folengo favors cloacal theories of origin ("Non Leonardus eam scoltat, procul imo recedit, cui minus una placet mulier quam trenta diavoi, ac genus humanum miserum esse per istud, quod pro sorte mala muliebri ventre caghetur" ["Leonardus does not listen to her, but draws far away from her, for he likes one woman less than thirty devils and holds the human race to be miserable on account of its misfortune at having been shat from a woman's belly," *Il Baldus* 17.68–71]).[12] But this excluded female sexuality and a gaping "other mouth" return in Book 17 of the *Baldus,* where the chaste Leonardus is assaulted by conjugal bears conjured up from Pandraga's magic book. Here the female grotesque acquires a subversive valence precisely as the

---

esametro di tono elegiaco viene immediatamente snaturato in una catena di ipertrofie di segno negativo il cui risultato comico scaturisce dall'alone evocativo della parola dialettale ma soprattutto dall'opposizione stilistica fra il punto di partenza e l'esito" ("An elegiac hexameter is immediately distorted in a chain of negative hypertrophies whose comic result arises from the aura of the dialectal word but above all from the stylistic opposition between the point of departure and the final outcome").

[12]See also Book 7.118: "postquam me matris panza cagavit" ("since my mother's belly shat me") and Book 25.289–91: "dunque fadigabant illam sterpare davantum / scilicet ex vulvae, velut est usanza, latebris, / ecce duos natos culi sporchissima bocca / retro cagat foedumque simul diffundit odorem" ("they labored to pull it out from in front, that is to say, from the lips of the vulva as is usual, when from behind, from the filthy mouth of the ass, were shat two newborns, spreading a fetid odor").

excluded element, the repressed that insists on returning in apparently innocent, folkloric form.

In Book 17 Leonardus, *radius honestatis* (ray of chastity) enters a forest in search of a lost companion and stumbles upon a *locus amoenus,* "lauri myrthique virentes" ("green with laurel and myrtle"), not unlike that where Venus finds Adonis in Ovid's *Metamorphoses,* or where Iulio and Simonetta meet in Poliziano's *Stanze della giostra.* While he dozes by a crystalline river, a "puella formosa" ("beautiful young girl") appears and is drawn to the handsome young man. This "puella formosa" is none other than Pandraga, immediately identified by the narrator as both "meretrix" and "maga." Pandraga, however, is a failed enchantress; when Leonardus awakes, he refuses her advances and is deaf to her pleas. Spurned and enraged, Pandraga resorts to her "quadernus diabolicus" ("diabolical book") and conjures up a pair of bears who will take revenge in her stead.

Why bears? The bear is, of course, one of the beasts of the hard hunt; but why the bear and not the boar? Had Leonardo listened to her pleas, he might have heard more than one Virgilian echo giving him cause to fear lions and tigers and bears:

> At Pandraga vocat retro:—Me aspetta, puellam,
> O puer, o formose puer, me aspetta puellam,
> non ego sum tigris, non sum leonissa nec ursa,
> non draco; mi pulcher Narcise, quid ah fugis?
> [*Il Baldus* 17.80–83]

[Pandraga called after him: Wait for me, the maiden, oh lovely young boy, wait for me, the maiden, I am not a tigress, I am no lioness nor she-bear nor dragon; my pretty Narcissus, ah, why do you flee?]

She is, of course, all of these things: her very name, Pandraga, indicates that she is "all-dragon," a superdragoness. The subtext here is Virgil's description of libidinous beasts in Book 3 of the *Georgics:*

> Omne adeo genus in terris hominumque ferarumque,
> et genus aequoreum, pecudes pictaeque volucres,
> in furias ignemque ruunt: amor omnibus idem.
> tempore non alio catulorum oblita leaena
> saevior erravit campis, nec funera volgo
> tam multa informes ursi stragemque dedere
> per silvas; tum saevus aper, tum pessima tigris.[13]

[13]*Georgics* 3.242–48, in *Virgil,* trans. H. Rushton Fairclough, rev. ed., 2 vols. (London: Heinemann, 1986).

[Yea, Every single race on earth, man and beast, the tribes of the sea, cattle and birds brilliant of hue, rush into fires of passion: all feel the same Love. At no other season doth the lioness forget her cubs, or prowl over the plains more fierce; never doth the shapeless bear spread death and havoc so widely through the forest; then savage is the boar, then most fell the tigress.]

In Virgil it is the lioness who is identified as negligent mother; in Folengo it is the she-bear: "Ursa ferox, et dira magis, se cazzat inantum; / quae male formattos ursattos liquerat antro" ("The ferocious she-bear rushes forward, even more frightful for she had left behind her malformed cubs" [*Il Baldus* 17.221–22]). These malformed cubs have a long history in Aristotle, Pliny, and Isidorus of Seville. Bears were thought to conceive "with mutual embraces like humans" and to give birth to a lump of flesh with no resemblance to a bear: after a thirty-day gestation period, the female supposedly gave birth to a small piece of eyeless, hairless white flesh; "gradually it is shaped by licking and is kept warm by being held to the chest, and life is breathed into it."[14] The she-bear licking her malformed cubs into shape was in fact Titian's *impresa* and exemplified the motto "natura potentior ars." And it was from this zoological "fact" that Isidorus drew his etymology of *ursus: ursus* was related to both *mouth* and *origin* since the mother bear shaped her offspring with her mouth (*ore suo*), and that was the bear's beginning, *orsus*.[15] The she-bear could thus be said to figure an original, maternal mouth.

Indeed, Folengo's she-bear is not only mother to her cubs. In Book 10, where Leonardus is introduced, we learn of his genealogy. In the Paganini edition Leonardus presents himself to Baldus as French: "Verum, mi Balde, fatebor / sunt mihi de clara francorum stirpe pa-

---

[14]Florence McCulloch, *Mediaeval Latin and French Bestiaries,* University of North Carolina Studies in the Romance Languages and Literatures, no. 33 (Chapel Hill: University of North Carolina Press, 1962), p. 94. See Pliny, *Natural History,* vol. 3, Books 8–9, trans. H. Rackham (London: Heinemann, 1967). Pliny reports (8.54.126): "Hi sunt candida informisque caro, paulo muribus maior, sine oculis, sine pilo; ungues tantum prominent. Hanc lambendo paulatim figurant" ("These are a white and shapeless lump of flesh, little larger than mice, without eyes or hair and only the claws projecting. This lump the mother bears slowly lick into shape").

[15]See Isidore de Séville, *Étymologies, Livre XII: Des animaux,* trans. Jacques André (Paris: Société d'édition "Les belles lettres," 1986), p. 107: "Ursus fertur dictus quod ore suo formet fetus, quasi orsus. Nam aiunt eos informes generare partus et carnem quandam nasci quam mater lambendo in membra conponit" ("The bear is so-called because it forms its young with its mouth: its beginning, as it were. For they say that it gives birth to its young unformed, a piece of flesh at birth that the mother, by licking, forms into limbs").

rentes" ("Truly, my Baldus, I will confess, my relatives are of illustrious French stock"). This parentage undergoes a change in the
later Vigaso-Cocaio edition, where he is instead "sanguine progenitus
claro de stirpe Colonnae / nanque Colonnesus pater est Ursinaque
mater" ("I am a descendant of the illustrious Colonna family, for my
father is a Colonna and my mother an Orsini" [*Il Baldus* 10.485–86]).
This modification is usually attributed to Folengo's desire to pay
homage to the two noble families with which he had had dealings: he
had been tutor to Camillo Orsini's son after leaving the monastery, and
he had frequented Vittoria Colonna's circle while in Naples.[16] But its
consequences are of more than biographical interest. Why make the
mother Orsini and the father Colonna? Here Folengo's own literary
genealogy seems to shape Leonardus' genealogy, for the name Orsini
already had been the object of onomastic play: one recalls *Inferno* 19,
where Pope Nicholas III, himself an Orsini, declares: "fui figliuol de
l'orsa / cupido sì per avanzar li orsatti" ("I was a son of the she-bear, so
eager to advance the cubs" [*Inferno* 19.70–71]). The she-bear was the
emblem on the Orsini family's coat of arms, and Leonardus, "Ursinaque mater," is yet another "figliuol de l'orsa," and is about to be
assaulted by his own mother. The she-bear begins the attack, and
Leonardus goes for the mouth:

> Cui punctam in ventrem torquet Leonardus, at illa
> destra sinistrorsum balzat scansando repente,
> inde super gambas derdanas ritta levatur,
> ongiatasque manus aperit panditque bocazzam.
> Barro sed in medium mostazzi, dando roversum,
> colsit eam tandem, fecitque tomare stravoltam,
> dentatamque simul spiccavit ab ore ganassam.
>
> [*Il Baldus* 17.222–28]

[Leonardus strikes a blow to the stomach and she immediately jumps,
dodging nimbly to the left and then, rising up on her hind legs, she opens
her clawed hand and throws wide her nasty mouth. But the baron deals
her a backhander full in her ugly face, and makes her fall stunned at the
same time as he severs a toothed jaw from her mouth.]

While the she-bear recovers, her spouse (and they are explicitly married
bears) takes her place in battle and plays the part of the Ovidian boar:

---

[16]For biographical details, see Giuseppe Billanovich, *Tra Don Teofilo Folengo e Merlin
Cocai* (Naples: Raffaele Pironti e figli, 1948).

Ursus adiratur, sociam videt esse feritam,
sanguine quae largo flores malnettat et herbas;
unde Leonardo stizza maiore sotintrat,
cumque manu dextra zampatam vibrat apertam,
quae, quantam gremiit faldam, de corpore squarzat,
nudatumque forat duris ongionibus inguen.
                    [*Il Baldus* 17.229–34]

[The bear, angered at the sight of his wounded companion, who soils the
flowers and grass with abundant blood, moves toward Leonardo with
greater fury and with his right hand strikes an open paw-blow which rips
from Leonardo's flank as much as it clawed, and with his hard claws
pierces his naked groin.]

In the earlier Toscolana edition, line 234 had read, "ac nudas rapido
carnes ungione penetrat" ("a swift claw penetrates the naked flesh");
the change in the Vigaso-Cocaio edition thus quite explicitly reinforces
the Ovidian reference: "trux aper insequitur totosque sub inguine dentes abdidit . . ." ("the fierce boar pursues [Adonis] and sinks his teeth
into his groin . . ." [*Metamorphoses* 10.715–16]). The attack on Leonardus' virtue has turned into a rape; what is implicit in both Ovid and
Folengo would, in fact, later be made explicit by Shakespeare, who
identifies the boar as sexual rival to Venus, insofar as it gores Adonis by
mistake as it tries to kiss him. If the bear delivers a boarish kiss, it is the
she-bear who will finish him off with a bear hug. As she sees her mate
die, she returns to the attack. Her strategy has changed, however, for,
missing a jaw, she has become as good as toothless and must rely on
her strong arms: "Est verum quod nulla suis in dentibus est
spes / stringere qui nequeunt, una mancante ganassa / sola stat in
duris sibi confidentia branchis" ("It is true that there is no hope in her
teeth, which she cannot clench since she is missing a jaw; her only faith
is in her strong arms" [*Il Baldus* 17.250–52]).

Se movet ursa levis, nunc huc nunc emicat illuc
mandrittosque omnes paladini reddit inanes,
quem dum destituit sanguis, sed maxima crescit
et magis atque magis virtus animosa guerero,
spada, gaiardiam non sueta capescere tantam,
hue peccat, medioque operae fit iniqua patrono.
Frangitur ad manicum, lamma cascante tereno,
infelixque puer dextram sibi sentit inermem.
Ambo statim currunt contra, se amplexibus ambo
fortibus abbrazzant: premit hic, permit illa fiancos,
ut non dura magis stringantur ferra tenais.

> Tandem affogantur pariter pariterque cadentes,
> sic sic complexi fato periere medemo.
> [*Il Baldus* 17.265–77]

[The she-bear moves nimbly, springing now here, now there, and rendering vain all the paladin's blows. He is losing blood, but though the warrior's courage grows ever more bold, his sword, not used to taking such force, alas, in the middle of the battle is unequal to its owner. The handle breaks and the blade falls to earth, and the unfortunate boy feels his right hand unarmed. Then both run at once toward the other and both hug in a powerful embrace: both he and she press flanks together no less than pincers hold fast hard iron. Finally they both suffocate and they both fall; thus entwined they perish of the same fate.]

Leonardus dies "amplexibus fortibus" ("in a powerful embrace"): remember, bears copulate like human beings. Pliny had been quite specific about their sexual habits: "Eorum coitus hiemis initio, nec vulgari quadrupedum more sed ambobus cubantibus conplexisque" ("Bears couple at the beginning of winter, and not in the usual manner of quadrupeds but both lying down hugging each other").[17] Leonardus and the she-bear die, lying on the ground "sic sic complexi" ("thus embraced"). Leonardus, "Ursinaque mater," is indeed raped by the mother. The inversion that occurs here is yet another instance of "displaced abjection": in this case an attack on women is figured as an attack *by* a woman, and specifically by the mother-muse in disguise.

Pandraga herself is another mother-muse in disguise; in the earlier Paganini edition her name was in fact Muselina ("little muse"). During the bears' attack, she withdraws to the muses' territory, the kitchen, where she participates in another scene of perverse motherhood. Like the she-bear that is her creation, she too has a mate, and a nearly toothless one at that:

> Bruttus erat vecchius, quo non manigoldior alter,
> tergore delphini facieque colore safrani.
> Densque suis nullus massellibus extat apiccus,
> nazzusque colat tanquam lambiccus aquarum.
> [*Il Baldus* 17.136–39]

[He was an ugly old man, and none was more a scoundrel; he had the back of a dolphin and a face the color of saffron. Not a single tooth stood straight in his jaw, and his nose ran like an alembic of water.]

17Pliny, *Natural History* 8.54.126.

Together, they drug and chain Falchettus; but Cingar, in search of his companions, comes upon them, and their battle takes the form of a repetition of the battle of the bears:

> Sed cum Falchetti grandem rammentat amorem,
> praestiter indretum scura se fronte retirat,
> et mostazzonem talem cito porrigit illi,
> atque manu replicans roversa vibrat un altrum,
> quod due denticuli cascarunt extra ganassas.
> In terram cadit illa ruens squarzatque capillos.
> arrabiata cridat stridosque ad sydera mandat,
> lamnetisque petras montagnae spezzat aguzzis.
> Ecce, senex crevatus, adest Beltrazzus: ad illum
> currebat strepitum, si currere dicitur ulla
> testudo, aut portans limaca in tergore stanzam.
> De passu in passu tussit, mollatque corezzam,
> sbolsegat atque sonat magno cum murmure cornum.
> Pro Satan, ut vidit sub Cingare stare morosam,
> quam male nunc pugnis nunc calcibus ille burattat,
> atque ad misuram carbonum donat acerbas
> Pandraghae sorbas asinamque melonibus ornat,
> irruit atque hosti currit, ceu porcus, adossum,
> dentibus et strictis, quorum pars maxima desunt,
> vult ingiottitum tribus in bocconibus illum.
> [*Il Baldus* 17.347–66]

[But when he (Cingar) remembers his great love for Falchettus, he quickly draws back with darkened brow and lands such a slap in her face and then turning to backhand strikes yet another, that two little teeth fall out of her jaw. She falls rolling to the ground and tearing her hair; angry, she cries and sends screams to the stars and breaks the mountain's rocks with her sharp wailing. Lo, the decrepit old man, Beltrazzus, approaches: at this shrieking he runs, if one can call running that of a tortoise or a snail carrying his room on his back. At every step he coughs and breaks wind, rasps and sounds his horn with much racket. By the devil, when he sees his love lying beneath Cingar, who now with punches now with kicks bolts her, and gives tons of bitter lumps to Pandraga and adorns the she-ass with melons, Beltrazzus rushes and runs at the enemy like a pig, and with clenched teeth, the greater part of which are missing, he wants to swallow him up in three mouthfuls.]

Cingar's attack repeats that of Leonardus: one blow full in Pandraga's face followed by a backhander ("in medium mostazzi, dando roversum") that knocks out her teeth. Seeing his mate in trouble, Beltrazzus comes to her rescue; with clenched teeth, most of which are missing, he wants to swallow Cingar up in three mouthfuls ("tribus in bocconibus"). Pandraga and Beltrazzus together figure not one but two toothless mouths that would devour their attacker. Their attempts are not as successful as those of the bears, however, and yet another beast responds to Pandraga's cries: Moloccus, to whom Pandraga is wont to feed her victims. This beast repeats the battle yet another time.[18] He seems to be produced as a compromise formation between cloacal theories of origin and the topos of the *bocca sdentata–vagina dentata*: conceived from foul dung ("turpi concepta ledamo"), he has a toothed mouth and vomits poison from both mouth and anus ("Dentiger ut porcus, cagnazzi more pilosus / moreque serpentum vomitat simul ore venenum / flammatasque simul schizzat de retro corezas" ["Toothed like a pig, hairy like a dog, he vomits poison from his mouth like a serpent and releases flaming farts from behind," *Il Baldus* 17.410–13]. He, too, would like to devour Cingar "tribus in bocconibus." As revenge for Leonardus' death, Cingar manages to kill Moloccus with the help of a centaur. And although Pandraga survives this attack, she will be burned at the stake in the next book.

But what has not survived is Folengo's muse. Pandraga is not only *maga* and *meretrix* but also muse and mother: the beasts that are her creations link her to both the motherly muses and the devouring bear. The *maga* and *meretrix* has invaded the muses' kitchen, sending the text into a downward spiral that will lead to the witches' pharmacy of Book 23, and to the pumpkin, "stanza poetarum" ("poets' room"), of Book 25.

If Leonardus was born *inter faeces et urinam,* his fate was to die *inter musam et ursam,* victim of the maternal "mouth" that formed him. The poet himself fares no better, for he too falls victim to that toothless mouth. The fate of the muse prefigures the fate of the poets: the witches' pharmacy is the perversion of the muses' kitchen, now occupied not by "divae . . . grassae nymphaeque colantes" ("fat god-

---

[18]These repetitions might account for Nino Borsellino's mistaken description of Leonardo's fate as "sbranato da tre orsi" ("torn to pieces by three bears"). Literally speaking, there are only two bears, but the bears' attack is figurally repeated three times. See Nino Borsellino, "Teofilo Folengo, maccheronici e fidenziani," in *Gli anticlassicisti del Cinquecento* (Bari: Laterza, 1973), p. 86. On the *Baldus* as structured by repetitions and reduplications, see Giorgio Bàrberi-Squarotti, "L'inferno del *Baldus*," in *Cultura letteraria e tradizione popolare in Teofilo Folengo: Atti del convegno tenuto a Mantova il 15–17 ottobre 1977,* ed. Ettore Bonora and Mario Chiesa (Milan: Feltrinelli, 1979).

desses and nymphs dripping with grease"), but rather by "scarcossae, sdentatae et lumine squerzae pinzocarae" ("bony, toothless, and cross-eyed old crones" [*Il Baldus* 23.505–6]). The poets imprisoned in the pumpkin are punished for the lies they tell by a barber who extracts one tooth for every lie:

> Quottidie quantas illi fecere bosias,
> quottidie tantos bisognat perdere dentes,
> qui quo plus strappantur ibi, plus denuo nascunt.
> [*Il Baldus* 25.639–41]

[Every day they must lose as many teeth as they tell lies, and the more that are torn out, the more grow anew.]

The poet's truthfulness is proportionate to his toothlessness. If we take this punishment as a Dantesque *contrappasso,* then we can deduce a particular sin from the form of the penance: punishment for falsehood is based on the topos of the *bocca sdentata* as figure of truth, and the mouth that would deny the truth of that *bocca sdentata* becomes itself a *bocca sdentata.* The poet can choose only to remain: "Zucca mihi patria est: opus est hic perdere dentes / tot quot in immenso posui mendacia libro" ("The pumpkin is my homeland: here I must lose as many teeth as I placed lies in my immense book" [*Il Baldus* 25.649–50]). The text has subverted itself for, toothless, the poet can no longer speak and must leave to another the task of recounting Baldus' adventures. The attempt to deny that truth is gendered backfires, and the poet's disavowal is written all over his mouth.

Indeed, we may recognize in the poet's alternately toothed and toothless grin—or, more probably, grimace—the disavowal of the fetishist.[19] The fetishist, of course, is also preoccupied by the truth-about-woman, for it is he who simultaneously affirms and denies her "castration." The poet's punishment appears to be ruled by this same fetishistic logic that allows presence and absence to coexist; the fetishist's simultaneous disavowal and affirmation of castration here become sequential and infinitely repeatable moments: presence of teeth, followed by absence of teeth, followed by presence as the teeth grow

---

[19]I am referring to Freud's discussion of the fetishist's *Verleugnung* in his essay entitled "Fetishism," in *The Standard Edition of the Complete Psychological Works of Sigmund Freud,* trans. James Strachey (1961; rpt. London: Hogarth Press, 1978), 21:152–57. See also Sarah Kofman's discussion of the fetishist's oscillation in "Ça cloche," *Lectures de Derrida* (Paris: Galilée, 1984), pp. 115–51.

anew, and so on. The punishment is, in other words, a narrativization of the logic of fetishism.[20] Like the fetishist, trapped by a hermeneutic model that cannot but see sexual difference as a question of presence and absence, truth and lie, castrated and not castrated, the poet is trapped in a pumpkin where presence and absence, truth and lie alternate endlessly. Yet even in his entrapment the fetishist also resists insertion into that model: there is no moment of final revelation of women's "castration" for the fetishist—only an endless oscillation between "castrated" and "not castrated." What has happened in Folengo's text also resists insertion into the hermeneutic model: now inscribed on the mouth that speaks lies, the truth-about-woman can no longer be figured as the toothless hag alone. What is "revealed" is instead the "truth" about the trap itself: the notion of truth as something hidden (which can then be revealed) necessarily implies a model of sexual difference in which woman stands as the privileged figure of absence. To refigure her is thus to rethink our notion of truth and break out of the hermeneutic "pumpkin."

[20]In "L'inferno del *Baldus*," Bàrberi-Squarotti notes that this punishment is Promethean. I would agree, but would add that it is Promethean in the sense that, like the myth of Prometheus and Pandora, it narrativizes the logic of fetishism. For an analysis of the Prometheus-Pandora myth as fetishistic, see Barbara Spackman, *Decadent Genealogies: The Rhetoric of Sickness from Baudelaire to D'Annunzio* (Ithaca: Cornell University Press, 1989), pp. 168–83.

Elena Ciletti

Patriarchal Ideology in the Renaissance Iconography of Judith

"Do you happen to know anything about Judith yourself, except that she cut off Holofernes' head; and has been made the high light of about a million of vile pictures ever since, in which the painters thought they could surely attract the public to the double show of an execution, and a pretty woman—especially with the added pleasure of hinting at previously ignoble sin?" This rhetorical question was put to his readers by John Ruskin in 1874, in defense of the decorous painting by Botticelli, *The Return of Judith to Bethulia* (fig. 1).[1] I would like to invoke it now, since the intervening century has given us new "vile pictures" on the subject (we are surely over Ruskin's "million" by now) and even more scholarly attention to Judith's presumed "ignoble sin." Since Ruskin's time it has become virtually impossible to raise the subject of Judith and Holofernes without recourse to the immense edifice of modern psychoanalytic theory on sexuality. Indeed, Freud's equation of decapitation with symbolic castration has alone assured Judith a prominent place in the psychoanalytic canon.[2] From this van-

I am grateful to Marilyn Migiel and Juliana Schiesari for their support, to James Crenner, Lee Quinby, Dan Ewing, Bonnie Bennett, and Judith Brown for their critical reading of this manuscript and suggestions for improvement, to Creighton Gilbert for his illuminating correspondence on difficult points, and to Susan Smith, Joseph Marino, and Graeme Taylor for bibliographic assistance.

[1]John Ruskin, *Mornings in Florence* (Kent, England: G. Allen, 1875), pp. 65–66; the text was written during a trip to Italy in 1874. I owe my awareness of Ruskin's interest in Judith and much of my early exploration of the subject to the far-ranging article by Jane Davidson Reid, "The True Judith," *Art Journal* 28:4 (1969): 376–87.

[2]Freud took up the story of Judith specifically in 1917 in "The Taboo of Virginity," in *The Standard Edition of the Complete Psychological Works*, trans. James Strachey (1961; rpt. London: Hogarth Press, 1953–74), 11:207–8; see also "Medusa's Head (1922)," in *Stan-*

Figure 1. Botticelli, *The Return of Judith to Bethulia,* c. 1470, Uffizi, Florence. Photo: Alinari/Art Resource.

tage point Ruskin's effort to disassociate his heroine from sinful sexual taint cannot fail to seem but a relic of Victorian chivalry. And yet I believe that his view has more than casual relevance for traditional and feminist historians of Renaissance culture, as well as for feminists in all disciplines working to untangle the traps of Freudian theory from its insights. With Ruskin's help, I wish to consider some Renaissance representations of Judith, including Botticelli's, and to ground them in contemporaneous literary and religious manifestations of the construction of womanhood. I will argue that the iconography of Judith in the Renaissance is informed by the intersection of humanism with patristic theology within the patriarchal dialectic of gender common to both. In the process I wish to stress that all images of Judith, visual and otherwise, including Freud's, participate in a complex, evolving intellectual history.

Furthermore, I must add at the start that ten years of reading, teaching, and writing about Judith imagery have convinced me that this is a subject that defies definitive formulation. It is no exaggeration to say that every aspect of the theme is riddled with puzzles which have inspired centuries (and in some cases more than a millennium) of controversy. The Book of Judith itself, with its problematical sources, versions, translations, historicity, and canonicity, is highly contested text. In spite of the passionate partisanship it has inspired, it has never been part of the Hebrew canon, and modern Christians consign it to the ambiguous category of the Apocrypha, whereby it is excluded from most Protestant bibles but included in the Catholic Vulgate.[3]

---

dard Edition, 18:273. For interpretations of Judith within the canonical psychoanalytic mode, the reader is directed above all to the journal *American Imago,* especially to Joseph W. Slap, "Artemisia Gentileschi: Further Notes," 42:3 (1985): 335–42; Graeme J. Taylor, "Judith and the Infant Hercules: Its Iconography," 41:2 (1984): 101–15; and Martin S. Bergmann, "Love That Follows upon Murder in Works of Art," 38:1 (1976): 98–101. The translation of this view into less technical terms can be represented by a general work such as Robert Melville, *Erotic Art of the West* (New York: Putnam, 1973), pp. 247–48. For a Freudian reading that incorporates a feminist critique, see Mary Jacobus, "Judith, Holofernes, and the Phallic Woman," in her *Reading Woman* (New York: Columbia University Press, 1986), pp. 110–36.

[3]It is not usually included in modern editions of the King James Version, for instance. For a general overview of the Apocrypha, see Bruce Metzger, *An Introduction to the Apocrypha* (New York: Oxford University Press, 1963), introduction and chaps. 17 and 18. See also, more briefly, "Introduction to the Apocrypha," in *New English Bible with the Apocrypha* (New York: Oxford University Press, 1976), pp. iii–vi; and "Apocrypha," in *Harper's Bible Dictionary* (New York: Harper & Row, 1973), pp. 24–25.

For the Book of Judith, the fullest treatment is D. Giuseppe Priero, *Giuditta* (Turin: Marietti, 1959), with a magnificent bibliography on pp. 30–34. More convenient brief

Similarly vexed is the history of the theological and moral interpretations of the protagonist's character; indeed, Judith would seem remarkable to us if only for the sheer quantity of opposing identities and
symbolic usages imposed on her across the centuries, from patriot to
Virgin Mary prototype to femme fatale.[4] Controversy also reverber-
ates throughout the rather fractious scholarly literature devoted to the
major examples of Judith iconography in the visual arts: one need only
think of the competing theories abut Donatello's heroic statue, for
instance, or the even more dramatic scrutiny of Gentileschi's intrepid
Baroque characterizations of the heroine.[5] Sometimes it seems to me
that all these convolutions have a way of simultaneously collapsing in
upon themselves and spiraling outward to encompass the whole
world. After all, to study Judith is not only to stray across disciplinary

studies are Metzger, *Introduction to the Apocrypha,* chap. 4; also the entries under "The
Book of Judith" in *Encyclopaedia Judaica* (New York: Macmillan, 1971), 10:451–55; *New
Catholic Encyclopedia* (New York: McGraw-Hill, 1967), 7:44–46; *Dictionary of the Bible,*
ed. James Hastings (New York: Charles Scribner's Sons, 1942), 2:822–24. I have found
particularly useful P. Giffin, "Judith," in *A New Catholic Commentary on Holy Scripture,*
rev. ed. (London: Nelson, 1969), pp. 403–6.

It is relevant to note that the status of the Apocryphal (or Deuterocanonical, to use the
Catholic term) books was a major issue in Renaissance theology in the wake of the
Protestant Reformation's rejection of them as noncanonical. The opposite position was
taken by the Catholic church; at the Council of Trent in 1546, the church designated the
Latin Vulgate, which had always included them, as the official Catholic Bible. For Trent
and the Vulgate decrees, see *New Catholic Encyclopedia,* 2:450–54; and, more fully,
Hubert Jedin, *A History of the Council of Trent,* trans. Dom Ernest Graf (Edinburgh:
Thomas Nelson and Sons, 1961), chap. 2.

[4]See, above all, André Marie Dubarle, *Judith: Formes et sens des diverses traditions,* 2
vols. (Rome: Institut Biblique Pontifical, 1966). A range of the possibilities can be
gleaned from the standard iconographic compilations: *Lexikon der Christlichen Ikonogra-
phie,* ed. E. Kirschbaum (Rome: Herder, 1970), 2:454–58; *The Oxford Companion to Art,*
ed. Harold Osborne (Oxford: Clarendon Press, 1970), p. 620; Louis Reau, *Iconographie
de l'art chrétien* (Paris: Presses Universitaires de France, 1955–59), 2:329–35. There is also
an iconographic survey in *Encyclopaedia Judaica,* 10:459–62; and a list of Judith paintings
in Metzger, *Introduction to the Apocrypha,* pp. 223–25. Medieval biblical illustrations are
covered by Frances Godwin, "The Judith Illustrations of the *Hortus Deliciarum,*" *Gazette
des beaux-arts* 36 (1949): 1–46. I have relied heavily on Frank Capozzi, "The Evolution
and Transformation of the Judith and Holofernes Theme in Italian Drama and Art
before 1627" (Ph.D. diss., University of Wisconsin–Madison, 1975). For a lively syn-
thetic treatment, see Marina Warner, *Monuments and Maidens* (New York: Atheneum,
1985), pp. 158–76. See also Jan Bialostocki, "Judith: Story, Image, and Symbol:
Giorgione's Painting in the Evolution of the Theme," in *The Message of Images* (Vienna:
Irsa, 1988).

[5]For instance, Jacobus, "Judith, Holofernes and the Phallic Woman," pp. 130–34;
Slap, "Artemisia Gentileschi," passim; Taylor, "Judith and the Infant Hercules," pp.
104–5; Marcia Pointon, "Artemisia Gentileschi's *The Murder of Holofernes,*" *American*

boundaries but also to address the conjunction of nothing less than our central conceptual dualities: woman-man, virtue-vice, art-artifice, appearance-reality, life-death. All I can hope to offer here is a minute stratum of this material, one step toward a cultural rather than a purely artistic history of Judith in the Renaissance. My concern throughout is not to provide new interpretations of the imagery but to enlarge the relevant historical context generally relied on by historians of Renaissance art and to underscore to others the manifold historicity of works of art.

For Ruskin, what was admirable about Botticelli's painting is its fidelity to its biblical source, of which he observed: "The idea of Jewish womanhood [is] there, grand and real as a marble statue. . . . There is somewhat more to be thought of and pictured in Judith, than painters have mostly found it in them to show you; that she is not merely the Jewish Delilah to the Assyrian Samson; but the mightiest, purest, brightest type of high passion in severe womanhood offered to our human memory."[6] He urged his audience to read the Book of Judith "with honorable care," even pointing out the key verses, precisely because he found most visual representations of it deficient. Following the spirit if not the letter of these instructions, let us turn first to the narrative itself, granting at the start that it subverts univocal interpretation at every turn.

Briefly condensed, the plot unfolds a story of the salvation of the nation of Israel by God acting through the unlikely agency of a woman. The setting is the reign of the deified Assyrian king Nebuchadnezzar, whose dreams of empire are thwarted by the Israelite town of Bethulia, the only holdout against his army under the general Holofernes. Under siege and cut off from its water supply, Bethulia is weakened to the verge of capitulation. The sole defense is offered by

---

Imago 38:4 (1981): 343–67; Elena Ciletti, "Ma questa è la donna terribile: Artemisia Gentileschi and Judith," paper presented to College Art Association (CAA) 1984 (*CAA Abstracts* 72 [Toronto]); Frima Fox Hofrichter, "A. Gentileschi's Uffizi *Judith* and a Lost Rubens," *Rutgers Art Review* 1 (1980): 9–15. The Uffizi *Judith* also figures prominently in the growing literature on women artists, most controversially in Germaine Greer, *The Obstacle Race* (New York: Farrar, Straus, & Giroux, 1979), pp. 189–91; cf. Roszika Parker and Griselda Pollock, *Old Mistresses: Women, Art, and Ideology* (London: Routledge and Kegan Paul, 1981). pp. 20–26. On Gentileschi's career, see the long-awaited monograph by Mary Garrard, *Artemisia Gentileschi: The Image of the Female Hero in Italian Baroque Art* (Princeton: Princeton University Press, 1989). Garrard's chapters 2 and 5 are directly relevant to the present study, with historical overviews of Judith iconography and of scholars' and artists' interpretations.

[6] Ruskin, *Mornings in Florence*, p. 67.

the pious and beautiful widow Judith, who leaves the life of seclusion and fasting she has adopted in the three years since her husband's death in order to enact a bold and secret plan. After ritual prayers and cleansing, she dresses in her best finery and sets out for the Assyrian camp with the permission of Bethulia's elders, accompanied by a maid who carries their provisions in a sack. Her claims of defection are accepted by the Assyrian guards, who lead her to Holofernes. In a highly charged passage Judith convinces the enemy general that she will assist him to victory over the Israelites, promising him, among other things, that "God has sent me to do things with thee at which the whole world will be astonished" (11:16).[7] He is immediately smitten, observing with delight at his apparent good fortune: "There is not such a woman from one end of the earth to the other, for fairness of face and understanding of words" (11:20). Of course this is no small irony, since Judith's assuring words run the range from double entendre to outright lie.

For three days the women hold themselves aloof from the life of the camp, eating only the food they brought from Bethulia and moving from the tent gallantly provided by Holofernes only to bathe and pray in the evenings. The climax of the tale occurs on the fourth evening, at a banquet staged in Holofernes' tent for the explicit purpose of seducing the seemingly docile Hebrew beauty. In the presence of soldiers and retainers, Judith quietly looks on as Holofernes drinks himself unconscious on "exceedingly much wine, more than he had ever drunk in one day since he was born" (12:20). When the others discreetly leave, Judith seizes his sword from his bedpost, prays for strength, and beheads him with two strokes. Her maid, waiting at the door, thrusts the head into the food sack, and the two women flee the tent, and the camp, undetected.

Safe within the gates of Bethulia, Judith describes herself as the humble agent of God's will and reveals the severed head to the assembled crowds with the triumphant cry: "And the Lord smote him

---

[7]I am quoting from the Greek Septuagint (the version of critical choice), in the translation by Morton Enslin and Solomon Zeitlin, *The Book of Judith* (Leiden: Brill, 1972), whose introduction is very useful for the history of Christian and Jewish Judith interpretations. One gets some idea of the inherent difficulties in working with the Book of Judith by comparing another modern Septuagint translation of the same passage: "If you follow my advice, God will do some great thing through you" (11:16), in *The New English Bible with the Apocrypha*. Cf. also the Vulgate in a Douay Version translation: "for if thou wilt follow the words of thy handmaid, the Lord will do with thee a perfect thing" (11:4) in *The Holy Bible* (Cleveland, 1961).

down by the hand of a woman. And as the Lord liveth, who watched over me on the way I went, my face deceived him to his undoing, and he wrought no deed of sin with me to defile me or cause me shame" (13:15–16). The loss of their general naturally results in the rout of the Assyrians and the victory of the Israelites. After celebrations in Bethulia and Jerusalem, the revered heroine retires to her own estate to live out her life in celibate virtue. The story closes with this tribute to the efficacy of her deed: "And there was no longer any who spread fear among the children of Israel throughout the days of Judith and for many days after she had died" (16:25). Even so compressed a synopsis as this makes it clear that Ruskin's vision of "high passion in severe womanhood" was not derived casually. We can understand how he sought in Botticelli's representation what he had found in the text: "the purity and severity of a guardian angel."[8]

This is not the place to take up the innumerable textual difficulties or early historical vicissitudes of the Book of Judith. Suffice it to say that it is generally now dated to the second century B.C.E.—that is, to the troubled Second Temple period—and assumed to be less history than encouraging political allegory for difficult times.[9] Indeed, in spite of generations of textual archaeology, the place names and cast of characters cannot be consistently matched to historic entities, and the very name Judith, meaning "Jewess," suggests a primarily symbolic dimension. Again, it seems that Ruskin was correct when he invoked "the idea of Jewish womanhood." Other ambiguities notwithstanding (and we shall return to these presently) the Book of Judith is a celebration of the special destiny of the Chosen People. Their laws are validated in Judith's strict dietary observance, their faith contrasted to Assyrian idolatry, and the irresistible might of their God confirmed by the entire episode.

For the most part, the early and medieval church embraced the laudatory textual depiction of Judith's motivations and actions. From the start, considerable stress was placed on the chastity of the heroine, rooted in her explicit denial of any "pollution" at the hands of Holo-

---

[8]Ruskin, *Mornings in Florence*, p. 67.

[9]On this point, see any of the sources on the Book of Judith listed in note 3. Especially helpful are *Encyclopaedia Judaica*, 10:451–61; Priero, *Giuditta*, pp. 11ff.; Metzger, *Introduction to the Apocrypha*, pp. 50–53; see also Enslin and Zeitlin, *Book of Judith*, pp. 28ff. Ruskin was obviously aware of but untroubled by exegetical controversy, noting in *Mornings in Florence*, pp. 66–67: "Now, as in many other cases of noble history, apocryphal and other, I do not in the least care how far the literal facts are true."

fernes.[10] For instance, in the Latin Vulgate Saint Jerome sharpened his sources' description of Judith's celibate later life in Bethulia, when "she knew no man all the days of her life after the death of Manasses her husband," by introducing these words with a phrase of his own invention: "And chastity was joined to her virtue" (16:26).

This, of course, comes as no surprise, given the early Christian exaltation of chastity and its concomitant condemnation of the dangers of female sexuality, which are the familiar oppositions of the patriarchal construction of femininity. The patristic literature abounds in misogynous accounts of female nature, based ultimately on Eve's sexual cupidity in Eden, with its resulting penalties for all women.[11] The enveloping of Judith in the mantle of exemplary chastity not only underscored her exceptional status but also made possible the historically dominant Catholic view of her as a prefiguration of the Virgin Mary. At least as early as the tenth century, the two women are paired in their triumphing over Satan—Mary through her chaste conception of Christ, who broke the reign of the devil on earth, and Judith through her chaste dispatching of the devil's emissary, the lewd, proud, and idolatrous Antichrist, Holofernes. Key phrases from the Book of Judith were adopted by the church for the liturgy of Mary's feast days, and throughout medieval art and theology there are invocations of this typology.[12] So emphatic was the equation of Judith and Mary that the Old Testament heroine could come to personify the quintessential Marian virtue of chastity itself. In thirteenth-century French medieval

[10]Among the church fathers who praised her chastity were Jerome, Tertullian, and Ambrose; see Dubarle, *Judith: Formes et sens,* chap. 5; and Enslin and Zeitlin, *Book of Judith,* pp. 48–49. For the development of chastity-related personifications given to Judith, see Garrard, *Artemisia Gentileschi,* pp. 280–89.

[11]Among the key proponents of early Christian misogyny, which was by no means monolithic or consistent, are Paul, Augustine, Jerome, Tertullian, and John Chrysostom. Some of their relevant remarks are usefully gathered in *Not in God's Image,* ed. Julia O'Faolain and Lauro Martines (New York: Harper and Row, 1973), pp. 128–36; fuller treatment is provided by Elizabeth A. Clark, *Women in the Early Church* (Wilmington, Del.: M. Glazier, 1983). I am indebted to a thoughtful discussion of Saint Jerome's misogyny and its immense importance in the Middle Ages by Jean Barr, "Women in the Vulgate," paper presented at Hobart and William Smith Colleges, Geneva, N.Y., on November 1, 1985. I have also profited from the reminder by Judith Brown of the complexities and even ambiguities in the patristic literature on women.

[12]It is from her association with Mary that Judith came to personify the church, especially in historic moments of combat with heresy, which could so easily be identified with Holofernes. In this way, during the Reformation and Counter-Reformation both sides claimed kinship with Judith and the Chosen People. Such linkages can easily assume political proportions, as when threatening medieval Vikings or Renaissance Turks are paired with the infidel Holofernes. See Edna Purdie, *The Story of Judith in German and English Literature* (Paris: Champion, 1927), pp. 40–43.

manuscript illuminations, for instance, Chastity is contrasted with Lust via the opposition of Judith to Potiphar's wife (fig. 2).[13] This time-honored association was not lost in the subsequent centuries on Italy, with its "Renaissance of chastity" for women.[14]

Furthermore, Judith's textually accurate chastity had long been pushed beyond its biblical dimensions in a popular tradition that transformed the widow into a virgin. It is in this guise that she first enters the realm of English literature, in the anonymous tenth-century epic fragment *Judith:* here her heroism and invulnerability are "predicated on her virginal purity" because for the medieval church, "virginity contained in itself extraordinary power."[15] It seems that there are some linguistic roots to this otherwise theological invention, since the name of Judith's town, Bethulia, has been seen as a derivation from a old Hebrew word for virgin.[16] The notion of Judith as a virgin was explicitly revived by Catholic apologists in the later Renaissance period. A well-known feature of the Counter-Reformation was the church's promotion of Marian devotion in the face of the Protestant rejection of Mary's special quasi-divine status, and this brought renewed attention to Mary's Old Testament prototypes. In the case of Judith, strenuous efforts were made to strengthen her relationship to Mary. Indeed, we find early-seventeenth-century exegetes crediting her victory over Holofernes not only to strength derived from her heroic virginity but also from her newly conferred immaculate conception as well.[17]

[13]For illustrations and interesting discussion of this iconography, see Ellen Kosmer, "The 'noyous humoure of Lecherie,'" *Art Bulletin* 7:1 (1975): 4–5.

[14]The phrase is Joan Kelly's, the title of the last section of her epochal revision of the history of women in the Renaissance, "Did Women Have a Renaissance?" reprinted in her *Women, History, and Theory: The Essays of Joan Kelly* (Chicago: University of Chicago Press, 1984), pp. 19–50.

[15]Jane Tibbetts Schulenburg, "The Heroics of Virginity: Brides of Christ and Sacrificial Mutilation," in *Women in the Middle Ages and the Renaissance,* ed. Mary Beth Rose (Syracuse: Syracuse University Press, 1986), p. 39. The fullest treatment of the patristic construction of the ideal of virginity is John Bugge, *Virginitas: An Essay in the History of a Medieval Ideal* (The Hague: Martinus Nijhoff, 1975); the "Judith" poem is mentioned on p. 51. See also Clark, *Women in the Early Church,* chap. 3. For the poem itself, in which Judith is Christian, see "Judith," in *Poems from the Old English,* trans. B. Raffel (Lincoln: University of Nebraska Press, 1960). Interesting discussions of it are provided by George Anderson, *The Literature of the Anglo-Saxons* (Princeton: Princeton University Press, 1949), pp. 133–34; and Purdie, *Story of Judith in German and English Literature,* pp. 27–31.

[16]A useful summary of the linguistic material is in Priero, *Giuditta,* pp. 81–83.

[17]An example is Diego de Celada, *Judith Illustris* (Lyons: Sumptibus Iocabi et Petri Prost, 1637), prologue and pp. 690ff.; this topic was addressed by Ciletti, "Ma questa è la donna terribile," pp. 5ff.

Figure 2. Parisian *Somme le roi*, Ms. 368, *Chastity/Judith & Holofernes and Lust/Joseph & Potiphar's Wife*, c. 1285, Fitzwilliam Museum, Cambridge, England. Photo: Fitzwilliam Museum.

In this persistent construction of a Mariological identity for Judith, we cannot ignore the disguised suspicion of the very sexual dangers against which she is so energetically marshaled. It is not just that moral paradoxes attend Judith's victory, by virtue of its dependence on duplicity, but also that her tactics utilize "feminine wiles." The Book of Judith abounds with sexual energy and imagery, much of it created and exploited by its protagonist. She flatters Holofernes' presumptions of seduction with calculated half-truths and untruths, and she dresses for the occasion. On this latter score alone we can trace the church's discomfort back at least as far as Saint Jerome in the fourth century. For the Vulgate he provided an explanation for Judith's costume elaborations missing from all other versions of the text: "the Lord increased her beauty," we are told "because all this dressing up did not proceed from sensuality, but from virtue" (10:4). "Feminine wiles" or not, it goes without saying that for the authors of the Book of Judith, it is self-evident that the end justifies the means. There is a war on, and the survival of the Chosen People is at stake. Judith is presented to us as the Lord's agent, a female David against an Assyrian Goliath. Repeatedly throughout the text her piety and humility are praised, and her predecessors in righteous vengeance against the enemies of Israel are invoked. The point of view of the Book of Judith itself offers no justification for the common modern designation of Judith's deed as "murder."[18] To label it thus is to make it a crime and therefore to adopt a resolutely unbiblical solidarity with the Assyrian cause. But the polemical story, not to mention its long afterlife in art and literature, reminds us that the apparently overt meanings of the text invariably contain the seeds of opposing interpretations, particularly when the story is concerned with "feminine wiles."

Consider, for instance, the reading by the Byzantine historian John Malalas in the sixth century, who wrote that at Judith's instigation she and Holofernes slept together in a secluded tent for three nights before she finally beheaded him.[19] Now, on one level this is an extratextual

---

[18]As by, for example, Pointon, "A. Gentileschi's *The Murder of Holofernes*," with justification on p. 366; Graeme, "Judith and the Infant Hercules," p. 104; Greer, *The Obstacle Race,* p. 190. For a modern Catholic view of the Book of Judith as "lacking the delicacy of the fully Christian conscience," see Giffin, "Judith," p. 404.

[19]In *Patrologia Graeca,* ed. J. P. Migne, vol. 97, cols. 260ff.; cited by Susan Smith in her extraordinarily useful study "'To Women's Wiles I Fell': The Power of Woman *Topos* and the Development of Medieval Secular Art" (Ph.D. diss., University of Pennsylvania, 1978), p. 21, note 16, which also remarks that the same idea was pressed in the fourteenth century by the German Meistersinger known as Frauenlob. (I can add a late

approach, since, as we have seen, the Book of Judith emphatically denies any sexual contact between the protagonists. For Malalas, the biblical Judith is the prototypical lady who "doth protest too much," a view encouraged by the church's own definition of all women as Eve's libidinous daughters. His is the position adopted by Freud, who also transcended the biblical account in search of a "truer" reality. He based his interpretation of Judith on the notorious play of 1840 by Friedrich Hebbel, in which a virginal Judith is frustrated by an unconsummated marriage and sexually drawn to Holofernes, who rapes her. She thus beheads him not out of patriotism but in revenge.[20] Freud explains his fidelity to Hebbel this way:

> Hebbel deliberately sexualized the patriotic narrative in the Apocrypha, for there Judith boasts after her return to the city of not having been polluted, nor is there any mention in the biblical text of her uncanny nuptials. But with the sensitive intuition of a poet Hebbel probably divined the primordial theme that had been lost in the tendentious story, and only gave back to the content its earlier currency.[21]

Freud suspects here that chronological as well as psychological roots pertain, and the Malalas precedent sharpens this historical resonance. Moreover, further adumbrations of Hebbel and Freud occur in both the patristic tradition and in the Renaissance, especially in the momentous reassertion of the formula woman = sex = sin = death in the fifteenth and sixteenth centuries.

It is well known that in Northern Europe art of the Reformation period, Judith came to be represented in a manner consistent not with her conventional medieval iconography but with its submerged opposite. In works by major artists such as Baldung, Cranach, Massys, and Lucas van Leyden, to name only the most obvious, we have difficulty recognizing either the familiar Jewish patriot or the Virgin Mary prototype.[22] Instead, we are explicitly asked to see the other side of the masculinist coin: a dangerous, erotic Judith. This is frequently signaled

---

Renaissance example in M. Bonacasa's *Ficta Iuditha et Falsa* [Verona, 1614], p. 18, where Judith is accused of "the perfidy of copulation.") Malalas (c. A.D. 491–578) included the story of Judith in his *Chronicle,* an uneven but immensely influential universal history. See Michael Grant, *Greek and Latin Authors 800 B.C.–A.D. 1000* (New York: H. W. Wilson, 1980), p. 272.

[20]*Judith,* in *Three Plays by Hebbel,* trans. Marion W. Sonnenfeld (Lewisburg, Pa.: Bucknell University Press, 1974), with useful introduction.

[21]Freud, "The Taboo of Virginity," in *Standard Edition,* 11:207–8.

[22]This moral and artistic climate is surveyed in the excellent article by Susan Smith and Larry Silver, "Carnal Knowledge: The Late Engravings of Lucas van Leyden," *Nederlands Kunsthistorisch Jaarboek* 29 (1978): 239–98. See also James Marrow and Alan

Figure 3. Jan Massys (1509–75, Antwerp), *Judith,* n.d., Koninklijk, Antwerp. Copyright A. C. L. Brussels.

Figure 4. Lucas Cranach the Elder, *Judith,* c. 1530.

Figure 5. Lucas Cranach the Elder, *Salome,* c. 1530, Szepmuveszeti Museum, Budapest. Photo: Foto Marburg/Art Resource.

by her untextual nudity, as in the painting by Jan Massys (fig. 3), or by her conflation, most familiar in Cranach, with Salome (figs. 4, 5), an archetype of destructive femininity.[23] The dramatically different circumstances and motivations of these two biblical characters, not to mention the results of their actions, are erased in favor of a presumed deeper truth: whenever women exert power over men, it is by definition sexual and lethal. Far from her earlier identity as Chastity, Judith can now come to hover like a presiding genius over prurient depictions of prostitution. In a print of this subject after Lucas van Leyden, for instance (fig. 6), an image of Judith carrying Holofernes' head looms from the background wall (or headboard) as a warning to men of the wages of the sin of lust so graphically depicted in the foreground, thereby linking the heroine to the whore.[24] Associations like this lead to her inclusion in one of the misogynist commonplaces of this period, the *Weibermacht*, or "Pernicious Power of Woman" topos.[25] In an en-

---

Shestack: *Hans Baldung Grien: Prints and Drawings,* exhibition catalogue (New Haven: Yale University Art Gallery, 1981), especially the entries on the various representations of Eve and witches. For a rich discussion of "negative" interpretations of Judith, within the context of the evolution of her iconography, see Garrard, *Artemisia Gentileschi,* pp. 289–301.

[23]See Warner, *Monuments and Maidens,* pp. 167–69. The important subject of the nude Judith still awaits definitive treatment. Susan Smith has addressed primarily the northern material in her "Vice or Virtue? The Nude Judith in the Early 16th Century," paper presented to CAA, 1977 (*CAA Abstracts* 46 [Los Angeles]); so did Peter Schabacker, briefly, in "Jan Van Eyck's *Woman at Her Toilet;* Proposals Concerning Its Subject and Context," *Fogg Art Museum Annual Report* (1974–76): 65–76. For interesting suggestions concerning the earliest Italian images, see Creighton Gilbert, "Signorelli and Young Raphael," in *Studies in the History of Art* 17 (1986): 121–24.

From the sixteenth century on, the iconographic confusion of Judith and Salome is common in Northern and Southern Europe; see, for instance, Titian's paintings (c. 1570) in the Detroit Institute of Arts and related versions, for which see Harold Wethey, *The Paintings of Titian* (London: Phaidon, 1969–75), 1:95, cat. no. 44. On Titian and Salome, see further Erwin Panofsky, *Problems in Titian, Mostly Iconographic* (New York: New York University Press, 1969), pp. 42ff. For the numerous Cranach depictions, see Max J. Friedländer and Jakob Rosenberg, *The Paintings of Lucas Cranach,* rev. ed. (Ithaca: Cornell University Press, 1978), nos. 32–33, 214–15, 230–34, 358–59; and Dieter Koepplin and Tilman Falk, *Lucas Cranach,* exhibition catalogue (Stuttgart, 1974), 1:413–20, 2:562–80. A famous modern case of Salome-Judith conflation can be seen in Klimt, for which see the explanation by Alessandra Comini, "Titles Can Be Troublesome: Misinterpretation in Male Art Criticism," *Art Criticism* 1:2 (1979): 50–54. On Salome representations in general, see Helen Zagona, *The Legend of Salome and the Principle of Art for Art's Sake* (Geneva: Droz, 1960), esp. pp. 13–22.

[24]This engraving has been attributed to the circle of Lucas, or "after" Lucas, since the nineteenth century. See F. W. Hollstein, *Dutch and Flemish Etchings, Engravings, and Woodcuts* (Amsterdam: M. Hertzberger, 1949), 10:244. It is not included in recent *oeuvre* catalogues of his graphic work.

[25]The best English treatment of this complex topic is Smith, "'To Women's Wiles I

Figure 6. After Lucas van Leyden, *Prostitution,* 16th century, Oxford. Photo: Courtesy of the Warburg Institute.

Fell.'" I have found useful also John B. Knipping, *Iconography of the Counter Reformation in the Netherlands* (Leiden: De Graaf, 1974), 1:47ff., 203ff. Of Judith he notes (p. 203): "It is practical to assume that Judith's heroic exploit was preceded by a seduction scene."

Although *Weibermacht* is generally treated as a Northern European phenomenon, Creighton Gilbert has recently posited a variant of it as the theme of a lost series of Neapolitan frescoes by Giotto (c. 1330); in his "Boccaccio Looking at Actual Frescoes,"

graved example after Heemskerck of this popular iconography (figs. 7, 8), we see her and a related Old Testament heroine, Jael, in the company of devious "sisters": Salome, Delilah, the daughters of Lot, the Queen of Sheba (luring Solomon to idolatry), and of course Eve. Another common protagonist in these schemes, but missing in this example, is Phyllis, who had been credited since the thirteenth century with transforming Aristotle into her sexual plaything. Holofernes thus sheds his traditional medieval identification with the devil and instead joins the ranks of saints and wise men, pathetic victims who have lost their heads (either literally or figuratively) to "feminine wiles." Male solidarity prevails over moral categories. Once a sexual dimension is acknowledged for the female character, her identity as a legitimate, active heroine is simply not possible.

Needless to say, it is not in the visual arts nor in Northern Europe alone that we find *Weibermacht* and related conceits. Rather, we can point to an immense body of literature in the fifteenth and sixteenth centuries reviving antique and early Christian misogyny. Important scholarship has made it increasingly apparent that on the subject of women, the humanist recuperation of and reverence for classical authors cannot simply be counted among the intellectual felicities of the age. Burckhardt's famous fantasy of sexual equality in Renaissance Italy notwithstanding, we are belatedly learning to see how the weight of classical authority served primarily to reinforce the debased status and nature conferred on women by the Judeo-Christian tradition.[26] It is true, of course, that humanism did evolve a "liberal" discourse of gender, the most familiar Italian contributor to which is Castiglione, but this development was fitful at best and largely the exception to the

---

in *The Documented Image: Visions in Art History,* eds. G. Weisberg and L. Dixon (Syracuse: Syracuse University Press, 1987), pp. 225–41. His compelling hypothesis needs to be taken up by historians of the Italian Renaissance.

[26]Jacob Burckhardt, *The Civilization of the Renaissance in Italy* (New York: Harper Torchbooks, 1958), 2:389–95. The beginning of the modern feminist revision of this position is generally dated to Joan Kelly's famous essay "Did Women Have a Renaissance?"; on humanist misogyny, see especially pp. 21, 35–41. An important predecessor was Ruth Kelso, *Doctrine for the Lady of the Renaissance* (Urbana: University of Illinois Press, 1956). The humanist recuperation of antique misogyny is also a leitmotif of Ian Maclean, *The Renaissance Notion of Woman* (Cambridge: Cambridge University Press, 1980). See also Hanna Fenichel Pitkin, *Fortune Is a Woman: Gender and Politics in the Thought of Machiavelli* (Berkeley: University of California Press, 1984); and Bonnie Anderson and Judith P. Zinsser, *A History of Their Own,* vol. 2 (New York: Harper & Row, 1988).

rule.[27] More common was the position espoused by treatises such as Tiraqueau's *De legibus connubialibus* of 1513, wherein classical authorities are yoked to medieval theologians, philosophers, and doctors in definitively establishing the legal basis of "woman's inferiority to man."[28] That inferiority easily collapsed into outright vice, especially where sexuality was concerned. Perhaps the most frightful Northern European formulation is Heinrich Kramer and Jacob Sprenger's *Malleus Maleficarum* of 1486, whose notorious misogynist ravings are well known. What I wish to stress here is that these authors cite classical as well as Christian sources for their conclusions that since women are "feebler in both mind and body, it is not surprising that they should come more under the spell of witchcraft," which itself "comes from carnal lust, which in women is insatiable. . . . Wherefore for the sake of fulfilling their lusts they consort even with devils." Furthermore, they characterize women as "a wheedling and secret enemy": "beautiful to look upon, contaminating to the touch, and deadly to keep."[29] In these phrases we recognize Judith as she was refashioned by the language of *Weibermacht,* and it is necessary to stress that the implications here extend far beyond the confines of Renaissance art or scholarship. We cannot forget that it was the very ideology that painted Judith as a bewitching femme fatale which sent contemporary real women to the stake.[30]

[27]See Garrard, *Artemisia Gentileschi*, pp. 141–54; Constance Jordan, "Feminism and the Humanists: The Case of Sir Thomas Elyot's *Defence of Good Women*," in *Rewriting the Renaissance,* ed. Margaret W. Ferguson, Maureen Quilligan, and Nancy J. Vickers (Chicago: University of Chicago Press, 1986), pp. 242–58; the editors of *Rewriting the Renaissance* discuss Burckhardt's misinterpretation in their introduction, pp. xv–xvi. See also Janice Butler Holm, "The Myth of a Feminist Humanism: Thomas Salter's *The Mirrhor of Modestie*," in *Ambiguous Realities: Women in the Middle Ages and Renaissance,* ed. Carole Levin and Jeanie Watson (Detroit: Wayne State University Press, 1987), pp. 197–218.

[28]Maclean, *The Renaissance Notion of Woman,* p. 5.

[29]Heinrich Kramer and Jacob Sprenger, *Malleus Maleficarum,* trans. M. Summers (London: J. Rodker, 1928); I have used the extensive excerpts of Part 3 in *Witchcraft in Europe, 1100–1700: A Documented History,* ed. Alan C. Kors and Edward Peters (Philadelphia: University of Pennsylvania Press, 1972), esp. pp. 114–27. The quoted passages are on pp. 120 and 127. Among the authorities cited by Kramer and Sprenger are Cato, Seneca, and Cicero, as well as the patristic fathers and the Bible. It is worth noting that in the brief passages praising women on p. 117, the authors invoke Judith.

[30]I owe the explicit connection of sexualized representations of Judith to witchcraft prosecutions, as well as many other fruitful ideas about related matters, to Smith and Silver, "Carnal Knowledge," note 146. An example of the traditional historical view of the phenomenon of witchcraft which virtually ignores gender is Hugh Trevor-Roper,

Figure 7. Philippe Galle after Maerten van Heemskerck, *Judith,* detail from *The Fatal Power of Women* (1610). Photo: from John B. Knipping, *Iconography of the Counter Reformation in the Netherlands* (Leiden: De Graaf, 1974) vol. 1, plate 38.

Coming back now to Botticelli's *Return of Judith to Bethulia* of around 1470 (fig. 1),[31] we see how the foregoing historical material, not to

The European Witch Craze of the 16th and 17th Centuries (New York: Harper & Row, 1967), pp. 90–192.

Interesting remarks on the importance of gender and nationality are provided by William Monter, "The Pedestal and the Stake: Courtly Love and Witchcraft," in *Becoming Visible,* ed. Renate Bridenthal and Claudia Koonz (Boston: Houghton Mifflin, 1977), pp. 119–36; and, more recently, his "Women and the Italian Inquisitions," in Rose, *Women in the Middle Ages and the Renaissance,* pp. 73–88. For an overview of the conflicting theories about gender and witchcraft, see the very useful Geoffrey R. Quaife, *Godly Zeal and Furious Rage: The Witch in Early Modern Europe* (New York: St. Martin's, 1987), chaps. 6 and 7.

[31]A convenient recent treatment of this and related paintings is Ronald W. Light-

Figure 8. Philippe Galle after Maerten van Heemskerck, *The Fatal Power of Women* (1610). Photo: from John B. Knipping, *Iconography of the Counter Reformation in the Netherlands* (Leiden: De Graaf, 1974) vol. 1, plate 38.

mention the contemporary nineteenth-century romanticism of people like Hebbel, provides some context for Ruskin's interpretation. It was the painter's refusal to hint at "previously ignoble sin" that Ruskin admired, with its corollary distancing of Judith from Delilah and "vile pictures," which must mean those contaminated by *Weibermacht*. It is telling that he had to overcome his own suspicions on precisely this score. He worried initially over what he perceived as the heroine's Salome-like step: "Judith, indeed!—say rather the daughter of Herodias, at her mincingest"; more attentive looking soon convinced him instead that "Sandro's picture is but slight; but it is true to her, and the only one I know that is."[32] One can understand some hesitation over Botticelli's decorative loveliness. Taken on its own, the painting may strike us primarily for a contemplative lyricism at odds with the vigorous drama of the biblical tale. But for Ruskin, the heroine's "sweet, peaceful motion" was but a function of her moral rectitude. Moreover, *The Return of Judith* must be seen with its pendant, *The Discovery of the Body of Holofernes* (fig. 9); the two tiny panels, currently placed back-to-back in the Uffizi, were apparently framed side by side in the Renaissance.[33] In *The Discovery* we find the gruesome horror missing from *The Return,* and we see immediately that the distinction makes good narrative sense. Together as a pair the two works thus create a nuanced historical dimension for a character whose visual representations are frequently conspicuous for the absence of the original literary setting. Thus, I think we might agree with Ruskin that in spite of the idiosyncratic grace of his style, Botticelli brings Judith closer to the overt spirit of the biblical text than the sixteenth-century northern examples we have just seen. This is even truer of some other Quattrocento Judiths, particularly those within the Florentine and/or humanist orbit.

In Botticelli's native Florence the most famous image of Judith was

---

bown, *Sandro Botticelli* (Berkeley: University of California Press, 1978), 1:26–30; 2:21–22.

[32]Ruskin, *Mornings in Florence,* pp. 65, 67. Ruskin thought a love of dancing a weakness in Botticelli. For his aesthetic motivations here, see Reid, "The True Judith."

[33]Their dimensions are approximately 31 × 24 cm. In the late sixteenth century they were described as framed together ("un dittico") in a gilt walnut frame (*Gli Uffizi: Catalogo generale* [Florence, 1979], p. 176); see also Lightbown, *Botticelli,* 2:21–22. It may be of some interest to note that in Ruskin's day they were hung directly below a head of Medusa attributed to Leonardo da Vinci (see Ruskin, *Mornings in Florence,* p. 64). That painting is now assigned to the seventeenth-century Flemish school; see *Itinerario fiorentino: "Le Mattinate" di J. Ruskin nelle fotografie di Alinari* (Florence: Alinari, 1986), pp. 87, 156. I owe this citation to Bonnie Bennett.

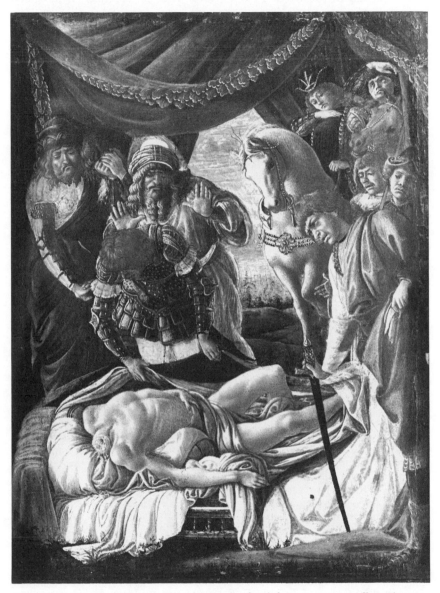

Figure 9. Botticelli, *The Discovery of the Body of Holofernes*, c. 1470, Uffizi, Florence. Photo: Alinari/Art Resource.

of course Donatello's vivid bronze statue of 1455–60 (fig. 10).[34] Placed in the garden of the Medici Palace soon after its creation, it has been interpreted in a variety of ways, both theological and political. On the basis of the relation between its reliefs and inscriptions on the base and the protagonists above, it has been seen variously as an emblematic Christian or Neoplatonic allegory of victory: of Sanctity over Lust, or Humility over Pride, or the Medici over their Florentine enemies, or Florence over its foreign foes.[35] In all of these cases it may also incorporate timely references to the Nine Worthies and the virtue fortitude. Despite, or perhaps because of, this iconographic density, the sculpture's symbolic power has readily been recognized and co-opted for various and sometimes opposing purposes. In 1495, for instance, the statue was removed from the Medici Palace to a conspicuous public position in Piazza della Signoria and provided with new inscriptions in order to celebrate the expulsion of the Medici from Florence and to serve as a warning to all tyrants. Judith's evolution toward a Florentine civic identity is not particularly surprising, given the overtly political nature of the biblical story itself. It is also a function of her long-standing pairing (both visual and conceptual) with David, who came to assume the status of a virtual patron saint in Renaissance Florence.

There were hints already in the fourteenth century of Judith's adaptability to contemporary Italian political propaganda. Most notably we can point to her invocation in 1347 by Cola di Rienzo in a circulating letter decrying the opposition to his short-lived republic in Rome: his enemies would be dispatched, he promises his readers, as Holofernes was by Judith.[36] The analogy may strike us as somewhat strained, but

---

[34]For this work's problematic dating, critical and interpretive history, and documentation, see above all H. W. Janson, *The Sculpture of Donatello* (Princeton: Princeton University Press, 1963), pp. 198–205. An important more recent treatment is that by Bonnie Bennett and David Wilkins, *Donatello* (Oxford: Phaidon, 1984), esp. pp. 82–90, 219–21.

[35]Many of these interpretations are summarized in Janson, *Sculpture of Donatello,* pp. 200–204, and incorporated by Warner, *Monuments and Maidens,* chap. 8. The Sanctimonia position is primarily associated with Edgar Wind, "Donatello's *Judith:* A Symbol of 'Sanctimonia,' " *Journal of the Warburg and Courtauld Institutes* 1 (1937–38): 62ff. A related view which also links Judith to the Virgin Mary and the Psychomachia is Hans von Erffa, "Judith—Virtus Virtutum—Maria," *Mitteilungen des Kunsthistorischen Institutes in Florenz* 14:4 (1970): 460–65. The Neoplatonic case was made by Laurie Schneider, "Some Neoplatonic Elements in Donatello's *Gattamelata* and *Judith and Holofernes,*" *Gazette des beaux-arts* 87 (1976): 41–48. Much psychoanalytic revisionism has been visited upon this work. See above all Laurie Schneider, "Donatello and Caravaggio: The Iconography of Decapitation," *American Imago* 33:1 (1976): 76–91, with discussions following on pp. 92–101; Jacobus, "Judith, Holofernes, and the Phallic Woman," pp. 127–30; and most recently Susan Smith, "Sex and Citizenship in Donatello's *Judith and Holofernes,*" paper presented to CAA, 1988 (*CAA Abstracts* 76 [Houston]).

[36]Quoted in Capozzi, "Evolution and Transformation of the Judith and Holofernes

Figure 11. Donatello, *Judith and Holofernes* (detail).
Photo: Alinari/Art Resource.

Figure 10. Donatello, *Judith and Holofernes*, c. 1455–
60, Palazzo della Signoria, Florence. Photo:
Alinari/Art Resource.

Theme," pp. 21–22. The same author records Cola's justifications later in 1347 for the
use of deceit in the pursuit of just causes, specifically invoking the example of Judith. He
cites Cola di Rienzo, *Epistolario,* ed. A. Gabrielli (Rome: Forzani, 1890), pp. 84, 155.

it was undoubtedly understood in Florence, at least by Cola's friend and critic Petrarch, who had himself written of Judith as a political exemplar.[37] Similarly, there is an obscure popular tradition which associates Donatello's *Judith* statue itself with a Quattrocento commemoration of a Trecento political event: the expulsion from Florence in 1343 of another failed civic reformer of the early Renaissance, the so-called duke of Athens.[38] In this way ancient linkages between Judith and classical Roman ideals of patriotic self-sacrifice were brought up to date in an incipiently humanist context.[39] By the early fifteenth century these associations were established and flexible enough to be brought to bear on the case of a modern heroine. In 1429 Christine de Pizan included Judith among the foremothers of Joan of Arc, having already employed the Old Testament patriot in her defense of all women in *Le livre de la Cité des Dames;* from this point on Judith was a "regular" in the "protofeminist" literature of the *querelle des femmes.*[40]

As we look at Donatello's statue, we cannot fail to be struck by the grim determination of the protagonist, played out in her gestures, facial expression, and, indeed, in the entire composition (figs. 10, 11).

---

[37]In a letter to the Empress Anna in which he praised the impact of various ancient women on political events. See Capozzi, "Evolution and Transformation of the Judith and Holofernes Theme," p. 21, citing Francesco Petrarca, *Le familiari,* ed. V. Rossi (Florence: Sansoni, 1942), 4:66. Petrarch also named Judith and Holofernes in his *Trionfi,* in the "Triumph of Love," the "Triumph of Chastity," and the "Triumph of Fame"; see *The Triumphs of Petrarch,* trans. Ernest Hatch Wilkins (Chicago: University of Chicago Press, 1962), pp. 22, 45, 83. They enter the secular visual iconography of the Renaissance through illustrations of these poems. In the Quattrocento this is often found on *cassone* panels and related decorative arts, usually in an erotic context; see Smith, "Sex and Citizenship." For the *Trionfi* in art, see Paul F. Watson: *The Garden of Love in Tuscan Art of the Early Renaissance* (Philadelphia: Art Alliance Press, 1979), esp. chaps. 2 and 5; also his "Virtù and Voluptas in *Cassone* Painting" (Ph.D. diss., Yale University, 1970), with useful remarks throughout on questions of the interactions of humanism, art, and ideas about gender.

[38]Recorded in Janson, *Sculpture of Donatello,* p. 200.

[39]Saint Augustine was apparently the first to link Judith to the heroic Roman era of the Tarquins; Capozzi, "Evolution and Transformation of the Judith and Holofernes Theme," p. 14. Judith was subsequently often paired with Lucretia.

[40]See Warner, *Monuments and Maidens,* pp. 164–65; Christine de Pizan, *The Book of the City of Ladies,* trans. E. Richards (New York: Persea Books, 1982), introduction and pp. 143–45. For the literature of the *querelle* initiated by Christine de Pizan, see Joan Kelly, "Early Feminist Theory and the *Querelle des Femmes,*" in her *Women, History, and Theory,* pp. 65–109; and Beatrice Gottlieb, "The Problem of Feminism in the 15th Century," in *Women of the Medieval World,* ed. Julius Kirshner and Suzanne Wemple (Oxford: Blackwell, 1985), pp. 337–61. One example, out of many, of a later citation of Judith in this context is Tomaso Garzoni, *Discorso sopra la nobiltà delle donne* (Venice: G. D. Imberti, 1588), p. 173.

There is an unyielding angularity about the statue which lends something of the inevitability of geometry to Judith's act.[41] This seems to be a Donatellian innovation, at least if we compare his immediate local predecessor in Judith iconography, Ghiberti. In the latter's small bronze figure set in the border of the *David and Goliath* panel on the famous Florentine Baptistry doors (fig. 12), a more fluid conception of heroism obtains (one that may well have later influenced Botticelli).[42] There are striking similarities between the two sculptural works, especially in the brandishing of the swords, but the overall tone is quite different. The greater vigor of Donatello's representation also has a lot to do with the moment depicted, since we apparently see his Judith in the act of decapitating her enemy, and she is physically convincing in the role.[43]

In her virile purposefulness, Donatello's *Judith* seems to take us away from the conventional associations of medieval Mariological iconogra-

---

[41]I am here co-opting a famous phrase by the Quattrocento Florentine humanist Giannozzo Manetti, who wrote in his *On the Dignity and Excellence of Man* "that the truths of the Christian religion are as clear and self-evident as the axioms of mathematics." For this reading and its relevance to fifteenth-century Florentine architecture, see Frederick Hartt, *History of Italian Renaissance Art*, 3rd ed. (New York: Abrams, 1987), p. 155. In the case of Donatello's *Judith* specifically, Janson remarked on "the rational geometric scheme" of the figure's relationship to the cushion on which she stands; Janson, *Sculpture of Donatello*, p. 204.

[42]The so-called Gates of Paradise were executed between 1424 and 1452. In the mass of documentation for the project, there is nothing that provides a date for the Judith, but the major reliefs are from 1429–37 and the rest was completed by 1448. See Richard Krautheimer and Trude Krautheimer-Hess, *Lorenzo Ghiberti*, 2nd ed. (Princeton: Princeton University Press, 1970), pp. 159–68. Of the border figures the authors say only that they "must have been cast somewhere along the way" between these two sets of dates.

[43]Janson, *Sculpture of Donatello*, p. 204, believed that what appears to be a cut in Holofernes' neck is a seam in the cast bronze; he therefore tends toward a ritual rather than a narrative identity for the sculpture. Bennett and Wilkins, *Donatello*, pp. 219–20, observed more recently: "Although scholars have sometimes been misled by an irrelevant casting flaw, which becomes too prominent in photographs, the recent relocation of the sculpture inside the Palazzo Vecchio makes possible a closer examination of the original, which reveals a deep open gash in Holofernes' neck." It is to be expected that the restoration of the statue, completed in May 1988, will spark a new wave of scholarly attention to many of the work's problematical issues. The laboratory reports on the internal structure of the base could resolve the controversy over the statue's reputed origins as a fountain, for instance, which might illuminate its elusive early history. Judith was not a common subject for Renaissance fountains, although she can be plausibly linked to water themes via her decisive rout of the Assyrian army, which meant the end of the siege-imposed drought for Bethulia. I am grateful to Bonnie Bennett and Claudia Lazzaro for suggesting these connections.

Figure 12. Ghiberti, *Judith*, c. 1430s–40s, Baptistry, Florence. Photo: Foto Marburg/Art Resource.

phy and into the world of humanist *virtù,* with its emphasis on civic action. And yet, this is an emphatically masculine world, one far removed from the domesticity by which Alberti defines the ideal woman in Book 3 of *Della famiglia.*[44] Moreover, whatever the sexual components of Donatello's sculpture, and the positioning of both Judith's foot and Holofernes' head cannot be ignored, his Judith is no icon of female allure. One has difficulty visualizing her plying "feminine wiles" at all. It would seem rather than Donatello is inviting us to consider a relevant convergence of humanist and patristic thinking that designated the gender of virtue as masculine. Saint Clement of Rome in the first century, the earliest patristic commentator on Judith, had put it succinctly, numbering her among those exceptional women who, "being strengthened by the grace of God, have performed numerous manly exploits."[45] He was broadly echoed throughout the Middle Ages and the Renaissance. In Trecento Renaissance Florence we meet the topos again in, for instance, Boccaccio, who chose the heroines in *De claris mulieribus* for their "manly courage."[46] In addition, we can locate the same tactic in the familiar patristic conceit which associated Judith with the apotheosis of female virginity. According to the church fathers, the ideal of virginity for women meant the repudiation of their intrinsically flawed sexual nature; this was such a heroic achievement that it entitled female virgins to something like spiritual equality with men and the accolade "virile" or even outright "male."[47]

[44]See the translation by Renée Neu Watkins in *The Family in Renaissance Florence* (Columbia: University of South Carolina Press, 1969), pp. 213ff. *Della famiglia* was written in the 1430s and revised in the next decade.

[45]Quoted in Capozzi, "Evolution and Transformation of the Judith and Holofernes Theme," p. 13, citing *The Ante-Nicene Fathers,* ed. Alexander Roberts (Grand Rapids: W. B. Eerdmans, 1950), 1:20. It is important to remember that the humanist revival of antique literature encompassed the early patristic writings. See Charles Stinger, *Humanism and the Church Fathers* (Albany: State University of New York Press, 1977). For some fifteenth-century Florentine artistic ramifications of this development, see Krautheimer and Krautheimer-Hess, *Lorenzo Ghiberti,* pp. 169–88.

[46]Giovanni Boccaccio, *Concerning Famous Women,* trans. Guido Guarino (New Brunswick, N.J.: Rutgers University Press, 1963), preface, p. xxxvii. Cf. discussions in Christine de Pizan, *The Book of the City of Ladies,* p. xxxv; Jordan, "Feminism and the Humanists," pp. 242–45; and her "Boccaccio's In-Famous Women: Gender and Civic Virtue in the *De mulieribus claris,*" in *Ambiguous Realities,* pp. 25–47. Jordan's analysis of Boccaccio's conflicted praise of the power of female eloquence—and its connections to chastity—is particularly appropriate to the case of Judith, whose dazzling words destroyed Holofernes. See also Valerie Wayne, "Zenobia in Medieval and Renaissance Literature," in *Ambiguous Realities,* esp. pp. 48–51. For links between Boccaccio's book and Giotto's frescoes on the "Fatal Power of Women" topos, see Gilbert, "Boccaccio Looking at Actual Frescoes," esp. pp. 237–38.

[47]Schulenburg, "Heroics of Virginity," p. 32. A fascinating recent treatment of this

It has always been abundantly clear that even on the surface the ani-
mating mechanism of the Book of Judith is the opposing of male and
female. At the core of the story is the reversal of prevailing patriarchal
gender codes, within the terms of the patriarchy, of course. What
makes the death of the mighty Holofernes remarkable, what gives it its
miraculous status, is that its agent was a "mere" female. Judith herself
repeatedly observes this, elaborating with some relish:

> The Lord Almighty hath foiled them by the hand of a female.
> For their champion did not fall by the hand of young men,
> Nor did the sons of the Titans smite him,
> Nor did towering giants lay their hands upon him;
> But Judith, the daughter of Merari,
> Undid him by the beauty of her face.
>
> [16:5–6]

The overt point of the story is the invincible power of the God of Israel,
and we are made to see that this is a power so great that it can even
overturn the "natural order" of gender-specific behavior.

Judith's exemplary status as a paradox of strength in weakness derives particular piquancy in the climate of humanism, where, as we
have seen, the revival of interest in classical antiquity meant renewed
currency and emulation of Greek and Roman dicta on female inferiority. For instance, directly relevant to the Renaissance cultivation
of *virtù* was Cicero's etymological foundation of that term in the word
vir (man), already known to medieval scholastics.[48] Such a linguistic
ploy is sustained by the entire body of antique scholarly opinion, taken
up by witch-hunters and humanists alike, which defines women as
physically imperfect (largely by virtue of their characteristic cold and
moist humors) and therefore intellectually and ethically limited. Because men are more robust, theirs is the capacity for action, which—
along with the superior male ability to reason—lies at the heart of

---

and related visual themes of direct relevance to the topic of Judith representations is
Margaret Miles, *Carnal Knowing* (Boston: Beacon, 1989).

[48]Maclean, *Renaissance Notion of Woman*, p. 53; his entire chapter 4 is relevant here. For
the reverse, deriving *vir* from *virtù*, see Warner, *Monuments and Maidens*, p. 65. The
question of gender designations for virtue was also alive for Renaissance defenders of
women. In the well-known discussions of *The Courtier*, for instance, we find an appeal
to grammar in the claim by Emilia Pia that women have more virtue than men:
"Consider that virtue is feminine whereas vice is masculine." Baldesar Castiglione, *The
Book of the Courtier*, trans. George Bull (Harmondsworth, England: Penguin Books,
1967), p. 201.

moral behavior and *virtù*. Consigned to naturally ordained passivity, "the woman is excluded from all moral behavior," and thus from the public realm.[49] (It seems relevant to point out in this context the sequestering of later Renaissance Florentine women in their homes, the extent of which practice excited comment even at the time.)[50] In such an intellectual and social atmosphere, Judith takes on an explicit function that fuses the secular with the religious to reinforce the ideology of gender difference. As Boccaccio put it:

> If men should be praised whenever they perform great deeds (with strength which Nature has given them), how much more should women be extolled (almost all of whom are endowed with tenderness, frail bodies, and sluggish minds by Nature), if they have acquired a manly spirit and if with keen intelligence and remarkable fortitude they have dared undertake and have accomplished even the most difficult deeds?[51]

Therefore a physically and psychologically believable Judith representation, such as Donatello's (and here the contrast with Botticelli is telling), must transcend the female norm to absorb enough *vir* to make her *virago*. I hasten to add that I mean *virago* in the Quattrocento sense in which it is applied to Caterina Sforza, closer to "Amazon" than to its subsequent designation of "scolding shrew."[52] Much the same can be

---

[49]Maclean, *Renaissance Notion of Woman*, p. 51.

[50]The remark in question is from 1610: "In Florence women are more enclosed than in any other part of Italy; they see the world only from the small openings in their windows." It is quoted by Judith Brown, "A Woman's Place Was in the Home: Women's Work in Renaissance Tuscany," in *Rewriting the Renaissance*, p. 215. See also Merry Weisner, "Women's Defense of their Public Role," in Rose, *Women in the Middle Ages and the Renaissance;* her note 29 cites an earlier draft of Brown's article. Historians are beginning to provide a long-overdue picture of the quotidian lives of Renaissance women; see especially Christiane Klapisch-Zuber, *Women, Family, and Ritual in Renaissance Italy,* trans. Lydia G. Cochrane (Chicago: University of Chicago Press, 1985); and Anderson and Zinsser, *A History of Their Own,* vols. 1 and 2.

[51]Boccaccio, *Concerning Famous Women*, p. xxxvii. Cf. a modern reformulation which makes the connection with Judith explicit: "If woman is generally considered to be weaker than man, her virtuous acts become as a consequence much more admirable, since the gap between her action and her true nature is greater than the gap in a man. It is clear from a variety of [Renaissance] texts that God delights in confounding the mighty by the agency of the weak: Judith, Deborah and Jael among biblical women all are figures for this." Maclean, *Renaissance Notion of Woman*, p. 21.

[52]It is worth quoting the view of Burckhardt, *Civilization of the Renaissance in Italy,* 2:391–92: "The highest praise which could then be given to the great Italian women was that they had the mind and courage of men. . . . The title *virago,* which is an equivocal compliment in the present day, then implied nothing but praise."

said of the late-fifteenth-century images of Judith by Mantegna.[53] In a northern Italian setting even more consciously humanist than Donatello's, Mantegna conceived of the heroine in virile terms, which might be construed as investing her with the capacity for moral behavior in the public realm normally denied to women. In his drawing of 1491, for instance, her physical strength is matched by an inner spirit of gravitas and dignity (fig. 13). In such representations, grammatical and moral cognates converge: *vir, virtù, virago, virginitas.*

This is dangerous territory by any account. The Book of Judith is careful to assure us that its central gender inversion is momentary, since Judith soon returns to her normal role of secluded, pious widow.[54] Decorum is thus violated primarily to be reaffirmed, a Renaissance phenomenon familiar to readers of Natalie Zemon Davis.[55] In fifteenth-century Florence the conservative Alberti shows us how the decorous ideal in the realm of behavior could impinge on representations of Judith in the realm of art. Giannozzo, the exemplary husband of *Della famiglia,* counsels his young wife that "we should have order and system in all that we do. It does not befit a woman like you to carry a sword, nor to do other manly things that men do."[56] In other words, whatever her power as a civic symbol, even overlaid with biblical and patristic sanction, the virago is no exemplar for actual women.

It should come as no surprise, then, to find Donatello's *Judith* under

[53]Mantegna was in Florence in 1466–67. A painting of Judith by him or close to his style was recorded in the Medici collections in an inventory of 1492. See Lightbown, *Botticelli,* 2:22. For Mantegna and humanism, see the monograph by Lightbown, *Mantegna* (Berkeley: University of California Press, 1986); the Judith representations are catalogue numbers 30, 52, 56, 156, 188, and 228. In this context it may be useful to observe that the source of one of the widely copied Mantegnesque Judiths is a Roman nymph sculpture in the Vatican; see Tilmann Buddensieg, "Raffaels Grab," in *Munuscula Discipulorum: Kunsthistorische Studien für Hans Kauffmann zum 70. Geburtstag* (Berlin: B. Hessling, 1968), p. 50, figs. 35, 42, 45.

[54]Enslin and Zeitlin devote Appendix I to her widowhood; *Book of Judith,* 180–81. It may be worth noting that the key figure in fifteenth-century Florentine religious life, Saint Antonine, revived the patristic celebration of widowhood. He preached that it was the preferred state for women. See Hartt, *History of Italian Renaissance Art,* p. 287.

[55]See "Women on Top," in her *Culture and Society in Early Modern France* (Stanford: Stanford University Press, 1975), pp. 124–51. Davis sees many Renaissance gender inversions as both undermining and reasserting the prevailing hierarchies. Many of her remarks, especially those on the virtuous virago, have direct bearing on the iconography of Judith.

[56]*The Family in Renaissance Florence,* p. 226. Alberti offers no scenario whereby carrying a sword would be appropriate for any woman. Even beyond the military question, the "liberal" Italian humanists generally drew the line at a public role for women. See Jordan, "Feminism and the Humanists," pp. 252–53.

Figure 13. Mantegna, *Judith*, 1491, Uffizi, Florence. Photo: Alinari/Art Resource.

attack on precisely these grounds. In 1503, during the famous delibera-
tions over the placement of Michelangelo's monumental statue of
David, attention naturally focused on the politically charged area in
front of Palazzo della Signoria, to which *Judith* had been moved ten
years earlier. One of the deliberators urged the substitution of the new
David for *Judith,* noting: "Judith is an omen of evil, and no fit object
where it stands, as we have the cross and lily for our emblems; besides,
it is not proper that the woman should kill the male; and, above all, this
statue was erected under an evil star, as things have gone from bad to
worse since then."[57] In fact, a version of this view prevailed: *Judith* was
moved, first inside the Palazzo della Signoria and soon after to the
adjacent Loggia dei Lanzi, and *David* was installed on her pedestal.[58]
One might well wonder if the conceptual impropriety of a woman's
killing a man could account for the rarity in Italian Renaissance art of
depictions of Holofernes' actual decapitation. As far as I know, Donatello's is the one such example among major artists of the period. In
Italy, at least, it seems that only the different psychic and stylistic
requirements of the Baroque could achieve something like common
currency for this charged image.

Among the deliberators on the placement of Michelangelo's *David*
was Botticelli. Having begun with him, I would like to chose with
him—not with his youthful *Return of Judith to Bethulia* but with one of
his last thoughts on the subject. In a late painting, the problematical
Calumny of Apelles (c. 1495), he included three images of Judith (fig.
14).[59] Behind the throne of Midas at the far right we see a statue of
Judith in a niche and above and below it narrative reliefs derived in part
from his earlier Judith painting of 1470. This is not the place to untangle the puzzle of this classically inspired allegory of truth, envy, and
justice, which was a product of the religious crisis of Botticelli's last
years. For the purposes at hand, let it be sufficient to observe that Judith
is installed here among an unusual grouping of antique and biblical
symbols of virtue. She thus participates in the quintessential intellectual project of humanism: the syncretic reconciliation of the classical

[57]Translated in *Italian Art, 1500–1600,* ed. Robert Klein and Henri Zerner (En-
glewood Cliffs, N.J.: Prentice-Hall, 1966), p. 41.
[58]Janson, *Sculpture of Donatello,* p. 201; on p. 99 we meet an echo in 1571 of the earlier
objection, in Francesco Bocchi's praise of Donatello's *Judith* for its "unusual boldness
and force, as well as the strength granted to her by God, for women do not ordinarily
accomplish such deeds."
[59]See Lightbown, *Botticelli,* 1:122–26, 2:88–92; and David Cast, *The Calumny of
Apelles* (New Haven: Yale University Press, 1981), chap. 1.

Figure 14. Botticelli, *The Calumny of Apelles,* c. 1495, Uffizi, Florence. Photo: Alinari/Art Resource.

and the Judeo-Christian traditions. But she can function to this effect on the complex intellectual level of the painting as a whole only if we understand the range of divergent and convergent meanings she had come to acquire by Botticelli's time. In this painting, then, Judith might be said to display the entire constellation of overlapping mores, dogmas, and ideals that constituted her iconographic evolution in the Renaissance.

For much of this paper I have co-opted Ruskin's agenda and attempted to enlarge his defense of Judith's character and reputation by insisting on its historical dimensions. At the close I must acknowledge the inherent limitations of such a project. The biblical Judith is, of course, a patriarchal creation. As a literary figure she may inhabit a richer range of human motivations than her Christian and psycho-analytic interpreters have given her credit for; but the Book of Judith's

operative polarity between her powerful chastity and Holofernes' debilitating lust is by definition a phallic conceit. In the words of one
critic, the "analysis of Judith's tyrannicide as an aspect of her sexual restraint is typical of reductive thinking about women."[60] The artistic
representations of the subject cannot, in the current state of our culture, fail to fall into the same traps: whether the artist sees Judith as
castrating femme fatale or invincible virgin-virago or any possibility in
between, it is patriarchal categories that prevail. At work here is a
powerful "set of representations which imposes itself as reality," as
Jacobus has acutely observed, building on the pioneering connecting of
ideology and iconography of Virginia Woolf.[61] In that famous passage
in A Room of One's Own—"Women have served all these centuries as
looking-glasses possessing the magic and delicious power of reflecting
the figure of man at twice its natural size"—I believe we can see the
varying images of Judith.[62] I think that what has made her such a
compelling figure is the ironic fact that the fathers of our culture have
consistently missed this point about her essentially specular function.
In their anxiety to assert their requisite double scale, which was actually there all along, they have periodically imposed on her image a
complex overlay of "correcting" distortions. The contentious evolution of Judith interpretations is the ongoing record of these attempts.

[60]Warner, Monuments and Maidens, p. 165.
[61]Jacobus, "Judith, Holofernes, and the Phallic Woman," p. 132.
[62]Virginia Woolf, A Room of One's Own (New York: Harcourt, Brace and World,
1957), p. 35. Garrard sees Gentileschi's Judiths as exceptions to such a claim, locating
them "beyond social or theological masculine control," in Artemisia Gentileschi, pp.
335–36.

Claudia Lazzaro

The Visual Language of Gender in Sixteenth-Century Garden Sculpture

In the Renaissance, as in antiquity, Natura was personified as a woman. The relationship was reciprocal: women were compared visually and verbally, in painting and poetry, with the forms of the natural world.[1] The association of nature with the female abounds in nature itself—that is, in the sculpted images in sixteenth-century Italian gardens, many of which personify aspects of the natural world. The female presence in monumental garden sculpture is striking, and the principal garden ornaments were often a pair of female and male images. The identification of nature with the female and the association of aspects of nature with either male or female suggest that in the Renaissance, gender played a significant role in the understanding of the natural world. Gender is conveyed not only through the identity of figures but also through unambiguous visual signs corresponding with female and male. We can speak of a female voice in visual language, which was used to convey analogies between the various ideas and

---

[1] For example, in the poetic conventions of metaphor the beloved is compared with aspects of nature. In Renaissance portraits the form of the female sitter is sometimes explicitly related to the natural forms of the setting. The most famous example is Leonardo's Mona Lisa, which expresses as a frequent theme in his thinking and scientific inquiries as well as in his paintings "the analogy between the reproductive processes of the female body and the generative powers of the natural world," as it has been described by Martin Kemp, *Leonardo da Vinci: The Marvelous Works of Nature and Man* (Cambridge, Mass.: Harvard University Press, 1981), pp. 261–70, 275. See also Laurie Schneider and Jack D. Flam, "Visual Convention, Simile, and Metaphor in the Mona Lisa," *Storia dell'arte* 29 (1977): 15–24, on the relationship of figure to landscape in both visual and conceptual terms; and Webster Smith, "Observations on the *Mona Lisa* Landscape," *Art Bulletin* 67 (1985): 183–99, for a more detailed analysis and also a discussion of the painter as poet.

71

activities that were understood as female in the code of the sixteenth century. If we fail to recognize this code, we will be unable to read the visual signs that function within it. Sensitized to the expressive means of gender, however, we can discern in some relief sculpture about nature not only contrasting visual signs but even a distinct system of representation.

In the Renaissance view human and natural worlds were inter-locked—practically, philosophically, morally, symbolically, in every way. Nature was perceived in relation to humans and as existing for their benefit. Plants and animals, for example, not only provided the food, medicine, clothing, and shelter on which human life depended, but also reflected and symbolized human virtues, moral and religious values.[2] Their relationship in gardens, similarly reciprocal, was ex-pressed, like much else in the Renaissance, as an interaction of art and nature: the raw materials of nature—trees, plants, water, stones—are shaped and manipulated by art.[3]

Since ancient times, human modification of the natural environment was called a second nature, and in the Renaissance, works of art were also termed a second or another nature.[4] The garden, however, was

[2]Keith Thomas, *Man and the Natural World: A History of the Modern Sensibility* (New York: Pantheon, 1983); Wolfgang Harms, "On Natural History and Emblematics in the 16th Century," in *The Natural Sciences and the Arts: Aspects of Interaction from the Renais-sance to the 20th Century: An International Symposium,* ed. Allan Ellenius (Stockholm: Almqvist & Wiksell, 1985), pp. 67–83; also discussed in Michel Foucault, *The Order of Things* (New York: Pantheon, 1971), chap. 2; originally published as *Les mots et les choses* (Paris: Gallimard, 1966).

[3]Vincenzo Borghini explained this interaction of art and nature in a similar example: "La natura dà il suo diamante, o carbonchio o cristallo et riunite altra materia rozza et informe, et l'arte gli pulisce, riquadra, intaglia, etcetera" ("Nature gives its diamond or ruby or crystal joined with other rough and shapeless matter, and art polishes, cuts, and engraves them"), in Marco Dezzi Bardeschi et al., *Lo Stanzino del Principe in Palazzo Vecchio: I concetti, le immagini, il desiderio* (Florence: Le Lettere, 1980), p. 31. On art and nature in Renaissance thinking, see Edward W. Tayler, *Nature and Art in Renaissance Literature* (New York: Columbia University Press, 1964); and A. J. Close, "Com-monplace Theories of Art and Nature in Classical Antiquity and in the Renaissance," *Journal of the History of Ideas* 30 (1969): 467–86. Much of the recent literature on Italian Renaissance gardens discusses the theme of art and nature, among them my article "The Villa Lante at Bagnaia: An Allegory of Art and Nature," *Art Bulletin* 59 (1977): 553–60.

[4]The ancient concept of a second nature, codified in Cicero's *De natura deorum,* is discussed in Clarence J. Glacken, *Traces on the Rhodian Shore: Nature and Culture in Western Thought from Ancient Times to the End of the Eighteenth Century* (Berkeley: Univer-sity of California Press, 1967), chap. 2, esp. pp. 144–49. Renaissance uses of the phrase in reference to art and poetry are cited by Jan Bialostocki, "The Renaissance Conception of Nature and Antiquity," in *Studies in Western Art,* vol. 2, *The Renaissance and Man-nerism,* Acts of the XXth International Congress of the History of Art (Princeton: Princeton University Press, 1963), pp. 28–29.

described by contemporaries not as a second but as a third nature, because nature is also an active, shaping force. In 1541 Jacopo Bonfadio explained that "la natura incorporata con l'arte è fatta artefice, e connaturale de l'arte, e d'amendue è fatta una terza natura" ("Nature incorporated with art is made the creator and connatural of art, and from both is made a third nature").[5] He conceived the interaction of art and nature in the garden as a dialectic and even a symbiotic system. Nature becomes the creator of art, and shares art's essence; it is not simply the object of the shaping human hand, but it also shares equally in the forming and ordering process. The garden is the incorporation of two essential aspects, art and nature, which together make a different sort of nature, a third nature.

In modern scholarship Renaissance gardens are characterized instead as an expression of man's dominance over nature. This view implies a separation between human and nature, locked not in a reciprocal relationship but in one of power, the latter dominated by the self-aware Renaissance "individual." Grammatically, the generic *man* is masculine, and power has been assumed to be a male prerogative. In the Renaissance, nature was emphatically identified with female and verbally paired with art, not man. Superimposing these two views, we can suggest that a conceptual model of male dominating female is the basis for our understanding of the human relationship with nature in the Renaissance. In literal terms, women as well as men owned and ornamented gardens; and metaphorically, writers in the fifteenth and sixteenth centuries did not articulate the relationship between human culture and the natural world as a hierarchical one.

The origins of the very different attitude toward the natural world embodied in the notion of dominance have been sought not with reference to Renaissance gardens but in a context relevant to this discussion. In *Man and the Natural World,* an illuminating account of the relationship between human and natural realms in England from the sixteenth through the eighteenth centuries, Keith Thomas suggests that the notion of man as dominating nature began in the late sixteenth

[5]Jacopo Bonfadio, *Le lettere e una scrittura burlesca,* ed. A. Greco (Rome: Bonacci, 1978), p. 96, and published in editions of Bonfadio's letters, and in *Lettere del Cinquecento,* ed. G. G. Ferrero (Turin: UTET, 1967), p. 501. Bartolomeo Taegio, in *La villa* (Milan: Francesco Moschoni, 1559), p. 94, also discusses the third nature. Both are cited by Alessandro Rinaldi, "La ricerca della 'terza natura': Artificialia e naturalia nel giardino toscano del '500," in *Natura e artificio,* ed. M. Fagiolo (Rome: Officina Edizioni, 1979), pp. 154–75, and by Alessandro Tagliolini, "Girolamo Fiorenzuola e il giardino nelle fonti della metà del Cinquecento," in *Il giardino storico italiano* (Florence: Olschki, 1981), pp. 295–308.

century.[6] Recent concerns with ecology have also prompted a search for the beginnings of our modern ideas of control and dominance over nature, by, among many others, Carolyn Merchant in *The Death of Nature: Women, Ecology, and the Scientific Revolution*.[7] Her thesis is that a change in the visual and verbal language used to describe nature signals a change in attitude toward it, and her discussion begins with the association of nature with the female. Merchant's approach warrants a more careful scrutiny of evidence than she has given, however; her conclusion that the modern attitude of dominance originated in the seventeenth century is based on a partial and biased analysis. In addition, in a study of frontispieces to botanical works, Gunnar Broberg finds that nature was personified as Diana of Ephesus until the mid-eighteenth century,[8] an image that we also find in sixteenth-century gardens, and one that embodies a concept of nature quite different from our modern one.

My own research unequivocally supports Broberg's view: with respect to gardens, the idea of man's domination over nature does not appear until long after the Renaissance. The mutually enhancing dialectic between art and nature, even nature's superiority, resounds repeatedly in texts of various sorts from the sixteenth through the eighteenth centuries. For example, Leonardo da Vinci, who suggests that the painter is almost another God, also speaks of the artist as an interpreter between nature and art.[9] A change in the way nature was viewed in the seventeenth century is witnessed by a new phenomenon, horticultural manuals. In one of the first such manuals in Italy, Giovanni Battista Ferrari's *Flora* of 1633, the final chapter is devoted to a competition between Art and Nature in the coloring of flowers. The con-

[6]Thomas, *Man and the Natural World*, chap. 1, where the sources he cites, however, are from the seventeenth century.

[7]Carolyn Merchant, *The Death of Nature: Women, Ecology, and the Scientific Revolution* (San Francisco: Harper & Row, 1980).

[8]Gunnar Broberg, "Natural History Frontispieces and Ecology," in Ellenius, *Natural Sciences and the Arts*, pp. 84–97. For the concept of nature embodied in the figure of the Goddess of Nature, see George D. Economou, *The Goddess Natura in Medieval Literature* (Cambridge, Mass.: Harvard University Press, 1972).

[9]*The Literary Works of Leonardo da Vinci*, ed. J. P. Richter, commentary by C. Pedretti, 2 vols. (Oxford: Phaidon, 1977), 1:79: "L'artifice viene quasi à dimostrarsi quasi un'altro Dio" ("the maker [of painting] comes almost to reveal himself to be almost another God"), and 2:257, painting "constringie la mente del pittore a trasmutarsi nella propria mente di natura et sia interprete infra essa natura e l'arte" ("compels the mind of the painter to transform into the very mind of nature, to become an interpreter between nature and art").

test concludes when Art, stunned by Nature's effects, concedes the palm of victory.[10] Almost a century later, in a treatise of 1726 on the history and cultivation of plants, Paolo Clarici's *Istoria e coltura delle piante,* gardens are still discussed within the traditional framework of the pairing of art and nature, very much as they were in the Renaissance. Nature is helped and served by art to become more fertile: pruning trees helps them to bear more fruit.[11] But man does not dominate nature.

Renaissance gardens were not characterized in terms of man's dominance until the early twentieth century, when this view was stated forcefully in two important publications. In Luigi Dami's *Giardino italiano,* published in 1924 and immediately translated into English, the primacy of man and disdain for the natural are presented as the essence of the sixteenth-century Italian garden.[12] In a major exhibition of the Italian garden in Florence in 1931, Renaissance gardens are characterized as "il continuo e ordinato e visibile dominio dell'uomo sulla natura" ("the continuous and orderly and visible dominion of man over nature").[13] This emphasis must reflect the social and political situation in Italy at the time, as well as the great enthusiasm in the early twentieth century for Renaissance gardens, and for historicizing gardens that aimed to emulate them. Since the 1920s the assumption that Italian Renaissance gardens expressed the dominance of man, which is the modern way of phrasing the superiority of art, has been unquestioned, along with other erroneous notions concerning the plants that filled them and how contemporaries conceived them.[14]

[10]Giovanni Battista Ferrari, *Flora overo cultura di fiori,* trans. L. Aureli (first Latin ed., 1633; Rome: P. A. Facciotti, 1638), chap. 6, "Miracolo della Natura maggior di quelli dell'Arte," pp. 466–74.

[11]Paolo Bartolomeo Clarici, *Istoria e coltura delle piante* (Venice: Andrea Poletti, 1726), p. 3.

[12]Luigi Dami, *Il giardino italiano* (Milan: Bestetti e Tumminelli, 1924), p. 22.

[13]*Mostra del giardino italiano,* exhibition catalogue (Florence, 1931), p. 23.

[14]For example, Francesco Fariello, *Architettura dei giardini* (Rome: Ateneo, 1967), p. 74: "Nato in un clima di magnificenza, il giardino del Cinquecento riflette il razionalismo umanistico dell'epoca, che afferma il dominio dell'uomo sul mondo sensibile" ("Born in a climate of magnificence, the sixteenth-century garden reflects the humanistic rationalism of the epoch, which affirms the dominion of man over the material world"); John Shearman, *Mannerism* (Harmondsworth, England: Penguin Books, 1967), p. 123: "The sixteenth-century garden is more obviously a product of man than of nature; it seems that the garden artist's material is not organic, or rather that it has no life that he does not give it"; and *The Oxford Companion to Gardens,* eds. G. Jellicoe, S. Jellicoe, P. Goode, and M. Lancaster (Oxford: Oxford University Press,

A critical examination of modern scholarship reveals that the attitude of dominance is of our own times, more imposed on than derived from the past. Justification for the man-dominated view of Renaissance gardens has been found in the words of the sculptor Baccio Bandinelli in 1551. When asked to design a fountain for the Boboli Garden in Florence, which was ultimately executed by Giambologna, Bandinelli agreed to make one worthy of the place, and in correspondence with a wall that was to be constructed, because "the things that one builds must be the guide and superior to those that one plants."[15] This phrase, rather than the words of many other contemporaries, has been selected by twentieth-century scholarship to characterize the Renaissance garden and the primacy of art, and man, in its creation. A similar bias is evident in modern discussions of the relationship between human technology and nature. The frequency in twentieth-century writings, especially in Utopian proposals of the 1960s, of such phrases as "domination of nature," "control of nature," and "conquest of nature" in reference to science and technology has been pointed out by William Leiss. In *The Domination of Nature*, Leiss offers some correctives to the displacement of this current view onto the past by distinguishing it in cultural terms from its beginnings in the seventeenth century.[16]

The transformation from a symbiotic relationship of two interlocked terms to the superiority of one over the other is not merely incorrect. It also has serious implications for how we understand the Renaissance and what we choose to examine in it. The period was indeed obsessed with competition and superiority—of the moderns to the ancients, of painting to sculpture, of poetry to painting. Contemporary accounts

1986), p. 284: "However, one of the features which was to remain central and constant in Italian gardens until the end of the 18th century was already apparent [in fifteenth-century gardens]—the subordinate role in the whole design played by plants, which were almost entirely evergreens," and p. 285: "Here [the Villa Medici at Castello], as elsewhere, there are two general themes: the superiority of art over nature and a celebration of the power and virtues of the patron."

[15]Giovanni Gaetano Bottari and Stefano Ticozzi, *Raccolta di lettere sulla pittura, scultura ed architettura*, 8 vols. (Milan: G. Silvestri, 1822), 1:93–94: "Le cose che si murano debbono essere guida e superiori a quelle che si piantano."

[16]William Leiss, *The Domination of Nature* (New York: George Braziller, 1972), pp. 12–15, and chaps. 2 and 3, esp. pp. 35 and 68. Since Francis Bacon is generally taken to be the key figure in a new attitude of mastery over nature in the seventeenth century, it should also be noted that his famous essay "Of Gardens" does not speak of them in terms of either the victory of art or the domination of man. Other correctives to a distorted understanding of the past can be found in Robin Attfield, "Christian Attitudes to Nature," *Journal of the History of Ideas* 44 (1983): 369–86, and above all in Glacken's learned and sensitive *Traces on the Rhodian Shore*.

accordingly describe a lively and playful competition between art and nature in gardens, but in this arena as in many others there was no clear winner. Gardens were not described in the military language of domination, conquest, and victory; this is true only of modern writing. In the Renaissance view one of the principal actions that art, culture, man, or the gardener performs on nature is not subduing but rather unveiling the order inherent there. It is not an order imposed on nature by human culture; the essence of nature is not altered, only revealed.

The dialogue, or balance of opposites, or pairing of complementaries, is a basic mode of verbal and visual expression in the Renaissance.[17] Paired concepts—nature and art, *fortuna* and *virtù,* country and city, and so on—are, like female and male, contrasting terms locked in perpetual relationship. Because only one half of a pair—art, or man—has predominated in the study of Renaissance gardens, much has been left out: nature as protagonist of the garden, as its very substance and its subject, often expressed through the female form as symbol of nature and embodiment of fertility. There has been little investigation of the planting in Renaissance gardens, or of nature as the principal theme of their statues, fountains, and other ornaments.[18] Most of the sculpture in gardens is specifically about nature, expressed through the human analogy of mythological figures and personifications, and often the same idea is told simultaneously through human forms and actual nature—water, earth, or trees. In the human analogy for understanding nature, the differentiation of male and female and their interaction are particularly significant. The characteristics of male and female were conveyed through a visual language that emphasized their difference and also expressed the cultural values embodied in those differences.

The modern interpretation of gardens rightly implies that male authority dominated culture and society in the Renaissance; yet, other orders besides the predominant male culture did have a marginal presence, and gardens were one appropriate place for them. The subordination of nature to art, or man, diminishes the importance of what is natural and innate, as well as of nature itself, in societal and cultural terms. Nature represented a different order from that of male culture, one explicitly identified as female to express the generative force in the

[17]For a discussion of one aspect of this topic, see David Summers, "Contrapposto: Style and Meaning in Renaissance Art," *Art Bulletin* 59 (1977): 336–61.

[18]See Claudia Lazzaro, *The Italian Renaissance Garden: From the Conventions of Planting, Design, and Ornament to the Grand Gardens of Sixteenth-Century Central Italy* (New Haven: Yale University Press, 1990), for the planting of Renaissance gardens as well as the role of nature in every aspect of garden design and ornamentation.

natural world; and one signifying, along with fertility and abundance, also sensuality, playfulness, freedom from social constraints, manners, and morals, and thus even sexual freedom, as well as inspiration for poetic endeavors.[19] All of these are freely expressed in gardens, if not always in the dominant culture. Gardens were the place for play, for getting drenched by hidden water jets, and for a loosening of both artistic and social rules of expression. Sculpture and other ornaments alluded to the Golden Age, or another earthly paradise where nature is undisturbed by human art. Nostalgia on the part of a sophisticated and urban society for a natural state, for a time not dominated by the requirements and restraints of civilization, is voiced in the dialogue between art and nature, and in their interaction in the planting, design, and imagery of gardens.

In Renaissance gardens, as in the frontispieces to botanical texts that Broberg examined, Natura was personified by Diana of Ephesus, an antique statue type which was well known in the sixteenth century and identified with the Goddess of Nature. Ancient statues of Ephesian Diana were displayed in Roman gardens; and at the Villa d'Este at Tivoli a modern statue closely modeled on the antique type originally stood as the centerpiece of the Fountain of Nature (fig. 1).[20] In the Renaissance this image was understood, as it had been since late antiquity, as "many-breasted," the multiple mammary glands symbolizing fertility (an interpretation only recently questioned).[21] The mythog-

[19]Contemporary writers stress the freedom and sensual pleasures of gardens, although cautioning that these are "honest" pleasures. On the association of gardens with love, see Terry Comito, *The Idea of the Garden in the Renaissance* (New Brunswick, N.J.: Rutgers University Press, 1978), passim; and for sexual license as part of the Renaissance understanding of the Golden Age and other earthly paradises, see Hiram Haydn, *The Counter-Renaissance* (New York: Charles Scribner's Sons, 1950; rpt., Gloucester, Mass.: Peter Smith, 1966), pp. 499–505; and Harry Levin, *The Myth of the Golden Age in the Renaissance* (Bloomington: Indiana University Press, 1969), chap. 2. For the role of gardens and their associated values in literature, see A. Bartlett Giamatti, *The Earthly Paradise and the Renaissance Epic* (Princeton: Princeton University Press, 1966).

[20]On Diana of Ephesus, see Phyllis Pray Bober and Ruth O. Rubinstein, *Renaissance Artists and Antique Sculpture: A Handbook of Sources* (London: H. Miller, 1986), p. 87. A Roman copy of this Hellenistic type, now in the Museo Capitolino in Rome, was in the Rossi Collection in Rome in the early sixteenth century and was described in 1514. Ancient statues of the Goddess of Nature stood in the Vigna Carpi and in Cardinal Ippolito d'Este's garden on the Quirinal in Rome, recorded by C. Hülsen, *Römische Antikengärten des XVI Jahrhunderts* (Heidelberg, 1917), pp. 77, 113. For Tivoli, see David R. Coffin, *The Villa d'Este at Tivoli* (Princeton: Princeton University Press, 1960), p. 18 and n. 10. The statue is identified in documents as the Goddess of Nature, and also as Fortune, underlining the relationship between nature and fortune in the Renaissance.

[21]*Lexicon iconographicum mythologiae classicae* (Zurich: Artemis, 1984), vol. 2, pt. 1, pp. 755–63, esp. p. 763. Benvenuto Cellini made a drawing for the seal of the Accademia

Figure 1. Diana of Ephesus, Villa d'Este, Tivoli. Photo: Ralph Lieberman.

rapher Vincenzo Cartari, in his manual describing the gods and goddesses of antiquity, *Le imagini de i dei de gli antichi,* described the goddess as covered with breasts, which signified, he added, that the
universe takes its nourishment from the earth.[22] In the sixteenth-century interpretation of this statue, the nourishing sexual characteristic of
the female body, emphasized by repetition, expresses the idea of nature
as generative, fertile, the source of all life. In the modern version at
Tivoli this is conveyed unambiguously: the problematic protrusions of
the ancient images are explicitly made breasts by the addition of nip-
ples and by the life-giving water that emerges from them.

While the ancient statue type of Diana of Ephesus had long been
understood as many-breasted, it was a Renaissance innovation to trans-
late the symbolic image into a literal one, and to use these spurting
breasts as the essential defining characteristic for other female images
representing generative nature as well. In the somewhat confused
Renaissance pantheon, Diana of Ephesus was also called Isis, and the
Earth was identified as Tellus or Terra Mater, the Great Earth Mother,
who was in turn conflated with the goddesses Cybele, Ceres, and Ops;
and all of these were represented with the essential symbol of nature's
sustaining character.[23] Ammannati's statue of Ceres (fig. 2), symbolizing the Earth, one of several sculptures in the monumental Fountain of
Juno, is indistinguishable in her body position, with hands squeezing
breasts, from the sculptor's representation of Ops.[24] Even Venus in her

---

del Disegno in Florence with the image of the many-breasted Diana. The legend indicates that in antiquity the goddess was "con molte poppe figurata" ("represented with
many breasts"), signifying the nourishing property of nature; Giovanna Gaeta Bertelà,
in *Firenze e la Toscana dei Medici nell'Europa del Cinquecento: Il primato del disegno* (Florence: Olschki, 1980), p. 99, cat. 159.

[22]Vincenzo Cartari, *Le imagini de i dei de gli antichi* (Venice: Vincentio Valgrisi, 1571;
facsimile ed., New York and London: Garland, 1976), p. 118: "Altri hanno detto, ch'ella
[Isis] è la terra . . . e quindi viene che facevano il corpo di questa Dea tutto pieno, e
carico di poppe, come che l'universo pigli nutrimento dalla terra" ("Others have said
that she [Isis] is the Earth . . . and therefore it came about that they made the body of
the Goddess all full, and heavy with breasts, just as the universe takes its nourishment
from the Earth"). He also indicated that an example of the many-breasted Diana type
was found in Rome under Pope Leo and could also be seen on a medal of Hadrian.

[23]Bober and Rubinstein, *Renaissance Artists,* pp. 85–86. Representations of Ops in an
engraving by Caraglio and a statue by Ammannati in Francesco de' Medici's Studiolo
in the Palazzo Vecchio are reproduced by Detlef Heikamp, "Ammannati's Fountain for
the *Sala Grande* of the Palazzo Vecchio in Florence," in *Fons Sapientiae: Renaissance Garden Fountains,* ed. E. B. MacDougall (Washington, D.C.: Dumbarton Oaks, 1978), figs.
35–38.

[24]On the Juno Fountain, see Heikamp, "Ammannati's Fountain," pp. 115–73; and
Malcolm Campbell, "Observations on the Salone dei Cinquecento in the Time of Duke

Figure 2. Bartolomeo Ammannati, Ceres, from the Fountain of Juno, Museo Nazionale del Bargello, Florence. Photo: Ralph Lieberman.

role as Venus Genetrix assumed the same pose. Cesare Ripa, in his iconographical handbook for artists, *Iconologia*, recommended depicting Terra, the Earth, with water shooting from her breasts to represent the springs and rivers that flowed from the earth.[25] In gardens, the breasts actually overflowed with water, and in Ripa's image, which seems inspired by those fountains, the liquid is interpreted similarly in terms of a natural phenomenon—the water that emerges from the earth—not simply the general life-giving property of nature. Ceres was similarly understood as signifying that the earth generates water.[26]

The inspiration for the images of women holding their full breasts derives from ancient statues of both Diana of Ephesus and Venus Pudica, but in the Renaissance they were fused into a new type, one more sensual than both sources. In the modest Venus, or Venus Pudica, one hand covers the breasts, another the genitals, the gestures assuming the double role of concealing and emphasizing. Even more emphatically, the pose of Ammannati's Ceres implies both invitation to gaze at her—in the presentation and display of her breasts, and in her step forward—and modesty, in the head turned to the side, counteracting the frontal body. Compared to that of Diana of Ephesus with her overburdened chest, Ceres' anatomy is represented naturalistically; but in contrast to the pose of Venus Pudica, her gesture of squeezing her breasts appears more artificial and symbolic than natural. The meaning of the image is conveyed first of all by the frankly symbolic nourishing action of her breasts, but also by the sensuality, enhanced by a hint of modesty, in her pose.

Artists were male, as were most, but not all, of the aristocratic patrons who commissioned garden sculpture, and the erotic appeal of female nudes was certainly one of the motives for these statues; but it was not the only reason for their presence.[27] Ceres was the centerpiece

Cosimo I de' Medici, 1540–1574," in *Firenze e la Toscana dei Medici nell'Europa del '500*, 3 vols. (Florence: Edizioni Medicee, 1983), 3:821–24.

[25]Cesare Ripa, *Iconologia* (first ed. without illustrations, 1593; Rome: Lepico Facij, 1603; facsimile ed., New York: G. Olms, 1970), p. 125: "La zinna, che scatorisce acqua, ne rappresenta i fonti, & i fiumi, che ella scatorisce" ("The breast, which shoots water, represents the springs, and the rivers, which shoot from it [the Earth]").

[26]Raffaello Borghini in 1584 explained the significance of the entire fountain as "il generar dell'acqua" ("the generation of water"), in which "Cerere figurata per la terra, la quale si premea le mammelle, e ne usciva fuor l'acqua" ("Ceres, representing the Earth, presses her breasts and water issues forth from them"), cited in Heikamp, "Ammannati's Fountain," p. 121.

[27]For the role of female nudes as providing delectation to a male audience in the context of painting, see John Berger, *Ways of Seeing* (London: British Broadcasting Corporation and Penguin Books, 1972), chap. 3.

of a monumental fountain originally intended for the Sala Grande of the Palazzo Vecchio in Florence, the seat of the ducal government, and later brought first to the Pitti Palace overlooking the Boboli Garden, then to the Medici Garden at Pratolino. Her sensual, generative pose reflects the culture's view of woman, but Ceres is not just woman; she is female and nature, and within a huge fountain dominated by female figures in a political setting, she functions as much more than merely an object of male desire.[28]

Many of the representations of nature and Earth are accompanied by animals, who symbolize nature but might also be considered a gender characteristic, since they were associated with women in both art and literature. The shaftlike lower body of the sixteenth-century statue of Diana of Ephesus at Tivoli, following its ancient prototype, is covered with images of animals in rows and compartments. Ceres, Ops, and, much more rarely, Venus Genetrix were also represented with animals at their feet; see, for example, the dogs at either side of Venus in a grotto of the Villa Lante at Bagnaia (fig. 3).[29] Animals live in caves and follow the laws of nature, not of civilization, and of instinct, not rationality. In Jacopo Bonfadio's letter in which he characterized the ordered gardens on the shores of Lake Garda as a third nature, he explained that in order to make the site on the lake perfect, nature also provided high, rugged, and menacing mountains, with caves, caverns, and fierce cliffs, the home of strange animals and hermits.[30] When Annibale Caro gave some suggestions for imagery inside a garden grotto or cave, he concluded that the best of all would be Circe turning Ulysses' men into animals.[31] Animals clearly denote wild nature, as these examples indicate. Equally important is the fact that the aspect of nature they symbolize was associated with the female, and in particular with female images whose sensuality and overflowing breasts imply yet another characteristic of nature.

[28]Campbell, "Observations on the Salone dei Cinquecento," pp. 822–23, points out the predominance of female imagery in this fountain, and associates the female principle in nature with the female half of the ruling Medici family, the Duchess Eleonora of Toledo.

[29]The identity of the statue at Bagnaia has been puzzling because of the combination of spurting breasts and dogs. In an inventory of 1588 only her action is described: "la statua di mezza getta per le Zinne" ("the statue in the middle shoots [water] from her breasts") (Rome, Archivio di Stato, Archivio Notarile, Tydeo de Marchis, v. 1078, March 29, 1588, f. 198v); but in all the printed views, from the earliest in 1596 by Tarquinio Ligustri, she is identified as Venus along with the unmistakable Neptune opposite.

[30]Bonfadio, Lettere, p. 97.

[31]Annibale Caro, Lettere familiari, 3 vols. (Florence: Le Monnier, 1959), 2:100.

Figure 3. Grotto of Venus, Villa Lante, Bagnaia. Photo: Ralph Lieberman.

The same paired visual signs, overflowing breasts and animals, used for the personification of Benignità (Benignity or Clemency), indicate a conceptual relationship as well between nature and this virtue. Ripa indicated that Benignità should be depicted with hands squeezing breasts that spurt milk, and with animals below to drink it (fig. 4). The generative and nourishing aspects of the Earth or nature are intimately related to giving freely. Both imply something innate, something that comes from within and emerges spontaneously. As Ripa explained, Benignità "preme dalle mammelle il latte, del quale bevono molti animali, perche è effetto di benignità, & di charità insieme spargere a-morevolmente quello che s'hà dalla natura" ("She presses the milk from her breasts, which many animals drink, because the effect of benignity, together with charity, is to spill lovingly that which she has by nature").[32] In his *impresa* for King Ferrandino, Paolo Giovio at-tributed to the king liberality and clemency, virtues which "come from nature, not from art."[33] To diminish the importance of nature (and of female) in this society is therefore also to dismiss other virtues and activities which share essential characteristics with nature, conveyed through a common visual language of gender in the code of the time.

Nature inspires poetry; and poetry, like nature, is fertile and flows freely. The reciprocal relationship is again expressed in representations of Poesia, for which Ripa also found appropriate the image of bare breasts full of milk, if not this time spurting (fig. 5). In this instance Poesia's breasts demonstrate the fecundity of conceits and inventions that are the very soul of poetry, and that also overflow spontaneously.[34] That poetry comes naturally Ripa explained by quoting the popular saying that poets are born and orators made, and by affirming that poetry's principal manners are not learned but infused in the mind.[35] In gardens, poetry and the inspiring property of nature were instead sym-bolized by the Muses. The garden is the place of poetry, often orna-

[32]Ripa, *Iconologia*, p. 43. It could also be noted that although there are obvious Christian counterparts to the imagery investigated here, they were virtually never discussed by Renaissance writers on gardens or related subjects.

[33]Paolo Giovio, *Dialogo dell'imprese* (Lyons: Rouillio, 1574), p. 39.

[34]Ripa, *Iconologia*, pp. 406–7. "Giovane bella . . . mostri le mammelle ignude piene di latte. . . . Le mammelle piene di latte, mostrano la fecondità de concetti, & dell'in-ventioni, che sono l'anima della Poesia." These characteristics of poetry are emphasized by R. J. Clements, *Picta Poesis: Literary and Humanistic Theory in Renaissance Emblem Books* (Rome: Edizioni di Storia e Letteratura, 1960), p. 34, who translates Ripa's last sentence as: "The breasts, turgid with milk, show the fecundity of conceits and in-ventions which are the very soul of poetry."

[35]Ripa, *Iconologia*, p. 215; and Clements, *Picta Poesis*, pp. 34, 48.

Figure 4. Benignità, from C. Ripa, *Iconologia,* 1603.

mented with a Mount Parnassus and called the home of the Muses, because of the inspiring property of nature, and also because poetry shares with the Earth a fertile and overflowing character. The relationship with nature was made more explicit by Cartari: he noted that Muses are often the same as nymphs, and nymphs frequently signify the water of springs and rivers that is good to drink.[36] In the Fountain of Parnassus at Bagnaia, the Muses shoot water not from their breasts

[36]Cartari, *Imagini,* p. 417.

Figure 5. Poesia, from C. Ripa, *Iconologia,* 1603.

but from their mouths, presumably spilling poetic conceits along with fresh spring water from the hills beyond.

Hybrid creatures, part animal and part human, are common inhabitants of Renaissance gardens as another vivid expression of the union of art and nature. An example at Tivoli combines spurting breasts, mythical animals, and an allusion to poetry (fig. 6). One of a pair, this image resembles a sphinx, but instead of the lion joined to a female head and chest, it has a horse's hooves and a winged body terminating in a curled fish tail. The winged horse within this hybrid recalls

Figure 6. Hybrid Fountain, Villa d'Este, Tivoli. Photo: Author.

Pegasus, who dug his hoof into the ground on Mount Parnassus and created the inspiring spring Hippocrene. The individual components express the generative, nourishing property of nature, the familiar association of female with animal, and the free flowing of both water and poetry. The pair of water-generating creatures, which recall the Fountain of Nature in the same garden, stand alongside the central axis at the head of the Fountain of the Dragons, the source of the water that cascades down the handrails of the great, sweeping oval staircase. Like the sphinx, which in the Renaissance symbolized, among other things, voluptuousness,[37] this composite image conveys its meaning through

[37]One of Andrea Alciati's emblems of 1555 explains that the sphinx represents ignorance, of which there are three causes, among them desire for worldly pleasures. Andreas Alciatus, *Emblems,* ed. P. M. Daly, 2 vols. (Toronto: University of Toronto

the separate parts, but also through the sensual and suggestive effect of the whole.

Tourists titter at these. Surely Renaissance cardinals and their friends did as well. An acknowledgment that the sensuality in the images discussed here was both potent and meaningful comes in its rejection by some of the very creators of the fountains. In his treatise on the "Nobility of the Ancient Arts," of about 1570–80, Pirro Ligorio, the designer of the garden at Tivoli, discussed the question of decorum through an imaginary contest of fountain designs.[38] In this competition the moralistic attitude voiced by Ligorio's fictive judges reflects the austere climate of the late sixteenth century. The designs that they considered dirty, lascivious, and otherwise disreputable included a nude Venus, Leda and the Swan, and a reclining female with water flowing from her breasts.[39] In 1590 the sculptor Ammannati pleaded that the statues of the Juno Fountain, which he had created almost thirty-five years earlier, including the shameless Ceres (fig. 2), be draped with golden leaves, because they might inspire indecent and ugly thoughts in those who admired them.[40] Their still decorous sensuality expressed the commonplace notion that the garden was a place of pleasure for all the senses, one that suggested another order of things, a natural state of men and women, social and sexual license.

Venus belongs to the set of female images in Renaissance gardens which express the fertility and life-giving aspects of nature through poses that are inspired by ancient models but were modified to enhance

Press, 1985), vol. 1, #188. See also Guy de Tervarent, *Attributs et symboles dans l'art profane, 1450–1600* (Geneva: Droz, 1958), p. 364.

[38]Pirro Ligorio, "Trattato di alcune cose appartenente alla nobiltà dell'antiche arti . . . ," discussed by David R. Coffin, "Pirro Ligorio on the Nobility of the Arts," *Journal of the Warburg and Courtauld Institutes* 27 (1964): 191–210, and published in *Scritti d'arte del Cinquecento,* ed. P. Barocchi, 3 vols. (Milan: Ricciardi, 1971), 1:1412–70.

[39]Coffin, "Ligorio," p. 200, and Ligorio, in Barocchi, *Scritti,* 2:1420, on Venus: "Questo disegno fu beffato da alcuni religiosi, i quali dissero che, per esservi Venere ignuda, era cosa sporca et obscena" ("This design was mocked by some friars, who said that, since there was a nude Venus in it, it was a dirty and obscene thing"); on Leda and the Swan (1426): also "cosa sporca" ("dirty thing"), and "deono le cose lascive essere usate e poste ne' luoghi che non sempre si veggono, benché sono degne di non essere in niun luogo permesse" ("lascivious things should be used and stationed in places that are not always seen, although they are fit to not be permitted in any place"); on the woman with water pouring from her breasts together with Pegasus (1428): "E per esser disgraziatamente finto, non piacque; essendo cosa [dis]onesta e sciocca, parve loro cosa insipida" ("And because it was miserably made, it did not please; being a shameful and silly thing, it seemed to them stupid").

[40]Heikamp, "Ammannati's Fountain," p. 143, and p. 166, document 45.

their sensuality. The Grotto of Venus at Tivoli was dedicated to voluptuous pleasure;[41] and, as we have seen, in her role as Venus Genetrix, the goddess symbolized generation and the source of water. Another antique Venus type was the indirect model for a bronze statue by Giambologna, originally created for a fountain in the Medici Garden at Castello (fig. 7).[42] Ancient statues of Venus Anadyomene holding strands of hair in each hand were unknown in the Renaissance, but Apelles' famous painting of Venus wringing her hair was familiar through a description by Sidonius, which inspired sixteenth-century representations of the theme.[43] In Giambologna's version, Venus wrings her hair with both hands on one side, an action well suited to the favored serpentine pose, since the twists of her hair echo the spiral of her body. The gesture is at the same time artfully conceived and naturalistic, and in the original fountain, water flowed from Venus' tresses. Her pose also exploits the sensuousness inherent in the serpentine line. From the principal point of view, Venus' chest is frontal, and her bent left knee seems to stride forward in opposition to the stasis of torso and straight right leg. She turns her head to her right, its curve repeated in her shoulder and swelling hip; her arms and flowing hair extend to her left and form right angles that frame and display her breasts. She is ripe, full, sensual, and dripping with water. In the garden at Castello, this Venus Anadyomene type personified the city of Florence, which, as Vasari noted, receives water from the local rivers.[44]

[41]Coffin, *Villa d'Este*, p. 34. The grotto originally had an ancient statue of the Capitoline Venus type stepping from her bath, and the manuscript attributable to the creator of the garden, Pirro Ligorio, indicates that it is dedicated to voluptuous pleasure (p. 144).

[42]The statue is dated either about 1560, by Charles Avery, *Giambologna: The Complete Sculpture* (Mt. Kisco, N.Y.: Moyer Bell, 1987), p. 130 and cat. 27; or about 1570, by Herbert Keutner, in *Giambologna, 1529–1608: Sculptor to the Medici*, exhibition catalogue, ed. C. Avery and A. Radcliffe (London: Arts Council of Great Britain, 1978), p. 80, who also noted that the pose derives from an engraving by Marcantonio Raimondi, for which see also Innis H. Shoemaker and Elizabeth Broun, *The Engravings of Marcantonio Raimondi*, exhibition catalogue (Lawrence, Kansas: Spencer Museum of Art, 1981), p. 68. Giorgio Vasari, *Le vite de' più eccellenti pittori scultori ed architetti*, ed. G. Milanesi, 8 vols. (Florence, 1887), 6:79, attributed the model to Tribolo before his death in 1550. For the statue and its restoration, see *Fiorenza in villa*, ed. C. Acidini Luchinat (Florence: Fratelli Alinari, 1987).

[43]On Venus Anadyomene and Renaissance knowledge of her, see Bober and Rubinstein, *Renaissance Artists*, p. 59. For Apelles' painting and the description by Sidonius, see Natalis Comes, *Mythologiae* (first ed., 1551; Venice: Comin da Trino, 1567), pp. 119–20.

[44]Vasari, *Vite*, 6:79, identified the figure as Florence: "una Fiorenza, a dimostrare che dai detti monti Asinaio e Falterona vengono l'acque d'Arno e Mugnone a Fiorenza" ("a

Figure 7. Giambologna, Fountain of Florence, originally Castello, Villa Medici (later Villa Petraia, removed for restoration). Photo: Alinari/Art Resource.

The statue's form and pose indicate as well that Florence, like Venus, is fertile because of the abundance of water generated in its surrounding countryside.

The pose of Giambologna's Venus, or more properly Florence, at Castello is related to that of another Venus he sculpted (fig. 8), brought to the Grotta Grande of the Boboli Garden in 1592.[45] Where the Castello figure reveals her breasts, the Boboli goddess covers them in a gesture of modesty, by bringing her right arm across to her left shoulder. The poses of both are inspired by Leonardo's lost painting of Leda with the Swan, and by the ancient statue types that influenced the Leda—Venus Pudica and Venus Crouching (fig. 9), where she is again associated with water, this time her bath.[46] In Renaissance images Venus rises to a standing position, but retains from her antique prototype the opposition of open and closed, bent and straight, as well as modesty through her raised limbs. Seen from the front, the Boboli Venus is modest; but the serpentine line encourages us to walk around, and on one side the bent leg seems to reveal rather than veil her genitalia, while on the other her twisted torso and extended arm similarly display her breasts.

While Venus steps from her bath, delicately balanced on the rocky mound beneath her, leering fauns peer over the rim of the vase. Jets of water once shot up from her rustic base into the vase, and more jets from the fauns' mouths spat water back toward Venus. Her pose emphasizes her sensuousness, and the grotesque heads act out just what the critics of such images seemed to have in mind. Their mood is like that of a painting Vasari proposed to make, with a nude and beautiful Venus and three Graces, and, hidden in the bushes, a satyr who, in contemplating their beauty, "si struggie nella sua lussuria, facendo occhi pazzi, et tutto astratto et intento à quello effetto" ("languishes in his lust, making lunatic's eyes, both distracted and obsessed").[47] The

---

Florence, to demonstrate that from the aforementioned Asinaio and Falterona Mountains come the waters of the Arno and Mugnone Rivers to Florence").

[45]For the transfer to the Boboli grotto, Archivio di Stato, Firenze, Fabbriche, vol. 44, c. 34r, noted by Detlef Heikamp, "The Grotta Grande in the Boboli Garden, Florence," *Connoisseur* 199 (1978): 42. Avery, *Giambologna*, pp. 218–21, and cat. 7, dates the statue about 1570.

[46]Bober and Rubinstein, *Renaissance Artists*, pp. 62–63, for the versions known in the Renaissance as well as Marcantonio's engraving after them. For ancient sculptures and Renaissance copies, including Leonardo's variations, see Wendy Stedman Sheard, *Antiquity in the Renaissance* (Northampton, Mass.: Smith College Museum of Art, 1979), p. 42.

[47]Vasari to Niccolo Vespucci, 1532, in Karl Frey, *Der literarische Nachlass Giorgio Vasaris*, 2 vols. (Munich: G. Müller, 1923), 1:2.

Figure 8. Giambologna, Fountain of Venus, Grotta Grande, Boboli Garden, Florence. Photo: Ralph Lieberman.

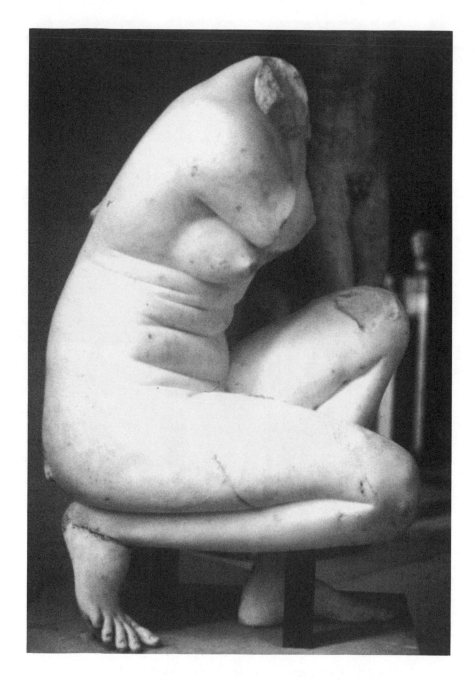

Figure 9. Crouching Venus, Louvre, Paris. Photo: Author.

subtle and graceful sensuality in the pose of watery, fertile Venus contrasts sharply with the crude and ugly fauns and their irreverent gesture. Together all these figures playfully invite lust along with sensuality into this damp cavern, to suggest metaphorically the generation of water that takes place here.

The contrast between masculine and feminine in personifications of nature is as important as female sensuality in expressing nature's generative powers in the garden. This is clear in Cosimo Bartoli's plans for an ideal garden, which include three pairs of male and female figures. The two principal statues represent Venus and Neptune, symbolizing heat and moisture, respectively, through which all things growing in the garden are generated.[48] Bartoli returned to the analogy in another context, where he discussed the birth of Venus from the sea foam following the castration of Uranus by Saturn. She was born through the union of moisture—the sea, and heat—the genitals of Uranus. The sea foam, Bartoli explained further, represents the rubbing and stimulus of lust in the coupling of female and male, or in the example of plants, of moisture and heat.[49] Sexual coupling is a metaphor for natural phenomena, but in Bartoli's account it seems rather the inverse: the

[48]Cosimo Bartoli, *Ragionamenti accademici sopra alcuni luoghi difficili di Dante* (Venice: Francesco de Franceschi Senese, 1567), p. 20v: "Voi sapete che tutte le cose che si generano, si generano mediante la calidità, e mediante la humidità. Io haveva preso Venere per essa calidità, e Nettuno per la humidità, accioche mediante queste due qualitadi, tutte le herbe et tutte le piante di questo Giardino, andassero di bene in meglio, multiplicando, e crescendo" ("You know that all things that are generated, are generated by means of heat, and by means of moisture. I have taken Venus to be heat, and Neptune to be moisture, so that by means of these two qualities all the herbs and all the plants of this Garden would go from good to better, multiplying and growing"). The context is a discussion of Bartoli's suggested improvements for a garden in via San Gallo, Florence, belonging to Giovan Battista Ricasoli, the bishop of Cortona.

[49]Cosimo Bartoli to Vasari, 1555, in Frey, *Literarische Nachlass,* 1:410: "Il qual Tempo overo Saturno dicono che castrò il Cielo et gli tagliò i genitalj et gli gitto nel mare, cio è cavò dal Cielo la possibilità et la faculta del generare. La qual mescolatasi col mare delle cose mondane, generò Venere di spuma marina: Cioè essa faculta del generare si transferi nella actione del congiungnersi insieme di tutte le cose creabilj mediante il calore, per il quale si intendono i genitalj, et mediante lo humore, per il quale si intende il mare; et la stiuma marina è presa per quello sfregamento et incitamento di lussuria nel congiungnersi insieme il mastio et la femina, o volete dire, come sarebbe nelle piante il congiugnimento del calore et della humidita" ("They say that Time, or Saturn, castrated Heaven [Uranus] and cut off his genitals and threw them into the sea, that is, he took away from Heaven the possibility and ability to generate. When the ability to generate was mixed with the sea of earthly things, it generated Venus from the sea foam: that is, the ability to generate transferred itself in the action of joining together all things capable of being created through heat, represented by the genitals; and through

understanding of generation in nature as the union of moisture and heat is inspired by the human model.

Similarly, different aspects of nature were characterized and distinguished according to gender, and were correspondingly represented by male or female images. Vincenzo Borghini described properties of the elements in terms of strongly contrasting gender differences: "per l'acqua metterei . . . due statue di donne, perché l'acqua è molto generativa, come per il fuoco gli torrei ambedue maschi che è attivissimo" ("for water I would put two statues of women because water is very generative, whereas for fire I would have both male, which is extremely active").[50] Paraphrasing Seneca, the mythographer Cartari characterized male and female aspects of each of the four elements: wind is masculine, while air that does not move and is always misty is feminine; the sea is masculine, while fresh water is feminine; fire that burns is masculine, while that which lights and causes no harm is feminine; the earth that is most hard, such as stones and rocks, is masculine, while soft earth is feminine.[51] Personifications of the elements, and various aspects of each, were sometimes represented by both male and female figures, but more often were fixed in their gender, in correspondence with the linguistic gender as well as with long tradition. Among the male personifications (corresponding with their masculine linguistic gender) are rivers, streams, mountains, the sea, the ocean, and lakes. The mountain, or *monte,* a hard part of the earth, and the sea appear in Cartari's male category as well. Feminine, in addition to Nature herself and the soft part of the earth, are freshwater springs and sources, as Cartari noted. These male and female images stood both in isolation and in pairs.

The poses of male and female personifications emphasize their gender differences, the female, as Borghini implied, sensual and static, none more so than the sleeping nymph (fig. 10). A common image of a

---

moisture, represented by the sea; and the sea foam is that rubbing and stimulus of lust in the joining together of male and female, or we might say, in the example of plants the joining of heat and moisture").

[50]Borghini in *Lo Stanzino,* p. 31. These refer to painted personifications in Francesco de' Medici's Studiolo in the Palazzo Vecchio.

[51]Cartari, *Imagini,* pp. 551–3: "Scrisse Seneca nelle sue questioni naturali, ove mette, che gli Egittij di ciascheduno de i quattro elementi da loro posti ne facevano due, l'un maschio, l'altra femina. Imperoche dicevano, che dell'aere il vento è il maschio, e la femina quello che non pare moversi, et è quasi sempre caliginoso: che'l mare è il maschio dell'acqua, e l'acqua dolce tutta la feminia: che del fuoco quello che abbruscia è maschio, e femina quel che luce, ne fa male alcuno: e che della terra è maschio il piu duro, come i sassi e gli scogli, a femina quella, che è piu molle, e si può continuare."

freshwater spring or source in the sixteenth century, these nymphs, lulled to sleep by the sounds of water, have a number of ancient precedents, both literary and artistic.[52] In Renaissance fountains they often represent, as Cartari indicated about nymphs in general, sources of fresh water, and, with the literalness that distinguished this period from antiquity, their presence generally denoted potable springwater. The courtyard fountain with the sleeping female in the Villa d'Este at Tivoli refreshes thirsty tourists even today with its fresh water, brought by aqueduct from the Rivellese spring.[53] The slumbering female at Tivoli is, in fact, Venus, since the two became interchangeable, her model an ancient statue type of a nymph of a spring which was well known in the Renaissance.[54] Again subtly altered from her ancient model, Tivoli's sleeping Venus suggestively raises her torso and tilts it toward the viewer, the breast that escapes beneath the protective arm blatantly framed by the supporting limb.

There is a long tradition in art, from the ancients to Picasso, of a sleeping female discovered by a male satyr, whose model is probably the story of Amymone, told by Hyginus in the *Fabulae*.[55] The young girl fell asleep while looking for water, when she was discovered by a satyr. In answer to her plea, Neptune drove him away, then seduced her and created a spring where he had thrust his trident into a rock. The parallel between their copulation and the generation of water is suggested through similar imagery in a garden grotto, the locus of both activities. At Bagnaia, in the Grotto of Venus, chambers on either side of the goddess are inhabited by sleeping nymphs and male figures— two satyrs and two humans, all in poses of climbing (fig. 11). The interior is cavelike, covered in small stones, and originally water

[52]The literature on the sleeping nymph includes Otto Kurz, "*Huius Nympha Loci:* A Pseudo-Classical Inscription and a Drawing by Dürer," *Journal of the Warburg and Courtauld Institutes* 16 (1953): 171–77; Millard Meiss, "Sleep in Venice," *Proceedings of the American Philosophical Society* 110 (1966): 348–82; Elisabeth B. MacDougall, "The Sleeping Nymph: Origins of a Humanist Fountain Type," *Art Bulletin* 57 (1975): 357–65; Phyllis Pray Bober, "The *Coryciana* and the Nymph Corycia," *Journal of the Warburg and Courtauld Institutes* 40 (1977): 223–39; and Bober and Rubinstein, *Renaissance Artists,* pp. 97–98.

[53]Michel de Montaigne, *Journal du voyage in Italie (1580–1581),* ed. A. D'Ancona (Città di Castello: Lapi, 1895), p. 327, and Antonio del Re, *Dell'antichità tiburtine* (Rome: Giacomo Mascardi, 1611), p. 7.

[54]One displayed in the Casa Galli in the early sixteenth century was apparently well known, and is discussed and illustrated in Bober and Rubinstein, *Renaissance Artists,* p. 98 and fig. 62.

[55]Hyginus, *Fabulae* 169, noted in the literature on sleeping nymphs in note 52.

Figure 10. Sleeping Venus Fountain, Villa d'Este, Tivoli. Photo: Ralph Lieberman.

Figure 11. Sleeping Nymph and Climbing Male in Grotto of Venus, Villa Lante, Bagnaia. Photo: Ralph Lieberman.

dripped from the walls, creating an oozing, damp, cool, and dark haven.[56] The conjunction of the female embodiment of the freshwater spring that nourished the garden, in her passive pose, and the active male figures suggests metaphorically that in this cave generation takes place through the union of opposite principles: male and female, active and passive, moisture and heat.

Male personifications of aspects of nature also derived from ancient types, and these too were modified into more active poses, or in six-teenth-century terms, stronger gender characteristics, just as ancient female types were made more sensuous. In fountain sculpture, water

[56]See Claudia Lazzaro Bruno, "The Villa Lante at Bagnaia" (Ph.D. diss., Princeton University, 1974), p. 77, and Frank Joseph Alvarez, "The Renaissance Nymphaeum: Its Origins and Its Development in Rome and Vicinity" (Ph.D. diss., Columbia University, 1981), pp. 148–49.

Figure 12. Stoldo Lorenzi, Fountain of Neptune, Boboli Garden, Florence. Photo: Ralph Lieberman.

Figure 13. Fountain of the River Gods, Villa Lante, Bagnaia. Photo: Author.

was again coordinated with human poses to reinforce their meaning. Neptune often physically activates the water, in contrast to the still figures of Diana of Ephesus, Ceres, and Venus, from whose breasts life-giving water emerges spontaneously. The statue of Neptune in the Boboli Garden overlooking the Pitti Palace (fig. 12) seems by his striding pose and energetic gesture to cause water to rush from his trident, as it does after a wet season when the water from a spring in the hills beyond is plentiful.

River gods, representing another source of water, were traditionally male, and closely followed several ancient prototypes placed in prominent locations in Rome. Ancient monumental statues of the Tigris and Nile rivers, only recognized as river gods in the late fifteenth century, were given a place of honor on the Capitoline Hill in 1517. The colossal Tiber and Nile rivers, not excavated until 1512 or shortly after, were

Figure 14. Bartolomeo Ammannati, Arno River, from the Juno Fountain, Museo Nazionale del Bargello, Florence. Photo: Ralph Lieberman.

displayed on fountains in the Statue Court of the Vatican Belvedere.[57]

[57]Bober and Rubinstein, *Renaissance Artists,* pp. 99 and 101–3, for all four ancient river gods.

Figure 15. Bartolomeo Ammannati, Spring of Parnassus, from the Juno Fountain, Museo Nazionale del Bargello, Florence. Photo: Ralph Lieberman.

These ancient statues inspired many modern versions in Renaissance villas and gardens, such as the pair at the Villa Lante at Bagnaia (fig. 13), which repeated the semireclining pose, resting on one arm, with one leg slightly raised. Renaissance river gods often held or leaned on a cornucopia, symbol of abundance, or a vase pouring water. At Bagnaia water flows from one to the next of the vases between them, so that the idea of a river is conveyed through an anthropomorphic representation and also with natural means—the cascade of water between the two river gods.

In Ammannati's Juno Fountain, Ceres (fig. 2) stood in the center, flanked by a male statue of a river and a female spring, whose contrasting poses exemplified their gender differences. In the original fountain, long disassembled, several statues arranged around an arc allegorized the generation of water, which was manifested in the Arno River (fig. 14) at the left, and opposite him the Spring of Parnassus (fig. 15).[58] It has been noted that the poses of both are reminiscent of Michelangelo's Times of Day in the Medici Chapel, but this inspiration is insufficient to account for the marked contrast in their body positions. Her pose, more reclining than sitting, is open and languid, and the vase rests suggestively between her legs. The tautly seated male Arno instead crosses the left leg firmly over the right. His right arm, raised above his head, is bent at a sharp angle to support the cornucopia behind his back. His left arm, in contrast to the flow of the Spring of Parnassus' arm, is extended rigidly, grasping the urn beside his legs.

Other male river gods in similarly active poses, which depart from the static ancient river-god type, reveal a strong influence of Michelangelo's sculpture; but, as in the Juno Fountain, their contrast with female figures cannot be explained simply as an emulation of a stylistic model. The crouching river gods on Giambologna's Oceanus Fountain in the Boboli Garden (fig. 16) are even more physically active than Ammannati's Arno in their bent, twisted, and contorted poses.[59] Their obvious derivation from Michelangelo's *ignudi* may be explained

---

[58]Tanai de' Medici in a letter of 1579 identifies them as the Arno River and the spring of Parnassus, since "Fiorenza habbia molto proprio la poesia, et Arno . . . fa fertile la città" ("Florence has very properly poetry, and the Arno . . . makes the city fertile"), and on the meaning of the entire fountain, he explained, "E tutto questo gruppo significa come nasce l'acqua, perchè la terra succ[h]ia l'aria, e poi getta fuori l'acqua, e ne nascono le fonti e i fiumi" ("And this entire group signifies how water is born, since the earth sucks the air, and then throws forth water, and from it are born springs and rivers"); cited in Heikamp, "Ammannati's Fountain," p. 121, and see also 130–33, on the style of the sculptures.

[59]The fountain was executed by Giambologna between 1570 and 1575; Avery, *Giambologna*, pp. 215–18 and cat. 9.

Figure 16. Giambologna, Oceanus Fountain, Boboli Garden, Florence. Photo: Ralph Lieberman.

by their own role as visually supporting figures for the standing Oceanus. The father of all river gods, Oceanus personifies the body of water encircling the Earth into which all rivers flow, thus sustaining it, as the composition of Giambologna's fountain suggests metaphorically.[60]

For the Medici Garden at Pratolino, Giambologna designed two personifications, of a river and a mountain, whose active poses identify them as representations of masculine aspects of water and earth, and specify their relationship to each other. The Mugnone River is similar in pose to the Boboli river gods, although less strained (fig. 17).[61] Seated, with right leg and left arm bent backward, and opposite limbs straining forward, his right arm reaches across his body to grasp the vase under his left foot. His body position is a mirror reflection of the personification of the Apennine Mountains above him in the garden (fig. 18). The related poses of these two figures provide visual confirmation of the geographical reality not only that rivers flow from mountains but also, more specifically, that the Mugnone has its source in the Apennines. In Giambologna's Appennino, art and nature become indistinguishable as personification and naturalistic mountain merge, modeled on images in ancient literature.[62] The Appennino drips water all over his hoary body, and, in a significant departure from ancient literary descriptions, he presses down with all his weight on the animal's head that emerges from his rocky base. Like Neptune thrusting his trident, the Appennino's action seems to activate the water that

[60]Malcolm Campbell, "Giambologna's *Oceanus* Fountain: Identifications and Interpretations," in *Boboli 90* (Atti del Convegno Internazionale di Studi per la salvaguardia e la valorizzazione del Giardino, Florence, 1989), in press, notes that although contemporaries identified the fountain figure as Oceanus, the attributes and stance of the standing figure associate it with Neptune and correspondingly with Grand Duke Cosimo de' Medici.

[61]The Mugnone dates from 1577–79; its pose was influenced by Tribolo's earlier river gods at Castello; Avery, *Giambologna*, pp. 221–23 and cat. 166.

[62]Ancient literary precedents include Virgil's description of the Apennines in the *Aeneid*, 12:701–3, discussed by J. H. W. Morwood, "Aeneas and Mt. Atlas," *Journal of Roman Studies* 75 (1985): 51–59; Ovid's "Atlas," *Metamorphoses* 4:656–62; and the story of the sculptor Dinocrates, who wished to shape Mount Athos into the statue of a man. Its representations in art are discussed by Werner Körte, "Deinokrates und die Barocke Phantasie," *Die Antike* 13 (1937): 289–312; and David Summers, *Michelangelo and the Language of Art* (Princeton: Princeton University Press, 1981), pp. 126–28. On Giambologna's statue, see Avery, *Giambologna*, pp. 221–23 and cat. 165; and for the theme of water in the garden, see my essay "From the Rain to the Wash Water in the Medici Garden at Pratolino," in *Renaissance Studies in Honor of Craig Hugh Smyth*, 2 vols. (Florence: Giunti Barbèra, 1985), 2:317–26.

Figure 17. Giambologna, Mugnone River, Villa Medici, Pratolino. Photo: Author.

Figure 18. Giambologna, Apennine Mountains, Villa Medici, Pratolino. Photo: Ralph Lieberman.

flows from the animal's head, as though he were squeezing a spring from the mountain's depths.

Examined with the traditional apparatus of art history, which has not been much concerned with nature, gender, or metaphorical language, these images reveal little of their subtle expressiveness, and can even be seriously misinterpreted. A more complex example, a relief carved out of the living rock at the Fontana Papacqua (fig. 19), which has defied interpretation by conventional means, instead easily yields its basic message when analyzed in terms of nature and gender.[63] On a steep slope of the hill town of Soriano nel Cimino at the site of a rushing natural spring, this relief employs similar personifications of the natural world, with their contrasting gender characteristics and associated significance, in order to represent the natural phenomenon that the Earth generates springs. With images carved in different scales and varied styles, the relief is dominated by a half-reclining female satyr with a striking archaic face, who is surrounded by several animals and sylvan creatures. The goat-legged woman with three children around her, one at her breast, recalls images of Tellus or the Earth, in which children are the emblems of her fertility. She is so represented in ancient reliefs, such as the Ara Pacis and the relief from Carthage in the Louvre (fig. 20).[64] The goat half of her body distinguishes the satyress at Soriano from ancient precedents. As Cartari explained in reference to Pan, however, the goat legs signify the earth,[65] and therefore in this image they reinforce the symbolism of its more traditional model.

The relief at Soriano has more than the principal figure in common with its ancient precedent: both include a naturalistic depiction of plants and animals together with personifications, all in varying scales, and seen from different points of view and positions in space. Another relief that does not follow the rules of one-point perspective in scale and depth is sculpted on the upper part of the niche behind the Sleeping Venus at Tivoli (fig. 10). The hilly landscape scene that must represent the setting of Tivoli itself includes trees, a distant castle, rustic structures, a shepherd with sheep, and on the right, flowing water and a

[63]S. Lang, "Bomarzo," *Architectural Review* 121 (1957): 427–30; Jacqueline Theurillat, *Les Mystères de Bomarzo et des jardins symboliques de la Renaissance* (Geneva: Editions les trois anneaux, 1973), pp. 143–53; and Marinella Festa Milone, "La triplice allegoria dell''acqua di papa': La fonte del Cardinal Madruzzo a Soriano nel Cimino," *Psicon* 8–9 (1976): 121–31. There are some useful suggestions in each of these, but as a whole I find them unconvincing and recommend reading them with caution.

[64]Eugenie Strong, "*Terra Mater* or *Italia?*" *Journal of Roman Studies* 27 (1937): 114–26; for the Paris relief, see *Lexicon iconographicum*, vol. 1, pt. 1, p. 380.

[65]Cartari, *Imagini*, p. 138.

Figure 19. Fontana Papacqua, Soriano nel Cimino. Photo: Ralph Lieberman.

mill, one on top of the other to the high horizon line. In these three examples—the reliefs from Carthage, Tivoli, and Soriano—the conventions of representation differ from those required in contemporary narrative painting; they belong not to the time or place but to the subject, which in all three is nature.

At the Fontana Papacqua the over–life-size reclining satyress is joined by the truncated form of a colossal bearded and horned male at the left of the relief. He assumes an Atlaslike pose of support, the sharp angle of his massive arm echoing and balancing the jutting rock at the upper right. In some ancient reliefs the Earth was paired with Atlas, the giant who supported the skies, and who, in Ovid's account, was

Figure 20. Tellus relief from Carthage, 2d century A.D., Louvre, Paris. Photo: Cliché des Musées Nationaux, Paris.

turned into a mountain.[66] Here the old satyr male in an active pose of support represents the hard and rocky aspect of the earth—the steep, volcanic hill on which the nymphaeum and the town of Soriano were built. Next to him Earth—the soft part—generates the water of the Papacqua spring, which bubbles up beneath her and below the terrace of the nymphaeum gushes out from the hillside. The relief is a metaphorical representation not only of the natural world but also of nature at this particular site, inspired by ancient reliefs with similar personifications, disproportions in scale, and confusion in spatial relationships.

[66]*Lexicon*, III, 1:2–49, s.v. "Atlas," no. 46, for the relief with Tellus, and III, 2, figs. 11–49. Ovid, *Metamorphoses* 4:627–62.

Figure 21. Moses Striking the Rock, Fontana Papacqua, Soriano nel Cimino. Photo: Ralph Lieberman.

On the wall perpendicular to this is a scene of Moses striking the rock (fig. 21), which is a narrative representation of the spring, and very likely of the role of the owner, Cardinal Cristoforo Madruzzo, in making its water available to the town. The Moses relief depicts a human acting on nature, and follows the conventions of an Albertian *istoria:* a single scale, proportional parts, one-point perspective, and horizon-line isocephaly, all of which, in Alberti's system, are determined in correspondence with the height of a man standing at a fixed distance from the scene. In contrast, the satyr-woman relief is strikingly lacking in these characteristics, just as her generative pose contrasts with his active one. These two reliefs represent the pair that come together in the garden—nature and art, or human action on nature, told through two different systems of representation.

Both art and nature are essential components of the garden and the contrast between them is deliberate and meaningful. The standards of one cannot be applied to both, however. Images of nature do not follow the same conventions of either representation or meaning as those of human culture. The satyr-woman relief has been found bizarre, mannerist, and enigmatic. In its own terms, though, in terms of nature, its style has models in antiquity, and its significance is clear and simple. But only if we accept that in the garden, the realm of nature, there is another presence besides art, besides man—another discourse and another mode of discourse, in which man is not the measure of all things.

Stephanie H Jed

Chastity on the Page:
A Feminist Use of Paleography

In her still timely and important essay "Notes on Women in the Renaissance and Renaissance Historiography," Joan Kelly elaborates her thesis that the emerging capitalist mode of production of the fifteenth-century merchant oligarchs of Florence gave rise to a new social relation of the sexes, a relation that was enacted in "two discrete but related realms," the "realm of social production" and the "realm of reproduction, the private family." As women of the entrepreneurial class were "increasingly confined to the domestic sphere," Kelly says, they were not only precluded from participating in the mercantile activities of their male relatives but were excluded as well from the "republican politics and humanistic culture" associated with these activities.[1] Even exceptional women who became accomplished humanists did so without modifying the "patriarchal and misogynous bias" of their classical learning.[2] In light of these conditions, Kelly deems it appropriate to speak of women's experience of the Renaissance not as a resurgence of individualism and creativity but rather as a "Renaissance of Chastity."[3] In this essay I will discuss a humanistic dialogue exemplifying this Renaissance of Chastity: the *Declamatio Lucretiae* by Coluccio Salutati, the humanist chancellor Florence from 1375 to 1406. I shall argue that the Renaissance of Chastity is represented not only in the thematics of this dialogue but also on the very pages of a manuscript reproduction

[1]Joan Kelly[-Gadol], "Notes on Women in the Renaissance and Renaissance Historiography," in *Conceptual Frameworks for Studying Women's History* (Bronxville, N.Y.: Sarah Lawrence Publications, 1976), p. 8.
[2]Joan Kelly, "Did Women Have a Renaissance?" in *Women, History, and Theory: The Essays of Joan Kelly* (Chicago: University of Chicago Press, 1986), p. 35.
[3]Ibid., p. 36.

of this text and in the cultural debates and discriminations surrounding the physical work of writing in fifteenth-century Italy.[4]

The considerations that follow are based on my encounter with a fifteenth-century Italian manuscript containing a copy of the *Declamatio,* which represents the Roman legend of the rape of Lucretia.[5] According to this legend Lucretia, an ancient Roman matron, was raped by the son of the tyrant and committed suicide in order to prove that she had resisted this act of sexual violence. It was Lucretia's chastity, violated by rape and verified by her suicide, that provided the impetus to Lucius Junius Brutus (the ancestor of Marcus Brutus, Julius Caesar's assassin) to expel the tyrants and establish republican liberties in Rome. Or at least this is the way in which the legend was codified in Livy's *Early History of Rome.*[6] From the time of its codification in Livy's text, the legend of the rape of Lucretia acquired a universal significance: in every age and place the act of sexual violence against Lucretia was represented and celebrated as the necessary prologue to republican freedom. By virtue of the frequent reproduction of this legend in the humanistic tradition, rape and liberation came to be connected to a relation of consequentiality, or rather in a narrative logic of sexual violence. Even modern interpretations of this legend tend to reinforce this logic by relating each reproduction of Lucretia's rape to the humanistic tradition as a whole and the values of freedom it claims to uphold.

[4]A more extensive treatment of the ideas in this essay may be found in my book *Chaste Thinking: The Rape of Lucretia and the Birth of Humanism* (Bloomington: Indiana University Press, 1989).

[5]I want to emphasize from the start that this is not an essay about the rape of Lucretia. Nor is it an essay about the anthropological or political significance of chastity in the actual social practices of fifteenth-century Florentines. I am not a social historian, and I do not pretend to be one in this essay. Rather, I focus, as a feminist literary critic, on a historically situated *encounter* in the 1980s with a fifteenth-century manuscript representing the rape of Lucretia in order to confront the question of chastity, not from the perspective of what it may have meant to its humanist proponents in fifteenth-century Florence, but rather from the perspective of humanism's reception and continued transmission in intellectual and cultural settings in the United States today. From this perspective, questions emerge which the Florentine humanists themselves did not ask and could not have articulated, given the fact that this moment and place in the transmission of humanism are quite different from the historical context in which they worked. And documentation about humanism is produced which can come into being only now, inasmuch as it responds to contemporary questions. These questions, in the case of my inquiry, regard the relation between the formation of the humanistic tradition and the representation of humanistic reading and writing practices.

[6]Livy, *The Early History of Rome,* trans. Aubrey de Sélincourt (London: Penguin Books, 1971), 1.57–58.

To retell the story of the rape of Lucretia in the present day is to enter into some sort of binding relationship with all of those readers and writers who somehow found the narrative of this rape edifying, plea-surable, or even titillating, and to be bound by the vision of those readers and writers to look at the rape as they did (and do)—as a paradigmatic component of all narratives of liberation. For in the pro-cess of reconstructing the meaning of Lucretia's rape in terms of re-publican freedom, women readers become not only part of the scene of violation but also agents in the reproduction of a violated body, a prod to prurience in a humanistic peep show. What means, then, do women readers have of displacing this text from its position in a lineage of texts connecting rape and freedom in a logic of sexual violence? One way to short-circuit the economy of pleasure afforded by reproducing the story of this rape is to interrupt its logic of sexual violence by changing our focus from the repeated representation of Lucretia's rape to the circumstances of writing in which the legend is, each time, re-present-ed. In my study of a fifteenth-century manuscript containing a copy of Salutati's dialogue, it became apparent that it was possible to interrupt this logic upheld by the legend of Lucretia's rape by relating the legend to the physical work of writing on the page and the systems of mean-ing in which such work was inscribed.

Many authors in different historical moments have reproduced the legend of Lucretia, but this reproduction further depends on the work of countless and anonymous writers, that is, scribes and printers whose agency was fundamental in the capillary dissemination of the logic of sexual violence represented by this narrative. Thus, if we focus on the work of writing by these scribes, rather than on the authors whose texts they reproduce, we can turn our attention from the *what* of this logic of sexual violence to *how* such a logic is transmitted in the hu-manistic tradition. If, for example, we begin by examining the work of an anonymous scribe who copied Salutati's text, we interrupt the tradi-tional practice of comparing different representations of Lucretia's rape while neglecting to question its codified meaning.

Instead of relating one reproduction of the legend of Lucretia to another, we can relate the social thematics of chastity and sexual vio-lence to the very formation of letters on the page, to the humanists' practices of handling texts, and to the contribution these practices made to the formulation of Florentine political and sociocultural pol-icies. On the basis of these alternative possibilities, I am interested in showing how feminist attention to the physical production of human-istic writing can present one avenue for building on Kelly's groundbreaking considerations of women's chastity and confinement to the domestic sphere in early capitalism. In following this line of thought, I am interested in expanding her use of the Marxian concept of the mode of production to include the production of writing. And, finally, I am interested in the possibilities available to feminist scholars for showing the intrinsic connections between humanistic writing and fifteenth-century Florentine economic structures, connections that continue to determine our own social relations of the sexes today. What follows here is one possible itinerary for relating the production of meaning in Salutati's *Declamatio* to the conditions and practices of writing in which this text was and continues to be produced and handled. Although the paleographic focus on the work of writing is by no means intrinsically feminist, perhaps it is possible for feminist readers to incorporate these techniques into a feminist frame.

The Historical Background

In the last years of the fourteenth century, historiographic perceptions about the origins of Florence began to change. Prior historiographic tradition held that Florence had been founded under the reign of Julius Caesar, thus tracing the origins of the city to imperial Rome. But by the late 1300s humanist historiographers and textual scholars had begun to develop the thesis that Florence was founded earlier, by veterans of Sulla's army, thereby making the city a direct "descendant" of republican Rome and an "heir" to republican freedom.[7]

In order to construct this new identity based on descent from the republican *virtus Romana*,[8] unsullied by any taint of imperial Rome, Florentine humanists searched for textual evidence that would support the thesis of the city's foundation under the reign of Sulla.[9] In this context it is not surprising that Salutati, the chancellor of Florence and a protagonist of humanism, would have tried his hand at representing the Lucretia legend. Written sometime before 1391, Salutati's *Declamatio Lucretiae* might be understood as a "literary" contribution to the historiographic reconstruction, several years later, of Florentine descent from republican Rome and to Florence's self-proclaimed politi-

---

[7]Hans Baron, *The Crisis of the Early Italian Renaissance: Civic Humanism and Republican Liberty in an Age of Classicism and Tyranny,* 2 vols. (Princeton: Princeton University Press, 1955), 1:51–52.

[8]Ibid., p. 47.

[9]Ibid., p. 52.

cal identity as the defender of Italian freedom against the tyranny of the
Milanese Visconti.[10] By reproducing, in this context of Florence's political identity, the rape on which Roman freedom depended, Salutati's
dialogue both strengthened the city's republican credentials and reinforced its filial descent from Brutus. For women readers, who are also
cultural descendants of the humanists, it is especially important to
reexamine this link between a legend of violence against a woman and
the Florentine ideal of republican freedom, for unless we do so, we too
end up reinforcing the narrative of Florence's defense of a freedom that
depends on rape.

The Manuscript Book and the Work of Writing

The manuscript book containing Salutati's *Declamatio Lucretiae* re-
sides in the Newberry Library in Chicago and is known there as 93.6
Humanistic Collection.[11] It is a typical humanistic miscellany including works of Roman history, a life of Virgil, and an "Invective" against
tyrants. The legend of Lucretia is represented three times in this manuscript. The book is bound in parchment over pasteboard, and the
writing surface is paper. The dimensions of the book are 217 by 135
millimeters. At least two of the watermarks—the configurations of a
human head and a bird—indicate that most of the paper may have been
produced in the area of Verona in the second half of the fifteenth

[10]Ronald G. Witt suggests that the *Declamatio* may have been composed at the same
time as the *Conquestio Phyllidis* (1367), because they both treat the theme of suicide;
Hercules at the Crossroads: The Life, Works, and Thought of Coluccio Salutati (Durham:
Duke University Press, 1983), p. 83, n. 23. We can say with more certainty that the
Declamatio was written before 1391, when Salutati cited it in a letter (*Epistolario di
Coluccio Salutati*, 4 vols., ed. Francesco Novati [Rome: Istituto Storico Italiano, 1891–
1911], 4:247). I do not mean to claim that this text is early evidence of the development,
on the basis of newly found classical sources (1402–3), of the Florentine ideology of
republican *libertas*. Rather, I see the *Declamatio* as one piece of evidence that this ideology
was formed in the context of an already established "literary" association.

[11]The *Declamatio* was printed as one of Aeneas Silvius' *Epistolae* (Milan: U. Scin-
zenzeler, 1496), epistola 427. Enrico Menestò has published a version of the text, along
with his Italian translation, and done the preliminary research for a critical edition. See
Enrico Menestò, "La *Declamatio Lucretiae* del Salutati: Manoscritti e fonti," *Studi medievali* 20 (1979): 917–24. I publish a facsimile edition, a diplomatic transcription, and my
translation of this text in my book *Chaste Thinking;* chapter 2 is devoted entirely to the
description and history of the humanistic miscellany containing Salutati's text and to
reflections on the epistemological possibilities opened up by the practice of manuscript
description.

century.[12] There are 177 constitutive pages plus two added pages at the beginning and two at the end.

This copy of the *Declamatio* conserved at the Newberry Library is written in "humanistic" script (or *antiqua*), and thus it gives concrete testimony about the transmission and diffusion of this handwriting several decades after the script's first exemplifications by Niccolò Niccoli and Poggio Bracciolini around the year 1400. By the time of the production of our "Humanistic Collection," *antiqua* had become the self-evident graphic expression of elite culture, a script no longer tied to the historical conditions of its inception. But concealed beneath the elegant legibility of this script is a complex problematic of chastity and contamination, particular to the historical moment in which it was developed. "Humanistic" script was a stylistic hybrid in which late Carolingian handwriting (eleventh and twelfth centuries) was contaminated by the use of Roman epigraphic capitals.[13] The product of this contamination, however, was considered to be "chaste."

The first humanists were intensely attentive to the effects different forms of writing had on their bodies. For Petrarch, whose own graphic preferences and practices opened the way to the elaboration of *antiqua,* these effects were especially troubling. In his letters Petrarch complains that the "unrestrained and licentious" ("vaga," "luxurians") handwriting of many of his contemporaries "caresses the eyes" and in doing so "afflicts and disturbs" them. *Because* the handwriting is seductive, he implies, it effects wear and tear on the body. Petrarch, always an aspiring ascetic, longs for a kind of handwriting that is "chaste and clear" ("castigata et clara"). He claims, however, that he prefers the Carolingian model, not because it is more "chaste" but because it is closer to the writing of the ancient Romans and thus more likely to offer orthographically and grammatically authentic readings. By shifting our attention from a moral attribute to the reference to antiquity, Petrarch clouds over the issue of chastity and the importance of this issue in his graphic preferences.[14]

Later humanists represent the *antiqua* writing as seductive in its own right; they praise the letters of *antiqua* for their ability "to attract" the eyes of the reader, to be more "willingly perceived" and more "pleas-

---

[12]C. M. Briquet, *Les Filigranes: Dictionnaire historique des marques de papiers dès leur apparition vers 1282 jusqu'en 1600,* 4 vols. (Leipzig, 1923), 15.619; 12.127, 128, 130, 135.

[13]Emanuele Casamassima, "Lettere antiche: Note per la storia della riforma grafica umanistica," *Gutenberg Jahrbuch* (1964): 18.

[14]Francesco Petrarca, *Le familiari,* ed. Vittorio Rossi (Florence: Sansoni, 1968), 23.19.8.

ing to the eyes." They justify this aesthetic preference, however, by claiming the form of "humanistic" letters to be "more chaste." A moral justification was invented to support an aesthetic preference. And this is at least part of the aesthetic–ethical dynamic behind the issues of graphic reform.[15]

The writing represented in the copy of Salutati's *Declamatio* that I examined descends from the passionate debates taking place in Florence in the late fourteenth and early fifteenth centuries about the beauty and goodness of certain forms of letters. Although the scribe was perhaps unconscious or semiconscious of the debates about graphic reform that had taken place among humanists of not too distant generations, he nonetheless reproduced the effects of those debates as he copied a late-fourteenth-century work about the rape of Lucretia in a humanistic hand. The very handwriting of the scribe evokes the issues of chastity and contamination represented by the narrative he inscribes. Because the forms of the letters themselves reinforce the meaning the rape of Lucretia has had in the humanistic tradition, it becomes difficult to question the meaning of this rape without investigating those graphic circumstances of chastity and contamination in which the story of Lucretia's rape is "naturally" reproduced. Just as Lucretia's kinsmen claim that Lucretia can remain chaste after she has been raped, so the humanists claim that their *antiqua* script replicates a chaste and ancient model uncontaminated by history.

Philology and the Work of Handling Books

In the area of textual editing, the Florentine humanists engaged in a similar contradictory project of making their texts "chaste" by contaminating them with their own "corrections." The texts of the Roman authors passed through the hands of the humanists, were submitted to their thoughts and judgments, underwent transcriptions, corrections, and editions, and were forged into a contemporary view of republican Rome to be transmitted onto the pages of Florentine political writing. The legends of republican Rome could not jump from the pages of the Roman authors to their proper place in Florentine public writing without the help of philological practice. And yet the contamination of textual traditions by the "chaste" interventions of the humanists gener-

---

[15]Emanuele Casamassima, "Per una storia delle dottrine paleografiche dall'Umanesimo a Jean Mabillion," *Studi medievali*, 3rd ser., 5 (1964): 541 nn. 26, 28; 543.

ally remains unexamined. Here, once again, we find that the humanist called their editions of texts *castigationes*[16] and conceived their work of castigating as a vindication of chastity after previous contaminations or errors. For the corruption of a text, in the minds of the humanists, was not unlike a rape. The threat lay not so much in the actual violation as in keeping the rapist's seed from reproducing.

In response to the threat of rape, the philological activity of the early humanists was soon translated into a moral commitment to the ideal of chastity. Terms for castigation, integrity, sincerity, and so on were invented to set the scene for editorial practice. And an editorial dialectic of contamination and castigation, represented by the humanists in relation to their handling of the Roman texts, can be discovered at the foundation of the Florentine ideology of liberty. Here again we find another structural support of the idea of liberty as an epilogue to sexual violence. The tendency of modern scholarship to exalt this connection between the humanists' "achievement of critical scholarship" and their "love of liberty"[17] discourages us from examining critically the violating and castigating practices that bind these two facets of humanism together.

In various moments of Salutati's text, the interlocutors of his dialogue express themselves in the philological language of the early humanists. Just as philologists abhorred the "violation of good books" by the corruption of scribes, so Lucretia abhors the violation of her self and her chastity. And when Lucretia laments the fact that for so many years, until the night of her rape, she had been successful in preserving her chastity intact, she speaks as if she has once been a text without defects, "sincere and unstained." In the same way, the philologists referred to a codex as "unstained," or *emaculatus* when speaking of a text that was correct or without flaws. And they considered a passage to be sincere, or *sincerus,* when it represented the outgrowth of a single branch in the genealogical tree of a textual tradition.[18]

When Lucretia's kinsmen try to convince her that her mind has remained chaste despite the violation of her body, they use the term *integer,* which was used by the humanists to refer to an untouched and, therefore, uncorrupt text. And there is a striking similarity between the

---

[16]Silvia Rizzo, *Il lessico filologico degli umanisti* (Rome: Edizioni di Storia e Letteratura, 1973), p. 276; Sebastiano Timpanaro, *La genesi del metodo del Lachmann* (Padua: Liviana, 1981), pp. 7ff.

[17]Hans Baron, *Humanistic and Political Literature in Florence and Venice at the Beginning of the Quattrocento* (Cambridge, Mass.: Harvard University Press, 1955), p. 20.

[18]Rizzo, *Il lessico filologico,* pp. 287, 215, 216.

attitude of the philologist and the attitude of Lucretia's kinsmen who wish to eliminate Lucretia's feeling of contamination and restore her "integrity." Although the objective of restoring a handled, copied, transmitted manuscript to an untouched, uncorrupt state seems, at best, contradictory, the philologists assumed that they were actually recreating "integral" editions.[19] In the same way, the kinsmen of Lucretia assumed that she could continue to cultivate her prior chaste and untouched state even though she had been raped.

In his analysis of the textual tradition of Boccaccio's *De montibus,* Vittore Branca points out that the philologist, intending to restore a text to a state prior to its having been contaminated by human hands, continues to handle and contaminate the text. Even if the readings supplied by the philologist are more "correct" than those supplied by the text's own tradition, the "correction" of a text means the demise of its "integrity"; for as a philologist "castigates," or makes the text "chaste," his own handling of the text constitutes a further contamination.[20]

The terms for handwriting and textual editing that the Florentine humanists elaborated to represent their relation to Roman texts contributed to their thinking about liberty as dependent on rape: the representation of these textual activities as vindications of chastity in the aftermath of violation, staining, and contamination limited to a great extent the meaning that the Roman legends of republican freedom could have for them. If practices of writings are so closely linked to thought, then different kinds of inscription and handling of texts could conceivably generate a different kind of thinking.[21] An alternative lexicon, based on other figures than those of violation and castigation, might lead not only toward an alternative mode of political thought but even toward the cultural reinforcement of alternative modes of

[19]Ibid., pp. 217, 277.

[20]Vittore Branca, "Copisti per passione, tradizione caratterizzante, tradizione di memoria," in *Studi e problemi di critica testuale* (Bologna: Commissione per i testi di lingua, 1961), pp. 78–79.

[21]It is important to point out here that scholars such as Eugenio Garin and Hans Baron have made a similar argument, demonstrating how the scholarly achievements of the humanists introduced a new kind of thinking to Western thought. The difference in my argument, I believe, is twofold. First, the focus on terms for the "practical" activities of handwriting and textual editing affords a different perspective from the one that focuses on the end results of such activities. And second, the practices of handwriting and textual editing, I argue, are themselves imbued with a rhetorical and ideological significance that helps to determine the repressive consequences for women of the kind of new thinking introduced by the humanists.

writing production. If we understand that historically certain kinds of graphic habits and cultural contexts have tended to attract the inscription of rape more than others, then we can construct different graphic habits that will attract the inscription of different kinds of stories.

In the selection of texts for his "Humanistic Collection," the scribe-compiler chose those texts that would be typically reproduced in humanistic script. Literary works in Italian, not pertaining to Greek and Roman antiquity, were "naturally" excluded from reproduction in his book. To see the culture of Florentine humanism from the perspective of the writing cultures it excluded[22] is the first step toward undoing, at the levels of language and relations of writing, the logic of sexual violence on which our own modern legacy of humanism depends.

Liberty, Force, and the Work of Mercantile Writing

In the period extending from the beginning of Salutati's chancellorship (1375) to the consolidation of power under Cosimo de' Medici (1434), the values of Florence's ruling oligarchy were represented by two writing cultures—that of the humanists and that of the merchants. These two cultures were distinct with respect to their graphic habits: while the humanists wrote in Latin, used "humanistic" handwriting, and imitated classical models of rhetoric and genre, the merchant oligarchs wrote in the vernacular, used "mercantile" handwriting, and affiliated their writing with the traditions of bookkeeping and notarial documentation. Despite such distinctions, however, humanistic and mercantile cultural efforts overlapped, for example, in their common support of the city's Studio or university, in the collection of important classical libraries, and in the experience of consolation in writing and study.[23] But because mercantile and humanistic handwriting represent

---

[22]The issue of "exclusion" is a problematic one for feminist literary historiography. As I noted earlier, the "patriarchal and misogynous bias" of classical learning did nonetheless produce humanistic women writers. And while the humanists aimed to exclude all traces of mercantile handwriting from their own, many humanists, coming from mercantile families, appropriated various aspects of mercantile writing for humanistic culture. This contradiction is more fully examined in chapter 3 of *Chaste Thinking*. The term *exclusion* is used here to refer to the ways in which Florentine humanists excluded the context of mercantile writing culture within which they wrote from their own textual representations.

[23]Lauro Martines, *The Social World of the Florentine Humanists, 1390–1460* (London: Routledge & Kegan Paul, 1963); see also Christian Bec, *Les marchands écrivains: Affaires et humanisme à Florence, 1375–1434* (Paris: Mouton, 1967), esp. pp. 362–64.

distinct graphic typologies, and because the merchants' books are generally conserved and transmitted within the confines of a family and do
not filiate in textual families, we tend not to see how the mercantile
work of writing forms part of the circumstances in which humanistic
texts such as the *Declamatio* were produced.

The humanistic ideology of liberty dependent on rape was related to
the writing culture of the Florentine merchants as well. The physical
features of the merchants' books, the composite methods by which
they represented their own concerns, and the terms in which they
described their own writing practices constitute a field in which we can
investigate the areas of overlap between mercantile and humanistic
values and examine the context in which humanism came to be represented as a separate and autonomous literary tradition—universal and
transcendent and, at the same time, closed and impermeable to contamination by other nonhumanistic types of writing.[24]

The practices of keeping thorough and accurate accounts of business
and of recording the kinds of reflections and representations of events
that linked the family's private well-being to public concerns were the
two principal components of the merchants' impulse to write. And the
interconnection they maintained between the keeping of accounts and
the recording of reflections produced a distinctive kind of logic, or
ragione, which enables us to link the reproduction of the legend of
Lucretia to the bookkeeping interests it served in fifteenth-century
Florence. The term *ragione,* implicated in a complex web of mercantile
associations and meanings, is most simply used as a synonym for *conto,*
or "account." Other uses of the term point to the tendency of this
"reason" to detach itself from the concrete practice of bookkeeping and
to attach itself increasingly to more abstract values, reflections, and
principles of social order.

In his book of *Ricordanze,* for example, Matteo Corsini uses the term
ragione as a synonym for property.[25] And for Morelli, *ragione* is both a
standard of justice to which people are urged to comply and the means
by which they are required to comply.[26] In the *Istoria di Firenze* of

---

[24]For my analysis in this section I am indebted to the work of Angelo Cicchetti and
Raul Mordenti, *I libri di famiglia in Italia* (Rome: Edizioni di Storia e Letteratura, 1985),
and "La scrittura dei libri di famiglia," in *Letteratura italiana,* ed. Alberto Asor Rosa, vol.
3, *Le forme del testo* (Turin: Einaudi, 1984). A more developed treatment of these ideas
may be found in chapter 3 of *Chaste Thinking.*

[25]Armando Petrucci, *Il Libro di Ricordanze dei Corsini (1362–1457)* (Rome: Istituto
Storico Italiano, 1965), p. 51.

[26]Giovanni di Pagolo Morelli, *Ricordi,* ed. Vittore Branca (Florence: Le Monnier,
1956), p. 238.

Gregorio Dati, *ragione* comes to be associated with a kind of narrative logic,[27] while other uses of mercantile *ragione* link this unique logic to Florence's reproduction of Roman liberty and honor[28] achieved in the aftermath of the rape of Lucretia.

Two Florentine institutions in this period, the Dieci di Libertà and the Monte del Comune, are directly involved in the relation, through the medium of the pen, between *ragione* and liberty. And later, every merchant of standing probably had some written relation with Florence's important institution of honor and *ragione,* the Monte delle Doti (established in 1425).[29] Finally, *ragione,* in the merchants' account books, memoirs, and *ricordanze,* comes to be associated with the "force" required for account books to prevail, in actuality, over the values and "realities" they claim to represent. In this way the merchant-oligarchs' work of writing functions as a means to regulate the values of liberty, force, and honor.[30]

In an often-cited passage of Alberti's *Libri della famiglia,* the interlocutor Giannozzo advises the merchant to keep his writing secret, protecting it even, or especially, from the eyes of his wife:

> Solo e' libri e le scritture mie e de' miei passati a me piacque e allora e poi sempre avere in modo rinchiuse che mai la donna le potesse non tanto leggere, ma né vedere. Sempre tenni le scritture non per le maniche de' vestiri, ma serrate e in suo ordine allogate nel mio studio quasi come cosa sacrata e religiosa, in quale luogo mai diedi licenza alla donne mia né meco né sola v'intrasse, e più gli comandai, se mai s'abattesse a mia alcuna scrittura, subito me la consegnasse. E per levarli ogni appetito se mai desiderasse vedere o mie scritture o mie secrete faccende, io spesso molto gli biasimava quelle femmine ardite e baldanzose, le quali danno troppo opera in sapere e' fatti fuori di casa o del marito o degli altri uomini.[31]

> [I wanted to keep only the books, my writings, and the writings of my ancestors shut up, then and ever after, in such a way that my wife could never even see them, much less read them. I always kept my writings not

[27]Gregorio Dati, *Istoria di Firenze dall'anno MCCCLXXX all'anno MCCCCV* (Florence: Giuseppe Manni, 1735), p. 66; Bec, *Les marchands écrivains,* p. 323.

[28]Baron, *Crisis,* pp. 155–56; Bec, *Les marchands écrivains,* p. 280; Martines, *The Social World,* pp. 25, 34, 254.

[29]Julius Kirshner, *Pursuing Honor While Avoiding Sin: The Monte delle Doti of Florence* (Milan: Giuffré, 1978).

[30]Dati, *Istoria di Firenze,* pp. 20, 123.

[31]Leon Battista Alberti, *I libri della famiglia,* ed. Ruggiero Romano and Alberto Tenenti (Turin: Einaudi, 1972), pp. 267–68.

in the sleeves of my clothes, but shut off and organized in my study almost as a sacred and religious thing. I never gave my wife permission to enter this place, neither with me nor alone, and I often commanded her that if ever she ran across some of my writing, to hand it over to me immediately. And in order to take away any desire she might have to see either my writings or my secret matters, I often criticized those daring and insolent women who spend too much energy in learning about affairs outside the house or about their husbands or other men.]

In this passage we can see, once again, the representation of a woman in relation to the work of writing. In the case of humanistic culture, we saw how the mode of production of writing was inscribed with figures of violation and castigation. As Lisa Jardine, Margaret King, and Albert Rabil have shown, exceptional women humanists, such as Isotta Nogarola, Cassandra Fedele, and Laura Cereta, who took up the pen, were necessarily inscribed within this system.[32] In the case of mercantile culture, there were also exceptional women writers, such as Alessandra Strozzi and Chiara Gambacorti, who were nonetheless inscribed by a misogynist mode of production of writing which regulated, by the force of figures, their daily activities and thoughts.

My purpose in pursuing this specific example involving the writing practices related to Salutati's transmission of the legend of Lucretia is to propose that the focus on the work or production of writing, seen in relation to the representation of women, can, in certain ways, be useful to feminist studies of the Italian Renaissance. By focusing on the work of writing, we can see how the production of a literary system in which *human* is equivalent to *male* begins with the very formation of letters on the page. We can examine the relative social freedoms or oppression of women in relation to the nonplace of women in the filial transmission of writing. And, perhaps most important, we can "decenter" the accepted "map of knowledge"—to use the formulation of Margaret Ferguson, Maureen Quilligan, and Nancy Vickers—by changing the mode of our own production of criticism to include nonliterary aspects of writing. The relation of this enterprise of "decentering" to possible feminist uses of paleography requires some final methodological considerations.[33]

[32]See Lisa Jardine, "Isotta Nogarola: Women Humanists—An Education for What?" *History of Education* 12 (1983): 231–44; Margaret L. King and Albert Rabil, Jr., eds. and trans., *Her Immaculate Hand: Selected Works by and about the Women Humanists of Quattrocento Italy* (Binghamton, N.Y.: Medieval and Renaissance Texts and Studies, 1983).

[33]See the introduction by Margaret W. Ferguson, Maureen Quilligan, and Nancy J. Vickers to their volume *Rewriting the Renaissance: The Discourse of Sexual Difference in Early Modern Europe* (Chicago: University of Chicago Press, 1986), esp. p. xxii.

The Work of Feminist Scholarship

The records of fifteenth-century Florence do not readily furnish data about questions of gender, female experience, and subjectivity, for these are "anachronistic" questions that concern those who ask them more than those who lived in early modern Florence. Various disciplines and methodologies, however, provide relevant information and important interpretations in which our own concerns are reflected, enabling us to draw different "maps of knowledge" that are historically related to our historical moment. My concern in this essay has been to take a small part of the knowledge we have about chastity as a social norm and practice in this period, to connect this knowledge to the work of writing, or the physical practice of forming letters on the page, and to explore the implications of this connection for feminist work on humanism. The methodological question that has informed my reflections on these issues has been: How can the concerns of a feminist reading subject be reflected in the legend of a rape celebrated as the prologue to freedom?

When we extend Kelly's notion of a Renaissance of Chastity to include the humanist's ideal of chaste handwriting and chaste texts, we are reminded that the "patriarchal and misogynous bias" which conditioned the lives of women in early capitalism also informed the structure within which literature was produced. At the same time as the chastity of women was cultivated "in the realm of reproduction, the private family," the chastity of texts was being cultivated in the production of philological or textual families. In order to derive the most chaste reading of the ancient Roman texts, the Florentine humanists began to elaborate those methods that would eventually produce the familial structure of modern philology. This structure ensured both the inscription of the author as a glorified father whose hypothetical will determined the chastity of his text and the definition of literature as that kind of writing which reproduces itself in families. One part of the feminist enterprise can consist in breaking down the power of the father and the family in determining the structure within which the meaning of Lucretia's rape is produced. The isolation of one copy of the *Declamatio* from the flow of authorial inscriptions and familial traditions of celebrating rape as a prologue to freedom offers one possibility for accomplishing this task.

A manuscript book containing the texts of authors such as Salutati is nameless and belongs to different, nonfamilial historical conditions. It speaks to us not as a Father but as the signs of different people who have touched, read, and modified both the material of the book and the thoughts and feelings it can produce for subsequent readers. While the thoughts of the author of the *Declamatio* are decidedly incompatible with the work of feminist research, there is some convergence between feminist work and the work of scribes who transcribed and assembled texts in such a way as to produce a certain meaning. In both cases, there is an effort on the part of the writer to collaborate in the production of meaning. As the scribe of the *Declamatio* worked to reproduce the meaning of Lucretia's rape codified by the humanistic tradition, so the feminist writer makes these efforts a part of her own narration.

In the representation of her experience of contact with the work of writing, the feminist writer can draw attention not only to *what* is represented by language but also to *how* such language is conserved in writing. This double focus enables her to see certain kinds of meaning as integrally related to particular modes of writing production, and, thus, to imagine different relations of writing as producing different kinds of meaning. In the case of the "Humanistic Miscellany," we cannot be sure of who assembled the texts or the purpose for which they were assembled. But by virtue of our contact with the work of writing in this manuscript, we become one of its intended readers, challenged to reassemble these materials of history in new configurations of meaning.

In her book *Alice doesn't,* Teresa de Lauretis underlines the necessity for feminists not only to study preestablished codes or sign systems, already in the habit of producing certain kinds of meaning, but also to represent their own experience of working through and interacting with these codes: "It is this work or activity which constitutes and/or transforms the codes, at the same time as it constitutes and transforms the individuals using the codes, performing the work."[34] By analyzing the work of writing required to reproduce the rape of Lucretia, feminist readers and writers can modify the preestablished codes or sign systems by which this legend is traditionally understood. In this context it seems that one possibility for feminist criticism of the Italian Renaissance is that of changing the focus from the literary offspring of a textual family to the work of writing required to produce it.

A direct physical encounter with the work of writing produces a particular kind of comprehension that provides a means of investigating the webs of signification in which figures such as Lucretia are caught. If the interpretation of texts representing Lucretia's rape places

---

[34]Teresa de Lauretis, *Alice doesn't: Feminism, Semiotics, Cinema* (Bloomington: Indiana University Press, 1984), p. 167.

feminist readers in the contradictory position of reproducing a scene of sexual violence, an examination of the work of writing offers the possibility of shifting the terms of interpretation to construct a different meaning. First, from the various marks of readers and owners of this writing, we can form a kind of composite picture of those who found the legend of Lucretia appealing or attractive, and then delineate our own difference, as readers, from them. In the physical marks of the humanistic handwriting of the scribe, we can perceive the contradictory position of those women who took up pens, writing themselves into hidden links in the chain of reproduction of humanistic culture. And we can interpret the aesthetic and ideological value of terms such as *chastity, violation,* and *castigation* as they were applied to humanistic handwriting in the fifteenth-century debates about graphic reform.

The study of scribal practices and errors provides one way to see (and touch) the mode of reproduction of the "bourgeois sex-role system" which, as Kelly noted, placed "man in the public sphere and the patrician woman in the home, requiring social virtues from him and chastity and motherhood from her."[35] We can examine the relation of this writing style to the interpretive practices of philology elaborated by the first humanists. And, finally, we can examine the relation of the culture characterized by "humanistic" script to other contemporaneous cultures of writing, most notably the culture of mercantile writing, excluded both then and now from the "literary" canon.

An examination of the work of writing by means of which the *Declamatio* was produced and transmitted can help the feminist reader break down the barriers between a text and its historical context in relation to her own conditions and practices of writing today. I want to emphasize that when I speak of feminist readers, I do not mean this in an entirely exclusive way. I am rather speaking of a gendered reading capable of being performed by men and women alike who are conscious of how their gendered interpretive and academic experience leads them to think and speak in gender-specific ways. While the humanists endeavored, as an important part of their program, to cover over the traces of the historical position from which they wrote, feminists and theorists of gender seek to underline the political effects of this concealment, attempting to privilege the ideological underpinnings of their own interpretive claims.

One way to expose the concealment of the historical and gendered conditions in which interpretation takes places is to focus on the work

35Kelly, "Did Women Have a Renaissance?" p. 38.

of writing and the contribution it makes to the production of meaning. Our disciplinary training, however, encourages us to segregate the task of describing the work of writing from the task of interpretation. The description of the work of writing is usually performed by scholars of codicology—the study of everything pertaining to the history of manuscripts—and of paleography—the study of everything pertaining to the history of writing. In the context of universities in the United States, the virtual elimination of these vast fields of knowledge from the curricula of studies in literature has kept the description of material contact with writing from being a subject of interpretive and theoretical inquiry. I would like to propose that a task still pending for feminist scholars of the Renaissance is the appropriation of paleography for our own ends. One way to change our relation to the production of meaning in the Renaissance canon is to change our relation to the work of writing.

II
THE POLITICAL ECONOMY
OF GENDER

Stanley Chojnacki

"The Most Serious Duty":
Motherhood, Gender, and Patrician
Culture in Renaissance Venice

"Educatio liberorum, pars uxorii muneris fructuosa et longe gra-
vissima" ("the upbringing of children, which is surely a rewarding and
by far the most serious of a wife's duties").[1] When the young Venetian
patrician Francesco Barbaro wrote these words in his erudite treatise on
marriage of 1415–16, he likely did not have in mind the complex
implications that they would have over the next century for the private
and public culture of the ruling elite to which he belonged. Although
convinced of the importance for family well-being of a wife's breeding
and character, Barbaro fully shared Venice's time-honored subscription
to the patriarchal principles of Roman law, encapsulated in the *patria
potestas*.[2] For him, as for most commentators then and later, mothers
contributed but fathers commanded; as Barbaro wrote, "Let the husband give the orders and let the wife carry them out with a cheerful
temper."[3] Indeed, for the Venetian patriciate the patriarchal ideal cov-

Research for this study was supported by the American Council of Learned Societies,
the Gladys Krieble Delmas Foundation, and the College of Arts and Letters and Department of History, Michigan State University.
    [1]*Francisci Barbari de re uxoria liber in partes duas,* ed. Attilio Gnesotto (Padua: Randi,
1915), p. 92. The translation is based on that of Benjamin G. Kohl, *The Earthly Republic:
Italian Humanists on Government and Society,* ed. Benjamin G. Kohl and Ronald G. Witt
(Philadelphia: University of Pennsylvania Press, 1978), p. 220. Barbaro's discussion
makes clear that he uses *educatio* in the sense that includes general upbringing as well as
pedagogy. On Barbaro, see Margaret L. King, "Caldiera and the Barbaros on Marriage
and the Family," *Journal of Medieval and Renaissance Studies* 6 (1976): 19–50, esp. 31–35.
    [2]On Venice's uninterrupted subscription to family principles of Roman law, see
Giorgio Zordan, "I vari aspetti della comunione familiare dei beni nella Venezia dei
secoli XI–XII," *Studi veneziani* 8 (1966): 127–94.
    [3]*De re uxoria,* p. 63; Kohl's translation, p. 193.

ered both private and public life. Husbandly dominion within the palazzo paralleled the central place of fathers in the functioning of the patrician regime. A man's membership in the elite rested on his documented descent from generations of patrician fathers, and the benefits he gained from patrician status depended on his paternal legacy: not just material assets but also the friendships, esteem, and social and political credit acquired by his father through involvement in the activity of his class.[4]

These traits made up the gender triptych of patriarchal, patrilineal, and patrimonial principles that formally governed family and regime. They give the strong impression that if any women had a Renaissance, it was not patrician women in Renaissance Venice. Yet gender and the relations between the sexes are complex matters with many dimensions and embracing both precept and practice. For a historian the insights offered by attention to gender come not just from ascertaining society's gender principles, but also from exploring the relationship between these and the practical activity of men acting as men and women acting as women. It is in this dialectical dynamic between gender norms and gender-interpretable behavior that much of what we think of as cultural change takes place—change of the kind implied in the complex question of a Renaissance for women.[5] Gender as an analytical concept is still in lively evolution, with no fixed consensus about its dimensions yet in place. This encourages exploration of varied configurations,

[4]The fullest discussion of patrician political practice is in Robert Finlay, *Politics in Renaissance Venice* (New Brunswick, N.J.: Rutgers University Press, 1980). On the establishment of the hereditary principle in the patriciate, see Frederic C. Lane, "The Enlargement of the Great Council of Venice," in *Florilegium Historiale: Essays Presented to Wallace K. Ferguson,* ed. J. G. Rowe and W. H. Stockdale (Toronto: University of Toronto Press, 1971), pp. 236–74. See also Stanley Chojnacki, "Political Adulthood in Fifteenth-Century Venice," *American Historical Review* 91 (1986): 791–810.

[5]See the seminal essay of Joan Kelly, "Did Women Have a Renaissance?" (1977), reprinted in *Becoming Visible: Women in European History,* 2d ed., ed. Renate Bridenthal, Claudia Koonz, and Susan M. Stuard (Boston: Houghton Mifflin, 1987), pp. 175–202. The broad strokes of Kelly's essay are given historical nuance in Susan M. Stuard, "The Dominion of Gender: Women's Fortunes in the High Middle Ages," ibid., pp. 153–74. For other considerations of change in the position of women during the Middle Ages and Renaissance, see Judith M. Bennett, *Women in the Medieval English Countryside* (New York: Oxford University Press, 1987), esp. the introduction; Merry E. Wiesner, *Working Women in Renaissance Germany* (New Brunswick, N.J.: Rutgers University Press, 1986); and Martha C. Howell, "Citizenship and Gender: Women's Political Status in Northern Medieval Cities," in *Women and Power in the Middle Ages,* ed. Mary Erler and Maryanne Kowaleski (Athens: University of Georgia Press, 1988), pp. 37–60.

mining its many rich veins in the interest of achieving an enhanced, more nuanced historical discourse.[6]

In this essay I would like to venture such an exploration, taking as my point of departure a configuration of gender as involving two sets of relationships, one between men and women, and one between individuals of each sex and the cultural norms governing gender. It seems to me helpful to picture these relationships as played out along the sides of a triangle, with reciprocal dynamics going on along each side. Along the horizontal base, men at one corner and women at the other interact under the influence of various cultural norms, chiefly that of patriarchy, but also according to the peculiar contingencies of individual circumstance, allowing or forcing greater or lesser conformity with those norms. The contingencies also figure in the other two dynamics. Individual men, grouped in this image at one of the bottom corners, and individual women, grouped at the other, both interact with the prevailing gender norms (or culture, or ideology: any term will do), which sit at the apex of the triangle. The action is reciprocal on all sides, for the subordination of individual women to patriarchal dominance depends on, but also influences, their relationships with men. With individual men the situation is the same, but in reverse: their conformity with the patriarchal model is expressed in, but in practice also depends on, their relationships with women. And gender ideology itself is subject to change on the basis of large-scale nonconformity with it in individual experience.

Among Venetian patricians, to ease away from such abstract schemes, the relationship between gender principles, gender in practice, and the direction of change may be observed concretely along three axes. One is influence within the family, and we may pose a focusing question about it: How closely did the legal endurance of the *patria potestas* correspond to a reality of paternal dominance in the home? The second axis runs

---

[6]My views of gender in historical analysis have been especially influenced by Sherry B. Ortner and Harriet Whitehead, "Introduction," in *Sexual Meanings: The Cultural Construction of Gender and Sexuality* (Cambridge: Cambridge University Press, 1981); Michelle Zimbalist Rosaldo, "Woman, Culture, and Society: A Theoretical Overview," in *Woman, Culture, and Society,* ed. Michelle Zimbalist Rosaldo and Louise Lamphere (Stanford: Stanford University Press, 1974), pp. 17–42; Rosaldo, "The Use and Abuse of Anthropology: Reflections on Feminism and Cross-Cultural Understanding," *Signs: Journal of Women in Culture and Society* 5 (1980): 389–417; Jean Bethke Elshtain, *Public Man, Private Woman* (Princeton: Princeton University Press, 1981); Jane Flax, "Postmodernism and Gender Relations in Feminist Theory," *Signs: Journal of Women in Culture and Society* 12 (1987): 621–43; and Joan W. Scott, "Gender: A Useful Category of Historical Analysis," *American Historical Review* 91 (1986): 1053–75.

through gender roles in patrician society at large: Did the deeply rooted patrilineal and patrimonial principles produce in practice male privilege and centrality, female subordination and marginality in the identities, activities, and relationships that made up patrician society? The third axis arrives at the symbolic forms in which patrician culture expressed itself at its broadest: Did the patriciate convey its dominant ideals in a symbolic vocabulary that is recognizably patriarchal? These are big questions, the interrelatedness of which draws attention to the linkage between manifestations of gender in the domestic setting and in the broader social, political, and cultural arenas, and to the dynamic friction of that linkage as it affected individual lives and identities.[7] They are too vast to be fully posed, let alone satisfactorily answered, here.[8] But it is possible to pick at them in a limited way. This essay inquires into patriarchy by looking at patrician mothers, and specifically their involvement in the shaping of their children's adult identities.

Just as gender elucidates its social and cultural context, so context is essential to understanding gender. Two matters of context must be kept in view when assessing gender in Venetian patrician culture. One is the paramount place of marriage.[9] From the late fourteenth century, patricians deepened their class's exclusivism, enacting a steady stream of laws that built an iron curtain of pedigree between themselves and the populace, with the patrician antecedents of a man's mother coming to be regarded as almost as important as those of his father in making valid his claim to patrician status.[10] This increased the stakes of matrimonial

[7]The complex interaction between gender, social placement, and individual identity is variously explored by Stephen Greenblatt, "Fiction and Friction," and Natalie Zemon Davis, "Boundaries and the Sense of Self in Sixteenth-Century France," both in *Reconstructing Individualism: Autonomy, Individuality, and the Self in Western Thought,* ed. Thomas C. Heller et al. (Stanford: Stanford University Press, 1986), pp. 30–52 and 53–63, respectively.

[8]This essay is part of a larger project exploring patrician politics, society, and culture, with special attention to gender, especially as it related to the liminal groups of women and young men. See, preliminarily, my "Patrician Adulthood," and also "The Power of Love: Wives and Husbands in Late Medieval Venice," in Erler and Kowaleski, *Women and Power in the Middle Ages,* pp. 126–48.

[9]On marriage in the patriciate, see Finlay, *Politics,* esp. pp. 81–96; Bianca Betto, "Linee di politica matrimoniale nella nobiltà veneziana fino al XV secolo: Alcune note genealogiche e l'esempio della famiglia Mocenigo," *Archivio storico italiano* 139 (1981): 3–64; Stanley Chojnacki, "Marriage Legislation and Patrician Society in Fifteenth-Century Venice," in *Law, Custom, and the Social Fabric in Medieval Europe: Essays in Honor of Bryce Lyon,* ed. Bernard Bachrach and David Nicholas (Kalamazoo: Medieval Institute Publications, 1990), pp. 163–84.

[10]See Chojnacki, "Marriage Legislation," on governmental definitions of the status requirements of patrician wives. Barbaro ranked the pedigree of the mother at least as high as that of the father in producing worthy offspring; *De re uxoria,* p. 41.

choice, making it more desirable than ever to marry within the class, but also to marry well within it, leading patricians to seek the richest, most influential and socially lustrous spouses possible for their children.[11] The concern with status was inseparable from concrete interest. The material advantages of membership in the elite were of pressing concern to patricians, and an elaborate business of patron-client relations, friendship cultivating, favor exchange, alliance forging, and bloc voting, all directed toward gaining or apportioning the remunerative government jobs and other privileges on which patrician families depended, was the main stuff of patrician politics.[12] In this high-stakes social world matrimony was the chief means of forging the associations through which families ensured their status and promoted their interests. Matrimony involved marriage portions; good marriages required big portions; and assembling these entailed the commitment of great chunks of family resources.[13]

The zeal for good marriages is tied to the second component of the context of patrician gender. The currency of matrimony, dowries, were the property of the women whose marriages they brought about. Husbands could invest their wives' dowries, and in fifteenth-century Venice one-third of the total marriage portion normally became the husband's property to keep.[14] But the bulk of these growing marriage portions belonged to the wives themselves, to spend, save, or distribute as they pleased during widowhood, and to bequeath to the heirs of their choice, whether they predeceased their husbands or not.[15] Wifely dowry

[11]Chojnacki, "Marriage Legislation."

[12]Finlay, *Politics;* on patrician dependence on political office, see Donald E. Queller, *The Venetian Patriciate: Reality versus Myth* (Urbana: University of Illinois Press, 1986).

[13]On assembling dowries, see Stanley Chojnacki, "Dowries and Kinsmen in Early Renaissance Venice," *Journal of Interdisciplinary History* 5 (1975): 571–600. For non-Venetian perspectives, see Diane Owen Hughes, "From Brideprice to Dowry in Mediterranean Europe," *Journal of Family History* 3 (1978): 262–96; Julius Kirshner and Anthony Molho, "The Dowry Fund and the Marriage Market in Early *Quattrocento* Florence," *Journal of Modern History* 50 (1978): 403–38; and Christiane Klapisch-Zuber, "The Griselda Complex: Dowry and Marriage Gifts in the Quattrocento," in Klapisch-Zuber, *Women, Family, and Ritual in Renaissance Italy,* trans. Lydia G. Cochrane (Chicago: University of Chicago Press, 1985), pp. 213–46.

[14]In the fifteenth century, marriage portions usually consisted of two-thirds strict dowry, to be returned to the wife, and one-third *corredum,* at that time an outright gift to the husband. The complex and evolving relationship of dowry to *corredum* (the latter in its twin dimensions as trousseau and as gift to the husband) is addressed in my larger study (see note 8). See, meanwhile, Chojnacki, "Marriage Legislation."

[15]The mechanisms guaranteeing women's rights to their dowries at marriage's end are too elaborate to discuss here; they are treated in my larger study (see note 8). The principal evidence is in the Venetian statutes, especially Book 4, chaps. 53–61, *Volumen statutorum legum, ac iurium D. Venetorum* (Venice, 1564), pp. 24v–29v; and Archivio di

wealth, growing in lockstep with families' matrimonial ambitions and safeguarded by statute and court, is central to gender in patrician family, society, and culture. It is the key to the way women discharged their "most serious duty," the launching of their children into the complex world of patrician adulthood.

Formally and prescriptively, fathers as patresfamilias had the principal responsibility for and authority over family strategy, including the planning of children's destinies.[16] In the pedigree-conscious climate of the fifteenth century, fathers exercising this authority merged the interests of family with those of lineage, the matrix of membership in patrician society, and the operating environment of the patriarchal triptych. The influence and motivations of fathers in the concentric settings of family and lineage are illustrated in the 1401 will of Gasparino Morosini.[17] Widowed three times, Gasparino had, among other kin, three living sons and a married daughter, a widowed daughter-in-law with two sons (Gasparino's grandsons), and an orphaned granddaughter by another deceased son. To each of these persons he had something to give, but he commanded as he gave. Setting up a generous investment fund for his youngest, underage son, Antonio, he declared that his two adult sons (Antonio's half-brothers) were not to complain, because they had already been provided for; indeed, of one of them, Nicolò, Gasparino said, "non digo niente" ("I say nothing"), because Nicolò had been so well set up at his emancipation.[18] Gasparino's strictures had added force because, beyond his own wealth, he had administrative control over the legacies that the elder sons had received from their respective mothers. And he flatly asserted that if they failed to treat the underage Antonio well, they would lose half their bequest from him, which would then go to Antonio.

Gasparino's authoritative largesse extended beyond his sons to the

---

Stato, Venice (hereafter abbreviated ASV), Giudici del Proprio, Diiudicatum, Reg. 1, 2 (1468–77); and innumerable notarial acts securing wives' rights to their husband's property against restitution of their dowries. See also Julius Kirshner, "Wives' Claims against Insolvent Husbands in Late Medieval Italy," in *Women of the Medieval World,* ed. Julius Kirshner and Suzanne F. Wemple (Oxford: Basil Blackwell, 1985), pp. 256–93; and Thomas Kuehn, "Some Ambiguities of Female Inheritance Ideology in the Renaissance," *Continuity and Change* 2 (1987): 11–36.

[16]On the authority of fathers, see Thomas Kuehn, *Emancipation in Late Medieval Florence* (New Brunswick, N.J.: Rutgers University Press, 1982).

[17]ASV, Archivio Notarile, Testamenti (hereafter abbreviated NT, followed by *busta* number and notary's name) 575, Gibellino, no. 675, 9 May 1401.

[18]On the continuing relationships between fathers and their emancipated sons, see Kuehn, *Emancipation.*

women in his life. To his widowed daughter-in-law, Maria, he bequeathed several properties, including the house where she was living, and he declared that his estate should bear the expenses of the upbringing of his two grandsons, who were also to share one-quarter of Gasparino's residuary estate (the other three-quarters going to his sons). He even bequeathed two hundred ducats toward Maria's dowry, should she decide to remarry: this is remarkable, since a remarriage might produce children who would compete for Maria's beneficence with her present offspring, Gasparino's grandsons. He further declared that if any of his sons should oppose his generosity toward Maria, he was to be disinherited.[19] Finally, to his orphaned granddaughter Franceschina he left the conspicuous sum of two thousand ducats in state bonds, to be used for her marriage, at age thirteen, to a "Venetian patrician worthy of her rank and acceptable to my sons Nicolò, Benedetto, and Antonio, and also to my cousins Bernardo and Barbon Morosini and my cousingerman Zanin Morosini."[20]

He enlisted the involvement of his sisters as well. One, a nun, he asked to care for Franceschina, keeping her in the convent until the girl was eleven, at which point his other, married sister was to take over, presumably to prepare Franceschina for her marriage. Gasparino also provided for Franceschina's living expenses; but despite his wide-ranging generosity in substance, the tone of the will, in this as in its other arrangements, is one of command. He was head of the extended family,

---

[19]Gasparino's unusual generosity toward Maria runs exactly counter to the remarrying "cruel mother" syndrome analyzed in the Florentine context by Christiane Klapisch-Zuber in her influential essay "The 'Cruel Mother': Maternity, Widowhood, and Dowry in Florence in the Fourteenth and Fifteenth Centuries," in *Women, Family, and Ritual*, pp. 117–31. Whereas the cruelty of the mother in Klapisch-Zuber's formulation consisted in her willing or coerced abandonment of her children after remarriage, Gasparino, though solicitous of his grandchildren by Maria, nevertheless benignly supported the prospect of her remarriage. It remains to be demonstrated that a remarrying Venetian mother was more likely than her Florentine counterpart to continue caring for the children of her first marriage. Gasparino himself was accustomed to cherish ties to in-laws even after remarriage; in an earlier will of 1374, written during his second marriage, he had bequeathed fifty ducats to each of the brothers of his deceased first wife, "per grande amor e raxion chio o portado sempre a quella caxa" ("because of the great love and interest I have always had for that house"). NT 1062, Della Torre, no. 300, 14 April 1374.

[20]"Vojo la se dia a quelo zentilomo venizian che sia dexevele ala so condizion e che sia de conttentto e azetto a mi fiuoli Nicolò Benedetto e Antuonio. E semelmentre sia azeto a miy cosini Barbon e Bernardo Morexini e mio coxin german Zanin Morexini, hover a la plu parte de questi." NT 571, "carte varie," 18 April 1401. (The May 9 will added codicils to the basic text of the April 18 will.)

mobilizer of its human resources, committed molder of the lineage's destiny. In short, he was the very model of a patriarch, solicitous of his living kin, mindful of the dead, but especially concerned with the young, both children and grandchildren, whose upbringing and future prospects he attended to in detail, applying moral and material leverage to ensure equity among his heirs, especially his sons by different mothers.[21] And as he made explicit in his instructions for his granddaughter, his authoritative concern extended to the enduring dignity of his lineage, to be secured by "worthy" marriages in which an array of agnatic kinsmen were to interest themselves. Gasparino resembles the patriarch ruling over what F. W. Kent calls in a Florentine context the "grand family."[22] As such he fills a quintessentially conventional male role. Yet virtually every one of his will's provisions (and those of other patrician patriarchs) can be found, though with significant differences, in the wills of wealthy, influential, self-confident patrician mothers.

Gasparino's solicitude over the needs of individual kin is a useful reminder that men did not mechanically follow a blinkered lineage interest. Nevertheless, male patricians were constantly reminded that their very social identity, to say nothing of their enjoyment of the benefits of elite status, was rooted in a title tied to the male line of descent. From the ritual at age eighteen that ascertained and registered their paternal descent to the mobilization of lineage loyalties and associations that gained them remunerative government posts and other privileges, men of the patriciate were labeled as their fathers' sons, and indeed had every reason to brandish the label and, like Gasparino, to transfer it, and the lineage orientation to which it was the key, to their own progeny.[23]

[21]The example of a father mediating equitably the legacies to his sons by their different predeceased mothers represents another alternative to the child-abandoning widow discussed as a model of Florentine wifehood by Klapisch-Zuber in "Cruel Mother." The remarrying widow was only one of several maternal typologies; in addition to women who, like Gasparino's three wives, preceded their husbands to the grave, many mothers remained head of household after their husband's death, giving a distinctive cast to their discharge of that role. See my discussion later in this chapter.

[22]F. W. Kent, *Household and Lineage in Renaissance Florence: The Family Life of the Capponi, Ginori, and Rucellai* (Princeton: Princeton University Press, 1977), pp. 29–36, 58–60.

[23]On the Balla d'Oro exercise establishing patrician adulthood, see Chojnacki, "Political Adulthood," and also "Kinship Ties and Young Patricians in Fifteenth-Century Venice," *Renaissance Quarterly* 38 (1985): 240–70. In 1405 the Venetian Great Council passed a law requiring candidates for office to be identified not only by given name and surname but by patronymic as well. ASV, Maggior Consiglio, Reg. (hereafter abbreviated MC) 21, Leona, f. 127.

The case of patrician women was different. As Christiane Klapisch-Zuber, Diane Owen Hughes, and Sharon Strocchia have emphasized, women's membership in the patrilineage was tenuous and temporary.[24] All married women belonged to two families, and most to two lineages, in some respects sequentially, moving from the natal to the marital *casa*, but in another sense simultaneously, retaining ties to each.[25] The complementary, countervailing, complexly interwoven lineage ties of married patrician women affected their relations with their variously aligned kin. Especially toward their children and grandchildren, dowry-possessing women projected influences that intersected the lineage orientation of men, alloying it with the values of what the anthropologist Meyer Fortes termed the "complementary line of filiation."[26] It is the exercise of the moderating influence of mothers in the discharge of "their most serious duty" of raising children to adulthood that is of interest for our understanding of patrician gender roles. For the participation of mothers, with their distinctive social orientation, in ostensibly patriarchal prerogatives affected the gender identities of their children.

[24]Christiane Klapisch-Zuber, "Cruel Mother," and "Kin, Friends, and Neighbors: The Urban Territory of a Merchant Family in 1400," in *Women, Family, and Ritual*, pp. 68–93. Diane Owen Hughes, "From Brideprice to Dowry," and "Representing the Family: Portraits and Purposes in Early Modern Italy," *Journal of Interdisciplinary History* 17 (1986): 7–38. Sharon T. Strocchia, "Remembering the Family: Women, Kin, and Commemorative Masses in Renaissance Florence," *Renaissance Quarterly* 42 (1989): 635–54. See also Ronald F. E. Weissman, *Ritual Brotherhood in Renaissance Florence* (New York: Academic Press, 1982), p. 33.

[25]Female testators often advertised their double affiliation: "Ego Victoria filia qd. domini Andree Victuri *ad presens* uxor nobilis viri domini Valerii Geno" ("I Vittoria, daughter of the late Lord Andrea Vitturi, *at present* wife of the noble Lord Valerio Zeno") (NT 857, Rizoto, no. 349, 31 July 1427; emphasis added); "Mi Franceschina fia fo del nobel homo miser Domenego Loredan *al prexente* spoxa del nobel homo miser Nicholo Chapelo" ("I Franceschina, daughter of the late noble messer Domenico Loredan, *at present* spouse of the noble messer Nicolò Capello") (NT 1238, Tomei, Part II, no. 292, 2 December 1464; emphasis added). The allusion to the temporariness of marital ties suggests a more durable natal than marital identification for these women. Other wives, however, emphasized the marital family connection: Briseida Pisani, wife of Nicolò Bragadin, while retaining close ties to her mother and brother (naming them as testamentary executors and leaving them bequests), nevertheless identified herself as "ego Briseida consors viri nobilis domini Nicolai Bragadeno" ("I Briseida, consort of the noble Lord Nicolò Bragadin"). Ibid., no. 17, 10 July 1438.

[26]Meyer Fortes, "The Structure of Unilineal Descent Groups," *American Anthropologist* 55 (1953): 17–41, at 34. On functional bilaterality in formally unilineal descent groups, see Jack Goody, *The Development of the Family and Marriage in Europe* (Cambridge: Cambridge University Press, 1983), pp. 6, 226; cf. Chojnacki, "Kinship Ties."

Male identity in patrician culture was essentially public. No sooner did a young man reach age eighteen than he was presented to public officials for an induction ritual, the so-called Balla d'Oro, that began his gradual passage into full adulthood, which was reckoned in terms of governmental activity.[27] The public nature of men's vocational activity and the economic dependence of, as officials noted, a "majority" of patrician families on government programs reinforced lineage discipline.[28] Fathers hurried sons into public life, and young manhood was a period of apprenticeship under the guidance of fathers and male kinsmen, whose political direction and economic support emphasized the benefits to be derived from cultivation of collective virtues: of the family, the lineage, the patriciate as a whole. Personal relations between fathers and sons in so highly structured a family culture make a fascinating subject requiring more study. But they were in any case enfolded within an ideology of mutually advantageous conformity to the requirements of lineage and regime. From this structure it was psychologically and materially difficult for either generation to extricate itself, with the result that the public gave form and substance to the personal, leading fathers to cultivate in their sons a conformist ideal of male adulthood, a male gender model in which, paradoxically, patriarchy dictated a narrow range of individual identity for men.[29]

Fathers' relationships with their daughters were inevitably different from those with their sons. The exclusion of women from the public life where fathers and sons consorted, and the convention that ushered daughters out of the natal household to marry in their mid-teens, make fathers seem remote figures in their daughters' lives. That helps to explain the apparent coldness with which fathers, or grandfathers such as Gasparino Morosini, negotiated marriages that took girls from the family hearth at a tender age and plunked them willy-nilly into the households and beds of male strangers.[30] It is wise not to universalize

[27]Chojnacki, "Political Adulthood."

[28]Official testimony about the dependence of a majority of patricians on office holding is in MC 34, Stella, f. 109v. The fullest treatment of governmental careerism among the patriciate is in Queller, *Venetian Patriciate*.

[29]On the tension between youthful expansiveness and adult conformity, see Chojnacki, "Political Adulthood," especially the references to liminality, pp. 806–10. See also the discussion of Richard C. Trexler, *Public Life in Renaissance Florence* (New York: Academic Press, 1980), chap. 5.

[30]Among testating parents in the sample of wills, thirty-four identified specific ages for their daughters' marriages. Their preferences ranged from age eleven or twelve to twenty, with a median age of fourteen to sixteen. See, briefly, note 53.

paternal stoniness: statements by fathers of warm affection for daughters do appear in the sources.[31] Moreover, fathers were under considerable pressure to forge advantageous family alliances by means of marriage; gathering a competitive dowry and bestowing a young daughter in marriage were two sacrifices that even tender-hearted patriarchs might be obliged to make. Nor were married daughters written off by their fathers or other family members. On the contrary, a father had a powerful practical reason for maintaining close ties to his daughter: the hope that she would return some of her dowry wealth to the natal family that had assembled it. For their part, young wives showed lingering ties to their fathers, for example, by making them executors and legatees of their wills, thereby attesting to the endurance of father-daughter bonds beyond the wedding day.[32]

Nevertheless, practical interest blended with cultural principles to make daughters instruments of the family strategies pursued by their fathers. Prevailing values tied men's honor to control over their womenfolk's sexuality; in practice, that limited women's approved gender roles to wifehood or enclosure in a convent.[33] Even that restricted

---

[31]In 1497 Francesco Morosini made a bequest to his daughter, who lived in a convent, "che io amo come lanima mia propria" ("whom I love as my very soul"). He urged the convent authorities (to whom he left a large bequest) to treat her well, "perche la dita mia fia mai non ho lassato haver senestro dapoi che le [i.e., lei è] li dentro nel dito monastier, per esserli sta bon padre e lei dolcissima fiola et esser el mio cuor proprio" ("because I have allowed no harm to befall her from the time she entered that convent, in order to be a good father to her, who is my most sweet daughter and my very heart"). ASV, Procuratori di San Marco, Commissarie de Ultra, B. 221, fasc. 1, Francesco Morosini, Register, 10 November 1497.

[32]Not yet systematically documented, this tendency emerges anecdotally: Isabetta Trevisan, married in 1417 to Filippo Foscari, named as executors of her 1419 will her father and a paternal uncle as well as her husband. Pregnant, she bequeathed to the unborn child six hundred ducats, which, if the child did not reach adulthood, were to go to her father and uncle, who in any case were named her residuary heirs; her husband was to get only one hundred ducats. NT 367, Angeletus, unnumbered, 4 January 1419 (1418 Venetian style); Marco Barbaro, "Libro di nozze patrizie," Biblioteca Nazionale Marciana, Venice, Codici italiani, classe VII, 156 (=8492) (hereafter abbreviated as Barbaro, Nozze), f. 189 left. Maria Barbarigo, married in 1450, named as executors of the will she drew up during her pregnancy in 1451 her father, a paternal uncle, and her husband. She bequeathed two hundred ducats to her husband, but the same amount each to her father and her mother and one hundred ducats to one of her brothers; her remaining hundred ducats she left to the child she was carrying, but if it died before reaching age fourteen, the money was to go to her brothers. NT 558, Gambaro, no. 220, 17 December 1451; Barbaro, Nozze, f. 368 left.

[33]On male honor and female vocations, see Julius Kirshner, "Pursuing Honor while Avoiding Sin: The *Monte delle Doti* of Florence," *Studi senesi* 89 (1977): 175–258.

vocational choice generally seems to have been made by the father, not the daughter. The large dowries that families were obliged to commit to favorable marriages, and the tender age at which women's vocations were decided, meant that factors other than a girl's preference dominated in her father's assessment of prospective sons-in-law; at the same time, many families simply lacked the wealth to arrange marriages for all their daughters, requiring fathers to force some into convents amid, as the preamble to one legislative act put it, "tears and wailing."[34] The evidence in fathers' wills shows that Gasparino Morosini was following custom in decreeing that the "gentleman" to whom his granddaughter Franceschina was to be married at age thirteen should be chosen by her male kinsmen.[35]

Mothers writing their wills applied the influence of their wealth in ways that both contrasted with and complemented the intentions of fathers, but with the ultimate effect of broadening the range of gender identity for both sons and daughters. Owing to their distinctive placement overlapping two lineages and families, women had greater flexibility in their family and kinship orientation than did men; indeed,

[34]ASV, Senato, Misti, Reg. 53, f. 70. This act, aimed at restraining dowry inflation, is discussed at length in Chojnacki, "Marriage Legislation." Motives for consigning daughters to convents are discussed in Richard C. Trexler, "Le célibat à la fin du Moyen Age: Les religieuses de Florence," *Annales: Économies, sociétés, civilisations* 27 (1972): 1329–50. Questions about the effectiveness of the religious life in guaranteeing male honor by preserving female chastity are raised by evidence of sexual activity in convents presented in Guido Ruggiero, *The Boundaries of Eros: Sex Crime and Sexuality in Renaissance Venice* (New York: Oxford University Press, 1985), chap. 4, "Sex Crimes against God."

[35]Nonetheless, Gasparino was more explicit than most about his lineage ties to the men he charged with arranging Franceschina's marriage. Men usually assigned the responsibility for their daughters' marriages to their executors, who normally included a large proportion of agnates, though by no means agnates alone. For example, Lorenzo Loredan: "Volio che mia fie . . . siano maridade o munegade segondo aparera a dischrezio de mio chomessarii" ("I want my daughters to be married or placed in a convent, at the discretion of my executors"), who were his three brothers, his wife, her father, and his sons when they reached age fourteen. NT 558, Gambaro, no. 86, 10 May 1441. Similarly, Andrea Arimondo provided that when his daughter turned fifteen, "lasso libertas ala maor parte de mii commessarii . . . al suo maridar a uno zentilomo de Veniesia" ("I give liberty to the majority of my executors [to make the appropriate arrangements] at her marriage to a Venetian noble"). ASV, Cancelleria inferiore (hereafter abbreviated CI), Miscellanea testamenti, notai diversi, B. 27, no. 2697, 13 August 1427. His executors were his mother, his four brothers, his wife, her parents, and her brother. On the involvement of wives and their natal kin in the determination of their children's futures, see my discussion later in this chapter.

such variety is a hallmark of women's wills. Women wrote more wills than men—in a sampling of 614 patrician wills more than twice as many, 431 to 183.[36] This seems chiefly a result of adjustment to the sharp social and thus affective changes in a woman's life as she proceeded through the uxorial cycle from young bridehood to mature wife and motherhood to widowhood. But it also reflects a woman's broader range of choice among potential recipients of her beneficence, a consequence of her more complex network of family ties, and it contrasts with the determinism apparent in men's wills, whose provisions followed a narrower path of family and lineage responsibility.[37] Whereas men's wills usually added a few special touches to the statutory conventions, sticking mainly to the male line, those of women included both greater variety among beneficiaries and less conventional—that is, less masculinely lineage-bound—patterns of bequests, to children and others. These different approaches to testation, revealing concrete differences in gender characteristics and showing women's confidence in institutional responsiveness to their intentions, enlarged the impact of women's dowry wealth beyond the economic to the social and cultural.[38]

To their sons, women offered a more ample social context for lineage affiliation. Husbands themselves frequently recognized the capacity of their wives to contribute to the lineage, enlisting them as collaborators in family strategy, naming them as executors of their estates, and committing to them, with inducements, the upbringing of the children, including control over their children's patrimonies—a mirror image of Gasparino Morosini's administration of the estates of his

[36]This sample is not scientific but simply the product of careful study over several years of all the wills I could read. Most but not all were drawn up by members, by birth or marriage, of sixteen patrician clans whose social and political experiences I am reconstructing in detail. I know of no statistical breakdown of surviving Venetian wills; but extensive work with the card index of wills in the ASV, as well as with the testament files of dozens of notaries, gives the overpowering impression that women left wills far more often than men.

[37]The Venetian statutes governing inheritance in cases of intestacy reflected patrilineal principles, favoring first children, then ascendants in the male line. Fathers who conformed to those principles could thus entrust their estates to the enforcements of the statutes. *Volumen statutorum*, bk. 4, chaps. 24–27, pp. 70v–74v. Mothers, whose intestacy was governed largely but not completely by the same rules, had reason in their more complex social placement to make their intentions testamentarily explicit. Ibid., chap. 28, p. 74v.

[38]For differences in men's and women's patterns of testation, see Chojnacki, "Dowries and Kinsmen," pp. 60–67.

wives.[39] For their part, mothers appreciated the inseparability of their sons' well-being from the matrix of the lineage. When, as often happened, widows sponsored their eighteen-year-old sons' patrician credentialing, they joined with their husbands' paternal kinsmen in seeing the young men through the ritual.[40] Women recognized the symbolic as well as the practical importance of lineage, for example, with regard to real estate: in 1401 the widow Beruzza Soranzo urged her son Girolamo to add one thousand ducats to the dowry of his sister Caterina, in return for which Beruzza would prevail on the girl to consign to Girolamo the share of the family palace that their father had left her. This is a wonderfully neat and revealing arrangement. It fattened the dowry that would enhance Caterina's social placement and, ultimately, her personal wealth, while at the same time giving Girolamo sole possession of the palace that identified him with his father's line. It also displays the contrast between fixed, locked-in male property, literally "immovable," and the more liquid, flexible, "movable" wealth that gave women's social relations greater agility.[41]

Mothers also supplemented their sons' lineage affiliation by strengthening the sons' ties to the mothers' kinsmen. Maternal uncles frequently joined with their widowed sisters in ushering nephews into official patrician adulthood. This practice served both parties. For young men it enlarged the web of friends and patrons whose support was necessary for success in the adult patrician world. To the uncles it offered a friendly vote in the council chamber as well as the prospect of economic cooperation, and through that some tangible benefit from the investment they had committed to their sister's dowry.[42] Young men who entered adulthood in these circumstances had a broader range of social options with which to fashion their identities, enlarging the basic lineage orientation, with the guidance of mothers serving as a key to flexible social

[39]See note 35; also Chojnacki, "The Power of Love," p. 132.

[40]Chojnacki, "Kinship Ties and Young Patricians."

[41]NT 575, Giorgio Gibellino, no. 704, 15 November 1401. Beruzza was the married sister whom Gasparino Morosini wanted to prepare his granddaughter Franceschina for marriage. The preference for men as heirs to immovable property and women as heirs to movables was clearly stated in the statutes governing intestacy. *Volumen statutorum,* bk. 4, chap. 15, p. 71v. On similar rules in Florence, see Kuehn, "Some Ambiguities of Female Inheritance," p. 28 n.4.

[42]Chojnacki, "Kinship Ties and Young Patricians"; Finlay, *Politics in Renaissance Venice,* pp. 87–89. Hughes, "From Brideprice to Dowry," pp. 284, 290, argues that the dowry regime diminished bilateral ties; she also notes, however, that men retained an interest in the woman to whose dowry they had contributed as well as in the affines it produced.

placement and the vocational advantages that it promised.[43] Encouraging that filial attitude was mothers' wealth and the capacity it gave them to smooth their sons' way, for example, by providing business capital and—interesting irony here—by pledging their own wealth for the safe restitution of the dowries of their daughters-in-law.[44]

Such mother-son associations softened the edges of patriarchy by giving mothers a role in guiding their sons into successful adulthood. This urges nuance in categorizing parental roles by gender, showing as it does that mothers could be directive, not merely supportive, in discharging their upbringing duties—even vis-à-vis their patriarchally privileged male offspring. For patrician social organization, it shows mothers enriching the basic kinship structure, interlacing formal patriliny with practical bilaterality. But dowry wealth had another effect on male gender identity, one with deep cultural and psychological as well as social significance: it narrowed men's chances to fulfill the patriarchal ideal of becoming husbands and fathers. That is, the heavy commitment of family wealth to daughters' dowries effectively deprived many of their brothers of the chance to marry: men from less influential or prestigious families, or members of fraternal groups that lacked the resources to guarantee the dowries of wives for all the brothers, or simply men into whose sisters' dowries had gone the wherewithal for taking on the responsibilities of patrician husband-hood. In the fifteenth century only three in five adult patrician men married.[45] Other reasons contributed, but the premium that high dow-

[43]On family and kin boundaries as the frame of adult identity, see Davis, "Boundaries and the Sense of Self."

[44]E.g., in 1430 Cristina Falier, widow of Nicolò Barbarigo, invested 1,300 ducats with her son, Andrea, who acknowledged that it was "pro meis utilitatibus" ("for my use"). CI, Busta 122, Marevidi, Protocollo, f. 15v. In a marriage contract of 1451 Marina, widow of Tomaso Donà, "se hobliga la mittade de tuti i suo beni" ("pledges one-half of all her property") as security for repayment of the dowry that her son, Nicolò, was to receive from his wife-to-be, Isabetta Querini; the total dowry to be repaid was 1,200 ducats. ASV, Giudici del Proprio, Vadimoni, Reg. 4, ff. 58v–59v.

[45]The exact percentage of adult male patricians who married, 62 percent, was gained by comparing marriage lists in Barbaro, Nozze (see note 32), with registrations for the Balla d'Oro (see note 23) among sixteen sample clans for the period 1410–90. This involved 952 registrants, of whom 540 married. ASV, Avogaria di Comun, Balla d'Oro, Reg. 162, 163, 164. To these were added 132 husbands recorded in Barbaro, Nozze, who did not register for the Balla d'Oro, making a total of 1,084 men, of whom 672 (62 percent) married. The practice among patricians of limiting male marriage for purposes of preserving the property of a group of brothers is discussed for the sixteenth through eighteenth centuries in James C. Davis, A Venetian Family and Its Fortune, 1500–1900: The Donà and the Conservation of Their Wealth (Philadelphia: American Philosoph-

ries placed on worthy husbands was an important one. In an indirect way, then, wealthy mothers fostered a schism in male gender identity, separating those who would assume the mantle of patriarchy from those who neither ruled families nor propagated their lineage (at least legitimately) nor presided over the integration of sons into patrician government and society. But mothers also had a more direct effect on the options of their sons, by way of their concern for their daughters.

As I have noted, fathers, by preference or necessity, generally treated daughters as prime instruments of family strategy. But, as if in compensation, mothers gave them concern, wealth, and latitude of vocation. A couple of examples convey the texture of this maternal influence. In 1415 Barbarella Contarini declared that her imminent marriage had been made possible by "her most benign and generous mother," who had provided the entire dowry: a good thing, she went on, "because of the meagerness [carentium] of my inheritance from my father."[46] In thus providing for her daughter's vocational destiny, Barbarella's mother was discharging an essential patriarchal responsibility. By supplying the material means that spelled the difference between Barbarella's being able to marry or not, she was also influencing—or, instead and significantly, giving Barbarella herself the chance to shape—the young woman's sexual identity.

A second case further displays this maternal power, here generationally doubled. In 1464 Petronella Falier, wife of Zilio Morosini, ordered in her will that as soon as her daughter Paolina turned fourteen, she was to be immediately married to a patrician ("subito in un zentilom"), to be chosen by her husband and her executors, the procurators of Saint Mark. Paolina's dowry was to consist of a one-third share of Petronella's estate (the other two-thirds to be divided between her son and her unborn child) and one thousand ducats which Paolina's maternal grandmother had bequeathed the girl. Yet, worried that Zilio might prove dilatory or even resistant, Petronella gave primary authority for the marriage arrangements to the procurators, who were to

---

ical Society, 1975), pp. 93–106. Davis cites sources asserting that the practice began in the mid-sixteenth century; the evidence just noted, however, suggests that it was already in effect in the fifteenth century.

[46]CI 56, Griffon, Protocollo I, f. 76v. In return for this maternal generosity, Barbarella transferred to her mother all her rights of succession to her father's estate. This case shows how, by discharging a paternal responsibility, a mother could lay claim to a child's share of a paternal estate.

carry out her intentions for Paolina whether Zilio liked it or not.[47] Remarkably, Petronella was asserting that a mother with enough wealth could prevail over her husband in deciding their daughter's marital future. It is impossible to know who would have won in litigation, but in the event, Paolina did get married two years later, at age fifteen or less, to a member of Petronella's natal lineage.[48]

Petronella Falier's influence came from female wealth, specifically her own and her mother's large contributions to her daughter's dowry, which it would have pained her husband to do without. But the dowry wealth of other mothers enabled them to influence their daughters' destinies in even more elaborate ways, by letting them choose their vocations. The 1479 will of Maria Bembo, wife of Girolamo Zane, illustrates this point. Toward the marriage portion of each of her three daughters Maria allocated six hundred ducats.[49] But she also allocated bequests to them if they should decide not to marry but instead elect the religious life ("nolent maritare, sed monacare"). That was not the end of it, however, for she offered them an even broader range of choice. If the girls chose neither marriage nor the convent ("nolent maritare nec monacare") but instead wished to remain spinsters, living with their father and brothers, then Maria's estate was to provide their expenses for food and clothing for as long as they lived. Moreover, if for some reason they could not live with their brothers, then each was to get an additional forty ducats yearly for housing expenses, and each who lived to age twenty-four under these circumstances would be able to dispose freely of an additional hundred ducats in her will.

Maria Bembo effectively underwrote for her daughters three different vocational choices, involving three different social situations and gender identities. Nor was she unique. Increasingly in the fifteenth century, mothers were offering daughters vocational choice and the economic means to exercise it.[50] Fathers were restrained from oppos-

---

[47]NT 1239, Tomei, no. 600: "ma tuto quel parera a diti commisarii sia fato in chaxo el padre dilatase el suo maridar" ("but my executors should take whatever action they deem appropriate in the event that her father delays arranging her marriage").

[48]Paolina's marriage to Luca Falier in 1466, when she could not have been more than fifteen (calculated from Petronella's will of 1464), is in Barbaro, Nozze, f. 327 right.

[49]NT 68, Bonicardi, no. 210, 16 May 1479.

[50]Francesca Loredan Capello bequeathed four hundred ducats to each of her daughters; but "ista condicio sit et intelligatur in filiabus meis que maritaverintur. Ille vero que monacaverintur aut *starent honeste in domo* habeant ducatos trecentos" ("this provision should be understood as applying to my daughters who marry. Those indeed

ing these maternal intentions because to make the good marriage alliances that served family interest, they needed the mothers' contributions to their daughters' marriage portions, most of which were actually paid out to husbands while the mothers, like Petronella Falier, were still alive. Indeed, in a remarkable development, which I believe shows the influence of wives on their husbands' attitudes toward their families, by the late fifteenth century fathers too were beginning to follow their wives' lead and themselves offer their daughters the choice between marriage and the convent, although, not surprisingly, they do not appear to have followed them into an acceptance of lay spinsterhood.[51]

Addressing the issue of female identity in early modern France, Natalie Zemon Davis suggests that giving oneself away in marriage, consciously accepting the imposed vocation, was a means by which women could attain a certain psychological autonomy, could carve out a personal identity, in a patriarchal society.[52] In the case of Venice, the

---

who become nuns or *live chastely at home* are to have three hundred ducats"). NT 1238, Tomei, pt. II, no. 292 bis, 6 October 1473; emphasis added. See also the wills of Isabetta Gritti da Lezze (ibid., no. 220, 4 May 1465), Fantina Contarini Morosini (NT 486, Gibellino, no. 204, 11 July 1435), and Isabetta Morosini, who bequeathed one hundred ducats to her granddaughter "o per so maridar, o se lie volese andar munega in monastier de oservancia voio lie i abia e posa far quelo lie vora, *e cusi se la vuol star in nel mondo sença maridarse, o, munegarse*" ("either for her marriage or, if she chooses to become a nun in an observant convent, I want her to have them to use as she wishes; and likewise if she elects to live a secular life without marrying or becoming a nun"). (NT 1156, Croci, no. 517, 23 October 1450; emphasis added).

[51]Although I have found no fathers explicitly endorsing spinsterhood for their daughters, Prodocimo Arimondo instructed that his daughter Pellegrina, "que ducit vitam spiritualem" ("who is leading a spiritual life"), was to live not in a convent but with her brothers, "et habeat vitum de bonis meis et vestitum et bene tractetur" ("and she is to have food and clothing from my estate, and be well treated"). NT 1239, Tomei, no. 606, 27 February 1474 (1473 Venetian style). More in line with the growing tendency to allow daughters vocational choice, Lorenzo Loredan left it "in libertade dele do mie fie zoe Chataruza e Ixabela se quelle volesse servir a dio" ("up to my two daughters, namely Cateruzza and Isabella, if they wish to serve God"), in which case each was to receive four hundred ducats; but "se veramente quelle volesse esser maridada, abiano de beni dela mia comessaria ducati 600 per suo dota" ("if indeed they wish to marry, each is to receive six hundred ducats from my estate for her dowry"). NT 1186, Groppi, no. 71, 29 April 1476. More munificently, Alvise Zane left his daughter Michela his entire residuary estate for her marriage portion, unless his wife bore a son, in which case Michela would get only (!) 3,500 ducats; but if Michela "vellet monacare solum habere debeat ducatos 1500" ("wishes to become a nun, she is to have only 1500 ducats"). NT 68, Bonicardi, no. 316, 7 April 1485.

[52]Davis, "Boundaries and the Sense of Self," p. 61. This essay lays out the components of the complex issue, central to social and cultural history, and especially to the

wealth of mothers was permitting some women to go even further, to elect the adult vocational and sexual identity of their choice. To be sure, even young women who could choose marriage rather than be thrust into it still had their husbands selected for them, with family interest, not psychological compatibility, the paramount consideration. Yet, the growing attention to female choice in the matter of marriage, by mothers above all but also by some fathers, is reflected in a gradual rise in the preferred marriage age for women. The evidence is sparse, but by the later Quattrocento the age at which parents wanted their daughters to marry had risen from the early teens—the fourteenth-century fashion—to the middle or late teens.[53] This delay may have been encouraged by fathers, for whom a married daughter's greater maturity made likelier a capacity to resist the influence of husband and father-in-law, thus enabling her to demonstrate tangible loyalty to the natal family. But mothers as well were influential in pushing back their daughters' marriage age.[54] The later a girl married, the more maturely considered her choice of vocation. And we may speculate that mothers may also have eagerly used their influence to spare their daughters the psychological distress, even terror, of coercive youthful marriage to a stranger.

A trend toward later marriage for women, toward a more considered measure of female adulthood and its implications, is one notable effect of the influence that propertied women were having on the upbringing and the adult identities of their children. Later marriages, larger dowries, and the choice of vocations altered the gender balance in patrician society, giving each successive generation of wives greater means of

---

benefits of a gender-sensitive approach to it, of the tension between individual identity and the group membership that both restricts and gives it shape. The conceptual and methodological problems involved in attending to both sociocultural context and the vagaries of individual circumstance and experience require much discussion, but they are helpfully clarified by Davis' essay.

[53]Of 361 wills of married patricians, most mentioned the age of majority (conventionally age fourteen) as the preferred marriage age. But among thirty-three parents who specified marriage ages between 1350 and 1500, those testating between 1350 and 1400 ranged in their specifications from eleven to seventeen years, with a median preferred age of thirteen; the preference of those testating between 1401 and 1450 ranged from age thirteen to twenty, with a median of fifteen; and between 1451 and 1500 from fourteen to eighteen, with a median of sixteen.

[54]The evidence is mixed on mothers' preferences; some seem to have favored early marriage for their daughters, possibly to free them from their fathers' control; but others favored delaying marriage, to give the daughters greater maturity in choosing and adapting to marriage.

affecting the culture of the ruling class. But the modification of male gender models through the direct and indirect action of mothers was equally significant for patrician culture. Alongside the patriarchal figure shaping the interests of family and lineage, his authority in the household mirroring his patrician entitlement to participate in Venice's government, the irreversible commitment to ever-larger dowries was now producing in increasing numbers alternative male types, notably the patrician bachelor, equally active in political affairs but lacking the titular family authority of his married brothers. As Guido Ruggiero has suggested, these bachelors may also have produced alternative sexual cultures, or subcultures, both heterosexual and homosexual.[55]

Indeed, for all male patricians the broad-ranging social orientation of influential mothers complemented and even displaced the narrow lineage configuration with strong loyalties to and involvements with a broad range of kin, maternal as well as paternal. Young men whose mothers forged close ties between them and their maternal uncles grew into full adulthood with an ampler kinship orientation, embracing a range of close, trusted associations beyond the boundaries of lineage. I have argued that this elaborate network of loyalties combined with shared exclusivism to promote the solidarity for which Venice's patrician regime was noted; I believe that this adds up to an important female impact on patrician politics, the public sphere putatively monopolized by men.[56]

In a sociopolitical elite such as Venice's patriciate the private and public spheres can be only artificially separated. It is therefore no surprise that the influence on patrician society at large of propertied women of clear intention found parallel expression within the private sphere of the conjugal family as well, in ways that caution against easy assumptions about patriarchal authority in practice. An act of the Venetian senate in 1535 noted that many men were no longer engaging in productive economic activity but were instead living off their wives' dowries.[57] Such men were adapting to the fact that patrician liquid wealth was gravitating into female hands, a consequence of steadily increasing dowries, the commitment by families of large portions of

---

[55]Ruggiero, *Boundaries of Eros,* pp. 137–40. See also Patricia H. Labalme, "Sodomy and Venetian Justice in the Renaissance," *Tijdschrift voor Rechtgeschiedenis* 52 (1984): 217–54, at 232–35.

[56]Chojnacki, "Kinship Ties and Young Patricians," esp. pp. 259–60.

[57]ASV, Senato, Terra, Reg. 28, f. 151r.

their wealth to their daughters' marriage prospects, and the provision by wealthy mothers for their daughters' adulthood. Without knowing more about individual marriages dominated by wifely wealth, one cannot conclude either that such husbands exploited their wives or, alternatively, that wives called the connubial tune. In either case, however, the inescapable fact is that these husbands were apatriarchally making a vocation of marriage.

Yet the nonconformity of individual men, whether bachelors or husbands, to a generalized model of the authoritative, directive patriarch does not mitigate the wholesale formal dominion of patriarchal institutions in Venice. However dependent on or even subject to this or that woman an individual male patrician might have been in practical matters, his sex gave him a share of the formal stature and prescriptive dominance that belonged exclusively to men as men. Michelle Rosaldo noted some time ago that female *power* does not dislodge male *authority;* no matter what leverage patrician mothers might have been able to exert on their families, the institutional and discursive framework of Venetian society accorded authority only to men—authority that no amount of female influence, wealth, and power could ever dislodge.[58] This asymmetry between firmly lodged principle and fluid, contingent practice reminds us how complex gender was in Venice, and remains in historical discourse about Venice and elsewhere. Indeed, it is the conceptual plasticity of gender, its potential to provide a coherent pattern connecting deeply ingrained patriarchal conventions with the Brownian movement of quotidian social relations guided by but also deviating from these conventions, that makes gender so valuable for a nuanced historical discourse embracing public and private life.

The anecdotal evidence presented herein shows Venetian patrician society as lacking absolute patterns of either patriarchal power or female subversion of it; of either exclusively patrilineal or effectively bilateral kinship orientation; of either paternal or maternal inheritance as the critical element in a child's future. Indicating above all that both sides of each pair constitute essential elements of the picture, the lack of compelling evidence either of sweeping patriarchy or of its absence reveals that patterns of gender identity in the Venetian patriciate were flexible, offering at least a range of choice, for women and for men.

[58]Rosaldo, "Woman, Culture, and Society," p. 21.

Although the possibilities of alternative gender identities were contained within the formal boundaries of patriarchy, their expression in the practical world of patrician adulthood owed much to—and therefore reveals the cultural importance of—propertied, socially influential, self-confident patrician mothers performing their most sacred duty.

Sharon T. Strocchia

Funerals and the Politics of Gender in Early Renaissance Florence

Historians have come to recognize that ritual and gender offer valuable new ways to study power and systems of social relations. Yet the connections between gender and ritual have remained largely unexplored. This essay examines how one set of rituals—those surrounding death and mourning—helped define and represent gender roles in early Renaissance Florence. As Florence became a territorial capital and budding cultural center between 1370 and 1435, changes in funerary style and mourning practices reflected and reinforced important changes in the distribution of political power, in the portrayal of cultural ideals, and in the relations between men and women. My objective here is to examine the ways funerals both represented and modified gender roles in the late fourteenth century, and then to explore how funeral practices in the early fifteenth century framed a new, idealized set of gender relations. I argue that funerals for men of the Florentine elite after 1400 promoted sharper distinctions in gender roles stemming from the consolidation of oligarchic controls and the public ideals of civic humanism.

Since gender is socially constructed, the meaning of gender roles and representations must be situated in the larger context of social arrangements and values. What shaped the representation of gender in late-fourteenth-century funerals was an overwhelming concern with social status. Around 1370 funerals for those above the level of artisan or shopkeeper regularly became occasions for a new flamboyance aimed at asserting personal and family status. This trend toward conspicuous consumption was brought on in part by reactions to plague, the relative fluidity of wealth, political corporatism, and social mobility.[1] In the 1370s and 1380s lavish wax displays, sumptuous bier cloths of gold and silver brocade, and luxurious outfits of purple silk and scarlet velvet dressing the dead became characteristic hallmarks of Florentine funerals, especially for affluent and politically influential men such as Niccolò Alberti, Palla Strozzi, and Francesco Rinuccini.[2] Enormous quantities of wax used in the cortege and requiem masses were further evidence of this showy taste. A number of these ceremonies carried hefty price tags, such as the 1,000 florins spent on Matteo Soldi's funeral in 1379, enough to provide basic subsistence for about seventy people for an entire year, or the whopping sum of 3,000 florins expended in 1377 for Niccolò Alberti's funeral.[3]

This conspicuous consumption was also used competitively by both old patrician families and newer elites to meet political and social aims. Running throughout the late Trecento was a tremendous social friction which at times erupted in overt conflicts, such as the Ciompi revolt of 1378.[4] In the competition for power and high standing, funeral pomp protected the status of established merchant and banking families against the inroads made by the "new men." At the same time, notaries, doctors, and affluent tradesmen also buttressed their newfound opportunities for political officeholding and social mobility with greater ceremonial pomp. A showy funeral display defended elite status, marked the arrival of political parvenus, and gave visible testimony that formal political categories of officeholding were not the sole means by which power was represented, distributed, or exercised. Given

[1] Gene Brucker, *Florentine Politics and Society, 1343–1378* (Princeton: Princeton University Press, 1962); John M. Najemy, *Corporatism and Consensus in Florentine Electoral Politics, 1280–1400* (Chapel Hill: University of North Carolina Press, 1982); Aliberto Benigno Falsini, "Firenze dopo il 1348. Le conseguenze della peste nera," *Archivio storico italiano* 129 (1971): 425–503. The bibliography on the economic effects of plague can be approached through Richard A. Goldthwaite, *The Building of Renaissance Florence* (Baltimore: Johns Hopkins University Press, 1980), pp. 335–45.

[2] These and other late-Trecento burials are described by the chronicler Guido Monaldi in *Cronica*, in *Istorie Pistolese* (Milan, 1845), esp. pp. 443–45, 464. Alberti's funeral is also recorded by Marchionne di Coppo Stefani, *Cronica*, in *Rerum italicarum scriptores* (Città di Castello: S. Lapi, 1903), 30:309. A fuller discussion of late-Trecento funerals appears in my unpublished manuscript, "Death and Ritual in Renaissance Florence."

[3] Monaldi, *Cronica*, pp. 443–44, 460. I have used the figure of fourteen florins set by Catasto officials in 1427 as the minimum required for annual subsistence for a single adult; Goldthwaite, *Building*, p. 348. The equation drawn between ceremonial costs and subsistence is designed only to give a rough sense of value rather than to peg ceremonies precisely to fluctuating wages and prices.

[4] Brucker, *Florentine Politics*, esp. pp. 50–56.

these multiple uses of funeral pomp, Florentines of means exercised little budgetary restraint when honoring their dead, despite the severe financial strains of warfare in the 1370s to the 1390s.[5]

These intense status concerns modified a rigid binary division between genders in late-Trecento funerals, which in turn pointed to the social valuation of women. In jockeying for greater social position, households of both new and older elites staged elaborate displays for women as well as for men. Pomp helped forge common, rather than gender-distinct, funeral styles, which were directed toward common family purposes. The sumptuary laws of 1384, for example, anticipated that women's funeral ceremonies had a similar potential for pomp and excess, and communal officials scrutinized the burials of affluent women, such as Bartolommea Baracci, for sumptuary violations, just as they did for men.[6] That Florentine men of means saw the value in burying their kinswomen well is systematically documented by communal permits allowing Florentines to surpass sumptuary limits. Of the 233 licenses sold by the commune between 1384 and 1392, about 30 percent were bought for women's funeral ceremonies, with "new men" honoring their dead kinswomen in numbers roughly proportionate to their overall representation.[7] Ecclesiastical account books, which provide a useful balance to family and state records, register the substantial revenues generated by women's funerals in the form of wax and palls customarily donated to churches.

The emphasis on material pomp as the chief indicator of status affected representations of the body, which stood at the center of gender differences. Most of the symbolic attributes such as flags, books, and spurs used to identify the dead in late-Trecento funerals were the province of men, since these symbols derived from corporate and institutional life. While symbols were often gender specific, however, the trappings of wealth were not. The bodies of both sexes resting on their

[5]The impact of warfare and forced loans on personal finances is less well understood than the problems facing the communal fisc; for the latter, see Anthony Molho, "Politics and the Ruling Class in Early Renaissance Florence," *Nuova rivista storica* 52 (1968): 401–20; idem., "The Florentine Oligarchy and the Balìe of the Late Trecento," *Speculum* 43 (1968): 23–51.

[6]Unless otherwise stated, all manuscripts cited are housed in the Archivio di Stato, Florence (hereafter abbreviated ASF). Statuti, 34, fols. 11v–13v; Manoscritti, 8, fol. 125r. For a discussion of Florentine sumptuary laws, see Ronald E. Rainey, "Sumptuary Legislation in Renaissance Florence" (University Microfilms, 1985).

[7]Provveditori e Massai del Comune, Campioni d'entrate e uscite, nos. 1–8. The commune began selling sumptuary exemptions for a base fee of 10.5 florins in 1384. The account book for 1389 is missing, and that of 1392 is incomplete.

biers were adorned with jewels, draped with brocades, and festooned with swags, much to the dislike of lawmakers, church officials, and moralists, who advised greater humility and economy in passing to the next world.[8] For both men and women, the corpse bedecked in finery and heavily ornamented projected a larger metaphor of a corporate body empowered by material wealth. I do not wish to suggest here that women's bodies were made the equivalent of men's, or that the differences between men and women were seen as politically unimportant. Rather, my point is that the representation of women's bodies contributed in significant ways to the assessment of a household's economic and social status.

Florentine women smiled on by fortune often readily acknowledged their association with wealth and exercised the power it represented through various legal and informal mechanisms. As testators, executors, and heirs, women disposed of property, selected individual burial sites, and contributed personal resources to their own funeral rites and those of others.[9] A certain Monna Filippa so placed herself in this prestige economy, for example, that the hospital of Santa Maria Nuova, as her executor, had to pay a sumptuary gabelle for her funeral excesses in 1390. During their lifetimes women frequently exploited funeral occasions through the manipulation of mourning routines and clothing. When the merchant Barna Ciurianni died in 1380, for instance, his mother, Piera, and two sisters agreed to share expenses for their mourning clothes with Barna's son so that their reputation would not be jeopardized.[10] Conversely, women of the propertied classes sometimes opted for burial in the religious habit of a tertiary, an inversion that turned their presumed role as status bearer on its head. Although Florentine women had little input into making the formal

[8]The statutes of the Capitano del Popolo (1322–25), for example, prescribed burial in a simple linen shirt, rather than in expensive clothing, and similar redactions continued through the revised communal statutes of 1415. *Statuti della repubblica fiorentina,* ed. Romolo Caggese (Florence: Galileiana, 1910), 1:223; *Statuta populi et communis florentiae anno salutis 1415* (Fribourg: Michael Kluch, 1783), 2:375–76.

[9]For women as commemorative patrons, see my article "Remembering the Family: Women, Kin, and Commemorative Masses in Renaissance Florence," *Renaissance Quarterly* 42 (1989): 635–54. Thomas Kuehn discusses the way women managed their property within the confines of legal guardianship in "'Cum Consensu Mundualdi': Legal Guardianship of Women in Quattrocento Florence," *Viator* 13 (1982): 309–33, and "Women, Marriage, and *Patria Potestas* in Late Medieval Florence," *Revue d'histoire du droit* 49 (1981): 127–47.

[10]ASF, Provveditori e Massai, Campioni, 6, fol. 310r/v; ASF, Manoscritti, 77, fol. 20v.

gender precepts enshrined in laws, institutions, and symbols, they nevertheless enjoyed a range of choices and mechanisms that modified gender roles in practice.

What also modified gender distinctions in funerals was age and position in the life cycle. Only adults, whether male or female, enjoyed these high funerary honors. The 1376 statutes regulating the activities of gravediggers officially signaled the lesser status of Florentine youth. These rubrics advised gravediggers to use discretion in levying fees for "young boys and girls, and the poor," the limited work of whose burials contrasted sharply with the heavy burdens incurred in burying "famous men, men of high estate, knights, and doctors."[11] Since the young simply could not match the social or political contribution of their elders, they were honored in commensurately limited fashion.

Although adulthood was a crucial determinant for funeral pomp, the concept of adulthood rested on different social criteria for each gender group. For Florentine women, marriage marked a coming of age in death as well as in life. As both church and communal records attest, high homage in funerals was reserved for women who had entered the social community through marriage, a transition generally made between the ages of sixteen and eighteen; girls who died before experiencing the gender-defining ritual of marriage fared poorly in terms of pomp, compared to their married counterparts.[12] About 60 percent of the sumptuary permits bought for women between 1384 and 1392 were targeted for wives who predeceased their husbands. For both acknowledged patricians and *gente nuova,* these were highly reflexive ceremonies that brought as much honor to husbands as to their recipients. Wives who died at the crest of the uxorial cycle were particularly privileged vis-à-vis mothers who survived their husbands; only ten of sixty-nine sumptuary permits (14.4 percent) were bought by sons for their mothers in this same period.[13]

[11]*Statuti dell'arte dei Medici e Speziali,* ed. Raffaele Ciasca (Florence: Vallecchi, 1921), p. 292.

[12]On Florentine demographic patterns, see David Herlihy and Christiane Klapisch-Zuber, *Tuscans and Their Families* (New Haven: Yale University Press, 1985). Gayle Rubin, "The Traffic in Women: Notes on the 'Political Economy' of Sex," in *Toward an Anthropology of Women,* ed. Rayna Reiter (New York: Monthly Review Press, 1975), pp. 157–210, argues for the centrality of marriage to gender differentiation. For an example of diminished pomp for an unmarried adolescent girl, see Conventi Religiosi Soppressi, 89 (Santa Trinita), 10, fol. 2r, dated 1405.

[13]ASF, Provveditori e Massai, Campioni, nos. 1–8. Of the sixty-nine permits honoring women, forty-two (60.8 percent) were bought for wives, and ten permits (14.4 percent) for mothers. The brothers Lionardo and Lambertuccio Frescobaldi, who were

Similarly, the funerals of young boys who died before reaching adulthood were overshadowed by ceremonies made for their elders. Measured on the scale of an individual household, the modest funeral for fifteen-year-old Borgognione Ciurianni in 1383 paled in comparison to the ceremony made for his father, Barna, three years earlier.[14] The subordinate position of sons to fathers is documented on an aggregate level by the meager number of sumptuary permits fathers bought for their sons' funerals. Between 1384 and 1392 fathers purchased only eight of 164 pertinent sumptuary licenses (4.8 percent) for their sons.[15] Nonetheless, these modifications based on age and place in the life cycle had their roots in a different gender concept than for girls. The entry of young males into the adult community and its corollary expression in pomp was not determined solely by marriage, as it was for girls, but depended instead on assorted achievements in business and government. For Florentines and Venetians alike, it was these achievements, rather than the married state, that established men's social identity as governors and in turn prepared young men for their gender roles as husbands and fathers, which began at the considerably later age of thirty-one or thirty-two.[16] Differing definitions of adulthood meant that a married woman who died in her early twenties might be honored with greater funerary display than a young man of similar age.

These contingencies of age, adulthood, and status made the formal and ideological boundaries dividing genders much more complex in practice. The pressing status concerns of shifting elites, coupled with available mechanisms for women's empowerment and the disabilities of youth, blurred a simple binary distinction between genders in multiple directions. The political and social circumstances of the late fourteenth century never overturned the fundamental principle of patriarchy governing the formal discourse of gender and public life. Yet these circumstances nevertheless pointed to a social valuation of women that paralleled the relative corporatism of the political regime.

---

members of an old and declining magnate house, each bought a permit for his wife's funeral, just as did the brothers Francesco and Stefano di Giovanni di Ser Segna, who enjoyed far shorter bloodlines. Campioni, 6, fol. 310r; 7, fol. 2r; 4, fol. 307v; 8, fols. 1r–9v.

[14]ASF, Manoscritti, 77, fols. 20v, 26r, dated 1380 and 1383, respectively.

[15]ASF, Provveditori e Massai, Campioni, nos. 1–8.

[16]Stanley Chojnacki, "Political Adulthood in Fifteenth-Century Venice," *American Historical Review* 91 (1986): 791–810. The special legal and ritual status accorded Florentine youths is discussed by Richard C. Trexler, *Public Life in Renaissance Florence* (New York: Academic Press, 1980), pp. 368–99.

Beginning in the first decade of the fifteenth century, however, new conventions were introduced into elite funerals that projected a sharper ideological split between genders. Innovations in funerary practice, such as Latin orations, consolatory letters, and stylistic shifts, formed part of a larger political rhetoric accompanying the transformation of Florentine politics from corporate to elitist. Through various modes of communication—formal political debates, public policy, humanist treatises, deathbed narratives, and funeral rites—an emerging oligarchy proclaimed its victories over "new men" and invoked a new familial language of rulership. Underlying this rhetoric was an emerging conception of state and society in which benevolent fathers ruled the parallel orders of polity and household.[17] What increasingly replaced a corporatist political ideology in the first third of the Quattrocento was a paternalistic notion that bound issues of gender and family to the consolidation of political power.

The most obvious examples of the way gender issues were integrated with the concerns of the regime can be found in public debates and policymaking. In response to the severe demographic problems confronting the city, lawmakers developed an administrative policy designed to regulate sexuality and to strengthen the institutions of marriage and the family. Between 1403 and 1433 the commune licensed female prostitution in an attempt to turn men away from the homosexual practices for which the city was famous; established a formal sodomy commission to prosecute homosexuals in the interests of achieving higher reproductive rates and punishing offenders; and set up magistracies to police convents, fund dowries for poor girls, and control the cost of women's finery, which was perceived as imperiling dowries and undermining marriageability.[18] These new magistracies

---

[17]Major works treating this transformation are Marvin Becker, *Florence in Transition,* 2 vols. (Baltimore: Johns Hopkins University Press, 1967–68); Gene Brucker, *The Civic World of Early Renaissance Florence* (Princeton: Princeton University Press, 1977), esp. pp. 262–82; Molho, "Politics" and "Florentine Oligarchy"; Najemy, *Corporatism*; and Ronald G. Witt, "Florentine Politics and the Ruling Class, 1382–1407," *Journal of Medieval and Renaissance Studies* 6 (1976): 243–67, who identifies the period after 1401 as witnessing an especially severe decline in political mobility. Dale Kent, "The Florentine *Reggimento* in the Fifteenth Century," *Renaissance Quarterly* 28 (1975): 575–638, analyzes the social complexity of political officeholding and influence.

[18]Richard C. Trexler, "La prostitution florentine au XVe siècle: Patronages et clientèles," *Annales* 36 (1981): 983–1015; Michael J. Rocke, "Il controllo dell'omosessualità a Firenze nel XV secolo: Gli 'Ufficiali di Notte,'" *Quaderni storici* 66 (1987): 701–23; Rainey, "Sumptuary Legislation," pp. 431–33. In 1421 the commune established a commission to police female convents (Conservatori dell'Onestà de' Monasteri), whose functions were taken over by the Ufficiali di Notte in 1433; Trexler, *Public Life,* pp. 378–

extended government intervention into previously unregulated areas of daily life, much as the Venetian republic did in the same period. Similar messages delineating proper gender behaviors peppered the fiery Lenten sermons of San Bernardino in 1424–25.[19] Both Bernardino's moral zeal and the judicial practice of the commune were aimed at establishing a "right order" in gender that would ensure appropriate behavior and demographic success.

As historians have discovered, however, political ideologies are expressed and implemented not only through concrete political action but also by means of symbolic representations. Given the explicit inclusion of gender issues in public discourse, it should not be surprising to find that a consideration of gender figured into such central devices for social and political communication as funerals and mourning. The new humanist conventions of funeral oratory, consolatory letters, and mourning practices, as well as shifts in funerary style among a male elite, all broached a particular view of gender as part of a larger ideology. These innovations of early fifteenth-century cult practice promoted a new valuation of civic activities that were seen as the exclusive preserve of men, while at the same time tying women more closely to a domestic context. New funerary practices by no means declared the political fortunes of all men to be equal; but they did work to posit a sharper split between public and private arenas while reasserting a male hegemony within each realm.

One of the ways this new civic ideology was represented was through a shift in funeral style for leaders of the regime. The funerals of eminent statesmen such as Vieri Guadagni, Rinaldo Gianfigliazzi, and Lorenzo Ridolfi downplayed the conspicuous pomp that had characterized the rites of their late-Trecento predecessors. Occupying a more central role instead were the trappings of political office and the apparatus of author-

---

80. Julius Kirschner and Anthony Molho are currently preparing a study of the dowry fund established in 1425; for now, see their essay "Il monte delle doti a Firenze dalla sua fondazione nel 1425 alla metà del sedicesimo secolo: Abbozzo di una ricerca," *Ricerche storiche* 10 (1980): 21–47.

[19]Venice established a special sodomy commission in 1418; Patricia Labalme, "Sodomy and Venetian Justice in the Renaissance," *Revue d'histoire du droit* 52 (1984): 217–54; Elizabeth Pavan, "Police des moeurs, société et politique à Venise à la fin du Moyen Age," *Revue historique* 264 (1980): 241–88. For a fuller discussion of these developments, see Guido Ruggiero, *The Boundaries of Eros: Sex Crime and Sexuality in Renaissance Venice* (Oxford: Oxford University Press, 1985). For Bernardino's attacks on homosexuals and related admonishments, see Michael J. Rocke, "'Sodomites' in Fifteenth-Century Tuscany: The Views of Bernardino of Siena," in *The Pursuit of Sodomy: Male Homosexuality in Renaissance and Enlightenment Europe,* ed. Kent Gerard and Gert Hekma (New

ity.[20] It would be mistaken to view such relative understatement solely as a response to high taxation or to the weakened business climate of the 1410s and 1420s, especially in light of late-Trecento consumption practices under equally trying economic circumstances.[21] These funerals for important statesmen, especially the dense cluster between 1425 and 1429, were significant reflections of the regime's patriotic style that also served symbolically to distance "new men" from the centers of political power.

In emphasizing this public, paternalistic dimension of power, statesmen's funerals also stressed both gender differences and a gender hierarchy. The stylistic twists in these elite funerals positioned a select group of men more visibly in a context of authority, while the trappings of wealth adorning affluent women's funerals isolated them in a context of goods and property far removed from esteemed civic affairs. Yet the place of affluent women in a prestige economy defined by pomp was also changing. At the same time that signs of public life became more dominant, the pomp invested in women's funerals declined among the Florentine elite as a whole. This trend can be traced systematically through communal sumptuary permits, whose number dropped dramatically in the early Quattrocento; more impressive still is the fact that there was not a single woman among those so honored.[22] This erosion in funeral display for elite women was offset to some extent by more impressive garb worn by female mourners, perhaps by a greater clerical presence at vigils and requiem masses, and occasionally by less material tributes such as tomb inscriptions. Nevertheless, these developments collectively describe shifting sources of economic and ideological power for women and men.

More explicit delineations of gender roles and their relative values came from Latin funeral orations. The classicizing Latin funeral oration

York: Haworth Press, 1989), pp. 7–31, and Trexler, *Public Life*, pp. 379–82. My thanks to Rocke for allowing me to read this and other work in manuscript.

[20]The funerals of Guadagni and Gianfigliazzi are recounted by Pagolo Petriboni, Biblioteca Nazionale di Firenze. Conventi Soppressi, C.4.895, fols. 117r-v and 114v, respectively. Lauro Martines, *The Social World of the Florentine Humanists, 1390–1460* (Princeton: Princeton University Press, 1964), pp. 240–41, cites communal appropriations for a number of funerals in the 1410s and 1420s, ranging from fifteen to twenty florins for lesser figures to thirty to fifty florins for leading statesmen.

[21]The state of the Florentine economy in the early Quattrocento remains a matter of debate; for two differing views, see Goldthwaite, *Building*, pp. 56–59, and Brucker, *Civic World*, p. 401.

[22]ASF, Provveditori e Massai, Campioni, 15, 18, 21, 24–27, 29, 30, 32, covering the period 1400–1429.

should be distinguished here from the funeral sermon, usually a thematic exposition on a scriptural verse, and from several other literary genres associated with mourning, such as private consolatory letters exchanged between individuals, or literary or poetic expressions of grief. Funeral orations formed part of the self-conscious imitation of classical antiquity that stood at the heart of Renaissance culture.[23] The first Florentine oration, composed for Salutati's funeral in 1406, set a precedent followed at chancellors' funerals throughout the Quattrocento.[24] Salutati's successor in the chancery, Leonardo Bruni, culled the propagandistic value of oratory in his 1428 eulogy for Nanni Strozzi, a citizen-soldier who died fighting in Florentine service against the duke of Milan. Like his panegyric on Florence, Bruni's tribute to Strozzi stressed the virtues of public service which made Florence and ancient Athens preeminent in their own day and in the grand sweep of history.[25] Florentine funeral oratory added another important differential in power between eminent civic leaders and those on the margins of the political process.

These same public ideals that gave oratory its eloquence also made Florentine funeral orations a gendered genre. Florentine humanists such as Bruni defined women, regardless of their learning or status, as outside the confines of politics and history, which were the only legitimate grounds for public praise. Hence Florentine humanists, unlike

---

[23]John M. McManamon, S.J., *Funeral Oratory and the Cultural Ideals of Italian Humanism* (Chapel Hill: University of North Carolina Press, 1989); on consolatory letters, see George W. McClure, "The Art of Mourning: Autobiographical Writings on the Loss of a Son in Italian Humanist Thought (1400–1461)," *Renaissance Quarterly* 39 (1986): 440–75.

[24]Salutati's oration was delivered by the communal notary Ser Viviano Viviani; "Diario fiorentino di Bartolomeo Corazza, 1405–1438," *Archivio storico italiano*, ser. 5, 13–14 (1894): 241. Leonardo Bruni was eulogized in 1444 by Giannozzo Manetti; "Oratio funebris in solemni Leonardi Historici, Oratoris, ac Poetae," in *Leonardo Bruni Aretini Epistolarum libri VIII*, ed. Lorenzo Mehus, 2 vols. (Florence: B. Paperini, 1741), 1:lxxxix–cxiv. For Matteo Palmieri's oration on Carlo Marsuppini in 1453, see ASF, Carte Strozziane, 2, 16 bis, fol. 16v. The eulogy for Palmieri, composed by Alamanno Rinuccini in 1475, is printed in Alamanno Rinuccini, *Lettere ed orazione* (Florence: Olschki, 1953), pp. 78–85.

[25]L. Bruni, "Oratio in funere Nannis Strozae Equitis Florentini," in Étienne Baluze, *Miscellaneorum* (Paris: Muguet, 1690), 3:226–48. The first half of the oration is translated in *The Humanism of Leonardo Bruni: Selected Texts,* ed. Gordon Griffiths, James Hankins, and David Thompson (Binghamton, N.Y.: Medieval and Renaissance Texts and Studies, 1987), pp. 121–27. For the ideological content of the oration, see McManamon, *Funeral Oratory,* pp. 95–97, and Hans Baron, *The Crisis of the Early Italian Renaissance,* rev. ed. (Princeton: Princeton University Press, 1966), pp. 412–13. McManamon (p. 24) notes that the Strozzi oration enjoyed wide diffusion in its own day, with twenty-four manuscript copies currently housed in Italian libraries.

their counterparts in several neighboring Italian courts, produced no public orations for women distinguished by their wealth, family, or erudition. Anonymous orators praised Elisabetta Malatesta in Pesaro (1405), for example, and Caterina Visconti in Milan (after 1410); at Rovigo, the great humanist Guarino da Verona lauded Margherita Gonzaga (1439), who herself had been educated by Vittorino da Feltre, and Antonio Lollio wrote at an unknown date in honor of the Sienese aristocrat Laudomia Piccolomini, sister of Pius II.[26] The second half of the fifteenth century witnessed an even greater number of orations written outside Florence for exceptional women. These court orations were not without their own particular ambivalences about female gender, especially regarding the thorny problem of women's political rule. Hieronymus Cribellus carefully hedged his praise for the tangled behaviors of Bianca Maria Sforza (1468), widow of the Milanese tyrant Francesco Sforza. Bianca restrained her grief at her husband's death in uncharacteristic fashion, and ensured an orderly transfer of dynastic and ducal authority by boldly seizing the reins of power in the absence of her son Galeazzo.[27]

Although Florentine humanists did not publicly eulogize women in funeral orations, they did sing their praises in private exchanges of consolatory letters. This personalized epistolary genre circumscribed in a practical way a wider public recognition of Florentine women's activities; moreover, the rhetoric used was often ambivalent and complex. Bruni's letter of consolation to Nicola de' Medici on the death of his mother, Bicie (1433), for example, praised her accomplishments while still working within the framework of gender ascriptions presented in his formal tract on *Economics* (1420).[28] Bruni highlighted Bicie's powers of administration and qualities of mind, which she put to good use on her family's behalf for almost forty years after her husband's death. In her practical abilities Bicie showed a business acumen similar to that of the Alberti women after the exile of their kinsmen in the 1410s and 1420s.[29] Yet while Bruni clearly admired Bicie's skillful handling of her husband's economic and social net-

[26]McManamon, *Funeral Oratory,* pp. 113–14, and appendix, pp. 249–92.

[27]John M. McManamon, S.J., "'Ut Crescat Laudat Virtus': Funeral Oratory and the Culture of Italian Humanism" (University Microfilms, 1984), p. 173. On the problem of women's political rule in an English context, see Constance Jordan, "Woman's Rule in Sixteenth-Century British Political Thought," *Renaissance Quarterly* 40 (1987): 421–51.

[28]Bruni's consolatory letter and excerpts from his *Economics* presented to Cosimo de' Medici are printed in Griffiths, *Humanism of Bruni,* pp. 300–317, 337–39.

[29]Susannah K. Foster, "The Ties That Bind: Kinship Association and Marriage in the Alberti Family, 1378–1428" (University Microfilms, 1985).

works, he placed an ideological gloss over her accomplishments. Bruni praised these meaningful forays into public affairs less for their own merits than to demonstrate how well Bicie had protected her son's patrimony and upheld the family's moral integrity.

In addition to the new rhetorical conventions of orations and consolatory letters, the culture of humanism also formulated a new model of grief and mourning that distinguished between gender roles in important ways. Humanists such as Salutati, Bruni, Manetti, and Marsuppini maintained that the moral authority and dignity of public officers required them to put away outward displays of emotion, including the visible expressions of grief that characterized Mediterranean mourning customs. They stressed instead an outward self-control accompanied by the inner consolations of philosophy and religion. Salutati gave initial instruction in this humanist "art" of mourning by leaving his wife's funeral in 1396 in order to administer the oath of office to incoming priors, as duty required. Salutati was by no means untouched by this death, or by that of his son four years later. Yet he proudly separated his inner feelings from the requirements of public office in an impressive show of control.[30] These acts of moral stamina were partly institutionalized in Bruni's chancery reforms of 1436, which denied signs of public mourning to members of the Signoria, principal communal officials, and their notaries. When Bruni died in 1444, his eulogist Manetti offered such decorum as a more generalized model for citizenship and manhood as well.[31]

This humanist formulation of public, masculine behavior contrasted sharply with women's customary role in mourning. Mediterranean cultures insisted that the dead be honored by visible expressions of grief such as ritual laments, tears, and gestures of despair, for which women were primarily responsible.[32] These deeply entrenched

---

[30]*Epistolario di Coluccio Salutati,* ed. Francesco Novato, 4 vols. (Rome, 1891–1911), 3:126–28, 133–42; 4:347–49; Ronald G. Witt, *Hercules at the Crossroads: The Life, Works, and Thought of Coluccio Salutati* (Durham: Duke University Press, 1983), p. 313; McClure, "Art of Mourning," pp. 444–51.

[31]Demetrio Marzi, *La cancelleria della repubblica fiorentina* (Rocca San Casciano: L. Cappelli, 1910), pp. 195–96; Manetti, "Oratio funebris." Manetti's praise for Salutati's admirable control, which was the model for Bruni's dignified demeanor, is printed in *Epistolario,* 4:513.

[32]For women's complex role in Mediterranean mourning rites, see Tommaso Porcacchi, *Funerali antichi di diversi populi et nationi* (Venice: Simon Galignani, 1574), pp. 5–8; Ernesto de Martino, *Morte e pianto rituale* (rpt. ed., Turin: Einaudi, 1975); Moshe Barasch, *Gestures of Despair in Medieval and Renaissance Art* (New York: New York University Press, 1976); and Sharon T. Strocchia, "Death Rites and the Ritual Family in

mourning practices gave women a ritual license that stood in direct opposition to the controlled public demeanor advocated by humanists. Petrarch was the first to decry the ritual license of grieving women and to emphasize their need for greater public decorum. "Order that wailing women should not be permitted to step outside their homes," he wrote to Francesco da Carrara in 1373; "if some lamentation is necessary to the grieved, let them do it at home and do not let them disturb the public thoroughfares."[33] Petrarch thus advocated stripping women of their customary prerogatives, or at least privatizing these expressions, in the interests of creating a more disciplined social body. The practical effects of these cultural conflicts became more apparent in the second half of the fifteenth century, when sumptuary laws in Florence (1473) and other Italian cities attempted to control women's unruly mourning behavior, probably with little success.[34]

In this brief sketch I have tried to show how the rituals of death and mourning formed part of an attempt to redefine the civic community and its ideals in the early fifteenth century. In focusing on a formative political ideology rather than on actual politics, however, I do not wish to imply that women as a gender group were categorically acted upon rather than being historical actors in their own right. Nor do I wish to suggest that the normative or idealized framework proposed by moralists, lawmakers, and humanists was ever entirely successful in erecting a clear binary division in practice. Even this scanty preliminary knowledge shows that Florentine women renegotiated gender precepts throughout the fifteenth century by skillfully exploiting their material circumstances, by allying themselves with extrafamilial institutions of church and state, and by using the power of patronage to insert themselves into larger social, spiritual, and perhaps even political arenas.[35] Moreover, it is clear that the interactive process of construct-

Renaissance Florence," in *Life and Death in Fifteenth-Century Florence,* ed. Marcel Tetel, Ronald G. Witt, and Rona Goffen (Durham: Duke University Press, 1989), pp. 120–45.

[33]Francesco Petrarch, "How a Ruler Ought to Govern His State," in *The Earthly Republic: Italian Humanists on Government and Society,* ed. Benjamin G. Kohl and Ronald G. Witt (Philadelphia: University of Pennsylvania Press, 1978), p. 78.

[34]ASF, Deliberazioni dei Signori e Collegi, Speciale Autorità, 34, fols. 126v–129r. Rome passed a new set of sumptuary statutes in 1471 that ordered women not to appear at the burial church in wild, disheveled, or disorderly fashion; Marc Antonio Altieri, *Li nuptiali,* ed. Enrico Narducci (Rome: C. Bartoli, 1873), appendix, p. xlviii.

[35]Gene Brucker, *Giovanni and Lusanna* (Berkeley: University of California Press, 1986); F. W. Kent, with Patricia Simons, "Renaissance Patronage: An Introductory

ing and modifying gender roles hinged on the behaviors of "private" man as well as on those of "public" woman.[36] The agenda for future research is a large and complex one. In order to develop a better understanding of the encounter between the precept and practice of gender, it is necessary to look at changes in the overarching framework of ideology and power that redirected gender in particular ways.

Essay," in *Patronage, Art, and Society in Renaissance Italy,* ed. F. W. Kent and Patricia Simons (Oxford: Oxford University Press, 1987), pp. 7–8.

[36]Stanley Chojnacki, "The Power of Love: Wives and Husbands in Late Medieval Venice," in *Women and Power in the Middle Ages,* ed. Mary Erler and Maryanne Kowaleski (Athens: University of Georgia Press, 1988), pp. 126–48.

Elizabeth S. Cohen

No Longer Virgins: Self-Presentation by Young Women in Late Renaissance Rome

Among the records of the criminal court of the Governor of Rome, the pope's chief municipal magistrate, for the years 1602–4 are testimonies taken in a dozen cases of rape of virgins.[1] Vivid narratives by young women of their loss of virginity appear as part of extensive interrogations of many witnesses.[2] In these accounts speak the voices, seldom audible to the historian, of nonelite early modern girls as they recount an intimate and traumatic personal experience. Microhistorical study of these documents permits the detailed reconstruction of the social and economic circumstances of victims of the crime, and it

---

[1]Except where otherwise noted, all the testimonies analyzed in this paper are taken from the Archivio di Stato di Roma, Tribunale Criminale del Governatore, Processi 1600–19, Buste 18–37 (hereafter cited as Processi, with *busta* and folio). The crime of rape appears classified in the documents either as *stuprum* or *defloratio*. Rape of acknowledged nonvirgins was seldom prosecuted in the governor's court; perhaps this crime did not seem a sufficient threat to public order to merit this high tribunal's attention. Nor was fornication a crime within its purview. A refusal of such jurisdiction by the preeminent criminal court of the city would be consistent with the Venetian evolution traced by Guido Ruggiero, *Boundaries of Eros: Sex Crime and Sexuality in Renaissance Venice* (New York: Oxford University Press, 1985), pp. 25, 95–96. Rape of married women registered in the category of adultery. Not all cases involving defloration came to court on those charges; one interesting exception was a libel suit against a young man who had written an illustrated, sexually explicit love letter to a neighbor girl, whom, almost incidentally, he had been visiting at night (Processi, B. 18, ff. 715–40). As will emerge, charges of rape might be brought to deal with a variety of situations; the apparent similarity before the law masks a much more diverse social reality.

[2]The rhetoric in these first-person accounts often contrasts with the formulaic quality of the state's rhetoric regarding rape, noted for fourteenth-century Venice by Guido Ruggiero, *Violence in Early Renaissance Venice* (New Brunswick, N.J.: Rutgers University Press, 1980), p. 158.

reveals the strategies of the people who brought the cases to court.[3] Against this background it is possible to assess the measure of freedom that girls could exercise in shaping their stories for the court.

According to the classifications of the law, these women all claimed to have suffered a similar form of assault; according to their culture, they were supposed to adopt established ways to describe this offense and heal its injuries. Nevertheless, their stories do not all sound alike. Close analysis of the form and rhetoric of these testimonies, read in the context of the shared milieu of early modern Rome and the specific familial situation of the participants, yields an appreciation of the particular texture of the individual experience for women of different personalities. The distress of rape, compounded by strong pressures from families seeking to remedy the social damage of a dishonored daughter, might seem likely to have overwhelmed a young woman's capacity to respond independently. While it is true that language, like behavior, may be severely constrained by social custom, institutional rules, and personal politics, it would be a mistake to underestimate the power of words to construct a sense of self and of psychological autonomy.[4] A woman who can talk about being raped possesses herself and her experience better than one who cannot put it into words. In her court testimony a young woman who had been raped could, by constructing an image of herself and her intentions, aspire to some control over her situation. With rhetorical self-assertion, some young women described their role in a particular dramatic event in a way distinct from what culture and social convention demanded. I suggest that this mod-

---

[3]The microhistorical approach proposes the close study of one or a few richly documented, but often obscure, moments of the past. Although the subjects for such study are frequently anomalous rather than representative of a class of phenomena, they can yield an understanding of the texture of experience which enriches our knowledge of the past. A compact statement describing the microhistorical approach is not yet in print, but well-known examples include Carlo Ginzburg, *The Cheese and the Worms* (Baltimore: Johns Hopkins University Press, 1980); Natalie Zemon Davis, *The Return of Martin Guerre* (Cambridge, Mass.: Harvard University Press, 1980); and Gene Brucker, *Giovanni and Lusanna: Love and Marriage in Renaissance Florence* (Berkeley: University of California Press, 1986). Thomas Kuehn, "Reading Microhistory: The Example of *Giovanni and Lusanna*," *Journal of Modern History* 61 (1989): 512–34, offers a telling critique of this type of narrative study but acknowledges that, properly done, it can yield fruit.

[4]On the importance of words in responding to rape, see Anna Clark, *Women's Silence, Men's Violence: Sexual Assault in England, 1770–1845* (London: Pandora Press, 1987), pp. 6–9. Speaking more generally, Stephen Greenblatt, *Renaissance Self-Fashioning: From More to Shakespeare* (Chicago: University of Chicago Press, 1980), p. 1, suggests that even where institutions restrict autonomy, a self may be fashioned.

est achievement, whether or not rewarded with practical consequences, marked a step on the path toward consciousness of self.

Scholars of both the history and literature of the early modern period have shown renewed interest in the problem of the understanding and presentation of the self.[5] Much study of individualism has focused on members of the literate elite who, from the sixteenth century, came increasingly to leave behind texts exploring self-consciousness. Natalie Zemon Davis, among others, has argued that the same kind of evolution of self-awareness, even though it was visible only in fragments, was occurring also among the less-educated ranks of society. She has described the construction of premodern identity as the interaction of two dimensions: on the one hand, social identity defined by affiliations and conventions, and on the other, individual identity framed from personal experience. Of the competition between these claims in the minds of ordinary folk she has written, "in a century in which the boundary around the conceptual self and the bodily self was not always firm and closed, men and women nonetheless could work out strategies for self-expression and autonomy; . . . the greatest obstacle to self-definition was not embeddedness but powerlessness and poverty."[6]

The examples from the judicial archives of late Renaissance Rome show young women who had not achieved closed, firm boundaries either for their conceptual or for their bodily selves. Nevertheless, some of those girls confronted the challenges of powerlessness and poverty with sufficient success to seize at least a measure of self-awareness. I shall explore the relationship between identity imposed from without by family and community and identity framed from within by an at least partially conscious self. To consider first the external constraints, I shall begin by looking at early modern Italian ideology surrounding sexuality and marriage, next survey the social fabric of papal Rome, and then focus on the criminal courts, their

[5]Thomas C. Heller et al., eds., *Reconstructing Individualism* (Stanford: Stanford University Press, 1986), offers commentary from many disciplinary perspectives on the history of and current thinking about the concept in its title. In addition, the conference at which this essay was first presented, "Autobiography and Biography: Gender, Text, and Context," held at Stanford University in April 1986, highlighted interest in the idea of the individual and the literary forms of its expression; but only a handful of papers addressed the historical origins of this complex of ideas. The concept of self-presentation is central to Greenblatt, *Renaissance Self-Fashioning,* and to several of the essays in Peter Burke, *The Historical Anthropology of Early Modern Italy* (Cambridge: Cambridge University Press, 1987), esp. chaps. 1 and 11.

[6]Natalie Zemon Davis, "Boundaries and the Sense of Self in Sixteenth-Century France," in Heller, *Reconstructing Individualism,* p. 53.

practices and preoccupations. Finally, I shall turn to the testimonies themselves to show how individual girls responded to these pressures.

Sexuality, and specifically virginity, figured importantly in the social process through which identity was worked out. In the mentality of ordinary seventeenth-century Romans, sexuality was not a categorically distinct, deeply private dimension of experience, but rather an asset with which to negotiate the best possible, or least bad, course through the stresses of early modern life. Fittingly, a common colloquialism for sexual intercourse was *negotiare,* from the family of words for doing business or selling things. Although such vocabulary should not lead us to interpret all sexual activity in the period as consciously mercenary or loveless, we should realize that sexuality served as a medium of exchange. Italian families married off their daughters to promote the collective social, economic, or political interest.[7] Virginity under such a regime resembled a commodity, pricey because difficult to keep.

Rules, based in the dominant religious and patriarchal ideologies of Italian society, governed acceptable sexual expression. A woman's social identity was defined largely by her relationship to males—as daughter, as sister, as mother, and especially as wife. According to the canons of moral codes, both Christian and honor centered, virginity was the essence of a young female's virtue. A good girl relinquished her maidenhead only under the mantle of legitimate marriage, contracted and ritually publicized under the supervision of family and community. Thus, not only did a nubile girl's virginity constitute an important asset in the calculation of her marriageability, but it also figured centrally in her community's measure of her identity and, perforce, in her own perception of self. Furthermore, the status and identity of "married woman" was in little part the creation of the bride herself, but was rather the gift and imposition of those in authority over her. While canon law required that a woman must consent freely to marriage, in social and cultural practice individual autonomy claimed little place.

In this ideological context intact virginity was valuable as a metaphor for control, a mark both of the family's ability to protect and discipline

---

[7]On attitudes toward the making of marriages, see David Herlihy and Christiane Klapisch-Zuber, *Tuscans and Their Families: A Study of the Florentine Catasto of 1427* (New Haven: Yale University Press, 1985), pp. 353–57; Christiane Klapisch-Zuber, *Women, Family, and Ritual in Renaissance Italy,* trans. Lydia G. Cochrane (Chicago: University of Chicago Press, 1985), esp. chap. 10; Julius Kirshner, "Preserving Honor while Avoiding Sin: The *Monte delle Doti* of Florence," *Quaderni di studi senesi* 41 (Milan: Giuffrè, 1978); Raul Merzario, *Il paese stretto: strategie matrimoniali nella Diocesi di Como, secoli XVI–XVIII* (Turin: Einaudi, 1981).

its members and of the girl's success in restraining herself. The capacity to exercise control at both levels counted as a desirable asset in the contracting of marriage alliances. The term *honorable* designated those families and persons who could defend their interests and reputations against threats from within and from without.[8] Given that an unmarried girl's virginity marked her honor, her loss of virginity, whether voluntary or involuntary, signified both shame and a measure of escape from the control on which the family constructed its collective self-esteem.

What, then, was the position of girls deflowered prematurely, illicitly, whether by choice or by force? Such were the raped virgins who came before the governor's court.[9] If virginity was a negotiable commodity, deals could also be made to compensate for its lack. A hymen lost could not be physiologically restored, but its social counterpart, honor, could be reclaimed.[10] To get bodily condition and social identity properly lined up again, a nonvirgin had to marry (preferably the

[8]Sandra Cavallo and Simona Cerutti, "Onore femminile e controllo sociale della riproduzione in Piemonte tra Sei e Settecento," *Quaderni storici* 44 (1980): 346–83, esp. 349–53; Guido Ruggiero, "'Più che la vita caro': Onore, matrimonio e reputazione femminile nel tardo Rinascimento," *Quaderni storici* 66 (1987): 753–75.

[9]For Italy, the principal discussions of rape are Ruggiero, *Violence*, pp. 156–70, and *Boundaries*, pp. 89–108. There are a few studies of rape elsewhere in the premodern West, but none match the Rome material closely in date. While there are common threads in premodern Western culture's understanding of rape, it is important to attend to differences in particular times and places. John Marshall Carter, *Rape in Medieval England: An Historical and Sociological Study* (Lanham, Md.: University Press of America, 1985), treats rape as a crime rather than an experience. Jacques Rossiaud, "Prostitution, Youth, and Society in the Towns of Southeastern France in the Fifteenth Century," in *Deviants and the Abandoned in French Society: Selections from the Annales,* ed. Robert Forster and Orest Ranum (Baltimore: Johns Hopkins University Press, 1978), esp. pp. 6–17, describes customs of collective rape and assesses pessimistically the social consequences for the victim. Cissie Fairchilds, "Female Sexual Attitudes and the Rise of Illegitimacy: A Case Study," *Journal of Interdisciplinary History* 8 (1978): 627–67, uses a large sample of *déclarations de grossesse* to analyze quantitatively and structurally sexual relationships that resulted in illicit pregnancies; the nature of the source privileges semipermanent liaisons, and only a few pregnancies resulted from rape. Nevertheless, her illustrative examples include situations that resemble a number of those in the Roman trials. The fine structure of rape as a transaction in a social context is discussed by Barbara S. Lindemann, "'To Ravish and Carnally Know': Rape in Eighteenth-Century Massachusetts," *Signs* 10 (1984): 63–82. Clark, in *Women's Silence*, goes farthest in exploring the interaction between society's and the victim's perceptions of rape.

[10]For example, a charitable institution in Bologna devoted itself not merely to the repentance of prostitutes but to their restoration to honorable—that is, marriageable—condition; see Lucia Ferrante, "L'onore ritrovato: Donne nella Casa del Soccorso di S. Paolo a Bologna (sec. XVI–XVII)," *Quaderni storici* 53 (1983): 429–527.

man who had altered her status, but if not him, another) or become a nun. While her maidenhead was normally one of the gifts a girl bestowed on her first husband, nonvirgins who had other valuables to offer could find spouses. For them the dowry was essential. Consequently, when families took the rape of their nubile daughters to court, they sought to repair the assault on their reputation by securing the offender as a husband or, sometimes preferably, by claiming a dowry with which to marry the girl to someone else.[11] Defloration did not, in the popular mind, definitively banish its victim to the margins of society; premarital sexuality, imposed or voluntary, did not necessarily create social pariahs. Many of the young women who told their stories to the officials were indeed marginal; but their accounts suggest that it was their circumstances of poverty and fragmented family that rendered them particularly vulnerable to sexual abuse, rather than their sexual misconduct that precipitated their social and economic deprivation.

Like the ideology of virginity and honor, the urban social milieu shaped the strategies and vested interests of the several participants in these trials and, in turn, molded their rhetoric. For the nonelite tradesmen, carters, notaries, and poor widows of Rome whose daughters were raped, their society, while not impersonal, was complex and fluid, disorderly and violent. Twentieth-century observers who seek to understand early modern people in this historical context must set aside modern presumptions about the requirements of social and psychological well-being; these Romans had routinely to cope with physical and social hardship unfamiliar to us. In the early seventeenth century the pope's city was a large, bubbling stew of Italians and foreigners, residents and pilgrims, courtiers and bureaucrats, mystics and tricksters, soldiers and artists, marketwomen and whores.[12] There, parents had far fewer resources than were available in the smaller, more cohesive setting of the village to regulate through community pressure the behavior of both daughters and their lovers; at the same time, girls were more at risk, and seducers and rapists could more successfully escape identification, or at least the obligation to restore

---

[11]Ruggiero, *Boundaries*, pp. 33, 102, 105, 107, provides examples from Venice of a similar general pattern. For a puzzling example from Rome in which the family's strategy did not cleanly fit this pattern, see Processi, B. 26, ff. 723–35.

[12]The best survey of Roman society remains Jean Delumeau, *Vie économique et sociale de Rome dans la seconde moitié du XVIe siècle* (Paris: De Boccard, 1957–59).

what they had stolen.[13] In the city a sense of collective responsibility, exercised through neighborhoods or groups of immigrants from the same village, probably did not evaporate entirely; but, especially for the fragmented families from whom the raped virgins typically came, local social discipline was difficult to enforce.[14] When lacking other social mechanisms adequate to their plight, urban parents sometimes enlisted the aid of the public courts in pursuing their family strategies; they hoped not necessarily to obtain some abstract justice or even punishment of the malefactors but rather, as I have said, to pressure the accused to marry the girl or provide a dowry.[15] When taking a sexual assault on a daughter to court, the family usually embedded its argument in the conventional ideology, which specified that a respectable girl had to be an unwilling victim who would resist offense to her honor and rely on her kin to protect her interests, which were the same as theirs.

Judicial practice also shaped the stories about rape. Legal procedures constrained all speakers to describe events in terms which were, if not always truthful, at least plausible, persuasive, and consistent with their particular interests in the conflict. Reconstruction of the circumstances of a case must take account of the divergent concerns of various witnesses. The magistrate's deputies made preliminary investigation of criminal accusations by interviewing—one by one—the principal participants and any other witnesses. Scribes took down their words verbatim. It is the records of these semiprivate interrogations, not testimonies in the public forum of open court, which the archives preserve.

---

[13]Cavallo and Cerutti, "Onore femminile," pp. 354–70; Ruggiero, *Boundaries,* pp. 28–29.

[14]In the thirteen cases examined for this essay, two victims were orphans, six had lost their fathers, three had lost their mothers; and in the remaining two cases, at the time of the crucial event one parent had been out of town. Such absences were common and further reduced families' ability to maintain control.

[15]Often we do not know how a case started; I presume, from internal evidence, that parents frequently entered the initial complaint, but only sometimes is there explicit indication. Also, the outcome of the trial is usually unobtainable. Nevertheless, odd incompletenesses in the testimonies—for example, the absence of any interrogation of the accused—prompts one to wonder if some cases never went very far because even the initiation of criminal action was sufficient to move the man to settle. See, for instance, Processi, B. 28 bis, ff. 417–26. The availability of extensive testimonies but not of final dispositions of cases reinforces my interest in how early modern Romans used the courts and behaved in them, rather than how the courts expressed and imposed the ideologies of the elite; this difference of opportunity gives a different focus from that found in Ruggiero, *Boundaries.*

One cannot tell how many families hired lawyers to assist in preparing girls for interrogation, although more people of lower social and economic position than one might think did resort to legal advice.[16] Presumably the rapists' victims were often coached about what the judge would want to know: although the question asking deflowered women to recount what had happened came phrased only in general terms, their responses so often incorporate the same several elements that I must assume prior prompting. The court wanted evidence that the victim had in fact been a virgin; thus, testimonies typically report pain and bleeding.[17] The magistrates sought corroboration of these facts from witnesses who had seen bloodied clothing or who had heard, from the girl herself or from neighborhood gossip, of her virginity and its recent sacrifice. Only sometimes did the judges order a physical examination by an experienced midwife. Resistance (whether a woman had cried out or fought back against her assailant) also interested the authorities.[18] Finally, the court was concerned about extenuating circumstances, in particular promises of gifts and, especially, of regularizing the situation in marriage.

Now let us turn to the testimony of the rape victims. Probably as a result of preparation, most of the women addressed the law's stipulations about blood, resistance, and promises; nonetheless, their stories varied. The girls spoke with differing language and with differing emphases; they added material to amplify their tales. Most interestingly, some expressed not only dismay, fear, and anger but also love and ambition, that is, personal feelings and intentions which fitted only in part with what their world would have had them say. For those women who, one way or another, gave up their virginity prior to marriage, there was often more at issue than the conventional expectations of society and family. For some, particularly for poor girls with slim prospects of a dowry, active sexuality promised greater and, especially, more immediate material rewards than custodianship of virginity. For others, the flattering attentions of a young man, even when he grew importunate, compensated for the risk of parental anger and

[16]Indeed, it was a man who was supposed to be helping with a lawsuit whom a poor, crippled widow charged with deflowering her fourteen-year-old daughter. See Processi, B. 35, f. 229, 233.

[17]On judicial practice regarding *stuprum* in Rome, see Prospero Farinacci, *Operum criminalium* (Nuremberg: Endter, 1676), pt. 5, sec. 4, pp. 710–27.

[18]The issue of the legal implications of consent, linked as it was to the matter of who was responsible for the girl's actions—herself or her family—remained problematic. In nearly all cases, however, the girl at least claimed to have resisted.

community scorn. In these and other situations nubile young women who came to the court's attention for having lost their virginity portrayed themselves as acting with some sense of their own will. Even in the aftermath of experiences in which standard morality and parental expectations, on the one hand, and the persistent demands and even physical force of would-be lovers, on the other, left girls scant room for maneuver, some of them spoke to the judges not as passive victims but as participants in the making of their own fate.[19] In adopting such a stance, these young women were often, at least implicitly, at odds with their kinfolk, who, in order to secure compensation, would cast responsibility onto others. Let us now look at some individual cases in order to trace the effects of society's external constraints and the girl's personal aspirations.

By way of a yardstick against which to measure other more self-assertive personalities, the first cases to consider concern two girls who seem most clearly the passive victims of assault. Olimpia lived with her mother, Marta, a poor widow, near the Trevi Fountain; her age is not given, but presumably she was in her early teens, for she reported having her first menstrual period in prison after her arrest.[20] The police captured her at the house of an aunt, possibly a fictive one, who had put her to bed with a man attached to the Flemish embassy. The investigation focused more on the older woman's procuring than on the girl's conduct, especially as Olimpia testified that she had already lost her virginity about a month earlier.[21] While her mother was away from the house, she had gone to the cellar to fetch water, when an unknown man, armed with a sword, entered, locked the door, assaulted her, gagging her mouth and covering her face, and threw her on the ground. The violence of his approach is unmistakable in the detail with which she noted the steps by which he came at her; indeed, in language uncharacteristically vivid in young women's descriptions of their attackers, Olimpia labeled him a "devil." In interesting contrast, her words recounting his specifically sexual abuse are almost terse, compared to the rhetoric in some other cases. "Mi alzò li panni et mi

---

[19]Cavallo and Cerutti, "Onore femminile," pp. 373–76, argue that as the seventeenth century progressed into the eighteenth, there was a tendency to shift responsibility for sexual conduct from the man, whose duty was enforced by the collectivity, onto the woman. While the information presented herein relates to a much narrower span of time, their contention, with its different perspective, is not inconsistent with my hypothesis of partial female autonomy.

[20]Processi, B. 23, ff. 992–1016.

[21]Processi, B. 23, ff. 997–1000, 1008–10.

sverginò, che mi fece uscire del sangue, che me ce lo mise su, ma io volevo strillare et non potevo, perche haveva turrata la bocca, et me doleva assai" ("He lifted my skirts, he deflowered me, he made me bleed when he pushed it up into me. I wanted to shout but I couldn't because of the gag, and it hurt me a lot"). She said what the court needed to know, but without embroidery. The injury, however, must have been considerable, for she could not walk for three days. Fearing her mother's anger, the daughter tried to cover up the event, but little by little had to confess. Oddly, five days later she suffered a second similar attack, although that time it did not hurt "too much"; because again her face was covered, she did not know if it was the same man.

Lacking an identifiable culprit, her mother could make no formal complaint. Without someone to accuse, public authority offered no means to assuage Olimpia's difficulties. She concluded, "Io direi per havere la dote, et non andarei a questo modo et con questi vestimenti che porto" ("I would say if I could, in order to have a dowry and not go about in this way and in these clothes"). She clearly associated her ill fortune with her poverty. In her mind, if the rapist could be found, she might have a chance to secure herself a husband and better clothes. Yet, to the outsider it is also obvious that her very poverty, which precluded her winning a husband to replace her dead father in the role of male protector, enhanced her vulnerability to sexual exploitation. Thus, fate delivered the twice-raped girl, bereft now of virginity as well as dowry, into the hands of her "aunt," the procuress. Here, certainly, was a girl whose rhetoric proclaimed her feeling of helplessness.

The second victim, Anna, a fourteen-year-old orphan, ward of the Ospedale di Santo Spirito, had suffered much from fortune even before she was raped.[22] When she reached the age of twelve, her institutional guardians contracted her as a servant to Madonna Lelia, a laywoman living a noncommunal religious life.[23] Madonna Lelia promised to provide dowry and see Anna married when she reached the age of twenty. Lacking the money to support her servant, Madonna Lelia arranged after six months for a Spanish woman to take over the contract. Two years later the Spaniard, seeking to unload her obligations, sent the girl to the Pazzarelli, the hospital for the insane, on the grounds that she was mad. Finding the accusation unwarranted and needing a temporary shelter for the girl nobody wanted, the authorities

[22]Processi, B. 28 bis. ff. 529–33.
[23]In Italian such an independent religious lay woman was called *pinzocca,* or sometimes *bizocca.*

at the Pazzarelli set Anna to serve the prioress of the hospital. While alone in the prioress's rooms, where no one else was allowed to come during the day, Anna was accosted by Sebastiano, the woman's son, a shoemaker by trade. As she told the story, he asked directly for "che fare" (sexual intercourse). She refused; laying on threat and blandishment, he grabbed her arm and began to sweet-talk her with promises of clothing. In that isolated part of the building her shouts went unheeded. She continued her account with a frank, step-by-step narrative of the rape, presumably coached by the wardens of Santo Spirito, who brought the lawsuit in an effort to make both the man and her delinquent Spanish mistress contribute toward a dowry. As Sebastiano forced himself into her, Anna reported, she cried and complained of pain, to which he answered that "non importava" ("it did not matter"). Afterwards, she cleaned herself up with a rag that became soaked with blood and informed him that he had taken her virginity. By this somewhat obvious assertion she declared that in her understanding he now bore special responsibility for her. Cad that he was, his only response was to warn her to tell no one.

The girl's subsequent conduct, however, suggests that for her the rape, even without prior contact, established a relationship in which the shoemaker was beholden to compensate her for her maidenhead, with gifts at least, and she was to allow him further sexual favors. The behavior of other women who suffered rape indicates that they shared this interpretation of the mutual obligations generated by the sexual encounter.[24] Possibly Anna and Sebastiano had flirted on earlier occasions and the rape was not so unprovoked as it was portrayed. Surely the plaintiffs would wish to present the girl in the role of victim. Nevertheless, she described the man's conduct as unsympathetic, and she indicated no interest in him apart from the things he promised to give her. And even in that she was disappointed, for, despite her reminders and his reiterated promises, the shoemaker abandoned her empty-handed and left town with his mother. Thus, Anna's tale demonstrates neglect and victimization; caught up in circumstances she could not control, she failed even to collect the little compensation that she was able to feel was her due.

The experiences of another fourteen-year-old servant girl, Menica, share some circumstances with Anna's, but Menica managed to take more control over her own life.[25] Her story emerges from a compli-

[24]See note 38.
[25]Processi, B. 36, ff. 1258–87.

cated case which began with charges of deflowering the girl made against her new employer, Bartolomeo Zaccardino, a physician in the small town of Morlupo. The accuser was Flaminia de Varii, a prostitute and Menica's former employer, who resented her departure. The servant testified that, as she had worked four years for Flaminia but was not content there, her contract allowed her to leave; she had sought a new position and, after a couple of days of negotiation, agreed to go with Bartolomeo to serve his wife. When the disgruntled Flaminia went to court, the doctor's wife arranged with Menica, who was apparently much happier in her new setting, to countercharge the courtesan with herself procuring the girl's loss of virginity.

In Menica's first appearance before the court, she recounted how Flaminia had left her alone in the house with a friend of hers, a priest. As he began to touch her cheeks and kiss and embrace her, she screamed, told him to stop, "che non me toccasse che sarebbe stato causa de farme gittare da quelle finestre" ("that if he touched me, I would throw myself out of that window"). He offered a ring from his finger, but she would have none of it. Nevertheless, "essendo huomo et gagliardo" ("being a man and vigorous"), he ultimately had his way. As he threw the fourteen-year-old onto a bed, raised her skirts, climbed on top of her, covered her mouth, unfastened his clothing, and forced apart her thighs, she yelled the whole time. While he caused her pain, at least he was gentleman enough, unlike Anna's assailant, to lend her his handkerchief to wipe up the blood. All the elements the court wanted to hear were included—resistance, pain, and blood. Whether Menica was reporting accurately or embroidering in order to reinforce her patron's defense is difficult to judge. As the case unfolded, it turned out that Menica had in fact been deflowered in circumstances very like those she described, but that the procuress had been not Flaminia but the girl's own mother, evidently a ne'er-do-well servant in another household. Like Anna, Menica never got the ring she had been promised and had even tried on; also like Anna, she was maneuvered into sacrificing her maidenhead on terms she could not control. But unlike Anna, whose destiny was shaped by the directors of the foundling hospital, Menica took her experience and put it to use in making her way in the world. Thus, she cooperated actively with her sympathetic new employers in response to a judicial challenge of which she had been the cause. A victim of her social vulnerability, but not a passive one, Menica manifested her inclination and ability to create for herself a place in the world.

At the other end of the spectrum from the "victims" of rape were the "opportunists." These were women who, though their families wished to present them in court as unfortunate objects of criminal assault, had quite deliberately negotiated their virginity for their own perceived advantage. In another case of misdirected accusations of virgin rape, Julia Ligie, originally from Udine, a crippled widow, charged Martio Fantuccio with sexual abuse of her daughter Cecilia, yet another fourteen-year-old.[26] Martio had been helping Julia with a lawsuit, and Cecilia had apparently acted as a messenger between them. Furthermore, Martio said, out of pity for the girl, whom he alleged to be somewhat dim-witted, he had given her work as a servant in his house. In Cecilia's account, in contrast, she had the first time resisted his invitation to enter his house, but at his second request she had gone with him, had sex with him, and received money and candy. Her report of these events was very direct and matter-of-fact. On discovering that her daughter has been staying at Martio's, Julia went to the authorities. Presumably she hoped thereby to get some compensation from him, although the tone of her complaint betrayed more outrage—especially as she felt she had been tricked—than scheming for gain.

For whatever reason, be it irritation with her mother's meddling or perhaps failure to understand the consequences, Cecilia subverted Julia's intentions when she testified. Not only had she not been forced to have sex with Martio, but she acknowledged that she had not even been a virgin, contrary to her mother's protestations. Her first lover had been a "Signore" Francesco Cecchi. Cecilia explained that during Carnevale (when much sexual misconduct seems to have occurred), two women approached her with a proposal. A man they knew was seeking the services of a virgin in return for the "most beautiful dresses" and dowry. Because she was a poor girl ("poverella"), said Cecilia, she agreed. Even under such a businesslike arrangement there was a bit of courtship which, as was so often the case in late Renaissance Rome, encompassed both the threat of violence and the conviviality of a shared meal. According to the girl's account, when Francesco first approached her, she declined. (This initial rejection she was to repeat later with Martio.) Thus, she asserted a measure of autonomy—first in making her own deal for her limited assets and then in not relinquishing them too easily. Her would-be lover then threatened to throw her on his horse and carry her off, but, content to play out the drama at some leisure, did not match actions to words. A week later Francesco

26Processi, B. 35, ff. 228–40.

reappeared and invited the two procuresses and the girl to dinner. After a pleasant evening the virgin Cecilia remained behind. While she described his lovemaking with much the same simplicity as she did Martio's, the aftermath merited a more florid rendering. "Io saltai fuori del letto per il male che me faceva" ("I jumped out of the bed for the pain it caused me"), she reported. Then she cried out so loudly that the servants came running. Francesco shouted at them to go back to bed and then had her another five times. There was so much blood that in the morning the servants said it looked like a "macello" ("butchery").

Thus, Cecilia kept her part of the bargain. The promises of a dowry, however, though reiterated by Signore Francesco after the evening of the bloody defloration, were typically hard to make concrete. Cecilia claimed that a "dottore," her "godfather," had looked into the matter and reported that some document had been written. When the girl herself later went to Francesco, however, he denied all obligation and threatened her with public whipping. With such an experience behind her, it is perhaps not surprising that Cecilia was content with a few scudi and some candies on the spot from Martio. While her gamble to ease her poverty by improving her chances of marriage had failed, perhaps inevitably, she had nevertheless tried, unbeknownst to her mother, to organize her own future. And even if she was not very clever, she presented herself before the judges as her own woman, not as her mother's pawn.

Two other young women who bartered their virginity for immediate material gain were Caterina, age twenty-three, and Domenica, age eighteen, daughters of Melchiore Piemontese, a carter.[27] The particular events that delivered these two into the hands of the court are unclear. It appears that Melchiore, suspecting his offspring of bad conduct, had resorted to the action of many early modern fathers of disobedient girls: for three months he had kept his daughters locked up. Prior to their arrest the two had escaped their imprisonment and had gone out in search of fresh air and recreation; their father had come after them with a knife and found them at a neighbor's house. Caterina's clothing was slashed, and a "Capitano Moretto" in the service of the governor had to intervene to quell the disturbance. Probably the public disorder was the source of the authorities' involvement. Nevertheless, when the affair came under formal investigation, the accused was no one involved in that fracas but rather "unknown carters," who supposedly

[27]Processi, B. 37, ff. 1389–95.

had raped the girls months before.[28] Melchiore was perhaps attempting to turn the consequences of his own violence to his advantage by directing the judges' attention to the alleged abuse of his daughters, which had provoked, even justified, his intemperate response. But his rather disgruntled children would be no party to such a scheme for his exoneration. As Caterina recounted;

> La verita e che io non sono vergine, perche mentre stavamo nell'altra casa dove sta lui [Lutio] vetturino questo mese di maggio prossimo passato mentre mio padre se ne stava in Trastevere a far mietere il fieno, un giorno stando un vetturino, che in casa ce ne veneva quando quattro quando otto et quando dieci vetturini, stando un giorno nella stalla, io mi affacciai da un busio che entra nella stalla dalla stantia di sopra et dissi "oh quanti dinari" et lui rispose "voletene che ve ne daro," all hora io dissi "di gratia," et esso disse "volete che venga su," et io gli risposi "venite su," et cosi sali su la mangatoia et entrò in un busio, et io laiutai a salire, et salito mi ricercò che io volessi fargli servitio di lasciarmi cognoscere che me lhaveria dato tre scudi . . . et poi comincio a basciarmi ad alzarmi le veste et alla sponda del letto cominciò a negotiare mi, che mi conobbe due volte, una dopo laltra, che la prima volta fece sangue et me fece male, che me fece gridare un poco ma non troppo, et la seconda volta mi dette manco fastidio.

> [The truth is that I am not virgin, because . . . last May while staying in the house of Lutio the carter, my father being in Trastevere to bring in the hay, . . . there coming to the house sometimes four or eight or ten carters, while I was one day in the stable I turned to a hole which opened from the upper room and said [to a carter standing below], "Oh, so much money," and he answered, "Do you want me to give you some?" I said, "Yes, please," and he said, "Do you want me to come up?" I answered, "Come on up," and so he climbed on the manger and through the hole, and I helped him. . . . He asked me if I wished to do him the service of letting him know me and that he would give me three scudi . . . then he began to kiss me, to lift my clothing, and on the edge of the bed he began to make love to me. He knew me twice, one time after the other; the first time it bled and it hurt me, so that I cried out a little but not too much, and the second time, it was less uncomfortable.]

Caterina thus made it very clear that the initiative was hers and that, while he did take her virginity, she had fully consented. On succeeding

[28]Interestingly, while Olimpia's mother, in the first case examined, thought it a vain effort to go to the authorities when there was no identifiable culprit, in this case the investigation went forward against "unknowns."

days she had similar dealings with several other carters and earned thirteen scudi, which she spent on a black shawl which, brazenly, she wore to testify. She offered no names to identify her lovers and (perhaps to spite her father) showed no interest in finding out who they were. Though less vivid, her sister Domenica's tale was similar. With markedly frank rhetoric both flaunted the convention that demanded that they adopt the pose of victims.

The testimonies of both Caterina and Domenica revealed much anger at their father, certainly for locking them up and for threatening them with a knife on more than one occasion; more strongly still, they expressed contempt for his failure to marry them off and for his hypocrisy in pretending not to know what was going on. To them Melchiore had obvious reason to be suspicious—where did the money for new clothes come from? And, if he were not suspicious, why imprison them? So, concluded Domenica, "Se nha havuto suspetto perche non ci maritava, tanto piu che io et Caterina gli dicevamo che ci levassero perche questi vetturini non ci lasciavono vivere" ("If he had suspicion, why did he not get us married, all the more because Caterina had told him to get us out of there since the carters would not leave us in peace").[29] Since their father had failed in his parental duty, the girls' testimony clearly implied, they had undertaken to make their own way and to construct a social identity on their own.[30]

In the courts of seventeenth-century Rome, conventional language to describe illicit sexual encounters included the phrase "per forza o per amore" ("by force or by love"); thus, the accused might deny obtaining sexual favors by either force or love.[31] The formula indicates some sense of alternative motivations. Perhaps most characteristic were situations in which multiple emotions entwined to shape behavior. For reasons of cultural ideology as well as of the demands of legal proceeding, as we have just seen, some measure of violence seems typically to have touched the loss of virginity. The court records provide few

[29]Processi, B. 37, f. 1395.

[30]A situation similar in a number of ways developed in Bologna and, because of the serious charge of sodomy involved, came on appeal to Rome. In that instance the artisan father of two motherless daughters of twenty-four and seventeen, upon discovering that they were carrying on with various gentlemen, demanded that the seducers "endower them, take them to wife, or put them in the Convertite [an institution to reform wayward women], so that my [sic] honor be restored." Processi, B. 28 bis, ff. 269–353.

[31]Processi, B. 23, f. 986v. Another suitor promised his chosen woman to have his way with her "per forza o per amore"; if she made herself available "per amore," she would be rewarded, but if it had to be "per forza," she would get nothing. Processi, B. 28 bis, f. 274v.

examples of defloration in which force was altogether absent (opportunists like Caterina and Domenica were exceptional). But the interplay of force and resistance did not preclude the influence of other and more positive feelings as well. In some girls' tales there is evidence that attraction and love, too, had their role.

The romantic Ludovica was, like Menica, another poor servant whose mother, Martha, lived elsewhere in the city and rarely showed interest in the girl.[32] Nevertheless, when Martha heard of the love affair between her fifteen-year-old daughter and her social superior Fabrizio Piccolomini, she probably entered the complaint that led to the trial. Fabrizio was a student of civil law with a benefice as canon in the Church of the Rotonda, as the Pantheon was then known. Yet the mother's intentions or strategy remain obscure. It was clearly not Martha but rather Olimpia, a matron of modest station who had charitably taken the girl in, who was the one actively working, outside the courts, to get from Fabrizio a hundred scudi for a dowry. Fabrizio, probably a well-meaning young man, initially seems to have been willing to promise the money, although only as an act of pure charity ("per l'amor di Dio"); although he acknowledged having made love with Ludovica, he denied the responsibility inherent in taking her maidenhead. Later, noting his limited finances, and presumably pressured by his family, he backed out of any commitment. Yet even his early responsiveness to Olimpia's demand suggested the unusually caring tone of the relationship, which emerged very explicitly from Ludovica's testimony. Her rhetoric was full of romantic love. She stated most clearly that when he deflowered her, he neither gave nor promised her anything, except, she added, the modest token of a pair of multicolored slippers. All discussion of compensation came later, and her phrasing dissociated her from those negotiations. Instead of material recompense, what Ludovica was eager to claim from her relationship with Fabrizio was the affection she felt for him and believed he reciprocated. Indeed, her testimony concluded with this touching peroration: "Io non ho conosciuto altro homo che lui, et ci semo voluti bene insieme, che come io lhavevo in braccio piangevo per tenerezza et lui ancora, insomma li volevo tutto il mio bene" ("I have known no man but him, and we loved each other, so that when I had him in my arms, I cried out of tenderness, and he also; all in all, I loved him with all that I had").[33]

Even though her account of the actual defloration contained the

[32]Processi B. 28 bis, ff. 539–59.
[33]Processi B. 28 bis, f. 543r-v.

typical elements of resistance, blood, and pain, the same theme of affection also illumined it. Ludovica had gone to serve in Fabrizio's parents' house, where she shared a bedroom with him and a bed with his two younger brothers.[34] As she reported, first he gave her caresses occasionally, and then,

> un giorno sonando lui il gravicembalo che non ci era altri in casa, gli dissi se mi voleva imparare di sonare, et lui rispose "volontiere," et cosi me avoltai li et lui mi bascio et mi piglio per la mano et mi meno di sopra in un altra stantia et li mi cominciò à basciare et io rebasciavo lui, che li portavo affectione et mi voleva negotiare, et io gli dissi "avertissi che voi sarette la ruina mia, che io sono zitella," et cosi per allhora mi lascio stare.[35]

> [One day, when there was no one else in the house, he was playing the *gravicembalo,* and I asked him if he would teach me to play. He replied, "Willingly," and thus I turned, and he kissed me, and took me by the hand, and led me upstairs to another room, and began to kiss me some more. And I returned his kisses, because I felt affection for him, and he wanted to make love to me and I said, "Know that you will be my ruin, for I am a virgin," and so, for then, he let me be.]

But as they continued to exchange caresses and to love each other, and because they slept in the same room, one night he came, undressed, and climbed into her bed. She again protested about her "ruin," but did not resist physically. Apparently not an experienced lover, the young cleric took several evenings' fumbling before he succeeded in entering her. Ludovica quoted him as wishing not to hurt her, but hoping that she would not scream and wake his parents. On the third night, when he finally broke through, she did feel a sharp pain and cried out; "'Ohime Fabrizio, che cosa hai fatto' et lui disse 'sta zitta, cor mio, sta zitta'" ("Alas, Fabrizio, what have you done?' and he said, 'Be quiet, my heart, be quiet'"). Thus, the young woman spoke consistently of responding with love to her seducer's initiatives. She assigned no blame and sought no reward. There was never any talk of marriage, which would have been quite unthinkable between an at least titular churchman, the son of a physician, and a serving girl. And little

[34]Sharing beds was normal in this period; whether a maidservant would commonly be assigned to occupy a bed with the young sons of the house is less clear.

[35]Processi, B. 28 bis, ff. 540–41. Did she literally wish to learn the instrument, or was there deliberate sexual innuendo in her request? His response and her compliance suggest that her expectations were not merely platonic.

interested in the efforts of her benefactors to secure the bit of dowry she deserved from one who had expended her only asset, Ludovica persisted in portraying herself as a generous, if perhaps naive, woman in love.

There remains to be considered virginity sacrificed on the road to marriage. In such stories the rape—if indeed it was always rape—occurred following some kind of courtship and was understood, at least by one of the parties, as a prelude to matrimony. These situations often parallel what Guido Ruggiero describes in "Fornication and Then Marriage," a chapter of *Boundaries of Eros*.[36] Such relationships came before the judges when the young man failed to meet commitments to marriage which the girl and her parents claimed he had made. Sometimes sexual intercourse, even where described in the usual vocabulary of force and resistance, probably was a deliberate ploy in a marital strategy. Adopted by the girl herself or by the couple together, defloration was a means to pressure his or her kinfolk into allowing a marriage to go forward; it might also pin an elusive admirer into the garb of a husband.[37]

Although in some of its circumstances Camilla's defloration recalled that of the victimized Olimpia, a close analysis of the former's self-presentation leads us to suspect strongly that she was pursuing a marital strategy of her own devising.[38] Camilla lived with her mother, Antonia, near Corte Savelli, one of Rome's major prisons. Her social station is not evident, but her suitor, Pierfelice di Terni, a young man recently come to town to apprentice to a notary, perhaps appeared to her an eligible mate. On Saint Lucia's day Camilla was home alone, making beds, when Pierfelice barged into the room. According to her testimony:

Serrò la porta dalla camera dove io ero et mi corse addosso et me abbracciò et me cominciò a fare carezze dicendo che io non dubitassi che me voleva sposare et che in ogni modo me voleva pigliar per moglie, et io dicendo che me lassassi stare accio non venisse mia madre, lui allhora per forza me buttò sopra la sponda del letto et me alzò li panni per forza et io vedendo questo me levai su a sedere et di novo feci resistenza dicendo che me lassasse stare et che non volevo in modo nessuno che me toccasse il

36Ruggiero, *Boundaries*, pp. 16–44.

37Thus, in Processi, B. 28 bis, ff. 417–26, Antonio, alias Tollo, a painter, was charged with the rape of a young virgin, whom all the neighborhood knew he wanted to marry but to whom his kin objected.

38Processi, B. 23, ff. 960–87.

qual di novo mi disse "non dubitar, io ti voglio sposar et pigliar per moglie," et di novo mi buttò sopra il letto et me alzò li panni alla sponda del letto et con una mano sua me teneva tutte due le mie mano et con laltra pigliò il suo membro et me lo appoggiò alla mia natura et spense forte che nello spengere me faceva male, che io gridai, che buttai uno strillo et allhora lui seguito a spegnere inanzi che sentendome io far male io buttai un altro strillo . . . che me dava dolor grande et tanto feci cosi fin tanto che lui hebbe fatto il fatto suo, se bene nel far che lui faceva io non voleva star ferma perche mi faceva male, ma lui diceva "non dubitare che questa cosa ha da esser la ventura tua, io te voglio sposare" et dopoi io me nettai alla mia camiscia quale imbrattai di sangue di una macchia grande di poco piu di una piastra fiorentina et dopo il detto vedendo che io piangeva me diceva "non piangere, non dubitare che voglio che sia la tua ventura che io te voglio sposar et pigliar per moglie" et che voleva farlo sapere a mia madre, che li haverebbe scoperto il fatto et domandate me per moglie.[39]

[He locked the door of the room where I was, threw himself at me, embraced me, and began to caress me, saying that I should not worry, that he wanted to marry me and by any means wanted to make me his wife. And I said that he must leave me be, that my mother might come. And then by force he threw me over the edge of the bed and raised my clothes by force, and I, at that, sat up and again resisted, saying to leave me be and that I didn't want to be touched in any way. Then again he said, "Don't worry, I want to marry you and take you to wife," and threw me again on the bed and raised my clothes, and with one hand held both of mine and with the other took out his member and placed it against my vagina and pushed hard. And in pushing he hurt me, so that I cried out and let out a yell, and then he continued to push and I screamed again . . . and it gave me great pain. And so he carried on until he had finished his business, during which I didn't want to stay still because it hurt, but he said, "Don't worry because this thing will make your fortune, I want to marry you." And afterwards I cleaned myself with my shift which soaked up a spot of blood a little bigger than a *piastra fiorentina*. Then seeing that I was crying, he said, "Don't cry, don't worry, I want it to be your [good] fortune, I want to marry you and take you to wife," and he wanted to tell my mother, to reveal everything and ask for my hand.]

In this elaborate narrative Camilla wished to establish several points: Pierfelice had taken her virginity by force; she had resisted—repeatedly; and he had promised—repeatedly—to marry her and even pro-

[39]Processi, B. 23, f. 962r-v.

posed to announce his intentions to her family, that is, to make the commitment public. All this was necessary to protect her reputation and, I infer, her self-respect. Even if the circumstances in part resembled those in Olimpia's case, Camilla's situation differed significantly. Pierfelice was not an unknown "devil" of an attacker but the nephew of an upstairs neighbor, who, by the girl's own admission, had flirted with her on several earlier occasions. Then he had declared himself "inamorato," but, she assured the court early in her testimony, she had not given him an "ear." This theme resurfaced at the end of her interrogation, when she insisted defensively:

> Nissuno me ha parlato mai de questo fatto [relazioni sessuali] ne meno ci e stato mezzano nissuno perche questo Pierfelice bazzicava qui in casa con l'occasione che ho detto di sopra [per fare visita alla zia et prendere il bucato pulito], et piu volte me diceva qualche parole come "bene mio, cor mio" et simile et anco per forza me haveva basciato tre o quattro volte . . . et nissuno se ne e accorto ne meno ne e stato consapevole alcuno.[40]

> [No one proposed this business (a sexual liaison) to me, nor was there any go-between, because Pierfelice frequented the building for the reasons that I gave above (to visit his aunt and collect his washing) and several times said a few words to me like "my good," "my heart," and the like, and also by force kissed me three or four times . . . but no one knew anything of it.]

As in her account of the rape, Camilla here seemed much concerned to portray herself as a young woman virtuous in intent, if no longer intact of body. Receiving admiring attentions from a young man, even when she spurned them, was something she felt she had to explain away. And she was anxious to deny participating in any arrangement to barter her favors, such as the go-betweens had urged upon Cecilia.

The unfolding of events subsequent to the rape showed the same preoccupation with maintaining and defending a self-image of virtue. According to Camilla, some days after taking her virginity Pierfelice returned and sought to repeat their encounter. While it was apparently common for women to acquiesce in such a situation on the grounds that the promise of marriage coupled with sexual intercourse constituted a binding relationship, Camilla did not see things that way.[41]

---

[40]Processi, B. 23, f. 963.
[41]See, for example, Processi, B. 28 bis, f. 423v; this girl's tale reflected considerable

When she refused Pierfelice's new advances and insisted that he marry her first, he stormed out angrily. The next day he came back; he spoke of his anger, and she reiterated that she did not want to see him again if he would not wed her as he had promised. The return of Camilla's mother interrupted the conversation. Pierfelice fled, leaving Camilla to face the parental ire alone. After berating the girl with such telling vituperation as "o figlia traditore"—she had "betrayed" her family— Antonia shortly sent to the Ospedale di Santo Spirito for a midwife to examine her daughter. Only then did Camilla abandon her pretense and confess all. Thus, Camilla may have had two purposes in her testimony. On the one hand, she was apparently sketching a strategy to arrange a marriage for herself. On the other, because she had gotten caught before manipulating her compromising experience to her intended end, she was certainly defending her conduct, as much perhaps to her mother as to the public represented by the court. Notably, in protesting her resistance to Pierfelice's sweet talk and later physical aggression, she never portrayed herself as weak or abused. Even after their sexual encounter, to which she may have objected as much for her having been bullied as for the threat to her honor, she did not relinquish her sense of autonomy.[42] She never resorted to the rhetoric of self-pity and shame with which her mother was overheard to upbraid Pierfelice's kinfolk: "Io son rovinata, io son vituperata, et . . . si batteva il petto dicendo che Pierfelice haveva levato l'honore a Camilla sua figliola" ("'I am ruined, I am condemned,' and . . . she beat her breast saying that Pierfelice had stolen the honor of Camilla, her daughter").[43] It was perhaps an ironic tribute to Camilla's force of

---

confusion about how to present herself. She described resisting the rapist, a young friend of the family, but refraining from making noise enough to rouse the whole neighborhood only because he promised marriage. She was more afraid of her father than of the assailant. For another case where there were no explicit marital plans but the suitor protested love as well as lust, see Processi, B. 188, ff. 715–40.

[42]For another young woman who portrayed herself as assertive, see the trial, in 1612 concerning the rape of Artemisia Gentileschi; this case occurs in the same series of judicial records I have examined here, and a transcript, translated into English, has been published in Mary Garrard, *Artemisia Gentileschi: The Image of the Female in Italian Baroque Art* (Princeton: Princeton University Press, 1989), pp. 403–87. It is never clear why Pierfelice only became angry and did not attempt a second rape; there are several possibilities. Perhaps he did have some feeling for Camilla and was not interested only in sexual comfort on any terms. His anger may have reflected his assumption that a girl, once sexually known, should be available thereafter. Perhaps her own mixed feelings, her desire for an admirer, for marriage, and for respect, caused her to send him confusing signals.

[43]Processi, B. 23, f. 972v. In general, the vocabulary of honor occurs in the mouths of

character that this case went farther than many. Both the young woman and her lover underwent the judicial torture to which the magistrates resorted when other means of establishing veracity failed.[44] Yet even that means did not elicit agreement on the facts, and the final resolution of the affair remains obscure.

To conclude, once one has experienced the shock and sympathy that all these testimonies on rape first inspire, what is striking to me is their variety. The stories of Menica, Caterina, Ludovica, Camilla, and the others are full of the diverse stuff of intensely personal experience. Very powerful cultural norms and legal practices shaped the tales in ways that tended to make them sound conventional; nevertheless, in ambitions, in strategies, in emotional rhetoric, the girls succeeded in assuming their own individual postures. All of these girls were the casualties of a society that abused them and left them scant means to help themselves. At the psychological level, as noted in the quotation from Davis with which I began, "powerlessness and poverty" might be expected to have deprived early modern people of the means to transcend identities defined by relationship and status imposed from without; young women confronted with those obstacles might well have failed to construct an internally rooted view of themselves as distinct from the roles they were given to play. For these reasons, because of the very weight of external pressure against which the raped virgins labored with few resources, their rhetorical self-assertions do them credit. Through language, at least, some such women could act for themselves.

---

parents and seldom in their children's. An exception is in Processi, B. 26, f. 727v. Other witnesses sometimes attributed feelings of shame to girls; for example, Processi, B. 18, f. 730.

[44]Such torture, its administration regulated by law, was a standard and legitimate procedure under Roman rules of evidence; see Edward Peters, *Torture* (Oxford: Basil Blackwell, 1985), pp. 67–73.

Carla Freccero

Economy, Woman, and Renaissance Discourse

In a striking and well-known passage, Karl Marx anthropomorphizes commodities to describe the capitalist predicament: "Commodities cannot themselves go to market and perform exchanges in their own right. We must, therefore, have recourse to their guardians, who are the possessors of commodities. Commodities are things, and therefore lack the power to resist man. If they are unwilling, he can use force; in other words, he can take possession of them."[1] Anthropomorphization of commodities follows from commodity fetishism, whereby "a definite social relation between men" assumes "the fantastic form of a relation between things" (p. 165). Marx goes on to say that "the characters who appear on the economic stage are merely personifications of economic relations; it is as the bearers [Träger] of these economic relations that they come into contact with each other" (p. 179). The commodity is "a born leveller and cynic, . . . always ready to exchange not only soul, but body, with each and every other commodity" (p. 179).

Marx could not (or did not wish to) avoid the gendered valence of his discussion. In a footnote to the passage on commodity possessors, he remarks humorously that in a twelfth-century French text, "femmes folles de leurs corps," or "wanton women," were included in the list of commodities at the fair of Lendit. Indeed, Luce Irigaray literalizes Marx's personifications in her discussion of the exchange of women. She declares that "heterosexuality is nothing but the assign-

---

[1]Karl Marx, "The Process of Exchange," chap. 2 in vol. 1 of *Capital: A Critique of Political Economy,* ed. Ernest Mandel, trans. Ben Fowkes (New York: Vintage, 1977), p. 178. All subsequent references to *Capital* are taken from this edition and are cited in the text.

ment of economic roles: there are producer subjects and agents of exchange (male) on the one hand, productive earth and commodities (female) on the other."[2] In a footnote to her discussion of *Capital* (chapters 1 and 2) she writes: "Will it be objected that this interpretation is analogical by nature? I accept the question, on condition that it be addressed also, and in the first place, to Marx's analysis of commodities."[3] She suggests that, whereas her critics will say that she develops her analysis of the "traffic in women" by analogy with Marx's theory of commodities, in reality his theory of commodity exchange may have been developed by implicit analogy to the (socially determined) difference between the sexes.[4]

Irigaray's challenge refers to the debate concerning the philosophic, psychoanalytic, and ultimately (ideo)logical priority of the structuring systems known as patriarchy and capitalism. It is, however, impossible to determine priority, either historical or (ideo)logical, in the structures of capitalist and patriarchal thinking within any social formation where the two coexist. Such a debate will not work to undo the logic of commodity and "woman" exchange on the level of ideology (which is not where the initial changes take place anyway), nor can it be particularly fruitful in informing practice in the present. To claim either a structural resemblance between Western economic discourse and the discourse on woman or a historical causality is to maintain a division between discourses which, in their practical realizations, are interstructured.

If gender and economy (in the modern sense of the latter term) are interstructured in Western discourse, Marx's delineation of the ideo-

---

[2]Luce Irigaray, *This Sex Which Is Not One* (Ithaca: Cornell University Press, 1985), p. 192.

[3]Ibid., p. 174.

[4]This argument resembles the Anglo-American Marxist feminist debate concerning the priority of origins in the formation described as "capitalist patriarchy." While it is generally agreed that patriarchy historically preceded capitalism, much theoretical work has focused on which is more fundamental to a (modern) political economy, and how one goes about extricating patriarchal from capitalist dynamics in a given social formation. See, among other studies, the collection edited by Lydia Sargent, *Women and Revolution: A Discussion of the Unhappy Marriage of Marxism and Feminism* (Montreal: Black Rose, 1981). Gayle Rubin, in her article "The Traffic in Women: Notes on the 'Political Economy' of Sex," interrelates the theories of Marx, Engels, Freud, Lévi-Strauss, and Lacan on the question of the "traffic in women" in an attempt to reconcile Marxist, anthropological, and psychoanalytic explanations of women's oppression; see Rayna Reiter, ed., *Toward an Anthropology of Women* (New York: Monthly Review, 1975), pp. 157–210.

logical effects of capitalist modes of production on the producer-owner-exchangers can be read in relation to women as well as to commodities. To do so is also to claim historical specificity for social constructs, gender in particular. This interstructuring has implications for feminist critical theorizing, particularly when it is "new historicist." I use that expression because, for those of us who attempt feminist analyses of our European cultural inheritance, historical investigation is politically interested in an explicit way. We are not simply rewriting history, "refiguring woman" in order to render her "visible." Rather, the rewriting of history becomes an enabling fiction, like that of Marx or Freud, in the production of counterhegemonic ideologies. Liberal humanist debates about whether or not women had roles to play in the economic and political life of the Renaissance, whether or not they were empowered within bourgeois society, beg the question of systemic class oppression and struggles for change. We know that some women were producers, and that some women have been economically and politically enfranchised. The uncovering of these facts by themselves has little effect on the notion of male superiority to the female, which includes the internalization of this ideology by women; such "discoveries" (like the white liberal "appreciation" of African-American culture) often serve class interests that resist the radical restructuring implicit in the designation of "women" as a category of struggle.

It has been convincingly argued that in early modern Italy capitalism became the dominant (though by no means the only) mode of production, while the family came to resemble its modern, predominantly northwestern form, the nuclear unit.[5] Of course, no social formation

[5]There is a vast body of material on the history of the family, beginning with Philippe Ariès' groundbreaking work *Centuries of Childhood: A Social History of Family Life* (New York: Vintage, 1962). I mention only that work which has proved directly useful to this study. See Richard Goldthwaite, *Private Wealth in Renaissance Florence: A Study of Four Families* (Princeton: Princeton University Press, 1968), and "The Florentine Palace as Domestic Architecture," in *American Historical Review* 77:4 (1972): 977–1012. Subsequent work on the family has presented a less monolithic view of family structures; see Peter Laslett, *Family Life and Illicit Love in Earlier Generations* (Cambridge: Cambridge University Press, 1977); David Herlihy and Christiane Klapisch-Zuber, *Tuscans and Their Families: A Study of the Florentine Catasto of 1427* (New Haven: Yale University Press, 1985); Christiane Klapisch-Zuber, *Women, Family, and Ritual in Renaissance Italy*, trans. Lydia G. Cochrane (Chicago: University of Chicago Press, 1985); Natalie Zemon Davis, "Ghosts, Kin, and Progeny: Some Features of Family Life in Early Modern France" in *The Family*, ed. Alice Rossi, Jerome Kagan, and Tamara Hareven (New York: Norton, 1978), pp. 87–114; Stanley Chojnacki, "The Power of Love: Wives and Hus-

has, at any given point in time, only one type of family arrangement (and Christiane Klapisch-Zuber has scrupulously corrected tendencies toward a monolithic view of the early modern family based exclusively on descriptions of ruling-class practices), nor does it have only one type of economy.[6] Perhaps it would be better to say that this is the period when the nuclear family gains hegemony as the preferred social unit, when finance capital and "primitive" accumulation coexist.[7]

The proliferation of literature on the family and on "woman" in the early modern period strongly suggests that certain transitions were being negotiated. Stanley Chojnacki, David Herlihy, Lauro Martines, and others have pointed out that early modern ideologies do not always correspond to actual practices, particularly in the case of gender, and they have focused their studies on the important political and economic roles some women played in Renaissance Italian societies.[8] These roles,

bands in Late Medieval Venice," in *Women and Power in the Middle Ages,* ed. Mary Erler and Maryanne Kowaleski (Athens: University of Georgia Press, 1988), pp. 126–48; Chojnacki, "Kinship Ties and Young Patricians in Fifteenth-Century Venice," *Renaissance Quarterly* 38 (1985): 240–70; see also the "Recent Trends in Renaissance Studies: The Family, Marriage, and Sex" section of *Renaissance Quarterly* 40 (1987), ed. Stanley Chojnacki. Finally, *Connecting Spheres: Women in the Western World, 1500 to the Present,* ed. Marilyn Boxer and Jean Quataert (New York: Oxford University Press, 1987), presents a useful overview.

[6]See, for example, Christiane Klapisch-Zuber, *Women, Family, and Ritual,* p. 3. Gene Brucker also makes this point in *Renaissance Florence* (New York: John Wiley, 1969). Marx discusses at length the coexistence of several modes of production in chapter 15 of *Capital,* while Michel Foucault makes this general point with regard to historical periodization in *The History of Sexuality,* vol. 1, *An Introduction,* trans. Robert Hurley (New York: Random House, 1978).

[7]Richard Goldthwaite, in a much-disputed thesis, has argued for a trend toward private wealth in the Florentine state with a concomitant focus on the individuals who make up the domestic social unit. See *Private Wealth* and "The Florentine Palace." Klapisch-Zuber, among others, takes issue with this theory in her chapter on "State and Family in a Renaissance Society," in *Women, Family, and Ritual,* pp. 1–22. These family characteristics pertain primarily, as Gene Brucker, among others, has pointed out, to the ruling classes, and vary as well from city to city in early modern Italy; see Brucker, *Renaissance Florence;* see also Klapisch-Zuber, *Women, Family, and Ritual.* David Herlihy has also taken care to focus on class differences when analyzing early modern family structures. See Herlihy and Klapisch-Zuber, *Tuscans and Their Families.*

[8]See, in particular, Stanley Chojnacki, "Patrician Women in Early Renaissance Venice," *Studies in the Renaissance* 21 (1974): 176–203, and "The Power of Love"; see also Lauro Martines, "A Way of Looking at Women in Renaissance Florence," *Journal of Medieval and Renaissance Studies* 4 (1974): 15–28. See also the collection *Women in the Middle Ages and the Renaissance,* ed. Mary Beth Rose (Syracuse, N.Y.: Syracuse University Press, 1986). David Herlihy, in his introduction to Klapisch-Zuber, *Women, Family, and Ritual,* takes issue with her view of women's powerlessness in Renaissance society.

however, as others have noted, were played out almost entirely within the domestic sphere, within enclosures. And the constraints placed on women's exercise of power are a function of a social formation, a masculine and feminine gendering of the economic and an economic relation to gender.[9]

Leon Battista Alberti's *Della famiglia,* a text engaged in the fiction of the domestic, articulates the construction of cultural ideologies of "woman" through the category of the economic.[10] This text is useful as a starting point because it makes explicit connections between economics and "woman" or the wife. My analysis is designed neither to point an accusatory finger at Alberti in particular, nor to "do justice to" the entire corpus of his work. Rather, it constitutes one entry into the text (among many) in which ideology can be read from a feminist point of view.

Alberti titles his third book "Oeconomicus," after Xenophon's Socratic discourse on the "skilled household manager"; indeed it might be said that his text, in its anxiety to divide public and private, the household and business, contributes to the eventual splitting off of economics from its etymological origin in the household and to the present-day division between economics (proper) and that redundant term "home ec." Alberti's imitation of the Greek renders all the more readable ideologies specific to the early modern context of the work. These ideologies continue to inform the relation between political economy and "woman" in today's patriarchal capitalism.

Alberti's is a nostalgic as well as an anxious and defensive text. The political exile of the Alberti family from Florence in 1387 and the lifting of the ban around the time that Alberti was composing the first three books in Rome form the context in which *Della famiglia* unfolds.[11] In spite of the exhortative preface, where he writes, "Tiene

[9]Judith Brown, "A Woman's Place Was in the Home: Women's Work in Renaissance Tuscany," in *Rewriting the Renaissance: The Discourses of Sexual Difference in Early Modern Europe,* ed. Margaret W. Ferguson, Maureen Quilligan, and Nancy J. Vickers (Chicago: University of Chicago Press, 1986), pp. 206–24. Peter Stallybrass, in the same collection, discusses the relation between gender and enclosure in "Patriarchal Territories: The Body Enclosed," pp. 123–42.

[10]I use the expression "engaged in the fiction of the domestic" to describe Alberti's dialogic staging of the treatise form so that its "literariness" is foregrounded. Although *Della famiglia* has often been read by historians as a direct transcription of contemporary merchant capitalist ideology, the rhetorical device of the dialogue necessitates a distancing from this method of reading. Everything is in quotation marks, as it were.

[11]The Alberti family was exiled from Florence in the 1390s. Leon Battista Alberti was born in Genoa in 1404, lived in Venice, and went to school in Padua and Bologna. According to the *Vita anonyma,* Alberti was secretary in the papal curia when he began

giogo la fortuna solo a chi se gli sottomette" (p. 9) ("Fortune masters only those who submit" [p. 30]), the theme and figure of exile as the source of the family's misfortunes return constantly in the dialogue. Fortune, ambivalently powerful as an emasculating force in this text, participates in the contradictory figuration described by Hanna Pitkin in *Fortune Is a Woman*.[12] Public politics is avoided as a topic for discussion so that, whereas Xenophon's *Oeconomicus* makes explicit its choice of household management as a peaceful art and sets it apart from the "warlike arts" of military and political occupations, *Della famiglia* turns defensively toward the private as a focus of obsessively detailed attention.[13] Landed wealth is the context of Xenophon's discussion, while Alberti's text stages the debate between commerce (or finance capital) and private property (or landed capital), overdetermined as it is by ruling-class values on the one hand and the fact of exile on the other.

As Gene Brucker has pointed out in *Renaissance Florence*, the state is not yet a distinctly separate entity apart from the ruling patriciate families; the split occurs, in Alberti's text, as a result of exile. In the *proemio* he invokes aristocratic and Rome-inspired values of honor, glory, and fame through public office as possessions or property which

---

Della famiglia and wrote at least the first two books in Rome before 1434, when he went to Florence, after the lifting of the ban. Alberti himself was illegitimate, although recognized by his father, after whose death in 1421 Alberti found himself without financial support from other members of the family. In these senses he is not "ideologically representative," either as a Florentine or as a member of the family business (Alberti did not become a merchant banker, nor did he marry and have children of his own). These factors may account for the particular framing of Alberti's discussion of the family, for the tensions between humanist and merchant throughout, and for the corresponding distancing from the mercantile position. All references in Italian to *Della famiglia* are taken from *Leon Battista Alberti: I primi tre libri della famiglia*, ed. F. C. Pellegrini and R. Spongano (Florence: Sansoni, 1946). English translations are taken from *The Albertis of Florence: Leon Battista Alberti's 'Della Famiglia'*, ed. Guido Guarino (Cranbury, N.J.: Associated University Presses, 1971).

[12]Pitkin describes a similar ambivalence in Niccolò Machiavelli's *Principe* with regard to the "couple" "virtù/Fortuna," and focuses on the gendering of this relation in that text. See Hanna Pitkin, *Fortune Is a Woman: Gender and Politics in the Thought of Niccolò Machiavelli* (Berkeley: University of California Press, 1984). Machiavelli's passage on fortune in chapter 25 also allegorically inscribes a relation to "woman" in political economy. See my essay "Rape's Disfiguring Figures: Marguerite de Navarre's *Heptameron* Day 1:10," in *Rape and Representation*, ed. Lynn Higgins and Brenda Silver (New York: Columbia University Press, forthcoming); see also John Freccero, "Machiavelli and the Myth of the Body Politic," unpublished ms.

[13]Leo Strauss, *Xenophon's Socratic Discourse: An Interpretation of the "Oeconomicus"* (Ithaca: Cornell University Press, 1970). All references to the *Oeconomicus* are from the translation by Carnes Lord in this edition.

cannot be taken easily from virile men (p. 13). Yet it is precisely that political power, those possessions, that have been taken from the family through exile.[14] This unmanning of the Albertis produces a tension throughout the work, between the good citizen content with "suo otio privato" (p. 281) ("the tranquility of [his] own private life" [p. 186]) and Lionardo's declaration that "non in mezo agli otii privati, ma intra le publiche experienzie nasce la fama" (p. 281) ("Fame crowns those who attend to public affairs, not those who enjoy the leisure of private life" [p. 186]).

In Book 3 the split between "politics" and "economics," between the statesman or civic humanist Lionardo, and Giannozzo, the experienced, commonsensical merchant, occasions a dramatic diatribe against holding public office, followed by an equally dramatic discourse insisting on the glories of statesmanship, one that nevertheless concludes, "Ma, poi che questo per ancora a noi non lice, restiamo di richieder[lo] . . . non seguiamo con desiderio quello che per ancora non accade potere con opere ottenere" (p. 283) ("But since this is not yet possible for us, let us not desire it . . . because it is useless to desire what we cannot obtain with our efforts at the present time" [p. 187]). The dispossession of the Albertis is both political and economic—a dispossession of landed wealth and an exile into commerce as well as a disenfranchisement from public office and an exile into private affairs. These losses, fears, and anxieties are later played out in the figure of woman.

The dispossession through exile is experienced as a feminization in the text. Giannozzo's appearance on the scene in Book 3 is marked by a recollection of his youthful pursuit of arms, in jousting and tournaments, which he mentions in order to distance himself and to praise, instead, *masserizia:* "Sancta cosa la masserizia" (p. 246) ("Thrift is a sacred thing" [p. 168]), he insists to the skeptical Lionardo. The anxieties of fatherhood, evoked in minute and attentive detail by Adovardo in Book 2, now surface with regard to "management."[15] When Lionar-

---

[14]In the *proemio* Alberti denounces the power of fortune yet constructs fortune as a powerful force. Symptoms of the anxiety about fortune's power over men manifest themselves in the repetition of the word *virtù*, which appears five times in the course of four sentences (p. 13). With regard to lost possessions, Giannozzo says, in Book 3: "Non ci ricordiamo al presente delle magnificentie Alberte, dimentichianci quelli edificii superbi et troppo ornatissimi" (p. 301) ("Let us not think at the present moment of the magnificence of the Alberti family. Let us forget those proud and ornate structures which today are in the hands of new masters" [p. 196]).

[15]In this book noble values and mercantile preoccupations coexist in uneasy relation to each other. Note the class anxieties expressed in the apparently irrelevant listing of the genealogical tree of the Alberti knights (pp. 258–60). Lionardo picks up on the

do asks Giannozzo which of the "cose private et domestiche, . . . due di casa, la famiglia et le ricchezze; due fuori di casa, lo onore et l'amistà" (p. 285) ("these private and domestic things of which you said there are four: family and wealth within the house, and honor and friendship outside" [p. 188]) he prefers, Giannozzo responds that the family is most important to him. In the discussion of commerce and managers, Giannozzo asserts, "vorrei molto spesso conoscere et rivedere persino alle minime cose, et qualche volta, benché io sapessi ogni cosa, di nuovo ne ridomanderei per parere più sollecito" (p. 321) ("I should often want to examine and verify even the smallest matters, at times even inquiring about things already known to us, so that I should seem more diligent" [p. 205]).

Shortly before the discussion of the wife begins, Giannozzo self-consciously creates a figure for himself, the spider, as the metaphor par excellence of the industrious bourgeois merchant. He thus constructs himself as mother, originator, and producer of a connecting web. It is interesting to see the way in which Giannozzo's "arachnology" works to reappropriate the feminization of "economics" as household management for the masculine. For although the image of the spider and its web is mythologically feminine, and, even in Giannozzo's account, the spider engages in a feminine (or at least feminized) activity, Giannozzo shifts the emphasis from the action of spinning the web to that of the spider's place within it: at the center. He is assisted, of course, by the masculine gender of the noun *ragno,* but his twisting of the metaphor is marked in the text itself. He says, "Non so, Lionardo mio, quanto questa mia similitudine ti dispiaccia" (p. 340) ("I do not know whether you like this similitude of mine, my dear Lionardo" [p. 214]).[16]

At this point in the dialogue a further division is made between public and private, and the wife appears to resolve the contradiction between commerce, now defined as "faccende di fuori" (p. 340) ("outside affairs" [p. 214]), or "cose publiche" (p. 340) ("public matters" [p. 214]) and "le domestiche," or the "domestic" economy of the home. This section most closely follows Xenophon's subtext, taking, therefore, as its explicit context not the "social world of the Florentine

repetition of the title "messer," thus making explicit the class conflicts of the third book. I am primarily interested in those ideological contradictions that do not receive attention within the work itself and the "political unconscious" (to use Jameson's term) that informs them.

[16]For a discussion of arachnology in the context of women's writing, see Nancy Miller, "Arachnologies: The Woman, the Text, and the Critic," in *The Poetics of Gender,* ed. Nancy Miller (New York: Columbia University Press, 1986), pp. 270–95.

Humanists," to use Martines' phrase, but ancient Greece.[17] The ideological specificities of the text thus become all the more marked in that
they constitute digressions from the Greek subtext. Giannozzo and
Lionardo together construct a rhetoric that virilizes men and feminizes
women in the process of dividing labor by sex. Giannozzo overcomes
the feminization implied by Lionardo's comments on domestic and
commercial occupations by developing a rhetoric of public circulation, virility, "traficare tra gli uomini" ("dealing with men in public"
[p. 215]), acquisition, against enclosure in the house, "otio" (leisure),
hoarding, effemination. Whereas Isomachos' discourse in the *Oeconomicus* simply divides household labor by sex, Alberti's text ex-
haustively genders economic occupations and insists on comparative
masculine superiority while applying diminutives to household affairs.
"Masserizia" thus becomes "masserizuole" (p. 342) ("little domestic
matters").[18] An anxiety that hints of projection reveals itself in the
examples of "some men":

> E quali vanno ravistando et disgruzolando per casa ogni cantuccio . . . et
> dicono essere vergogna niuna né fare ingiuria ad alcuno se procurano e
> facti suoi o se danno sue legge et suoi costumi in casa sua, . . . ma pure io
> non posso darmi a credere che agli uomini occupati in cose non feminili
> stia bene essere o mostrarsi tanto curiosi circa a queste tali infine mas-
> serizuole domestiche. [pp. 341–42]

> [I see many men who go around looking and searching in every corner of
> the house and allow nothing to remain hidden . . . They say there is no
> shame in looking after one's own affairs and that they harm no one by
> establishing within their homes those rules of conduct which seem ap-
> propriate to them . . . But I cannot bring myself to believe it is proper for
> men busy in manly occupations to be, or show themselves to be, so
> solicitous of these unimportant domestic matters. (p. 215)]

Later he will contradict himself, returning to this feminized preoccupation and insisting that he know everything that goes on within the
house (p. 349).

Lionardo colludes, but his own rhetoric of virility continues to uphold the *magnati* values of political and military participation, thus in

---

[17]The Guarino edition carefully documents Alberti's extensive use of Xenophon's
chapters on "Gynaikologia" in the *Oeconomicus* (*The Albertis of Florence*, p. 338).

[18]Other examples of obsessive gendering and the insistence on masculine superiority
can be found in the repetition of "più" in Lionardo's speech (p. 342) and the use of
adjectives such as *virile, feminine, effeminate, manly*, and so on (pp. 342–43).

the guise of agreement continuing to feminize commercial preoccupations:

> L'uomo difenda la donna, la casa, e suoi, et la patria sua, non sedendo, ma exercitando l'animo, le mani con molta virtù per sino a spandere il sudore et il sanguc . . . questi . . . i quali si stanno il dì tutto tra le feminelle, o che si pigliano ad animo tali simili penseruzzi feminili, certo non ànno il cuore maschio né magnifico, et tanto sono da biasimare costoro quanto e' dimostrano più piacerli sé essere femina che uomo. [p. 343]

> [Let men defend their women, their homes, their families, and their country, not sitting idly, but striving with their minds and their hands with great valor, shedding sweat and blood . . . these idlers who spend the whole day among women and take to heart such trifling matters fit only for women do not have a virile, generous heart, and they are to be blamed in accordance with their preference for being women rather than men. (p. 216)]

The loss of status and political power occasioned by exile, the feminization and anxiety associated with commercial and domestic preoccupations, and a "helplessness" with regard to fortune are displaced and projected onto gender difference so that "men"—these Albertis—can construct masculinity in opposition to the feminine they create.

Giannozzo tells Lionardo how his wife came to be a household manager and a "madre di famiglia" ("mother"), not primarily, he insists, because of any quality of her own but "molto più per miei amonimenti" (p. 344) ("even more through my instruction" [p. 216]). Unlike the Greek text, however, where each gender's place is fixed and ordained by a divine order the husband dictates to his wife, this discourse laboriously constructs an object (the wife) that continues to elude the subject's complete grasp.[19]

There is always the threat of dispossession or expenditure through the woman's body and, more specifically, through one of her two mouths. This threat appears first as potential betrayal within the sanctuary of the house. The public-private division must be constructed

---

[19]The Greek subtext does not "naturalize" gender inequality; it declares the sexual division of labor to be divinely ordained; see Strauss, *Xenophon's Socratic Discourse*, pp. 32–33. This ordering of inequality is more familiar in a slave society or in a caste system than in incipient capitalism, where exploitation depends on the alienation of the labor of free people. Christianity has a role to play as well; the ethics of Christianity work to some extent against divinely ordained inequalities so that there may be a need to euphemize the control of women.

again, within the house, which has now become the space of both economics and politics: a political economy. The wife may see the manifestation of her husband's wealth, its fetishes, as it were, which are locked away in the bedroom: "tutte le mie fortune domestice gli apersi, spiegai et mostrai" (p. 346) ("I showed her all the treasures of my household" [p. 217]), but the process of acquisition, the signs of production, are concealed:

> E libri et le scritture mie et de' miei passati mi piacque et allora et poi sempre avere in modo rinchiuse, che mai la donna le potesse non tanto lègere, ma né vedere; sempre tenni le scritture non per le maniche de' vestiri, ma serrate, et con suo ordine allogate nel mio studio quasi come cosa sacrata et religiosa. [p. 346]

> [I kept only the ledgers and business papers, my ancestors' as well as mine, locked so that my wife could not read them or even see them then or at any time since. I never kept them in my pockets, but always under lock and key in their proper place in my study, almost as if they were sacred or religious objects. (p. 217)][20]

The fear that women will talk is associated with their circulation; Giannozzo immediately gives an example of a woman who goes about interrogating other men concerning the whereabouts of her husband, and concludes: "[Sono] pazzi per certo, se credono la moglie ne' facti del marito più essere che il marito stessi tenace et taciturna. O stolti mariti, quando cianciando con una femina non vi ramentate che ogni cosa possono le femine excepto che tacere" (p. 348) ("They are mad . . . if they think a wife can guard a secret with greater jealousy and silence than her husband. O foolish husbands, is there ever a time when you chat with a woman without being reminded that women can do anything but keep silent?" [p. 218]). He invokes again twice the image of the "grotesque" body of woman as lower class, gesticulating,

---

[20]This sacralization of the economic testifies to fears of women's access to power through the economic. Stanley Chojnacki has pointed out to me that there is some evidence that the Alberti women may have been running the family business during the period of exile; see the work of the historian Susannah Kerr Foster on the Alberti family, "The Ties That Bind: Kinship Association and Marriage in the Alberti Family, 1378–1428" (University Microfilms, 1985). Chojnacki's own work has focused on the complex meanings women's access to economic power had within the Venetian patriciate and the equally complex responses this access may have generated in men. See especially "Kinship Ties and Young Patricians in Fifteenth-Century Venice," and "Patrician Women in Early Renaissance Venice." For a study of woman's relation to the production of writing in fifteenth-century Italy, see the work of Stephanie Jed in this volume.

open-mouthed, circulating in the streets; the images multiply as he strives to contain the threat.[21]

Finally, Giannozzo goes so far as to attempt to structure his wife's desire: "In questo letto fa, moglie mia, mai vi desideri altro uomo che me solo, sai" (p. 351) ("You will never wish for any other man in this bed but me" [p. 219]). His remark, and Lionardo's subsequent questioning, "Come, Giannozzo, insegnastili voi queste cose?" ("And how did you teach her these things, Giannozzo?" [p. 220]), occasion a joking exchange that brings Xenophon's text into play once again, on the subject of cosmetics. Giannozzo replies: "Che? Forse adormentarsi senza uomo altri che me appresso? . . . Certo sarebbe cosa da ridere se io gli avessi voluto insegnare dormir sola. Non so io se quelli tuoi antichi il sepporo insegnare" (p. 351) ("What things? How to sleep with no one but me? . . . It would have been very droll if I had tried to teach her to sleep alone. I do not know whether those ancient authors of yours knew how to teach it" [p. 220]). Lionardo says that the ancients, by condemning the use of cosmetics, did, however, teach women not to appear more dishonest than they were. But the *Oeconomicus* precisely does not concern itself with infidelity; there is no suggestion that wives may have desires other than to obey. The passage on make-up in the *Oeconomicus* serves as an example of how Isomachos' wife obeyed him "quickly in some matter after hearing it only once" (p. 44).[22]

The opposite occurs in Giannozzo's account. In this social formation, where lineage and patrician status are constructed upon the ex-

[21]Peter Stallybrass and Allon White revise Bakhtin's notions of the grotesque and classical bodies by including gender in the application of these notions to cultural formations. See *The Politics and Poetics of Transgression* (Ithaca: Cornell University Press, 1986). Mary Russo explores the relation of "grotesque" to "woman" in "Female Grotesques: Carnival and Theory," in *Feminist Studies / Critical Studies,* ed. Teresa de Lauretis (Bloomington: Indiana University Press, 1986), pp. 213–29.

[22]The departures from Xenophon's text are particularly marked in the narrative example used to condemn the use of cosmetics. Isomachos recounts his conversation: "Would I then seem more worthy to be loved, . . . if instead I smeared myself with vermilion, applied flesh color beneath the eyes, and then displayed myself to you and embraced you, all the while deceiving you and offering you vermilion to see and touch instead of my own skin?" (p. 45). The discourse of masculine virilization in Alberti's text renders such an example taboo, not to mention the repression of sodomy and homosexuality in early modern Italy. Here, then, is another instance in which intertextual comparison may stress historically determined ideological specificities in a text. That the example should then become the adornment of a statue and involve the rhetoric of valorization indicates the extent to which the (female) body has become commodified.

change of women, "private property" is never secure. Yet, as Luce Irigaray points out: "Mothers, reproductive instruments marked with the name of the father and enclosed in his house, must be private property, excluded from exchange. . . . As both natural and use value, mothers cannot circulate in the form of commodities without threatening the very existence of the social order."[23] These contradictory conditions—contradictory for both the man and the woman—inform the "cruel mother" phenomenon that Christiane Klapisch-Zuber describes.[24] They produce contradictory and unstable symbols on the level of cultural production as well, as Catherine Clément has noted in relation to the myths of the sorceress and the hysteric.[25]

The invective against cosmetics becomes the occasion for mapping these contradictions onto the body of woman. First, Giannozzo launches into the argument that cosmetics are an unnecessary adornment for the wife, who ought to be "ornat[a] di pura simplicità et vera onestà" (p. 355) ("adorned with pure simplicity and true honesty" [p. 221]). Chastity alone in a woman pleases God, the family, her children; immodesty dishonors them and incurs God's wrath. Praise received as a result of immodest adornment is really blame, and men will pursue a woman so adorned to her ruin and eternal damnation. He tells her this; then, "per rendella bene certa" ("to make her very certain of this fact"), he illustrates with an example. There is an ornate statue of a saint "posta nel mezo del tabernaculo" (p. 356) ("[standing] in the center of the tabernacle" [p. 222]). If, he says to her, you were to smear it with ointments and then wish to sell it, how much do you think you would get for it? "Rispose ella: 'Molti pochi'" ("'Very little,' she replied"). That's right, he says, because whoever buys the statue would not buy it

[23]Irigaray, *This Sex Which Is Not One*, p. 185.

[24]Klapisch-Zuber, "The 'Cruel Mother': Maternity, Widowhood, and Dowry in Florence in the Fourteenth and Fifteenth Centuries," in *Women, Family, and Ritual*, pp. 117–31. Klapisch-Zuber describes how young widows were reclaimable by their kin for recirculation on the marriage market, whereas children belonged to the deceased husband's family. The latter would, of course, attempt to retain her, and her departure was often seen as abandonment. The contradictory conditions of woman as private property and woman as exchangeable commodity also inform the discourse on infidelity. In this case the necessity for women to circulate is disguised and displaced as women's willful desire to be unfaithful. I owe this insight to Louise Fradenburg.

[25]Hélène Cixous and Catherine Clément, *The Newly Born Woman* (Minneapolis: University of Minnesota Press, 1986), p. 7: "Societies do not succeed in offering everyone the same way of fitting into the symbolic order; those who are, if one may say so, between symbolic systems, in the interstices, offside, are the ones who are afflicted with a dangerous symbolic mobility. . . . And more than any others, women bizarrely embody this group of anomalies showing the cracks in an overall system."

for the cosmetics on it but because he "appregia la bontà della statua et la gratia del magisterio" (p. 356) ("appreciates the value of the statue and the skill of the sculptor" [p. 222]). And if you continued to so decorate it, he pursues, would you make it more beautiful? "'Non credo,' disse ella" ("'I don't think so,' she said"). "'Anzi,' dissi io" ("'On the contrary,' I said"), and he goes on to enumerate the disastrous effects such a process would have on the ivory of the statue. This laboriously extended dialogue is a dilation of the proposition that if makeup can destroy hard ivory, it surely must wreak havoc on the delicate cheeks of a woman.[26]

The construction of the ideal, saintly woman out of precious metal and ivory objectifies her in the Petrarchan manner. The objectification appears here in degraded form, not as courtly but as domestic, a saintly household ornament, only faintly reminiscent of the Penates or household gods of the ancients. The merchant has commodified women's beauty; no longer incarnated in a "real" body nor idealized in an aristocratic rhetoric, beauty is a thing of value whose worth must be assessed in market terms. This process of objectification mirrors, in reverse, Marx's commodity anthropomorphization and genders it.

Against this construction, another woman appears. Giannozzo, "ancora perché ella più mi credesse" ("to make her believe me even more"), points to a neighbor, "la quale tenea pochi denti in bocca, et quelli pareano di busso tarmato, et avea gli occhi al continuo pesti, incavernati, il resto del viso vizzo et cenericcio, per tutto la carne morticcia et in ogni parte sozza" (p. 357) ("I asked her about a neighbor of ours who had only a few teeth left in her mouth, and those seemed of rotten wood. Her eyes were sunken, always livid; the rest of her face was dry and ashen, her complexion completely lifeless and dull" [p. 223]). This "hag," so to speak, manifests the ravages of makeup. Giannozzo asks his wife if she would like to look like her. Oh, no, says she. "Why, because of her age?" he says, determining the reason for her negative response. He then asks his wife to guess the woman's age. She replies that she thinks the woman must be the same age as her mother's balía (wet nurse), whereupon Giannozzo replies that she is thirty-two, two years his junior.[27]

---

[26]I have tried to reproduce the tone of domination in my account of the conversation. Giannozzo uses a variety of discursive techniques to overwhelm, silence, and contain the woman in his reported conversation with her. These techniques foreclose the possibility of alternative interpretations of his example of the painted statue and determine what his wife's response will (have to) be.

[27]The age gap is seventeen to nineteen years; the wife is from fifteen to seventeen

The "demonized" contrary of the ivory and silver statue (although the demonization is domesticated as well) is not only gendered and "real" (that is, she is a neighbor, has an age, and so on), a woman rather than an idol, but she is also of a lower class.[28] The comparison thus constructs contraries in order to contain the threatening mobility of human "goods," whether that mobility is construed as the promiscuity of women or as the revolt of the lower classes. As such, the comparison also literalizes by breaking down into its two components the containment strategy that motivates it; on the one hand, Giannozzo displays the desired product of his strategy (the ivory statue); on the other, he describes the threat (a lower-class woman) against which his defense, the statue, is constructed.

One element of the image escapes this control and raises again the question of whether a woman's self-construction as attractive to other men (and her self-circulation) can be successfully contained. Giannozzo says of the neighbor that "solo in lei poteano alquanto e capelli argentini guardandola non dispiacere" (pp. 357–58) ("the only thing about her which could be somewhat attractive was her blond [silver] hair" [p. 223]), thus tacitly admitting the erotic effect of appearances. His final argument, that cosmetics are worn to attract strangers ("gli strani") seems more to the point. Lionardo asks him if his wife obeyed, whereupon Giannozzo recounts the tale of her infraction. Cosmetics, circulation, talkativeness, attraction all combine as he says that at a wedding celebration "troppa lieta s'afrontava a qualunque venia, et così a chi andava si porgeva, a tutti motteggiava. Io me n'avidi" (p. 359) ("my wife got all made-up and received everyone gaily, chattered with all, and paid compliments to them as they left. I noticed it" [p. 223–24]). His final strategy is sadistic humiliation, as when he asks, "Come t'imbrattasti così il viso?" (p. 360) ("How did you get your face so dirty?" [p. 224]), thus causing his wife to run out of the room crying.

The invective against cosmetics is usually based on a nature-artifice opposition. Giannozzo appeals to the example of the Alberti girls (of his own family), who wash their faces with plain water and are "frescozze et tutte vive" (p. 358) ("[of] a clear complexion and lively color"

---

years old, and Giannozzo is thirty-four. Although he reveals the hag's age as though she were surprisingly young, it does not seem out of the question that thirty-two would indeed seem old to his adolescent wife.

[28]That is, she is compared to the mother's wet nurse. See Klapisch-Zuber, "Blood Parents and Milk Parents: Wet Nursing in Florence, 1300–1500," in *Women, Family, and Ritual,* pp. 132–64, for a survey of the groups that supplied wet nurses for the Florentine ruling class.

[p. 223]). It is also an argument for plain speaking as opposed to rhetorical ornament, which is thus construed as deceitful. Yet at the heart of the natural in this invective stands a statue—an ornate one at that. Likewise, this encomium of the natural abounds in rhetorical artifice. Giannozzo's speech reveals that the natural is constructed upon the artificial and vice versa, and thus exposes the ideological bases of his argument. Indeed, it might be argued that all containment strategies, to the extent that they attempt to "resolve" a logical contradiction, are so vulnerable.

Certain oppositions, symptomatic of a transitional political economy, come to be inverted in this text, which permits their revalorization. Thus the oppositions—between public politics and private wealth, landed property and exchange, the country and the city—shift in valence; civic responsibility, as contrasted with avarice and hoarding, becomes instead the corruption of public politics as opposed to the honesty of economic pursuits. Landed property is the quintessentially secure form of wealth, yet it is vulnerable to theft, whereas exchange may produce wealth. In the case of these oppositions the dialogue aims not at containment but at renegotiation. Alberti depicts a scene of intraclass struggle between men, a subjective renegotiation of contradictions by the agents of those contradictions. The contradiction mapped onto bourgeois "woman" in this text demonstrates, however, that this particular consolidation of class identity depends on a gendering of class definitions. In order to be a commodity, that is, to accrue value, "woman" cannot be the agent of her own exchange but must be instead the product of her exchanger, while to be of use-value she must be, "naturally," a woman.

Contradictions are not necessarily less productive for being contradictions, whether on the material or cultural level. The uneasiness of the emergent capitalist, his feminization and alienation, did not bring this mode of production to an end. The dispossession of Leon Battista Alberti did not cause him to disappear from history. The contradiction between woman as an absolutely noncirculating use-value (the mother) and an exchangeable commodity (the daughter) did not extinguish the social order based on the exchange and circulation of women, while the Pygmalion myth has not entirely lost its power to contain unruly merchandise.

Patriarchy, like "power" or hegemony, is never absolute.[29] Yet the

[29]My understanding of hegemony and power derives from Gramscian and Foucauldian uses of the terms. Peter Stallybrass notes of hegemony that it is "a process in which

continued gender and class struggles of today testify to the persistence of its discourses and practices. And whatever the economic, political, and social importance of some classes of women, who negotiate within the social order that oppresses them and who, like myself, are empowered to criticize that order publicly, global female enfranchisement is far from imminent.

---

the dominant groups have to negotiate with and respond to both each other and to the subaltern classes and in which the discourses and practices through which alliances are formed are never given in advance"; "The World Turned Upside Down: Inversion, Gender, and the State," in *The Matter of Difference: Materialist Feminist Criticism of Shakespeare*, ed. Valerie Wayne (Brighton: Harvester, forthcoming). See also *Culture, Ideology, and Social Process*, ed. Tony Bennett et al. (London: Batsford, 1981), p. 192: "Gramsci rejects the cruder and more orthodox Marxist conceptions of 'class-domination' in favour of a more nuanced and sophisticated coupling of 'force and consent' (or 'coercion plus hegemony' as he puts it). He is primarily concerned with the ways in which a whole complex series of cultural, political and ideological practices work to 'cement' a society into a relative—though never complete—unity." Michel Foucault, in *The History of Sexuality*, defines power in terms of the mobilization of force relations, thus also providing a more fluid notion of the exercise of power (or domination) within a social formation.

III

WOMAN AND
THE CANON

Marilyn Migiel

The Dignity of Man:
A Feminist Perspective

For w.

The phrase "the dignity of man" will have a decidedly humanist ring
for most readers, evoking the illustrious humanist scholars Giannozzo
Manetti, Pico della Mirandola, Marsilio Ficino, and Pietro Pomponazzi, who participated in the philosophical debates about man's
nature, his place in the universe, his freedom, and the purpose and
conditions of human life.[1] My point of departure for a feminist reading
is a marginal perspective on the issues at stake in this Renaissance
philosophical debate. The work I have chosen to examine is a "litcrary"
and not a "philosophical" one; it is in Italian rather than in Latin;
strictly speaking, it is not humanist but "popularizing"; and finally, its
author is a minor figure some might call provincial: Giovan Battista
Gelli. As will become clear soon enough, this very marginality raises
questions relevant to feminist readings of Renaissance literature.

Giovan Battista Gelli can be said to have been a success story of the
Renaissance. Born in Florence in 1498, a man of humble origins who

[1]For discussions of the dignity of man, see Giovanni Gentile, "Il concetto dell'uomo
nel Rinascimento," in *Il pensiero italiano del Rinascimento,* vol. 14 of *Opere* (Florence:
Sansoni, 1968), pp. 47–113; Charles E. Trinkaus, *Adversity's Noblemen: The Italian Hu-
manists on Happiness* (New York: Columbia University Press, 1940); idem., *In Our
Image and Likeness: Humanity and Divinity in Italian Humanist Thought,* 2 vols. (Chicago:
University of Chicago Press, 1970); Ernst Cassirer, *The Individual and the Cosmos in
Renaissance Philosophy,* trans. Mario Domandi (New York: Harper & Row, 1963); Paul
Oskar Kristeller, "The Philosophy of Man in the Italian Renaissance," and "Ficino and
Pomponazzi on the Place of Man in the Universe," in *Studies in Renaissance Thought
and Letters* (Rome: Edizioni di Storia e Letteratura, 1956), pp. 261–78, 279–86, and
Kristeller, "The Dignity of Man," in *Renaissance Thought and Its Sources* (New York: Co-
lumbia University Press, 1979).

made his living as a shoemaker and hosier, he became a notable figure in Florentine intellectual life. Inspired by Dante's *Commedia,* he undertook the study of the liberal arts and of Latin at the somewhat advanced age of twenty-five. His acceptance into the intellectual circles of his time gives some evidence of his intellectual accomplishments: he participated in the meetings at the Orti Oricellari; he became a member of the Accademia degli Umidi in 1540, and when it was transformed a year later into the Accademia Fiorentina, he was one of the founding members; later he served as one of the Academy's consuls. In 1553, by special appointment of Cosimo I, he was assigned to undertake a more systematic commentary on Dante's *Commedia* than he had carried out up until that time. He had arrived at Canto 26 of the *Inferno* by the time he died in 1563.

Today, Gelli is considered a minor author of the Italian Cinquecento, and it sometimes seems that he is remembered more for the position he took in the debate on the *questione della lingua* (he was in favor of spoken Florentine) than for anything he wrote. His main literary works, *I capricci del bottaio* (*The Caprices of a Cooper* [1546]) and *La Circe* (*Circe* [1549]), won immediate popularity in his own time and have continued to be read over the centuries, but they currently remain outside the mainstream of critical interpretation of Italian Renaissance literature, and even farther outside the line of vision of non-Italianists.[2]

Scholars have frequently expressed admiration for Gelli and his intel-

---

[2] *I capricci del bottaio* was reprinted several times after it was published in 1546; it was translated almost immediately into French and Spanish. By the end of the sixteenth century, *La Circe* had appeared in several editions, some of them with more than one printing. Translations into French, Spanish, and English appeared within six years of its original publication; German and Latin translations were published during the first two decades of the seventeenth century.

The only study of Gelli in English is Armand L. De Gaetano, *Giambattista Gelli and the Florentine Academy: The Rebellion against Latin* (Florence: Olschki, 1976). Italian studies of *La Circe* are to be found in the following publications: Carlo Altucci, *"La Circe* del Gelli," *Annali dell'Istituto superiore di scienze e lettere di S. Chiara* (1951): 3–84; Carlo Bonardi, *Giovan Battista Gelli e le sue opere,* vol. 1, *Giovan Battista Gelli: "La Circe"* (Città di Castello: S. Lapi, 1899); Carlo Bonardi, "Le orazioni di Lorenzo il Magnifico e l'inno finale della *Circe* di G. B. Gelli," *Giornale storico della letteratura italiana* 33 (1899): 77–82; E. Hatzantonis, "Il potere metamorfico di Circe quale motivo satirico in Machiavelli, Gelli e Bruno," *Italica* 37 (1960): 257–67; Luigi Russo, "Novellistica e dialoghistica nella Firenze del Cinquecento," *Belfagor* 16:3 (1961): 261–83, and 16:5 (1961): 535–64; Nicola Tarantino, "La *Circe* e i *Capricci del bottaio* di G. B. Gelli," *Studi di letteratura italiana* 13 (1923): 1–56; Roberto Tissoni, "Per il testo della *Circe* di G. B. Gelli," *Studi di filologia italiana* 20 (1962): 99–136; Aurelio Ugolini, *Le opere di Giambattista Gelli: I dialoghi, le comedie, le opere minori* (Pisa: Francesco Mariotti, 1898).

lectual accomplishments. But in some cases, as in the following description of *La Circe*, written by Roberto Tissoni, one begins to wonder what value such regard has:

La *Circe* incontrò subito vivo e largo interesse. Doveva piacere: per la sua "facilità" e piacevolezza di lettura, per la stimolante cornice fantastica, per la serena semplicità con la quale si riconducevano alla loro radice umana e al giudizio, modesto ma infallibile, del buon senso le più gravi questioni di "filosofia morale." I popolani vi trovavano il loro piccolo convivio di sapienza ed erano orgogliosi del modesto calzaiolo che aveva voce in capitolo tra i dotti che facevan corona al grande Cosimo (tanto da leggere, acclamato professore, i grandi poeti all'Accademia fiorentina, orgoglio della città) e pure non dimenticava le sue umili origini, e metteva al servizio dei meno fortunati compagni tutta la dottrina acquisita, in un fervido apostolato di divulgazione culturale. Né i letterati di professione potevano non guardare con simpatia, o almeno con benevolenza, a tanta verginità di intelletto e di sentimenti, a tanto onesto desiderio di sapere, a tale tesoro di buone qualità morali.[3]

[*Circe* met immediately with a lively and widespread interest. It was inevitable that it should be liked: for its "facility" and pleasure of reading, for the exciting, fanciful setting, for the quiet simplicity with which the most serious questions of "moral philosophy" were brought back to their human source, and to the modest but infallible judgment of common sense. The people found here their small feast of wisdom and they were proud of the modest hosier who had his say among the educated men who surrounded the great Cosimo (so much so that he, an acclaimed professor, read the great poets at the Florentine Academy, the pride of the city). And still, he did not forget his humble origins; he put all of his acquired learning at the service of his less fortunate companions, in a passionate apostolate of popular cultural transmission. Nor could the professional men of letters fail to look with sympathy, or at least with benevolence, upon such virginity of intellect and feeling, such honest desire for knowledge, such a treasure of good moral qualities.]

---

[3]Tissoni, "Per il testo della *Circe*," p. 108. In a later version of this statement that appeared in Tissoni's critical edition of Gelli's *Dialoghi* (Bari: Laterza, 1967), Tissoni makes a number of interesting revisions. He eliminates the quotation marks; he draws a finer distinction between Gelli and his work, and has the professional men of letters focus on Gelli's *libretto* rather than on Gelli himself; Gelli's "verginità di intelletto e di sentimenti" is replaced by the little book's "purità di intelletto e di sentimenti." Most important, the contrast between the *popolani* and the intellectuals is now marked as a contrast between the *incolti* (who might well include more than the *popolani*) and the well educated. See *Dialoghi*, p. 397. All translations are mine unless otherwise noted.

Tissoni's expressions of esteem are guarded and double-edged. He distances himself from Gelli's work with a sprinkling of quotation marks; he focuses on the pleasure *La Circe* offers rather than on its worth; he emphasizes the benefits to the uneducated masses rather than to the literary elite. Indeed, it appears that the professional men of letters did not express appreciation of Gelli's learning or engage in intellectual debate with him. Rather they express "simpatia, o almeno . . . benevolenza" ("sympathy, or at least . . . benevolence"), and for what? Above all, for "verginità di intelletto e di sentimenti" ("virginity of intellect and feeling")! Such "verginità," preserved by an "onesto desiderio di sapere" ("honest desire for knowledge") and a fine "tesoro di buone qualità morali" ("treasure of good moral qualities"), marks Giovan Battista Gelli as the token woman of the Florentine Academy.

I dare say that in a patriarchal culture minor authors are always, in a sense, women with respect to the powerful literary tradition into which they fail to insert themselves. Someone might object, perhaps, that by saying this I fail to recognize that critics' faint praise may be the gracious substitute for an acknowledgment of literary worth they feel that they cannot accord Gelli as a minor author. No one has suggested that Gelli displays a literary talent equal to that of the major authors of his time, and I do not intend to contest such an opinion. But twentieth-century readers of Gelli are often as inspired by ideological concerns as were the inquisitors who set about to identify the unorthodox assertions in Gelli's *Capricci del bottaio*.[4] One senses that Gelli, as a writer who straddles the line between intellectual and working classes, comes to be lauded for having stayed in his place, for having "enlightened" the masses without provoking open class antagonism or disturbing the division between mental and manual labor. The opening sentence of one critic's essay is a telling one: "Il Gelli ha diritto alla nostra ammirazione per aver atteso allo studio senza tralasciare il mestiere di calzettaio" ("Gelli has a right to our admiration for having dedicated himself to learning without giving up his trade as hosier").[5]

My attempt to rethink Gelli's place in Renaissance culture—and, by extension, the place of all minor authors in the literary canon—is motivated by the belief in the critical value of a marginal perspective on

---

[4]For an insightful reading of the Inquisition's inscrutable understanding of dialectics, as revealed in its interpretation of Gelli, see Paolo Valesio, *Novantiqua: Rhetorics as a Contemporary Theory* (Bloomington: Indiana University Press, 1980), pp. 142–44.

[5]Tarantino, "La *Circe* e i *Capricci del bottaio*," p. 1.

the dominant ideologies in human history. My discussion is based on a reexamination of *La Circe*. The few commentaries on Gelli's dialogue abound in description and summary, perhaps because the dialogue is presumed to be so simple and straightforward that it does not require critical elucidation. This may be the reaction to minor literary work, but, as we shall also see, it can be characteristic of the silence that is so crucial to the production of a powerful ideology.

> Platone fu quegli che rendeva gratie alli Dei di tre cose, che l'havessero fatto rationale, e non fera; huomo e non donna; che fosse nato in Atene, e non altrove. Altri però le mutano dicendo che fusse nato Greco e non barbaro, e nato al tempo di Socrate, e non prima, né dopoi.[6]

> [It was Plato who gave thanks to the gods for three things: that they made him a rational being, and not a beast; a man and not a woman; and that he was born in Athens, and not elsewhere. Others, however, alter these things, saying that he was born Greek and not a barbarian, and born in the time of Socrates, and not before or after.]

At the beginning of *La Circe*, Ulysses makes a pact with the sorceress for whom the dialogue is named: any of the Greeks whom Circe has transformed into animals will be allowed to assume once again their human form and to return to Greece with Ulysses if they wish to do so. Ulysses, supremely confident of his ability to gather this group, does not even consider the possibility that there will be any opposition. But the first ten animals to whom he speaks argue that they are much happier as animals, and would never return to being men. Ulysses is annoyed by their refusal, which, according to him, shows the lack of reason that leads them to deny the dignity of man and the superiority of free will over necessity. Finally, Ulysses succeeds in finding an Elephant—formerly a Greek philosopher named Aglaphemus—well disposed toward returning to Greece and reclaiming the honor that manhood and philosophy offer.

In the course of his dialogues with his bestial interlocutors, Ulysses argues explicitly for the human over the brutish, perfection over imperfection, reason and free will over nature and instinct. Implicitly, however, he argues an upper-class, phallocentric, and misogynistic view-

---

[6]This statement is to be found at the beginning of Girolamo Gioannini da Capugnano's commentary on the Third Dialogue. See Giovan Battista Gelli, *La Circe, aggiuntevi le annotationi, & argomenti da Maestro Girolamo Gioannini da Capugnano Frate Predicatore* (Venice: Altobello Salicato, 1589), p. 35.

point. He fires nasty remarks about manual laborers (pp. 159, 163) and about women (pp. 208, 210, 211); he is quick to question the animals' limited patriotic affections (p. 197); he repeatedly attacks his interlocutors for their limited experience, their lack of reason, their faulty perception, and their self-deception.[7] Evidently Ulysses perceives Greek manhood as the highest form of humanity.

Neither side can be said to be free of false consciousness, however. Both Ulysses and the animals assign nature a key role as they struggle to present their own views as ideologically neutral. Ulysses, by continuing to believe that inequality is the product of natural forces rather than cultural conditioning, is able to dismiss the possibility that man is responsible for the oppression of other men and women. Ulysses' blind spot becomes particularly apparent when he continues to discount human motives even after a conversation with the Hind which is quite enlightening. He remarks:

> Io non so qual sia la cagione per la quale la natura, la quale si dice che non erra mai, ha fatto tanto differente la femmina dal maschio solamente nella specie umana. Se io riguardo infra gli uccelli, di tanto valore è l'uno quanto l'altro, o veramente è di tanto poco meno, che quasi non si conosce. Né si pensi alcuno che la femmina, nel covar l'uova o nello allevare i figliuoli, voglia durare punto più fatica del maschio. E il simile avviene ancora negli animali terrestri, e in quegli che vivono nelle acque, per essere, come io ho detto, di tanta virtù e di tanta forza la femina quanto il maschio. Ma nella specie umana la donna è di tanto minor valore e di tanto minor forze de l'uomo, che quelle virtù che sono in lui, o elle non sono in lei, o elle vi sono tanto imperfette, che a pena vi si riconoscono. [p. 220]

> [I don't know for what reason Nature, who is said never to make a mistake, has made female and male so different only in the human species. If I look at birds, one is as worthy as the other, or the difference is so small as to be insignificant. Nor does anyone think that the female, in hatching eggs or in raising the young, will endure any more hardship than the male. And the situation is similar among land animals, and in those animals that live in the water, for, as I have said, the female is equal to the male in ability and in strength. But in the human species, woman is so much less able and is so much weaker than man, that those powers found in him are not in her, or if they are, they are so defective as to be practically unrecognizable.]

[7] All references to *La Circe* are made to the critical edition in Giovan Battista Gelli, *Dialoghi,* ed. Roberto Tissoni (Bari: Laterza, 1967).

This statement leads to the convenient scapegoating of a female Nature, and permits Ulysses to put male conscience at rest:

> Dolghinsi adunque della natura, che l'ha così fatte, e non si dolghino di noi, se par loro essere più tosto nostre serve che nostre compagne: perché questo non nasce né dalle forze né da la tirannide nostra, ma dal poco valore e animo loro, per il quale, temendo di non sapere o poter vivere senza noi, si arrecano sotto l'imperio nostro, stando volontariamente sotto quel giogo; dove se elle fussino de la medesima nobilità d'animo o del medesimo valore che siamo noi, non le potremo noi tener per forza giamai. [p. 220]

> [Let them complain about Nature, that made them this way, and let them stop complaining about us, if it seems to them that they are our servants rather than our companions. Because this situation is not born of our force or our tyranny, but from their limited valor and spirit, so that they, fearing that they would not know or could not live without us, place themselves under our rule and stand voluntarily beneath that yoke. For if they were of the same nobility of spirit or of the same valor that we are, we would *never* be able to hold them by force.]

But if from our point of view Ulysses' masking social forces as natural ones reeks of bad faith, the animals are in many ways no less guilty. They too slyly attempt to situate themselves outside ideology by identifying their own voices with that of Nature. Thus, the Oyster of the First Dialogue exclaims, "Io non so che cosa sia logica; pensa come io posso esser logico! Io favello in quel modo che m'ha insegnato la natura" ("I don't know what logic is, so how could I be a logician? I speak as nature has taught me to speak" [p. 153]). While it might seem that the Oyster is right, because animals must in all cases follow Nature's rule, the Oyster's statement is in fact sophistic. Pearls may be the work of Nature, but all pearls of discourse—even when placed in the shell of an Oyster—are necessarily rhetorical and ideological in character.

The two notions of nature that emerge in *La Circe*—two different ways of responding to the dilemma of individual difference within which inequality and alienation loom large—are irreconcilable. Ulysses' humanity, blessed by dignity, freedom, and a true nature that is divine, is untroubled by class and sexual difference. It transcends such difference and the problems stemming from it. Man is therefore not constrained by such external obstacles as power struggles and material difficulties, the inevitable result of human existence on earth. The animals, by contrast—especially those in the first half of La Circe—see the human existence they reject as shaped primarily by power relations foreign to the natural world. They claim to have found a Utopia in which class and sexual antagonisms are nonexistent. (I would point out, however, that even though Nature has eliminated power struggles from among animals of the same species, it permits the power struggle among animals of *different* species. The animals consider such conflict natural, and therefore acceptable.)

The tongue-in-cheek presentation of the first four animals, whom Ulysses meets in Dialogues 1–3, suggests that the reader is being encouraged to side with Ulysses. The animals appear rather comical because their current condition reflects so obviously the human state from which they proudly claim liberation. The Oyster was formerly a fisherman named, appropriately enough, Ittaco; the Mole who now burrows blindly in the earth was a peasant who worked the land; a former physician is now a Serpent, commonly seen as a symbol of health, precisely for this animal's ability to shed its skin; and a man who was a jack-of-all-trades has become a Hare, an animal renowned for its changeability.[8]

In general, the animals of the first half of the work are more given to lamenting the material conditions of their human existence. They discuss the advantages of their new lives as animals: since Nature provides all for them, they do not have to work constantly, and they do not have to worry about homes, clothes, cures for illness, food, childbirth or child rearing. The four animals who appear in the second half of La Circe (the Lion, Horse, Dog, and Calf of Dialogues 6–9) focus more on metaphysical questions. In particular, they reflect on fortitude, temperance, prudence, and justice, and they debate whether virtue born of necessity is as admirable as virtue born of free will. As a result, these animals have even been seen as symbols of the four cardinal virtues.[9] The reader is encouraged to see these animals as ones that are "higher up" in the chain of being. Galen cites these four animals several times as representative of the quadrupeds, which occupy "a position midway between the perfectly prone and wholly erect animals."[10]

The animals' concerns vary according to a pattern that appears to be determined by gender. The first four animals Ulysses meets are ones

[8]On this, see note 16.

[9]Enzo Noè Girardi, "Giambattista Gelli," in *Letteratura italiana: I minori* (Milan: Marzorati, 1961), p. 1121.

[10]Galen, *On the Usefulness of the Parts of the Body,* trans. Margaret Tallmadge May, 2 vols. (Ithaca: Cornell University Press, 1968), 1:160. See also p. 157.

whose names are of feminine gender in Italian: Ostrica, Talpa, Serpe, Lepre. The Hind (Cerva) of the Fifth Dialogue is the only animal in *La Circe* who was formerly a Greek woman; not by chance, I think, she occupies the central place in the series of eleven animals with whom Ulysses speaks. In the second half of *La Circe* the animals concerned with virtue bear names of masculine gender: Lione, Cavallo, Cane, Vitello. The thematic division that places the animals with names of feminine gender on the side of materiality and the animals with names of masculine gender on the side of metaphysics is in fact quite striking. We are reminded that all discourse about the earthly and the commonplace can be textualized as "woman's discourse."

I do not believe that we need to belabor the issue of the tenuous relation between grammatical gender and sex.[11] The issue at stake in *La Circe* is a different one. Metamorphosis changes more than bodies (depriving them of human form), more than minds (depriving them of reason). A renunciation of manhood necessarily implies a renunciation of the symbolic order that organizes human signification (at least in part) by codifying sexual and gender difference. What happens when a man, a *uomo*, becomes an *ostrica, talpa, serpe,* or *lepre?* Otherwise phrased, what happens to an individual—an individual whose being has always been defined as masculine by the masculine generic applied to the individual of undetermined sex—when he enters a linguistic order that defines the individual of as yet undetermined sex as a *she?*

In referring to the (male) animals who bear female names (the Oyster, the Mole, the Serpent, and the Hare), Circe adopts feminine gender when she speaks of them in their current state and masculine gender when she speaks of them in the past tense, as men who were once Greeks.[12] Similarly, Ulysses usually respects the gender of the animals'

[11]Such defenses appear to be a requirement of any discussion about abstractions of feminine gender, as in Hanna Fenichel Pitkin's *Fortune Is a Woman: Gender and Politics in the Thought of Niccolò Machiavelli* (Berkeley: University of California Press, 1984). Pitkin's cautious introductory point that "there may be a psychological tendency among speakers of a language with gender, if they personify an abstraction, to imagine its sex in accord with the word's gender. . . . But . . . it is quite common in gender languages for a personification to have the sex opposite to the word's gender" (p. 131) is well taken. Nevertheless, just as Pitkin goes on to argue that in Machiavelli's case certain abstractions are personified as female, I argue later in this essay that the blur between human and animal status in *La Circe* makes for a blur between gender distinctions.

[12]In the First Dialogue Circe avoids the problem of marked gender by speaking of the Oyster and the Mole together: "Parlerai con loro" ("you shall talk with them" [p. 150]). In referring to the Serpent of the Second Dialogue, Circe begins by using the feminine gender ("parlerai un poco con quella Serpe che viene attraversando la strada inverso noi" ["you shall talk a bit with that Serpent that is crossing the road toward us"]) and

names when he speaks of them in the third person, but he adopts masculine forms when he addresses them directly.[13] In some cases speakers have several options. Because *serpens* was both masculine and feminine in Latin, *il serpe* existed alongside the preferred *la serpe* in Cinquecento Italian. Circe refers to the Serpent as "quella Serpe," while Ulysses opts for the masculine form ("questo Serpe" [p. 165]).[14] Although *il lepre* existed along with *la lepre,* and continues to exist in some modern Italian dialects, the masculine form *il lepre* does not appear in *La Circe.* Nevertheless, the issue of gender confusion is brought to the fore and thematized in the dialogue with the Hare.

There is no intimation of the Hare's sexual or gender confusion until near the end of the dialogue; indeed, both the Hare and Ulysses have occasion to use masculine gender in speaking to and about this animal.[15] But upon hearing the Hare's final refusal to return to its human state, Ulysses snaps: "Io non voglio che tu dica tanto ostinatamente così. Non vedi tu animal vile che tu sei, e di tanto poco conoscimento, che tu non sai pur se tu sei maschio o femina?" ("I won't have you speak so obstinately. Don't you see, contemptible animal that you are, and of so little knowledge, that you don't even know if you are a male or a female?" [p. 192]). Ulysses here appears to be alluding to the fact that some ancient writers considered the hare to be hermaphroditic.[16]

---

then switches to the masculine forms even in the same breath: "Se ben mi ricorda, colui che io transmutai in lei era greco; e egli ti soddisferà forse assai meglio che non hanno fatto questi. E io per questa cagione gli concedo facultà di poter risponderti e parlare" ("If I remember correctly, the man I transformed into her was Greek; and he will perhaps satisfy you better than have these others" [p. 165]). At the beginning of the Third Dialogue she says to Ulysses, "Parlerai con quella Lepre che tu vedi che pasce all'ombra di quella quercia: và là, e chiamala, ché io le ho conceduto il favellare" ("You shall speak with that Hare whom you see feeding in the shade of that oak: go there, and call her, for I have granted her speech" [p. 181]).

In translating the pronouns that refer to animals with names of feminine gender, I deliberately use *she* and *her* rather than the *it* of a fluent English translation.

[13]As he moves to speak with the Mole ("quella Talpa"), he announces, "Io voglio accostarmi un poco più a lei, e chiamarla" ("I wish to move a bit closer to her, and call her" [p. 158]).

[14]Elsewhere, in referring to serpents generally, Ulysses speaks of "le Serpi" (p. 201), as does the Dog in a later dialogue (p. 249). Ulysses' shift from masculine singular to feminine plural here can be compared to a similar instance in Baldassarre Castiglione's *Libro del cortegiano* 1:9.

[15]See in particular the exchange on p. 183 of the *Dialoghi.*

[16]John Boswell notes that Pliny (8.81.218) cites Archelaus as stating that rabbits are hermaphroditic and that they conceive while pregnant ("superfetation"). Aelian (*On Animals* 13.12) relates that the male hare bears young and "has a share in both sexes." See Boswell, *Christianity, Social Tolerance, and Homosexuality: Gay People in Western*

The Hare dismisses Ulysses' insult summarily: "Sì voi non lo sapete, che vi par così intendere ogni cosa; ma noi lo sappiamo benissimo" ("You certainly don't know it, you who fancy you understand everything; but we know it quite well" [p. 192]). Ulysses does not let the insult drop, however, for he adopts a feminine adjectival ending in his next comment: "Tu hai paura d'ogni cosa e fiditi solamente nel fuggire; e nientedimanco tu sei dipoi *giunta* da molte sorti d'animali" ("You're afraid of everything and you have faith only in flight; and even so you fall prey to many kinds of animals" [p. 192; emphasis mine]). The desired effect appears to be that of forcing the Hare to admit its femininity, and it does: "Tu faresti tanto, che mi parrebbe essere *miserissima:* dove, per non conoscere tante cose, mi pare essere *felicissima*" ("You would bring me to thinking that I am most miserable; while, by not knowing so many things, it seems to me that I am very happy" [pp. 192–93; emphasis mine]). Ulysses responds with a charged invective against men who, because of their cowardice, are not really men. The Hare declines to debate this with him; but in its parting comment, the Hare flaunts its femininity at Ulysses: "Avendo io veduta quella erbetta in quel bel colle che ci è a rincontro, e avendo fame, sono *forzata* di lasciarti" ("Having seen those greens on that nice hill that is opposite us, and being hungry, I am forced to leave you" [p. 193; emphasis mine]). The Hare's assumption of the feminine voice recalls the Oyster's use of the feminine in a similar context: "Non mi dare più molestia: perché io voglio, poi che io mi sarò *cibata,* richiudermi e riposarmi alquanto" ("Don't bother me anymore: for I wish, after having eaten, to close myself up and rest for a while" [p. 157; emphasis mine]).[17] The Hare's use of the feminine form is particularly striking because it appears when the Hare uses the verb *forzare,* the very verb the Hare had used with a masculine ending when it refused Ulysses' offer of retransformation into the human form at the beginning of the dialogue: "A me non la restituirai tu già, se io non sono però *forzato*" ("You won't restore it to me, unless I am forced" [p. 183; emphasis mine]).

Ulysses does not respond specifically to these moments of linguistic deviation. Such gender scrambling must remain incomprehensible— outside metalinguistic discourse, that is—to the likes of Ulysses, for he

---

Europe from the Beginning of the Christian Era to the Fourteenth Century (Chicago: University of Chicago Press, 1980), p. 139, note 7.

[17]The Oyster used a masculine form (*cibato*) in the first edition of *La Circe.* In both the second and third editions, the Oyster uses the feminine form *cibata;* see *Dialoghi,* p. 481.

remains outside the understanding that his intellectual and moral position is founded on difference. But Ulysses is not entirely deaf to this
voice of resistance; he registers it, as do the editors of La Circe, who—
although they remain silent about the significance of this linguistic
deviation—have demonstrated remarkable integrity as philologists by
registering these moments that might easily have been blanked out.
Ulysses has from the beginning sensed that the animals are perma-
nently contaminated in some way by the feminine, for he believes that
Circe controls the decisions of these men turned beasts: "In fine, io ho
a far con bestie; e se ben Circe rende loro il poter favellare e risponder-
mi, secondo che pare a me, ella non rende loro il cervello: perché
considerano solamente certe cose minime, e non quel che importa"
("In the end, I am dealing with beasts; and even if Circe gives them the
ability to speak and to answer me, it seems to me that she doesn't give
them any brains: for they consider only certain things that are minor
and not what matters" [p. 179]). Rather than dismiss Ulysses' mistrust
of Circe, we might acknowledge that in a sense all of the animals that
refuse Ulysses' offer are "feminine," precisely because these animal
voices are the ones that Circe, woman par excellence, permits unwilling ears to hear. It seems to me that it may be possible to link anxiety
about this feminine contamination to readers' desire to identify Gelli
and Ulysses, even when the animals present legitimate criticisms of
society that Gelli himself might have voiced.[18] It is when Ulysses'
interlocutors are female (as in the case of the Hind and Circe) that the
temptation to assume that Gelli adopts Ulysses as his spokesman is
particularly strong, thus reinforcing the notion that masculine authority ought not get too entangled in a dialectical critique identified as
feminine.

As concerns Ulysses, the attempt to belittle and feminize the potentially troublesome opposition and to suggest that its desires are unrea-
sonable is concomitant with accounting for individual difference in
light of one privileged term: male wholeness. The individual who
rejects the authorized conception of the self's proper role in society
will soon be cast as a being less than a man, that is, as an animal or as a
woman.[19] Ulysses sees his inability to persuade the animals of his

[18]For an example of a reading in which the distinction between Ulysses and Gelli is
lacking, see De Gaetano, Giambattista Gelli, pp. 191–99.

[19]The analogy man : animal :: man : woman is recognizable as having a place in
classical medical literature, as shown by this representative statement taken from Galen's
On the Usefulness of Parts 2:630: "Now just as mankind is the most perfect of all animals,
so within mankind the man is more perfect than the woman."

convictions as a sign of an uncertain relation to reason, a sure sign of *someone's* defect. Shortly after his first encounters with the animals, Ulysses remarks:

Io non so se io son desto, o pur s'io sogno; se io sono desto, certamente che io non son più quello Ulisse che io soglio, dapoi che io non ho saputo far credere a nessuno di questi due la verità. E soleva pur persuadere già a i miei Greci tutto quel ch'io voleva! Ma penso ch'e' venga il difetto da loro: perché io mi sono abbattuto a due che non son molto capaci di ragione. [pp. 162–63]

[I don't know if I am awake or if I am dreaming. If I am awake, certainly I am no longer the Ulysses I usually am, since I have not been able to make either of these two believe the truth. And I used to be able to persuade my Greeks of everything I wanted! But I think that the defect lies in them: because I have come across two who are not very good at reasoning.]

Yet, from the viewpoint of both the Hare and the Oyster, the feminine voice appears as the definitive refusal of Ulysses' offer of human company and society, the voice of resistance to Ulysses' male ideology and his support of male-dominated institutions.[20] Both sides here work to contribute to the articulation of the concept of the dignity of man within the analogy man : animal :: man : woman, an analogy that depends on a shift from the masculine generic in the first part of the analogy to a sexually specific term in the second half.

The declaration of an indissoluble bond to the earthly, and to the minor, woman's voice permits the demystification of all discourse that purports to be free of the material. As a rule it is woman—represented here by the Hind of the Fifth Dialogue, among others—who is able to put into question man's relation to his property. Ulysses has attacked the animals for their excessive attachment to material goods, and has criticized them simultaneously for their lack of the "property" that would make them truly human: reason. And yet, when his property— some of it very earthly property—is put into question, his reaction is quite different. Partly because the Hind exposes her own dependence on material goods less than she exposes man's dependence on property, she deftly draws Ulysses into revealing patriarchy's concerns for estab-

[20]François Rigolot has studied a similar kind of gender scrambling in the poetry of Louise Labé. See his "Gender vs. Sex Difference in Louise Labé's Grammar of Love," in *Rewriting the Renaissance: The Discourses of Sexual Difference in Early Modern Europe,* ed. Margaret W. Ferguson, Maureen Quilligan, and Nancy J. Vickers (Chicago: University of Chicago Press, 1986), pp. 287–98.

lishing proper relationships that ensure the patrilinear transmission of wealth. Ulysses justifies his denial of sexual freedom for women, for example, by defending a man's right to know where his property is: "Dimmi un poco: pàrti ei ragionevole che l'uomo lasci quelle facultà e quegli onori che egli s'ha acquistati con la sua fatica e con la prudenza, a uno che non sia suo figliuolo?" ("Tell me: does it seem reasonable to you that a man should leave those things and those honors that he has acquired with his labor and his prudence, to one who is not his child?" [p. 215]).

Questions about language and about interpretation, although they may not seem immediately related to the Hind's exposure of the patriarchy's roots in property relationships, emerge with a vengeance in this dialogue. These questions regard the relative authority of cultural voices in conflict. The significance of language is remarked on at the beginning of the conversation with the Hind, the first animal to rejoice in the reacquisition of language. But the relative valorization of different voices emerges soon after. Upon discovering that the Hind's point of view is opposed to his own, Ulysses promptly marks her discourse as one of the "female" genre, the result of a "voglia di cicalare" ("desire to chatter") that can be dismissed as insignificant (p. 210). The Hind counters with arguments designed to reveal men's manipulation of language; she questions Ulysses' notion of "insignificant" cultural data, and highlights his partial presentation of linguistic and proverbial lore. In a sense she puts into question Ulysses' control of language, since she succeeds in exposing Ulysses' shifting relation to the cultural ideology that proverbial lore expresses and his uncertain control of that popular and maximatic "literature."

The specter of uncertain control brings forth a response designed to reassure. Man's property and his properties—material goods, children, wives, labor, reason, consciousness, culture—can be maintained if everyone stays in his or her place. Ulysses hastens to cut the Hind off when she declares that women would be capable of great deeds in the public arena, as well as in the domestic one:

> Non andate più là: ch'e' non vi avvenissi come a quel calzolaio, che, avendo biasimato una statua per avere i coreggiuoli delle scarpette al contrario, e essendone lodato, prese poi animo di biasimarla in non so che altre parti; onde gli fu detto: "Non passar più su che la scarpa, ché questo non appartiene a te." [p.213]

> [You (women) stay right there: so that it wouldn't happen to you as with that shoemaker, who, having criticized a statue because its shoelaces were done the wrong way, and having been praised for that, was then cou-

rageous enough to criticize it in some other parts. Whereupon he was told: "Don't go beyond the shoe, because those things do not belong to you."]

The alienation of woman, like that of manual laborers, is established in the division of labor, brought home here with a line that would certainly have had autobiographical resonance for our author, himself a *calzolaio*. The gender division, like the division of mental and manual labor, lies buried at the heart of the concept of man's freedom, and must remain misunderstood for man to believe himself free.

From the reader's perspective, Ulysses emerges worse in this dialogue than in many others. His explicit misogyny weakens his argument, and the contrast between his stated morality and the double standard reflected in his personal behavior reflects negatively on him. (Penelope, for example, is a forgotten figure until the issue of woman is definitively settled in Ulysses' mind at the beginning of the Sixth Dialogue. Then the Lion, in the course of making pleasant small talk, inquires after Ulysses' wife.) By contrast, the Hind's critique is limited to certain issues that put Ulysses in a negative light but do not devastate his arguments as they might. She does not consistently use Ulysses' arguments against him in the best possible fashion. For example, when the Hind attacks Ulysses for the double standard and Ulysses responds (as I have noted) that women cannot be allowed sexual freedom because to do so would fail to ensure men of the certainty of transmitting their acquired wealth to their own children, the Hind agrees with Ulysses that it is not fitting for men to pass on wealth to children who are not theirs, and after doing so, the Hind takes up another line of attack: that men do not pay much attention to children when they are young. The objection that fails to arise here is this: Why is it proper for the wife to transmit the fruits of her labor to children who are not *hers,* but whom her husband has fathered and has recognized as his own? Such an objection would grapple with Ulysses' argument rather than confirming the economic supremacy of men; it would raise the question of why it is assumed that women's labor in the home does not create wealth but only preserves wealth acquired by males outside the home. My point here is not to revile the Hind for being a poor debater or a poor feminist. Rather, it seems to me important to note that Gelli's dialogue is progressive inasmuch as it permits various animals to voice certain kinds of dissatisfactions, but conservative inasmuch as it quickly muffles any social critique that addresses the really crucial issues.[21]

---

[21]This combination of ideologically progressive and conservative elements is to be found also in the animals' linguistic practice. Although the animals on occasion use the

Such discourse exists in dialectical relation to the possibilities of historical change within a given economic and social system. Thus, if the Hind were indeed able to formulate such an objection about alienated labor, there would already have been more than a germ of feminism in the Italian Renaissance. Furthermore, a pointed critique of property relations, such as that which we find in Marx and Engels, seems to permit further historical change, but is also itself permitted by changes in economic structures.

Like the animals, but in a more pleasant fashion, Circe prods Ulysses toward a realization of how ideological man's view of other men is.[22] Hers is a thankless task, however. As Ulysses and the former Elephant Aglaphemus exit from the text, they engage in a peculiar bit of name-calling. Circe is proclaimed the "fraudolente e sagace donna" ("fraudulent and shrewd woman" [p. 289]), the "malvagia incantatrice" ("the evil enchantress" [p. 289]) from whom they flee at the end of the work; Aglaphemus attributes to her the responsibility for deceiving all those who do not live by the rule of reason and free will. The assumption is clear: no man would of his own will renounce his manhood. But where is the threat presented by the feminine here? In epic poetry deceptive seductresses and sorceresses modeled on Circe (Falerina in Boiardo's *Orlando innamorato*, Alcina in Ariosto's *Orlando Furioso*, Acratia in Trissino's *Italia liberata dai Goti*, Armida in Tasso's *Gerusalemme liberata*) often appear as obstacles to the establishment of a patriarchal civil order: they seduce men, deceive them, and render them effeminate and powerless. But the Circe of Gelli's dialogue is from the beginning unthreatening: polite, reasonable, accommodating.[23] Ulys-

---

feminine generic in the singular, the generic pronoun in the plural seems to remain masculine, suggesting that animal society remains organized according to patriarchal norms even when some concessions are made on the question of which singular pronoun is considered to be the generic one.

[22]For example, after Ulysses returns from speaking with the Oyster and the Mole at Circe's encouragement, Circe says pointedly: "Non pensare che io abbia fatto ancora questo a caso; ché io ho voluto che tu cominci a vedere che ancora in quegli stati bassi, che sono stati già tanto lodati da molti de' vostri scrittori, sono tante incommodità, che i più vili e imperfetti animali che si ritruovino stanno meglio di loro: e eglino te ne hanno assegnato le ragioni" ("Don't think I've done this by chance; for I wanted you to begin seeing that in these base conditions, which have been so praised by many of your writers, there are so many troubles, that the most contemptible and imperfect animals alive are better off than they are; and these animals have listed the reasons for this" [p. 164]).

[23]Robert Adams notes that "it is only at the end of the last dialogue that Aglaphemus is allowed to slip into the conventional invective against her" and explains this by

ses does not have to convince Circe in order to win the right to take his companions, appropriately retransformed into men, back to Ithaca. She announces quite simply, "Dipoi che tu avrai intesa la voglia loro, vieni a me, e io farò quel che tu vorrai" ("After you have heard their wishes, come to me, and I will do what you want" [p. 150]).

"I will do what you want": it seems that Ulysses has access to the ultimate performative. This accommodating statement makes it sound as if all of Ulysses' desires will be fulfilled. He appears to resemble the prelapsarian man in Pico della Mirandola's fable of creation—man as the being to whom "it is granted to have whatever he chooses, to be whatever he wills."[24] In describing the freedom and the free will of man, Pico tells how the Creator took man as a creature of indeterminate nature, placed him in the middle of the world, and conferred upon him the power to fashion himself:

> Nec te caelestem neque terrenum, neque mortalem neque immortalem fecimus, ut tui ipsius quasi arbitrarius honorariusque plastes et fictor, in quam malueris tute formam effingas. Poteris in inferiora quae sunt bruta degenerare; poteris in superiora quae sunt divina ex tui animi sententia regenerari.

> [We have made thee neither of heaven nor of earth, neither mortal nor immortal, so that with freedom of choice and with honor, as though the maker and molder of thyself, thou mayest fashion thyself in whatever

---

suggesting that "the possibility looms large that this rhetoric is one more ironic hedge against the intelligence of Aglaphemus. Certainly he is too priggish an elephant for his ungenerous words to influence our judgment of the enchanting Circe. On the whole, one could not ask for a fairer (in every sense of the word) temptress." See Adams' introduction to Giovanni Battista Gelli, *The Circe*, trans. Thomas Brown and Robert Adams (Ithaca: Cornell University Press, 1963), pp. xl-xli.

[24]Giovanni Pico della Mirandola, "Oration on the Dignity of Man," trans. Elizabeth Livermore Forbes, in *The Renaissance Philosophy of Man*, ed. Ernst Cassirer, Paul Oskar Kristeller, and John Herman Randall, Jr. (Chicago: University of Chicago Press, 1948), p. 225. The Latin original reads "cui datum id habere quod optat, id esse quod velit." See Giovanni Pico della Mirandola, *De Hominis Dignitate, Heptaplus, De Ente et Uno*, ed. Eugenio Garin (Florence: Vallecchi, 1942), p. 106.

I would emphasize, as does Kristeller in his *Renaissance Thought and Its Sources*, that "it has been argued quite often that Pico seems to attribute to man an unlimited freedom, and thus to deny, at least by implication, the Christian doctrines of grace and predestination. This view may easily be exaggerated, for Pico never denies these doctrines, and even in this passage we should not overlook a significant detail: the often quoted words about man's freedom are addressed by God to Adam upon his creation, that is, before his fall. Hence, we might stretch the point and insist that Pico describes man's dignity before the fall, and somehow leaves it undetermined to what extent this dignity has been affected by the fall and by original sin" (p. 175).

shape thou shalt prefer. Thou shalt have the power to degenerate into the lower forms of life, which are brutish. Thou shalt have the power, out of thy soul's judgment, to be reborn into the higher forms, which are divine.][25]

The dedicatory letter of *La Circe,* addressed to Cosimo I, reveals Gelli's debt to Pico on this point:

In potestà de l'uomo è stato liberamento posto il potersi eleggere quel modo nel quale più gli piace vivere, e, quasi come un nuovo Prometeo, trasformarsi in tutto quello che egli vuole, prendendo, a guisa di cameleonte, il color di tutte quelle cose a le quali egli più si avvicina con l'affetto; e finalmente, farsi o terreno o divino, e a quello stato trapassare che a la elezione de il libero voler suo piacerà più. [p. 145]

[In the power of man has been freely placed the ability to choose the way in which he likes best to live, and, as if he were a new Prometheus, to transform himself into everything he wishes, taking on like a chameleon the color of all those things to which he comes closest in his affections; and finally, to make himself either earthly or divine, and cross over to that state which is most pleasing to the choice of his free will.]

"Prometeo" appears in the place of "Proteo," a substitution some editors and translators of *La Circe* correct without further ado, assuming that Gelli intended "Proteo" because Pico also compares man to a chameleon and to Proteus.[26] How strange, nevertheless, that this "mistake" was not corrected in the second or third editions of *La Circe,* editions published within Gelli's lifetime. The few who comment on the substitution do so without offering an explanation for it.[27] The

---

[25]Pico, *De Hominis Dignitate,* p. 106; and in Forbes' English translation, in *Renaissance Philosophy of Man,* p. 225.

[26]Pico, *De Hominis Dignitate,* p. 106; p. 225 in Forbes, *Renaissance Philosophy of Man.*

[27]Tissoni, who leaves "Prometeo" in the text, remarks on his decision to do so: "Gli errori e le confusioni culturali sono, a livello testuale, intangibili, perché appartengono anch'essi 'all'unica concreta realtà storica che qui interessi: quella della mente di colui che credette vero quel falso'" ("Errors and cultural confusions are, at the textual level, intangible, because they too belong 'to the only concrete historical reality that interests us here: that of the mind of the person who believed that false thing to be true'"). Tissoni is citing a statement made by Luigi Firpo, "Correzioni d'autore coatte," in *Studi e problemi di critica testuale* (Bologna: Commissione per i Testi di Lingua, 1961), p. 147. Firpo goes on to say, "E in ogni caso non è compito della filologia ricostruire il *vero* delle cose, bensì il *certo* dei testi" ("In any case, it is not philology's task to reconstruct the *truth* of things but rather the *certainty* of texts").

prominence of the myth of Prometheus in other Renaissance discussions of the dignity of man would suggest that Gelli may indeed have intended "Prometheus" even though the rest of his argument recalls a passage in which Pico della Mirandola mentions Proteus.[28] If "Prometeo" is a lapsus, it is not an insignificant one, however, for it reminds us that there are limits on man's power to become whatever he wishes and to have whatever he desires. The Promethean man is a being for whom the origins of culture are linked with the act of theft and with the gods' punishment of that transgression. In one version of the myth Zeus responds to Prometheus' transgression by sending a woman, Pandora, into Prometheus' happy, all-male world. In another version of the myth, Zeus punishes Prometheus by binding him to a rock and sending a vulture to eat his liver.[29] Barbara Spackman has pointed out the centrality of castration to the story of Prometheus and Pandora, a myth she reads—along with Gabriele D'Annunzio—as a powerful myth of transgression.[30] We might say that behind every Proteus there is a Prometheus; that is, behind every being who glories in newfound liberties there is the shade of a being who pays for cultural progress and liberation.[31]

Inserted into a reading of La Circe, the Prometheus myth reminds us that whatever the positive aspects of the freedom of choice, and whatever the spiritual gain from the return to the social order, there is a

[28]Ernst Cassirer has discussed the importance of the Prometheus legend in Renaissance discussions of the dignity of man, and has shown how this motif came to be fused with the "Adam motif." Cassirer focuses in particular on the shaping of the Prometheus legend in Boccaccio, Ficino, and Bovillus. See his Individual and the Cosmos in Renaissance Philosophy, pp. 92 ff., especially pp. 95–96.

[29]This episode of the wounding of Prometheus is recounted in Hesiod's Theogony ll. 507ff., while the creation of Pandora is recounted in Hesiod's Works and Days ll. 54ff., and in Theogony ll. 570ff. On the Prometheus myth, see Jacqueline Duchemin, Prométhée: Histoire du mythe, de ses origines orientales à ses incarnations modernes (Paris: Société d'édition "Les belles lettres," 1974).

[30]Barbara Spackman, Decadent Genealogies: The Rhetoric of Sickness from Baudelaire to D'Annunzio (Ithaca: Cornell University Press, 1989), pp. 168–83. My sensitivity to the lapsus in Gelli's dedicatory letter was sparked by this discussion of the Prometheus myth.

[31]On the way in which a feminist perspective forces us to revise our notions about progress in history, and particularly about periodization, see Joan Kelly, "Did Women Have a Renaissance?" in Women, History, and Theory: The Essays of Joan Kelly (Chicago: University of Chicago Press, 1984), pp. 19–50. Particularly relevant is Kelly's stated premise: "To take the emancipation of women as a vantage point is to discover that events that further the historical development of men, liberating them from natural, social, or ideological constraints, have quite different, even opposite, effects upon women" (p. 19).

price to be paid. Ulysses and Aglaphemus pay that price for their return to their homes. They have no doubts; they are able to accept their manhood without irony, and they remain convinced that their dignity and freedom can in all cases and under all circumstances be maintained without loss to any other being.

The loss is there, and is registered in the peculiarities of the final dialogue, where the affirmation of the dignity of man is accompanied by signs of textual flattening. Aglaphemus, though perhaps not a dolt, is not as quick a discussant as one might have hoped for. As Armand De Gaetano points out,

> Since the interlocutor here is a philosopher we should expect the debate to be heated and to contain the best arguments from the opposition. Instead, whereas the fisherman, the peasant, and the other characters had given Ulysses a very difficult time, the philosopher does actually little to challenge the arguments of his adversary, and the dispute becomes a mere monologue uttered by Ulysses with the philosopher putting in an occasional remark just to break up the monotony.[32]

Moreover, the final hymn that Aglaphemus sings as he rejoices in his human form, "Oda questo hymno l'universa natura del mondo" ("Let the universal nature of the world hear this hymn") reveals yet another possible moment of "textual collapse." As Carlo Bonardi has shown, this hymn is, like one of Lorenzo de' Medici's *Orazioni*, "Oda questo inno tutta la natura" ("Let all nature hear this hymn" [p. 287]), a loose translation of a passage from Hermes Trismegistus, and in Aglaphemus' voice we may hear the overtones of a man adhering to a party line.[33]

Giovan Battista Gelli had portrayed a world quite unfamiliar to the reader by creating characters who depart from traditional molds—a Circe who is not deceptive and seductive, a Ulysses whose rhetorical powers do not command immediate capitulation, and an array of ani-

[32]De Gaetano, *Giambattista Gelli,* p. 219.

[33]See Bonardi, "Le orazioni di Lorenzo il Magnifico." Bonardi does not venture beyond the most superficial philological identification, but I believe that it is significant that Gelli chose to strike a Medicean stance here. Although the intertextual relations between Gelli's writings and the historical and cultural context of Medicean Florence is outside the bounds of this essay, it seems to me that the area of research could prove a fruitful one. I am grateful to Elena Ciletti for information she has given me concerning the possible significance of the Medici *impresa,* the yoke with the motto N/SVAVE (or SVAVE), for my interpretation of Gelli, information that has sparked my current study of the historical and political echoes in Gelli's dialogue.

mals that go beyond the expected swine. This counters the general effect that results from casting the story of Circe and Ulysses in a homey and informal Florentine that may seem to render the story more familiar and accessible to the common reader. The dialogue relies on this process of defamiliarization in order to clear new avenues of critical thinking about the essence of human nature and human existence. But the conclusion of the dialogue reaffirms the traditional conception of Circe as evil seductress, an interpretation not supported by textual evidence but well documented by the *idées fixes* of the tradition.

It is especially upon reading the final dialogue that one sees clearly the extent to which the previous dialogues depend on the articulation of difference, frequently cast as sexual difference. I would have the reader recall an earlier, instructive moment—the moment when Ulysses asks Circe whether she is of the opinion that it is better to be a beast than a man. Circe replies, "Questo non vo' io già determinare, né anco tu debbi pensare che io lo creda; perch'io mi sarei ancora io trasmutata in fiera come io ho fatto loro. Ma se io dicessi quel che di' tu, i ragionamenti sarebbon finiti" ("I don't want to decide this, nor ought you to think that I believe this is the case; because I would have changed myself into an animal as I have done with them. But if I were to say what you say, the discussion would end" [p. 196]).[34] The presence of Circe preserves the possibility of dialectic; silencing her is the necessary accompaniment to the affirmation of the manhood that Ulysses and Aglaphemus choose. Ironically, however, as Ulysses and Aglaphemus opt to relinquish bestiality and to dedicate all to the cultivation of a spiritual life—admittedly a victory for a humanist point of view—they bring into being a work that is entitled not *Ulisse,* not *Aglafemo,* but *La Circe.*

Need I spell out my reasons for naming my own essay as I do? What has happened to "the dignity of man" now that "a feminist perspective" has been adjoined to it? As we have seen, the feminist perspective has no proper "place" in *La Circe,* for it emerges at various levels of the discourse. Indeed, the power of the feminist perspective—like that of Pico's man blessed by dignity—consists in being able to resist confin-

[34]What Circe tells us here is similar to what Barbara Johnson has noted in our own time: "If human beings were not divided into two biological sexes, there would probably be no need for literature. And if literature could truly say what the relations between the sexes are, we would doubtless not need much of it then, either." See Barbara Johnson, *The Critical Difference: Essays in the Contemporary Rhetoric of Reading* (Baltimore: Johns Hopkins University Press, 1980), p. 13.

ing categorizations, in being able to occupy the place of the animals as well as that of higher beings. Moreover, the terms of my title are not necessarily in opposition, for the Renaissance philosophical debate on the dignity of man is not necessarily misogynist. Inasmuch as it resists the explicit misogyny of Innocent III's *De miseria humane conditionis* (*On the Misery of the Human Condition*), it works in the same direction as "the feminist perspective."[35] *La Circe* makes clear the underlying ideological assumptions and implications of a *particular* rhetorical application—a misogynist and exclusivist application—of the debate on the purpose and conditions of human life. I hope that my commentary on the previously unperceived ironies of *La Circe* will lead us to ask how many other ironic discourses have also fallen on deaf ears. But irony cannot be predictable, readable; and, as we take our stand to deconstruct the discourses that have turned authoritarian and oppressive, we may not always be able to ascertain which place we occupy.

[35]Lotario dei Segni (Pope Innocent III), *De miseria condicionis humane,* ed. and trans. Robert E. Lewis (Athens: University of Georgia Press, 1978). (This modern edition uses a somewhat different title.)

Juliana Schiesari

The Gendering of Melancholia:
Torquato Tasso and Isabella di Morra

In an already celebrated and somewhat infamous essay, Stephen
Greenblatt seems to impugn the validity of applying psychoanalytic
criticism to Renaissance texts. In his critique psychoanalysis is understood as that which presupposes a "continuity of selfhood," which is,
however, the mere "historical effect" of the early modern redefinition
of the relation between "body, property, and name."[1] According to
this logic, then, psychoanalysis cannot legitimately be used to explain
the "causes" of a selfhood whose very definition not only precedes
psychoanalysis but is also presupposed by it. Thus, for Greenblatt,
psychoanalysis would be not simply "irrelevant," or even an "anach-
ronism," but "causally belated, even as it is causally linked: hence the
curious effect of a discourse that functions *as if* the psychological categories it invokes were not only simultaneous with but even prior to
and themselves causes of the very phenomenon of which in actual fact
they were the results."[2]

A more attentive look at Greenblatt's argument reveals, however,
that a certain kind of psychoanalysis is utterly pertinent to the study of
early modern literature. While Greenblatt is right to reject the
ahistoricism of those psychoanalytic approaches that posit a "univer-

---

[1]Stephen Greenblatt, "Psychoanalysis and Renaissance Culture," in *Literary Theo-
ry / Renaissance Texts,* ed. Patricia Parker and David Quint (Baltimore: Johns Hopkins
University Press, 1986), p. 221. For a critique of Greenblatt's historicist approach as
implicated in a denial of gender and racial difference, among other differences, see
Marguerite Waller, "Academic Tootsie: The Denial of Difference and the Difference It
Makes," *diacritics* 17 (Spring 1987): 2–20.

[2]Greenblatt, "Psychoanalysis," p. 221.

233

salizing mythology"[3] or the depth psychology that uncovers the same invariant motivation (that is, repressed sexual desire) behind all human behavior and in all cultural and historical periods, his argument about the developing Renaissance paradigm of the self as derived from the institutional accrediting of one's external persona is strikingly congruent with the Lacanian revision of psychoanalysis. This revision rejects the hypothesis of a self-contained and self-originating psychological subject and instead grounds subjectivity in the "discourse of the Other."[4] Within the Western world that *symbolic* Other is the social institution of patriarchy which organizes, through a determined set of injunctions and prescriptions (the "symbolic order"), the very nomenclature of family relations, to which Lacan refers—in the shorthand that is his—as the "nom du père": the father's name, which is also the powerfully interdictive "no" of paternal authority.[5] Within this revised Freudian schema the phallus, as a *metaphor* for the "nom du père," would be a principle of sexual differentiation which is at least as social as it is biological.[6] No longer the deep, dark "subconscious" of traditional or vulgar Freudianism, the Lacanian "structural unconscious" is what "exceeds" the subject, or "decenters" its supposed centrality, by ascribing the very core of its individuality to a mirror reflection of

[3]The critique seems less apt in regard to Freud or to psychoanalysis in general, as Greenblatt would seem to have it, than to that renegade of psychoanalysis, Jung, whose monistic positing of a "universalizing mythology" in the form of his famous archetypes was directly responsible for his split with Freud. Also see Greenblatt, "Psychoanalysis," pp. 217–18. While on p. 221, Greenblatt explicitly mentions Lacan with approval, he does not overtly explore the possibilities of a Lacanian reading and continues to attack a "straw man" version of psychoanalysis.

[4]See Jacques Lacan, "Subversion of the Subject and Dialectic of Desire," in *Écrits: A Selection,* trans. Alan Sheridan (New York: W. W. Norton, 1977), pp. 292–328, esp. p. 312; Fredric Jameson, in "Imaginary and Symbolic in Lacan: Marxism, Psychoanalytic Criticism, and the Problem of the Subject," in *Literature and Psychoanalysis: The Question of Reading Otherwise,* ed. Shoshana Felman (Baltimore: Johns Hopkins University Press, 1977), pp. 338–95, defines the Lacanian "structural" unconscious in opposition to "the classical image of the Freudian unconscious as a seething cauldron of archaic instincts" (p. 365). This understanding of the Freudian subject as one whose psyche is embedded in an ahistorical primal organization must be criticized for its assumption that a given subject's entry into the world of exchange is wholly predetermined by its personal history. Thus, Greenblatt would be correct to refuse *the* ahistoricism of such "psychoanalytic" readings that view the subject's experiences as simply what pours out of that "seething cauldron of archaic instincts."

[5]See Lacan, "Function and Field of Speech and Language," in *Écrits,* esp. pp. 65–68.

[6]See Jacqueline Rose, "Introduction II," in *Feminine Sexuality: Jacques Lacan and the école freudienne,* trans. Jacqueline Rose, ed. Juliet Mitchell and Jacqueline Rose (New York: W. W. Norton, 1982), pp. 38–40.

something external to it,[7] and hence, although Lacanians do not always draw this conclusion, to the particularity of a social order or of a historical moment.[8]

According to Greenblatt, psychoanalysis "can redeem its belatedness only when it historicizes its own procedures," and indeed, the *uncritical* application of any conceptual schema to any object of analysis is invariably suspect.[9] In its strongest forms, however, psychoanalysis is not the application of a set of concepts (castration anxiety, penis envy, the Oedipal triangle, and so on) to a given subject matter. Rather, psychoanalysis is itself a critical approach whose terms and procedures are always and already unendingly revised *in their very implementation*. It is the "interminability" of the analysis (and not some fixation on the phallus) that most forcefully marks the work of the later Freud as well as of Lacan, and explains much of their so-called obscurity.[10] If, as Greenblatt states, the Renaissance is that period which undertakes "the prepsychoanalytic fashioning of the proprietary rights of selfhood" which makes the later invention of psychoanalysis possible, then not only is psychoanalysis indeed capable of shedding *some* light on the literature of that period, but the psychoanalytic reading of such texts— also and necessarily—transforms the very theory that carries out the interpretation through contact with those texts that seem to prefigure psychoanalytic categories.[11] Psychoanalysis, if you will, is less a theory than a *practice* of interpretation that lends an ear to what is not said, to what is "repressed."

The difficulty (and urgency) of such a self-transformative critical practice when brought to bear on historical texts at the very inception

---

[7]See Lacan, "The Mirror Stage," in *Écrits*, pp. 1–7; also see John Brenkman, *Culture and Domination* (Ithaca: Cornell University Press, 1987), esp. pp. 157–58, for an analysis of the mirror stage as that moment which is fraught with conflict, given that the gestalt of the image in the mirror is one of wholeness the fictionality of which is belied by the child's recognition of its dependence on *others*. Thus such "autonomy" is questioned, just as the child's acquisition of and dependence on language are not acts of "self-sufficiency" but of "participation" and "interaction" (p. 157).

[8]Cf. Brenkman, *Culture and Domination,* who states: "The importance of Lacanian theory lies precisely in the fact that it restates the psychoanalytic problem in *social and cultural terms,* while at the same time maintaining the integrity of the psychoanalytic experience" (p. 151; emphasis mine).

[9]Greenblatt, "Psychoanalysis," p. 221.

[10]On the notion of "interminability," see Sigmund Freud's late "Analysis Terminable and Interminable," in *The Standard Edition of the Complete Psychological Works of Sigmund Freud,* trans. James Strachey (London: Hogarth Press and the Institute of Psycho-Analysis, 1964), 23: 209–53.

[11]Greenblatt, "Psychoanalysis," p. 223.

of the modern notion of selfhood is compounded when the historical perspective is doubled by a feminist one. For, just as the autonomy of the subject is historically compromised by the symbolic order within which it is located, so too the centrality of the phallus to that order is contested by a feminism that hears what remains unspoken within, or is repressed by, Western patriarchy: the voices of women. Again, if the very conditions of the patriarchal subject were first made possible in the Renaissance, then the combined feminist and psychoanalytic criticism of texts from that period is urgent, not only for a greater understanding of the Renaissance but also for the radicalization of psychoanalysis itself. In sum, the psychoanalysis of Renaissance texts is possible—even necessary—insofar as it allows or wills the transformation of its own conceptual apparatus through the twin displacement of feminist criticism and the confrontation with older texts.

Finally, any psychoanalytic approach to Renaissance material must also take note of Freud's indebtedness to the works of that period in the elaboration of his own most cherished principles. Whether we consider (critically or uncritically) Freud's studies of Leonardo and Michelangelo or the prominence of various Shakespearean figures throughout his works, psychoanalysis has since its very inception been involved in rereading the Renaissance. The key, formative role played by Renaissance texts (exceeded only by the world of Greek mythology) in the development of Freud's thought is less surprising than it may at first seem, given that Freud appears at the historical end of that great era of Cartesian selfhood (defined by the autonomy of a self who needs only to "think" in order to know he "is") whose first stirrings, following Greenblatt, would have been laid down during the Renaissance, and given too that Freud undertakes what has been called a Copernican revolution (another Renaissance reference!) in our notions of selfhood. The psychoanalysis of Renaissance texts is thus implicated in the very genealogy of psychoanalysis, a situation that is less a vicious circle of mutual implication than the necessity—and the possibility—of a critique of psychoanalysis from *within* psychoanalysis itself.

For instance, Freud's famous essay of 1914, "Mourning and Melancholia," whose title already evokes the familiar topos celebrated in the famous etchings of Dürer, the character of Hamlet, the poetry of Tasso, and the *Anatomy* of Burton, can also be shown to bear more than a casual complicity with the Renaissance discourse on melancholia.[12] For Freud, the act of mourning is the affective reaction of grief to a concrete

---

[12]Freud, "Mourning and Melancholia," in *Standard Edition,* 14: 243–58.

loss such as the death of a loved one. It is a way of recuperating the ego's investment of libido in the lost object through a ritual of commemoration and farewell. In contrast to this normal, if somewhat uninteresting, psychological labor is an eminently "pathological"—if not highly romanticized—state of melancholia, wherein a subject, as Freud tells us, acts *as if* he were mourning some loss, whose exact nature remains, nonetheless, and to all concerned, obscure and nameless. Whereas the mourner has no trouble pointing to what needs to be mourned, the melancholic cannot readily explain the source of his feelings.[13] Because of the melancholic's inchoate source of unhappiness, we can assume that there is the need for an analysis and therapy that will lift the subject's repression and allow him consciously to articulate what it is that is troubling him. (The classic scenario would be a morbid fixation on the mother, whose primal fantasmatic loss can never be avowed by an ego who internalizes that loss into the very definition of its being, who thus perpetually "mourns" a self that never was, and hence borders on a state of pathological narcissism.)[14]

The psychoanalytic cure would seem to be hampered and complicated in the melancholic situation, however, by one of the peculiarities of this neurosis: the very garrulousness of the patient, whose nearly limitless capability for self-criticism and abnegation subtends an "insistent communicativeness which finds satisfaction in self-exposure."[15] It is clear that the famous "talking cure" comes up against an unusual

[13]In "Mourning and Melancholia" Freud argues that even if in some cases of melancholia it is *clear* that the illness is due to the loss of a loved object or to the loss of a more ideal type, there also exists another type of melancholic situation in which "one feels justified in maintaining the belief that a loss of this kind has occurred, but we cannot see *what* it is that has been lost, and it is all the more reasonable to suppose that the patient cannot consciously perceive what he has lost either" (p. 245; emphasis mine).

[14]Freud posits the following scenario as one way to explain such a loss: "An object-choice, an attachment of the libido to a particular person, had at one time existed; then owing to a real slight or disappointment coming from this loved person, the object-relationship was shattered. The result was not then a normal one of withdrawal of the libido from this object and a displacement of it onto a new one, but something different, for whose coming-about various conditions seem to be necessary. The object-cathexis proved to have little power of resistance and was brought to an end. But the free libido was not displaced onto another object; it was withdrawn into the ego. There, however, it was not employed in any unspecified way, but served to establish an *identification* of the ego and the latter could henceforth be judged by a special agency, as though it were an object, the forsaken object. In this way an object-loss was transformed into an ego-loss and the conflict between the ego and the loved person into a cleavage between the critical activity of the ego and the ego as altered by identification." Freud, "Mourning and Melancholia," p. 249.

[15]Ibid., p. 247.

obstacle here in this pathological verbosity, whose discursive plenitude can be said to rejoin a long-standing tradition of melancholia understood as a source of intellectual and artistic creativity, precisely through its conversion of emotional loss into creative productivity.[16] So, while Freud's text is remarkable for the distinction it draws between mourning and melancholia, it nevertheless stops short of understanding that a certain type of melancholic fixation can be read as being constituted through the desire to idealize loss *as* loss, to perpetuate and even capitalize on that sense of loss. What Freud's analysis does not seem to bear out is that the melancholic model can be understood not simply as the "incorporation" of a lost object of desire, but also as an incorporation of loss which needs to be endlessly reproduced as loss to sustain its myth.[17] By privileging a nostalgic ideal that is also kept absent and

[16]An excellent source for the discussion of the origins of melancholy as a sign of extraordinary intellectual and artistic creativity is the canonical work by Raymond Klibansky, Erwin Panofsky, and Fritz Saxl, *Saturn and Melancholy* (New York: Basic Books, 1964). Also see the classic work by Robert Burton, *The Anatomy of Melancholy* (Oxford: Cripps, 1621). Burton's seventeenth-century propensity for encyclopedic knowledge yielded a study of the various types of melancholy, which range from clinical descriptions of melancholy as a physiological illness to that melancholy which seemed also to afflict men of intellect, among whom Burton (following upon the Ficinian legacy) counted himself. Not only does Burton in the very opening pages of his book identify himself as a scholar who has lived "a silent, sedentary, solitary, private life, *mihi et musis* in the University" (p. 2), but, following the tradition inaugurated by Ficino, he most explicitly aligns his fate with the planet Saturn: "Saturn was lord of my geniture" (p. 3). Thus, the very book on melancholy is the product of an avowed melancholic temperament: "I wrote of melancholy, by being busy to avoid melancholy" (p. 4). One ought to keep in mind, however, that his melancholy, or what he refers to as his "Mistress 'melancholy,' my Aegeria, or my *malus genius*" (p. 5), is nonetheless of a "higher" order than the mere depressive state of those others whose depression is not linked to creative expression. Also see Michael O'Connell, *Robert Burton* (Boston: Twayne, 1986), who points out that Burton's interest in melancholy came from what Burton claimed to be "the center of all discourse" (p. 41). What I find interesting about this "melancholic subject" is that melancholy becomes a way to talk about subjectivity and even more so to create a subject—one who identifies himself as artistic, intellectual, or whatever—out of what had, according to the Galenic tradition, been viewed primarily as a clinical and debilitating illness with no transcendent value. Thus, even in Freud we can see two sides of this illness. On the one hand, Freud gives us the clinical picture of this pathology, but, on the other hand, by referring (as I will argue) to Hamlet's visionary talents, he points to a cultural apotheosis of its victims as a sign of their special nature. The question I must ask myself, and which is the organizing theme of my essay, is just where, if, and how women fit into this "creative" form of melancholic illness.

[17]On the "incorporation" of a lost object as theorized by Freud, see "Mourning and Melancholia," esp. pp. 248–50. Also see Giorgio Agamben, *Stanze: La parola e il fantasma nella cultura occidentale* (Turin: Einaudi, 1977), pp. 1–43, who argues that what is

deferred, the self not only reconverts the loss into self-display but also legitimates that display as part of a cultural myth—that of the melancholic intellectual and artist—whose roots reach well back into the Renaissance.

More than just the undesirable *disease* that humoral medicine had traditionally diagnosed as caused by an excess of black bile, melancholia had come by the Renaissance to be perceived also as an eloquent form of mental disturbance—a special, albeit difficult, gift—as hierarchically superior to mere depression as the individuals afflicted by it were to those whose sadness was only the passing effect of unfortunate circumstances, such as illness, poverty, or the loss of loved ones.[18] Aristotle had already attributed the melancholic temperament to great men: "Why is it that all those who have become eminent in philosophy or politics or poetry or the arts are clearly of an atrabilious temperament, and some of them to such an extent as to be affected by diseases caused by black bile, as is said to have happened to Heracles among the heroes?" Among the other great *men* said by Aristotle to have been afflicted by melancholy were Ajax, Bellerophon, Empedocles, Plato, and Socrates.[19] But it was the Florentine philosopher Marsilio Ficino, a self-described melancholic, who revised such negative or at least ambiguous assessments of the melancholic temperament by insisting that those who were born under the unlucky planet Saturn, as he himself had been, were especially gifted. In a letter addressed to Giovanni Cavalcanti, Ficino states his desire to find a way to rethink Saturn's possible influence over melancholic temperaments: "Saturn seems to have impressed the seal of melancholy on me from the beginning. . . . Either I shall say, if you wish, that a nature of this kind does not issue from Saturn; or, if it should be necessary that it does issue from Saturn, I shall, in agreement with Aristotle, say that this nature is a unique and

at stake in melancholia is a fantasmatic capacity to make it seem *as if* an object of desire had been lost (p. 26). While I would agree with Agamben on this point, Agamben himself, like the melancholic, seems to place an extraordinary value on the hypostatization of a lost object of desire as a way to eroticize the loss. What Agamben fails to take into account is the way in which such fantasy implicitly belies an eros dependent on the negation of women's subjectivities since the figure of the "feminine" is always, in some way, at stake in these kinds of object relations. Furthermore, in so doing, Agamben occludes the political and social realities of disempowerment by arguing that in melancholia the object is neither lost nor appropriated (p. 27).

18Stanley W. Jackson, *Melancholia and Depression from Hippocratic Times to Modern Times* (New Haven: Yale University Press, 1986), esp. pp. 99–103.

19See Aristotle, *Problems* 30, in *The Complete Works,* ed. Jonathan Barnes (Princeton: Princeton University Press, 1984), 2: 953a–57a.

divine gift."[20] To the extent that his interpretation of the Aristotelian category of melancholy aligned it with the Platonic notion of divine frenzy, it permitted the reencoding of melancholy by situating its "impairment" as creative power.[21] Underscoring the view that the melancholic's depression stemmed from a nostalgia for the lost sphere of the heavens, Ficino added other great men to Aristotle's list but insisted most especially on the man of letters[22]: "Of all scholars, those devoted to the study of philosophy are most bothered by black bile, because their minds get separated from their bodies and from bodily things. They become so preoccupied with incorporeal things, because their work is so much more difficult and the mind requires an even stronger will. To the extent that they join the mind to bodiless truth, they are

[20] *The Letters of Marsilio Ficino,* trans. members of the Language Department of the School of Economic Science, London (London: Shepard-Walwyn, 1978; rpt., New York: Gingko Press, 1985), 2: 33–34. See also Klibansky, Panofsky, and Saxl, *Saturn and Melancholy,* esp. pp. 254–74. Another source that traces the historical influences of classical texts on Renaissance notions of madness and melancholy and their promulgation through Ficino's rereading of Plato and Aristotle in his *De Vita Triplici* is Rudolf and Marge Wittkower, *Born under Saturn: The Character and Conduct of Artists: A Documented History from Antiquity to the French Revolution* (New York: Random House, 1963). Other useful studies are Ioan Couliano, *Eros and Magic in the Renaissance,* trans. Margaret Cook (Chicago: University of Chicago Press, 1987), esp. pp. 42–52; Agamben, *Stanze,* pp. 1–43.

[21] While Plato did not deal with the melancholic humor as a positive virtue per se, he did manifestly influence Ficino. To see this, one need only read Plato's discussion of the four types of madness in the *Phaedrus.* The last type of madness, the amatory, which according to Plato is also the highest, derives from passionate souls whose friendship ought to be sought over more sane ones: "This kind of madness is a gift of the gods, fraught with highest bliss." See *The Collected Dialogues,* ed. Edith Hamilton and Huntington Cairns, trans. R. Hackforth (New York: Random House, 1961), 245 b, c. For Marsilio Ficino's discussion of poetic madness, see his *Commentarium in Phaedrum,* in *Marsilio Ficino and the Phaedran Charioteer,* ed. and trans. Michael J. B. Allen (Berkeley: University of California Press, 1981), pp. 65–129. The most pertinent passages are found in chap. 4, "De furore poetico ceterisque furoribus et eorum ordine, coniunctione, utilitate," pp. 83–87. Also see Paul Oskar Kristeller, *The Philosophy of Marsilio Ficino* (New York: Columbia University Press, 1943), esp. pp. 211–14, where Kristeller explicitly discusses the paradoxical condition of Ficino's doctrine on melancholy. For a discussion of Ficino's Platonism, see Michael J. B. Allen, *The Platonism of Marsilio Ficino* (Berkeley: University of California Press, 1984).

[22] See Marsilio Ficino, *De Vita Triplici,* trans. Charles Boer (Dallas: Spring Publications, 1980), esp. pp. 6–11; also see Marsilio Ficino, *Commentary on Plato's Symposium on Love,* trans. Sears Jayne (Dallas: Spring Publications, 1985), for his views on the relationship between love, madness, and melancholy, which is found in its most noble form in Socrates (Speech 6). Also see Agamben, *Stanze,* p. 21, who situates a pathological eros and melancholy in Ficino's *De Amore.*

forced to separate it from the body. Body for these people never returns except as a half-soul and a melancholy one."[23]

Not only did Ficino cast the melancholic situation in terms of an attempt to reconnect body and soul (or in modern, psychoanalytic terms, the lost object and the ego), but he also by the same token conditioned the way in which depression and feelings of disempowerment could become reencoded as a special virtue for the literati, that is, for the men of genius. Depression for "qualified" men became a sign of spiritual greatness, which in turn empowered such men to capitalize on difference by making of that difference a difference that counts. The *Homo melancholicus* might be seen as mad; but a blessed lack or holy curse signifying proximity to God granted him cultural and literary legitimacy. The "victim" of such a malady was thus able to identify his illness as a gift of inspiration. In other words, depression became translated into a virtue for the atrabilious man of letters. And it is significant that melancholia—at least this form of it—became an elite "illness" which afflicted men precisely as the sign of their exceptionality, as the inscription of genius within them. Out of its distress the masculine ego is preserved and even affirmed through literary and cultural production. Thus, as early as Ficino and as late as Freud, melancholia appears as a specific cultural form for male creativity, one whose narrative turned the experience of disempowerment into a representational artifact.[24]

---

[23]Ficino, *De Vita Triplici*, p. 7.

[24]Cf. Burton, *Anatomy of Melancholy*, who, in the chapter entitled "Symptoms of Women's Melancholy," writes: "Many of them cannot tell how to express themselves in words, or how it holds them, what ails them, you cannot understand them, or well tell what to make of their sayings; so far gone sometimes, so stupefied and distracted, they think themselves bewitched, they are in despair" (p. 48). This particular view of women as less articulate than men in describing the source of their distress rejoins my analysis and critique of melancholia as a gendered "illness." While, of course, both women and men *can* be depressed, a certain discourse of melancholia has historically been linked with a topos of expressibility and has accordingly given to men a means to express their sorrows in a less alienated way. Luce Irigaray, in *Speculum of the Other Woman,* trans. Gillian C. Gill (Ithaca: Cornell University Press, 1985), argues that "the economy and frailty of the girl's or woman's ego make it impossible for the melancholic syndrome to establish a firm and dominant foundation" (p. 71). According to Irigaray, this is particularly so because for the girl or woman there is no adequate access to a "signifying economy, to the coining of signifiers" by which she could represent herself, and she is therefore excluded in her desire for origin (p. 71). In distinction to Irigaray's premise, Kaja Silverman, *The Acoustic Mirror: The Female Voice in Psychoanalysis and Cinema* (Bloomington: Indiana University Press, 1988), makes a case for female melancholia as taking place at the onset of the castration complex in women (see esp. pp. 154–59). My

Freud's long-range indebtedness in "Mourning and Melancholia" to the tradition inaugurated by Ficino is evidenced by his attributing to the melancholic a moral—hence superior—quality, but his indebtedness is more manifestly mediated by that other avatar of Renaissance melancholia, the character of Hamlet. Among others, the figure of Hamlet falls squarely within this Ficinian tradition, a tradition that is to be understood as an ethos of suffering, and that points to the (male) subject's difficult—and extraordinary—encounter with the "martyrdom" associated with "true greatness": "[The melancholic] has a *keener eye for the truth* than others who are not melancholic. . . . For there can be no doubt that if anyone holds and expresses to others an opinion of himself such as this (an opinion which Hamlet held both of himself and of everyone else), he is ill, whether he is speaking the truth or whether he is being more or less unfair to himself" (emphasis mine).[25] Freud in his analysis is pleased to uncover something virtuous and exceptional in Hamlet, whose illness makes of him a speaker of truths and a visionary. In other words, Hamlet's melancholic humor elevates him above ordinary men—as in Ficino's model. It is what we could call an *accredited pathology,* justified by the heightened sense of conscience which the melancholic putatively or ostentatiously displays: "Dissatisfaction with the ego on moral grounds is the most outstanding feature."[26]

Freud further posits *within* the individual psyche of the melancholic a structure of dominance and disempowerment: "We see how in him one part of the ego sets itself over against the other, *judges it critically,* and as it were, *takes it as its object.* . . . What we are here becoming acquainted with is the agency commonly called 'conscience' " (emphasis mine).[27] Here, the critical agency of the moralizing conscience functions in terms of an objectification, which positions a superior moral side of the psyche over and against a lesser "immoral" one. As Freud says later in

---

intention, however, is not to set up some polarity within this model, between male and female melancholia, nor to argue the existence of male melancholia as precluding the possibility of female melancholics. My intention, rather, is to show how the *discourse* of melancholia legitimates that neurosis as culturally acceptable for particular men, whose eros is then defined in terms of a literary production based on the appropriation of a sense of lack, while the possibility of such appropriation is denied women.

[25]Freud, "Mourning and Melancholia," p. 246. As Jacqueline Rose points out, "The relationship of psychoanalysis to Hamlet has in fact always been a strange and repetitive one in which Hamlet the character is constantly given the status of a truth, and becomes a pivot for psychoanalysis and its project." Jacqueline Rose, *Sexuality in the Field of Vision* (London: Verso, 1986), p. 133.

[26]Freud, "Mourning and Melancholia," p. 248.

[27]Ibid., p. 247.

his essay, "The ego may enjoy in this the satisfaction of knowing itself as the better of the two, as superior to the object."[28]

My feminist suspicion that this object judged by a "superior" and "moral" instance is situated in the same way as woman in classic phallocentrism (that is, as a devalued object, as abject and at fault) is corroborated if we look again at the Renaissance text of Hamlet, and especially at the role given the female figures in it. While the gloomy prince continually desires the attentive gaze of others, the women in the play (Gertrude and Ophelia) are the persistent objects of his aggression and derision. In fact, Hamlet's brooding mourning has been situated by psychoanalytic readers within an Oedipal structure whereby the feminine is both desired and devalued. Thus, Hamlet's melancholia points to an overinvested tie to his mother, Gertrude, which is certainly not her fault nor that of any other woman.[29] Spurned and ridiculed, Gertrude and Ophelia lose all, even their lives. Yet, it is the question of Hamlet's sense of lack that makes Shakespeare's tragedy so compelling for male subjectivity: Hamlet underscores the possibility for men to display loss, thus encoding a gendered bias within the melancholic syndrome. Concomitantly, the women's losses are delegitimated or made to seem insignificant by men's melancholic display of loss.[30]

---

[28]Ibid., p. 257. While Freud is arguing at this point in terms of a cure for the melancholic that would entail a mental separation from the incorporated object of loss, the subject at that moment still remains locked in a polarized conflict between the ego and an object that it seeks to dominate.

[29]As Jacqueline Rose astutely remarks: "The fact that Hamlet constantly unleashes an anxiety which returns to the question of femininity tells us above all something about the relationship of aesthetic form and sexual difference, about the fantasies they share— fantasies of coherence and identity in which the woman appears repeatedly as both wager and threat. . . . The problem of the regulation of subjectivity, of Oedipal drama and the ordering of language and literary form—is not, to put it at its most simple, the woman's fault." Rose, Sexuality in the Field of Vision, p. 139; emphasis mine.

[30]See Elaine Showalter, "Representing Ophelia: Women, Madness, and the Responsibilities of Feminist Criticism," in Shakespeare and the Question of Theory, ed. Patricia Parker and Geoffrey Hartman (New York: Methuen, 1985), pp. 77–105. In addressing the question of how Ophelia has been historically represented, Showalter remarks that the Elizabethans would have diagnosed Ophelia's behavior as a "female love-melancholy, or erotomania," which needs to be contrasted with that other type of melancholy for which "Hamlet himself is a prototype" and "hero." One could, however, easily say that Hamlet too suffers from some type of lovesickness, as many psychoanalytic critics have argued. I think what needs to be underscored here is that, as Showalter has suggested, "the epidemic of melancholy associated with intellectual and imaginative genius curiously bypassed women," and "women's melancholy was seen instead as biological and emotional in origin" (p. 81). Also see Jacques Lacan, "Desire and the Interpretation of Desire in Hamlet," trans. James Hubbert, in Literature and Psycho-

In Freud's "Mourning and Melancholia," it is striking that the only named subject of melancholia is Hamlet. The other examples Freud provides are mere *types* of women such as the deserted bride or the self-deprecating wife, suggesting that, for Freud, Hamlet's pathology exceeds mere depression.[31] In Hamlet there is a claim to a status beyond the commonplace. This notion of a privileged lack functions to produce a specifically male-oriented subjectivity which invests its eros by appropriating the putative lack of some other, in particular, by appropriating the feminine. (By "feminine" here I mean not some essence of woman but the social constitution of her by and within patriarchal culture as the traditional object of desire.)[32] In other words, the polarization mirrored in the Freudian model places the melancholic subject—say, Hamlet—in a privileged position vis-à-vis the feminine. The critical function of the moralizing conscience, split as it is, is symbolically defined in terms of its power to reduce an other to control its difference, but then the moralizing conscience becomes dependent on that now delegitimated "inferior" other in order to eroticize its own subject position by bemoaning its fate. That unnamed, feminized, objectified, inferior other is the condition for the morally superior, male subject of melancholia, the grandeur of whose name is a function of his expressive self-criticism—that is, criticism of that devalued other. Yet this conscience which both Ficino and Freud attribute to the *Homo melancholicus* is dialectically aggravated through the ego's warring over the object of loss such that it is the loss itself that becomes the dominant feature and not the lost object.[33]

---

analysis. Lacan rereads Freud's "Mourning and Melancholia" in terms of Hamlet's lack of proper mourning, but he too (like Freud) situates the feminine as the object of a judgmental male gaze in his discussion of the relation between Hamlet and Ophelia.

[31]Freud, "Mourning and Melancholia," pp. 245, 248.

[32]Joan Kelly, in *Women, History, and Theory: The Essays of Joan Kelly* (Chicago: University of Chicago Press, 1984), has remarked that "femininity" can be understood "as an internalization of inscribed inferiority" (p. 6). To speak about women in this way is to understand the position of inferiority *as socially determined* while, at the same time, arguing the need for women to be self-defined: "In short, women have to be defined as women. We are the social opposite, not of class, or caste, or a majority, since we are a majority, but of a sex: men. We are a sex, and categorization by gender no longer implies a mothering role and subordination to men, except as a social role and relation recognized as such, as socially constructed and socially imposed" (p. 6). Femininity is in itself a problematic concept which indeed can be reduced to the fact of sexual difference, at the same time that "femininity" designates the kind of subject position imposed on women under patriarchy.

[33]The question that begs to be asked is: to what degree does the psychoanalytic analysis of melancholia remain within a Ficinian tradition? I will treat this issue in a book-

Melancholia thus appears as a gendered form of ethos based on or empowered by a sense of lack; at the same time, it finds its source of empowerment in the *derealization* of the historical reality of women's disempowerment and of the ritual function that has traditionally been theirs in the West: that of mourning.[34] That is, the ideology of melancholia appropriates from women's subjectivities their "real" sense of loss and, in Lacanian terms, recuperates that loss, whose sense both philosopher (Ficino) and psychoanalyst (Freud) attribute to moral superiority, for the dominating function of the Symbolic. In turn, that recuperation legitimates the male in his "excessive" suffering, even in his appropriation of the so-called feminine position (but wherein women remain the oppressed and even nameless other).[35] Even if sexual difference is questioned within the melancholic subject, any ambiguity of gender turns out to be recuperated by male power as moral conscience, artistic creativity, or heightened sensitivity, and the melancholic thus remains situated both in reaction to and in complicity with

---

length study I am writing, "The Gendering of Melancholia: Feminism, Psychoanalysis and the Symbolics of Loss in Renaissance Literature."

[34]Diane Owen Hughes, "'Invisible Madonnas?' The Italian Historiographical Tradition and the Women of Medieval Italy," in *Women in Medieval History and Historiography,* ed. Susan Mosher Stuard (Philadelphia: University of Pennsylvania Press, 1987), pp. 25–57, has shown how a feminine symbolic became obviated by a masculine one: "the ordering of the commune, an exclusively male corporation whose earliest laws not only excluded women from membership but also sought to limit their dominance in the private sphere, restricting those marriage festivities, mourning ceremonies, and birth celebrations that had accorded women a central role" (p. 31); also see Sharon Strocchia's essay in this volume.

[35]Such a male appropriation of a *male* representation of women, which then doubly excludes women, can be seen in Ficino: "To achieve poetic madness (the madness that may instruct men in divine ways and sing the divine mysteries), the soul of the future poet must be so affected as to become almost *tender* and *soft* and *untouched* too. The poet's province is very wide, and his material is varied; so his soul (which can be formed very easily) must subject itself to God. This is what we mean by being 'soft' and 'tender.' If the soul has received alien forms or blemishes because of its ability to be formed so easily, then it cannot be formed in the meantime by the divine forms; and this is why Socrates added that the soul must be completely 'untouched,' that is, unblemished and clean." *Commentarium in Phaedrum,* in Allen, *Marsilio Ficino and the Phaedran Charioteer,* p. 82. A very interesting reversal of this notion, wherein women are seen to be that which "corrupts," but which nevertheless betrays a similarity with Ficino's appropriation of "femininity," is described by Freud in reference to critical appraisals of the Mona Lisa: "the most perfect representation of the contrasts which dominate the erotic life of women; the contrast between reserve and seduction, and between the most devoted tenderness and a sensuality that is ruthlessly demanding—consuming men as if they were alien beings." "Leonardo da Vinci and a Memory of his Childhood," in *Standard Edition* 11:108. On this passage, also see Rose, *Sexuality,* p. 127.

patriarchy. Women, by contrast, become dehistoricized by being the mere object of patriarchal desire. The historical and political reality of women in such a scheme remains obfuscated by their absorption into discourses that superimpose a transcendental lack over women's own losses. The superiority of the *Homo melancholicus* thus lies in his privileged understanding and in the exceptional marginalization or alienation which gives him cultural legitimacy.[36]

Given the preceding realignment and revision of Freud in terms of the Renaissance ethos of melancholia, and the possibility provided by the simultaneous reading of psychoanalytic and Renaissance texts for a feminist critique of the discourse of melancholia, I would like to analyze the gendered construction of the melancholic artist as a privileged subjectivity, less abstractly perhaps, in the following pages through the contrastive examples offered by the relatively unknown *canzone* written by Isabella di Morra, "Poscia che al bel desire hai troncate l'ale," and Torquato Tasso's famous "Canzone al Metauro."[37]

---

[36]In his book *Disease and Representation: Images of Illness from Madness to AIDS* (Ithaca: Cornell University Press, 1988), Sander L. Gilman asks why melancholics in medieval and Renaissance icons are often women: "The superficial reason is grammatical: melancholia is a feminine noun. . . . The female is perceived as being especially prone to exaggeration of emotional states; thus she becomes the icon of melancholia" (p. 19). Yet this characterization of femaleness is, I would suggest, itself appropriated from discourses which relegate a hypersensitivity and thus a hyperexclusivity to the exceptional *male* artist, poet, philosopher and so on. Gilman convincingly argues that "the social status of 'love sickness' shifts from the nobleman to the woman, from the top of the social ladder to its bottom" (p. 100). I hasten to add, however, that the notion of lovesickness does not so easily slide from top to bottom; otherwise there would be no Tasso, no Hamlet, no Nerval, no Baudelaire. I suggest instead that the modeling of melancholia privileges a certain type of self that represents itself as lacking. This lack legitimates a literary production grounded on the notion of the exceptional man of letters whose "feminizing" illness is culturally empowering, thereby excluding women from this "higher" form and reducing woman's "depression" to nothing more than a clinical illness. For one example of such a prevalent stereotyping of melancholia into higher and lower forms, see Julia Kristeva, *Soleil noir: Dépression et mélancolie* (Paris: Gallimard, 1987). In chapter 3, "Figures de la dépression féminine," Kristeva presents us with clinical examples of depression, all of whom are women. In the following four chapters, however, we read of the "great" representors of melancholia: Holbein, Nerval, Dostoyevski. All are men and all are artists. Kristeva does, however, conclude her book with a chapter on Duras. The strategies and compromises involved in this exceptional representation of a female melancholic obviously remain to be analyzed.

[37]My source for Isabella di Morra's *canzone* is *Poesia italiana del Cinquecento,* ed. Giulio Ferroni (Milan: Garzanti, 1978), pp. 250–52. For Torquato Tasso's "Canzone al Metauro," see Torquato Tasso, *Poesie,* ed. Francesco Flora (Milan: Ricciardi, 1952), pp. 813–18. All further references to these poems will be cited in the text. The translations of

Isabella di Morra, born in 1520, was the daughter of Giovanni Michele di Morra of Favale, who was forced to leave the kingdom of Naples after he had sided with the king of France against Charles V of Spain. He lost all his rights in the kingdom of Naples and went to live in France. Isabella was kept like a prisoner by her brothers in their castle of Favale; she wrote her poem sometime during this period. She was murdered by her brothers in 1546, after they had discovered that she was having an affair with a certain Don Diego Sandoval De Castro, whom they also murdered.[38]

Isabella di Morra's biography is interesting not only for our understanding of the context of her poem, but also for the unexpected parallels with Tasso's fate as textualized in his "Canzone al Metauro," written in 1578. Like Isabella di Morra, Tasso wrote his poem in a state of exile and isolation. But Tasso's poem was written during one of his *self*-imposed exiles from Ferrara, one year prior to his imprisonment in Sant'Anna. The poem recalls Tasso's youth, when his father, Bernardo, had also been obliged to leave the kingdom of Naples for having sided with the French against Charles V. Eventually following his father into exile, Tasso left his mother, Porzia, in Naples, where she, like Isabella, was kept a prisoner by her brothers and may have been subsequently murdered by them. In fact, Bernardo Tasso believed that Porzia's brothers had killed her in order to keep her dowry for themselves.[39]

Tasso are my own; translations of Isabella di Morra, with some modifications, are from *The Defiant Muse: Italian Feminist Poems from the Middle Ages to the Present*, ed. Beverly Allen, Muriel Kittel, and Keala Jane Jewell (New York: Feminist Press, 1986), pp. 10–14.

[38]See Ferroni, *Poesia italiana del Cinquecento*, p. 249; Giovanni Caserta, *Isabella Morra e la società meridionale del Cinquecento* (Matera: META, 1976); Benedetto Croce, *Isabella di Morra e Diego Sandoval de Castro* (Bari: Laterza, 1929).

[39]For a detailed account of this crisis, see Angelo Solerti, *Vita di Torquato Tasso* (Turin: Ermanno Loescher, 1895), 1, chap. 1. See also Margaret W. Ferguson, "Torquato Tasso: The Trial of Conscience," in *Trials of Desire: Renaissance Defenses of Poetry* (New Haven: Yale University Press, 1983), pp. 54–136. Ferguson gives an excellent psychoanalytic reading of the Oedipal crisis which runs like a leitmotif throughout Tasso's life and in his major works. Among critics who have discussed the "Canzone al Metauro," see especially Ferguson, pp. 74–77; Antonio Daniele, *Capitoli tassiani* (Padua: Antenore, 1983); Karlheinz Stierle, "Episches und lyrisches Pathos: Torquato Tassos *Canzone al Metauro*," in *Interpretation: Das Paradigma der Europäischen Renaissance-Literatur: Festschrift für Alfred Noyer-Weidner zum 60 Geburtstag*, eds. Klaus W. Hempfer and Gerhard Regn (Wiesbaden: Franz Steiner, 1983); Lynn Enterline, "Armida's Lap, Erminia's Tears: In the Wake of Paternity and Figuration in Tasso's *Gerusalemme Liberata*," paper presented at the colloquium "Refiguring Woman: Gender Studies and the Italian Renaissance," Cornell University, April 8–9, 1988.

A cruel Fortune casts her unhappy spell in both poems. "Poscia che al bel desire hai troncate l'ale," composed of six stanzas of eleven lines each and a valediction of five lines, is addressed to "cruel Fortune" ("crudel Fortuna" [2]), who is identified as the source of all the poet's pain. The poet continues: "Così, a disciolta briglia / seguitata m'hai sempre, empia Fortuna, / comminciando dal latte e de la cuna" ("Thus with loosened reins / oh pitiless Fortune / have you always pursued me / beginning from mother's milk and from the cradle" [20–22]). She is "qui posta da ciascuno in cieco oblio" ("Placed here by everyone in blind forgetfulness" [11]). The terrible irony of that phrase is compounded and emblematized by the effective oblivion into which Isabella's poem had fallen, at least until recently. Even though her poem was published in an anthology in 1556 in Venice, it was not until Benedetto Croce rediscovered her in 1929 that some attention has been given to it.[40] She had been, therefore, lost to the world, unheard and unread.

Fortune has drawn the poet from her beloved father, the only person who could restore her to her "proprio stato" (own state or proper state [34]), the only person who could rescue her from oblivion and restore her to a place within the social framework from which she might be seen and perhaps heard. Indeed it is a community that Isabella di Morra desires. She tells Fortune, "Se nodrita già, fossi in cittade, / avresti tu più biasmo, io più pietade" ("if I had been nurtured in the city, / you would have more blame and I more pity" [54–55]). But in the community in which the poet finds herself—among people she calls "gente irrazional, priva d'ingegno" ("irrational people, deprived of intelligence" [8]), presumably her brothers and, in general, the inhabitants of the Basilicata—the poet has no voice. She also remains unheard by the king of France, the "gran Re" ("great king" [71]), as well as by the man whom she calls "Cesar," a title she uses negatively for Charles V, whom the pope had proclaimed as an heir to Augustus Caesar and Charlemagne. This new Caesar becomes the interdictive power who does not allow her father to help her: "Cesar gli vieta il poter darmi aita: / o cosa non più udita, / privar il padre di giovar la figlia!"

---

[40]I would like to thank Rinaldina Russell for bringing to my attention earlier anthologies which included poems by Isabella di Morra: *Rime di diversi signori napoletani e d'altri: Libro settimo* (Venice: Giolito de' Ferrari, 1556), and *Rime diverse d'alcune nobilissime e virtuosissime donne* (Lucca: Busdrago, 1559). The similarity of the two poems leads one to suspect that Tasso had read her poem, especially if one considers that Tasso's library was well stocked, and he certainly must have been familiar with the two anthologies in which her work appeared.

("Caesar forbids him to help me: / o thing never before heard, / to deprive the father of means to help his daughter!" [17–19]). The multiplication of addressees—Fortune, the king of France, the inhabitants of the Basilicata, her father, and Charles V—would inspire one to believe that a viable community exists that would recognize the poet's grief. Yet her "interno male" ("inner ill" [5]) speaks of the forced suppression of her victimization which, by virtue of her being a woman, denies her entry into the world of symbolic exchange as a viable contender for a voice of grief. Her "interno male" libidinally expresses the impossibility of her social determination; that is, relations of power exist without her while they exercise their dominance over her.

Torquato Tasso's "Canzone al Metauro," an unfinished sixty-line poem in three stanzas, also attacks Fortune. Tasso says, "Me dal sen de la madre empia fortuna / pargoletto divelse" ("Me from mother's breast impious Fortune / a child divided" [30–31]), and insists on Fortune's persecution of him since the time of his birth: "Ohimè! dal di che pria / trassi l'aure vitali e i lumi appersi / in questa luce a me non mai serena, / fui de l'ingiusta e ria / trastullo e segno" ("Alas! From the day that I first / drew in the vital air and opened my eyes / in this light to me never serene, / I was the plaything and sign / of unjust and evil [Fortune]" [21–24]). Fortune is in direct conflict with the poet's ego: the *me* that begins his line of woeful separation from the mother. What is at stake is *his own* persecution, *his own* loss of the mother. And instead of *his* mother, Tasso speaks of *the* mother, turning her into the abstract principle of his loss. That loss is loudly heard and displayed, not only in the fiction of the poem but also throughout the history of Tasso's work.

While Tasso mourns the loss of his mother as *his* loss, as the loss he experiences of her love, Isabella di Morra mourns the loss suffered *by* her mother—a mother whom she identifies as "misera madre" ("unhappy mother" [57])—and for the loss suffered by a father who is denied the means of helping his daughter. Both poems raise a pressing question: Whose loss is it?

For Isabella, the lament frames the scenario within which—as well as through which—she is excluded and forgotten. The psychic economy of loss can be seen in the exclamation "o cosa non più udita! privar il padre di giovar la figlia." Loss is everywhere, but none of it is hers to claim. She can only lament her condition of disempowerment. Her loss is dependent on her father's power; she sees her loss to be his. As she situates loss elsewhere, she demarcates the way in which her psyche is implicated in the Other as the negative space of loss. Her psychic position must be read in terms of her social position, in terms of the Other's (patriarchal) power. Both her psychic and social realities clearly demarcate the relations between dominance and forced submission which she, from her dislocated place, articulates and which paradoxically allow us to read what is at stake in her lament: the economy of gain and loss whose vectors cannot be determined except from without. It is her father's loss; it is the gain of Charles V and the king of France. (I might add here parenthetically that even her father had not lost; we know from her biographers that he went to live happily ever after in Paris with a good pension, but wholly uninterested in Isabella's fate.)[41]

After the poet's initial address to Fortune, she writes: "Dirò con questo stil ruvido e frale / *alcuna parte* del interno male / causato sol da te" ("I will tell in this crude and weak style / *some part* of the internal ill / caused by you alone" [4–6; emphasis mine]). Her "internal ill" can remain privatized only to the extent that her voice, her text, has no public arena. Her text thus cannot be externalized, or "published," as an artifact of the self. It cannot be externalized as such because the speaking and writing subject is female; were she actually in a public arena (that is, a court), she would still have another signifying economy than would a male court poet.[42] As if to exacerbate the poet's exclusion from the public sphere, she says that she can tell only "*some part*" of this "internal ill." The lack of further qualification or explication renders the poet's statement extremely complex: she may be suggesting that her pain is so great that it could never be fully described, or that there is no social space within which her lament could be heard, or she may also be suggesting that the language available to her is itself insufficient to communicate such pain.[43] Perhaps it is also her ability to extend her sorrow to include others that makes her pain seem only *partially* representable.

Di Morra says: "Qui, non provo io di donna il proprio stato"

---

[41]Caserta, *Isabella Morra.*

[42]Furthermore, there is a subtext here which suggests that to attempt to represent her loss would be impossible since by virtue of her being a woman, and both literally and psychologically locked away, she remains subject to what Lyotard refers as the *différend,* as "that something [which] asks to be put into phrases, and suffers from the injustice of not being able instantly to be put into phrases." Jean-François Lyotard, "The *Différend,* the Referent, and the Proper Name," trans. Georges Van Den Abbeele, *diacritics* 14 (Fall 1984): 7.

[43]See Elaine Scarry, *The Body in Pain: The Making and Unmaking of the World* (New York: Oxford University Press, 1985).

("Here, woman's rightful place I do not experience" [34]). Her father's return would restore her to her "proper station," where, we may assume, Isabella di Morra would reclaim the dowry she needed to marry. This would allow her to reclaim as well her own proper state ("proprio stato"). This proper and independent state, however, is neither, since it depends on her positioning by and within a patriarchal order. There a woman might function merely as an object of exchange whose value is crudely measured by the monetary value of her dowry. Her "proprio stato," far from being some state proper to her, might be no more than capital for male investment. Or rather, since she desires to attain a position that is by virtue of its construction already prefigured as lacking the full autonomy of male selfhood, her desire becomes inconsequential. In other words, the expression of her "inner ill" cannot surface from the suppression and reclusion she finds herself in, and her social as well as discursive disempowerment would remain, whether or not patriarchy reinstates her in her "proprio stato," precisely because it is patriarchy that decides.

Yet we could also argue that the "proprio stato" refers less to the poet's symbolic role within society than to her libidinal position as a desiring subject (as an object of desire, and even as one desiring to be desired). She writes, "Tutta ho passato qui cieca ed inferma, / senza saper mai pregio di beltade" ("Blind and infirm, I have spent all [my youth] here, / without ever knowing praise of beauty" [25–26]). Thus, for her, her subjectivity would be constructed over and beyond the comprehension of herself as an object of desire, through knowing praise for her beauty. A certain narcissism is at stake, but it is a narcissism, as we shall see, decidedly different from that of a poet such as Tasso. Isabella di Morra's narcissism is marked by a desire to return to one of the only "public" spaces available to her—as an object of desire. Such a feminine narcissism is obviously fraught with problems. On the one hand, and from a standard patriarchal position, the poet's narcissistic investment of her own ego cannot fetishize it as the image of autonomous selfhood, since her "proprio stato" designates her within the male world as one who "essentially" lacks. [44] On the other hand, her desire to be desired, to be the *subject* of her own desire—that is, to know the "value" or "praise of beauty" ("pregio di beltade")—works

---

[44]On the notion of feminine narcissism, see Sarah Kofman, *L'énigme de la femme: La femme dans les textes de Freud* (Paris: Galilée, 1980); also, Naomi Schor, "Female Fetishism," in *The Female Body in Western Culture,* ed. Susan Rubin Suleiman (Cambridge, Mass.: Harvard University Press, 1985), pp. 363–72.

against her victimization's being accepted simply as something essential or "natural" to her condition, since this desire does originate from herself. Her desire to know the *value* of her beauty and to hear *praises* of her beauty—"pregio di beltade"—is also a desire to be a referent in others' discourse, to oblige someone else to speak of or to her. Yet, because she has no symbolic *place of her own,* no truly proper *proprio stato,* she cannot ever fully succeed in presenting herself as a desiring subject. The poet's feminine desirability depends on her being the object of another's desire, just as her "feminine" loss is ultimately understood as belonging to an other.

In spite of these oppressive effects of patriarchal law, one can nevertheless argue that Isabella's *canzone* indeed resists patriarchal norms, first, because the text *has been written,* and second, because by positing a plurality of addressees (Fortune, her father, her mother, the inhabitants of the Basilicata, and the embedded addressee of Fortune, the king of France), Isabella's *canzone* refuses to accredit any one male figure as the hierarchical center of phallic dominance. If, as Freud has shown, more than one phallus implies castration,[45] then the multiplicity of subject positions figuratively decenters the phallus from its position as the organizing principle behind the distribution of social roles to the extent that the situation of woman is no longer merely that of *not* being man, of not being in a relation of absolute difference from man, of being the other of man.[46] At the same time, in place of a hierarchy where one father stands for another in a series of substitutions ultimately grounded in some symbolically primal or transcendental Father (such as God or king), we see rather a dispersion of a shifting historical and political ground of differences in gender and even of differences *within* gender differences. The metaphoricity of patriarchal substitution would be impugned by her addressing a community which she would have as different than it indeed is but against the conflation of whose differences she nonetheless inveighs.

The invective in her *canzone* is born of the realization that her predicament is the result of the undifferentiating ignorance of those others who, like her brothers, no doubt see themselves as the immediate representatives of patriarchal law, as unthinking metaphors of the Father, and hence as the invested protectors of the symbolic order, (self)-

---

[45]Freud, "Medusa's Head," in *Standard Edition* 18: 273–74.

[46]For a discussion of such subjectivities constituted—engendered—by a multiple, heterogeneous field, see Teresa de Lauretis, *Technologies of Gender: Essays on Theory, Film, and Fiction* (Bloomington: Indiana University Press, 1987), p. 1 and passim.

empowered to imprison or even murder those who go against that order. Blame here is justly placed on the ignorance of those who cannot understand her, that is, on the empowered:

> S'io mi doglio di te si giustamente,
> per isfogar la mente,
> da chi non son per ignoranza intesa,
> i' son, lassa, *ripresa*.
> [50–54; my emphasis]

> [If I complain of you so justly
> to relieve my mind,
> by those who through ignorance misunderstand me,
> alas, I am *reproved*.]

This moment of understanding can be seen to be where the "real" is situated, that is, where the censorship of the victim occurs even as it is stated. Contradicting the patriarchal norm that defines her in terms of lack, and accused through the ignorance that stands in for the so-called Law (of the Father), her poetic lament questions that law which denies her the space of articulation. The anger in her invective against the ignorance of the powerful thus belies any essentialist victim's discourse, as she follows in the tradition of other women writers of that period, as well as those earlier humanist women, who inveighed against the injustice they suffered from male authority.[47]

---

[47]Although she is truly locked away, her luckier contemporaries were also, but perhaps more subtly, denied access to the public space. One need only think of the treatises of Bruni or even of Castiglione, who, on the one hand, extol women's virtues and their ability to learn, but who, on the other hand, edify the final verdict for women: marriage in order to become the perfect *donna di famiglia* in support of their courtier-husband's social affairs. An argument that needs to be made (and which has been made) is that in the sixteenth century, as the state was being formed as an autonomous entity, women were steadily excluded from the public space and became, as we read in Baldassare Castiglione's *Libro del Cortegiano*, in *Opere di Baldassare Castiglione, Giovanni della Casa, Benvenuto Cellini*, ed. Carlo Cordié (Milan: Ricciardi, 1960), the emblem of the perfect lady, almost a mirror of the courtier (except that she was exempt from arms). The public increasingly became the space for men, and the home, as the locus of the private, the space for women. On this issue so much has been written that I will cite only a few representative sources: Joan Kelly, "Did Women Have a Renaissance?" in her *Women, History, and Theory*, pp. 19–50; Lillian S. Robinson, "Woman under Capitalism: The Renaissance Lady," in *Sex, Class, and Culture* (New York: Methuen, 1978), pp. 150–75; Peter Stallybrass, "Patriarchal Territories: The Body Enclosed," in *Rewriting the Renaissance: The Discourses of Sexual Difference in Early Modern Europe*, ed. Margaret W. Ferguson, Maureen Quilligan, and Nancy J. Vickers (Chicago: University of Chicago

Thematizing, as the texts of those women do, the problematic space of an articulation that constantly risks the fall back into inarticulateness for lack of an accredited locus in the phallocratic order, Isabella's poem mourns a victimization that is political, social, historical—and prosaic. By prosaic I mean that it evokes neither the special status of its poet nor an eroticized poetics of lack as melancholic idyll. This is not to suggest that Isabella di Morra is devoid of eros, for her very desire to know herself as an object of value and beauty is in itself an erotic longing for love and appreciation. But the difference lies in the way in which erotic desire is recuperated. Her desire for poetic expression is not a desire to display (whether critically or uncritically) the melancholic ego of loss but one that desires a community wherein she can be a participant, that desires not a pre-Oedipal indifferentiation but the indefinite exchange of social and discursive differences. The longing for her father is one that looks toward the father for the future, for liberation from her status as abject, rather than nostalgically toward any fixated past. For the father here (both literal and symbolic) is not a space to occupy but simply, for Di Morra, a possibility of self-determination.[48] This is an ambiguous line which women have historically had to cross and re-cross, a line between their imbrication within patriarchal values and their resistance to such determination.

This ambiguity raises again the problematics associated with the voice of melancholia. Unlike Isabella's mournful desire to be heard, the melancholic imagination is legitimated by a cultural mythology empowering male fantasy in terms of a divine illness. The subject of melancholia assumes a place within the symbolic order where the fixation on loss can be converted into a representation of the ego which vies both for and against the father's love. In classic phallocentrism loss is often linked to the maternal and to death, and functions fan-

---

Press, 1986), pp. 123–42; Sarah Kofman, *Le respect des femmes* (Paris: Galilée, 1982); Margaret L. King, "Book-Lined Cells: Women and Humanism in the Early Italian Renaissance," in *Beyond Their Sex: Learned Women of the European Past*, ed. Patricia M. Labalme (New York: New York University Press, 1980), pp. 66–90. On the issue of women's education, see especially Leonardo Bruni, "De studiis et litteris," in *Vittorino da Feltre and Other Humanist Educators*, trans. and ed. William H. Woodward (New York: Bureau of Publications, Teachers College, Columbia University, 1963), pp. 119–33.

[48]It is noteworthy that during the Renaissance a strong bond established itself between young girls and their fathers since it was often the father who took care of his daughter's education (as it was in Isabella's case; see Caserta, *Isabella Morra*). Margaret King has argued that as educated girls became learned women, they were often frustrated in their hope for an extended intellectual *and* public role. As women they inevitably had two choices: to marry, or to take vows. King, "Book-Lined Cells," pp. 66–81.

tasmatically as the expression of desire for a return to something other. For those who see themselves as disempowered, loss is imbued with nostalgia. When articulated from a melancholic "male" position, this loss becomes a pretext for an aesthetic and even political project that continually derealizes the feminine by recasting loss in terms of a golden age, one that I would wager women themselves have never known.

Such an Oedipalized narrative of loss can be found egregiously played out in Tasso's "Canzone al Metauro." As I noted earlier, the poet describes the necessity of having to follow his father, Bernardo, into exile, leaving his mother, Porzia, behind in Naples. The lamenting hero of this narrative is Tasso, the *Me* separated from the mother. He is the one to whom loss and lament are said exclusively to belong: "Or che non sono io tanto / *ricco* de' propri guai che basti solo / Per materia di duolo? / Dunque altri ch'io da me dev' esser pianto?" ("Now am I not so / *rich* of my own woes that I alone suffice / for material of grief? / Therefore, do others by me need to be lamented?" [48–50; my emphasis]). It is the word *ricco* that points here to the differential economics at work in the gendering of melancholic mourning.

In Isabella di Morra the feeling of loss extends beyond her own loss, for she also feels the loss of her mother, and even extends pity to her brothers. It is a loss that remains socialized, aware of others. Although this socialization can be seen as a mere negative result of the cultural conditioning of women, I would rather read it in an ambiguous manner. It might indeed be negative if it were seen to be the only capacity— one overladen with sentimental value—ascribed to women's social roles. But one might also read this social libido as a critical one which makes no claim to a nostalgic collapse of difference.

Even in Tasso's poem the Oedipal is not resolved as the end to a happy story. Although Tasso movingly describes his traumatic separation from the mother in terms of his having to follow his father, the poet can nonetheless assume a significant role in his narrative. In other words, Tasso, unlike Isabella, is able to insert his loss within the Law of the Father. For Tasso, fathers become the addressees who legitimate his position in regard to them, while "the" mother, the fantasm of the symbolic female, is internalized as the muted figure of alienation, lack, and even death. This exiles women as other, and creates of femininity a negative pole.[49] The notion of the "feminine" can easily appear as

---

[49]Rose states: "As the place onto which lack is projected and through which it is simultaneously disavowed, woman is a symptom for the man" (p. 72). Thus, the mother is simply the hidden face of a phallic desire wherein the feminine figures as the

Freud's critical object, which "conscience" judges and against whom it can feel morally superior, since access to the male-dominated symbolic order, to patriarchal subjectivity, is dependent on a split from or renunciation of woman. The notion of the "feminine" thus becomes that in contradistinction to which cultural empowerment can measure itself.

For Isabella, fathers function as representatives of the Law, as "equivalences of subject positions" in whose identity or differences her socially constructed identity is literally, prosaically, at stake.[50] For her, it is not a question of Oedipal narrative, of linearity, but rather of the mere possibility of enunciating. For Tasso, desire is knotted nostalgically to the mother as fantasm; she is evoked not because of her death/murder but because he desires to return to his own birthplace, marked by the tomb of Parthenope. "Sassel la gloriosa alma Sirena / appresso il cui sepolcro ebbi la cuna: / così avuto v'avessi o tomba o fossa / a la prima percossa!" ("The glorious, nurturing siren / near whose sepulcher I had my cradle knows: / If only I had had a tomb or a grave / at the first blow" [27–30]).[51] Tasso's melancholic mourning is focused on the mother, whose own loss is appropriated as if it were his own. He positions his body and his text under the sign of loss, as the sign of the suffering beloved. The libidinal connection between the poet, the mother, and the poet's loss is situated at the nexus between womb and tomb. The mother allows entry into the

---

fearful place of lack and of castration, as "the child's desire for her which does not refer to her but beyond her, to an object, the phallus, whose status is first imaginary (the object presumed to satisfy his desire) and then symbolic (recognition that desire cannot be satisfied)." Rose, *Sexuality in the Field of Vision*, p. 62. In pathological mourning, however, it is precisely the deferral of desire which creates an eros of nostalgia, which becomes the sign of the subject's entrapment in the imaginary. "Woman," or "Mother," figures simply as a fantasmatic object, as a pretext for a transcendent relation to other-worldliness such that the "feminine" becomes a mere idea for phallic organization and does not imply a social relation between subjects.

[50]The phrase "equivalences of subject positions" is borrowed from Ernesto Laclau and Chantal Mouffe, *Hegemony and Socialist Strategy* (London: Verso, 1985), who intend by it "an ambiguity penetrating every relation of equivalence: two terms, to be equivalent, must be different—otherwise, there would be a simple identity. On the other hand, the equivalence exists only through the act of subverting the differential character of those terms" (p. 128).

[51]See Ferguson, *Trials of Desire*, pp. 71–75. Ferguson argues that the siren is an analogue for Tasso's mother in "being a woman deserted and indirectly killed and the epic hero is for Tasso always in some sense guilty of murdering Eros" (p. 75). Certainly eros is murdered to the extent that woman is denied, but is this eros not recuperated in Tasso's poem through the reinscription of his mother's death onto his own eros, that is, as the eros of loss, and the aestheticization of her death?

economics of recuperation, allowing him to relive his losses repeatedly. Continuity is thus foremost localized in the desire to return to some sort of originary state. This originariness is represented through a corporeal tie with the mother: the "knots" that bind him to her: "Ch'io non dovea giunger più volto a volto / fra quelle braccia accolto / con nodi così stretti e sì tenaci. / Lasso! e seguii con mal sicure piante / qual Ascanio o Camilla, il padre errante" ("That I was no longer to reach her face to face / held between those arms / with knots so tight and so tenacious. / Alas! And I followed with insecure footsteps / like Camilla or Ascanius, the wandering father" [36–40]).[52]

Leaving aside the obvious Oedipal crisis, engendered by the "cutting" of the knot in consequence of the father's departure, which also takes away the son, let us look at how this moment becomes the focal point at which the Oedipal narrative is sutured. The "knots" represent a corporeal loss since they are the knots of the mother's embrace; they call attention to the morbidly erotic bond even as they *derealize* the specificity of her loss and victimization. A symbol of permanent lack, she becomes the means through which the poet's "loss" of her is nothing more than a pretext for the aestheticization of loss. Insofar as such an appropriation may indeed produce a discourse based on an ambivalent rivalry with the father, this ambivalence requires recourse to yet *another* discourse, which attempts to reinscribe Oedipal narrative in terms of the poet's own desire to be the exclusive object of the father's love, to be the chosen son. For, in the last stanza of Tasso's *canzone,* it is Tasso's relation to his father that is played out, a father whom he apostrophizes in the final lines: "Padre, o buon padre, che dal ciel rimiri / egro e morto ti piansi, e ben tu il sai, / e gemendo scaldai / la tomba e il letto: or che ne gli alti giri / tu godi, a te si deve onor, non lutto: / a me versato il mio dolor sia tutto" ("Father, oh good father, who looks down from the sky, / I cried for you, weak and dead, and well you know it, / and with moans I warmed / the tomb and bed: now that you in the high circle rejoice, to you is owed honor, not mourning: / let it be enough for me to have poured out all my pain" [55–60]). The unfinished *canzone* ends here, suggesting that the poet's mourning is anything but fully poured out.

---

[52]These knots, *nodi,* serve to sexualize the male ego in terms of his narrative. They eroticize the woman (in Tasso, his mother's death) and therefore derealize the specificity of her loss and victimization. The victim becomes an instance of aesthetic production. See my essay "The Victim's Discourse: Torquato Tasso's *Canzone al Metauro,*" *Stanford Italian Review* 5 (Fall 1985): 189–203.

Certainly this relation is inspired by the melancholic tradition. By appropriating his mother's death as if it were his own loss and victimization, Tasso becomes the Oedipal prince not only of his lyric but also of modern notions of disenfranchised subjectivity. The male subject finds satisfaction in his melancholic voice precisely because this voice incorporates as well as appropriates the dissonances found within patriarchal power relations. Tasso thus becomes the possessor of the voice which expresses both the struggle for dominance and the necessity of submission. Through this voice he is legitimated in *his* rearticulation of *his* victimization through the prestigious position of one who incarnates *the* alienated and creative subject of literary production. Having incorporated his mother's real victimization, he makes it his own by designating himself as the preferred victim of patriarchy; at the same time he continues his Oedipal dialogue with patriarchy by romancing the father and eroticizing those maternal knots. Lack as a place to be "occupied" serves as an efficacious means to bring the prodigal son back into the folds of established procedures. Incorporating the mother's loss thus saves patriarchy for patriarchy.

Tasso's biographer Giambattista Manso, and later Goethe, glorified Tasso as the quintessential heroic model for an alienated genius who suffers from both unrequited love and hostile politics. Countless articles and books have been written on Tasso's poetry. Many of Tasso's critics have been fascinated with his language and metaphor, often remarking on the prevalent erotic feeling that his work evokes. He has been romanticized as the melancholic *per eccellenza* of the late Renaissance, as one who embodies the poetic spirit of alienation and disempowerment, whose suffering modeled an eros of lack: melancholia. Few have raised the question of what there is in his work that privileges lack as the motivation of eros.[53] The cultural acquisition of loss for

[53]Critics who have dealt with Tasso's compulsion to privilege lack include Mario Fusco, "La question des obstacles dans la *Jérusalem délivrée*," *Les langues neo-Latines* 248 (1984): 55–76; and N. Jonard, "L'érotisme dans le *Jérusalem délivrée*," *Bergomum: Bollettino della Civica Biblioteca di Bergamo* 78:3–4 (1984): 43–62. On the relation between melancholia and loss in Tasso, see Ferguson, *Trials of Desire*, esp. pp. 123–26. In "Clorinda's Fathers" (forthcoming in *Stanford Italian Review*), Marilyn Migiel argues that the price Tancredi must pay for Clorinda's death is perpetual sorrow: "He first considers suicide, turning the guilty hand against himself. But he deems this too merciful, because it would bring his grief to an end. The solution left him is to become a "misero mostro," for this punishment allows him to reenact repeatedly the horrible act of killing Clorinda and simultaneously punish himself for doing so." In Tancredi we thus see the melancholic syndrome at work whereby the murder of Clorinda is recuperated into an eros of lack and loss and whereby the incorporation of this lost object of

individual gain helped to forge a newly arising individual subjectivity and to reencode melancholia as a particular form of male creativity. Not only does this form of exclusive sensitivity build its particular hegemony on notions of loss and lack predicated on the appropriation of the feminine—predicated, that is, on the *derealization* of women's experiences as historical reality—but such loss is also granted a privileged place of recuperation within Western aesthetics when uttered by the disenfranchised male poet. Tasso's discourse of victimization is mediated through the story of women; Porzia's and Isabella di Morra's stories are lived—and forgotten—as historically determined abjection. The stories of these women, like the women themselves, are therefore reduced to the function of the maternal, a position necessarily associated with the abject in classic phallocentrism. Tasso, by appropriating their "position" through an act of pathological mourning, denies, in a sense, *their* historical and sexual difference.

My reading thus suggests that melancholia is not simply a pathological condition of either medical or psychological interest, but a historically specific discursive practice that differentiates along gender lines (or *at least* along gender lines, but perhaps also along those of class, race, and nationality) between those "losses" that are considered significant and those that are not. Furthermore, the "significant" losses of the melancholic are themselves appropriated from what, from *his* standpoint, can only be called insignificant others. Caught in the bind of an expressive inexpressibility, only to have it expressed by others as if it were their own, the latter in their plight point to the suspect quality of Freud's distinction between mourning and melancholia, which implicitly subtends a historical opposition between woman and man, hushed and garrulous, prosaic and poetic. My psychoanalytic reading of some Renaissance texts thus points to a historicization of the Freudian categories and undertakes a revisionist and feminist critique of psychoanalysis while, I hope, demonstrating and advancing the critical rigor and validity of the psychoanalytic approach.

The comparison of the lyric poems by Tasso and Di Morra also serves to illustrate the relationship of women to the canon (at least in the late Italian Renaissance) as their exclusion from it by a melancholic

---

desire is reinscribed as the eros of a gendered pathos which legitimates the melancholic in his excessive suffering. See also Lynn Enterline, "Armida's Lap, Erminia's Tears: In the Wake of Paternity and Figuration in Tasso's *Gerusalemme Liberata,*" who argues that the loss of Tasso's mother is recast into the figure of Armida, who then mourns this loss for him. Tasso thereby situates mourning itself in a precise "feminine" register.

"male" pathos. I would like to stress, however, that this lack of representation is not a mere epistemological gap but a systematic repression that occurs through the nonattribution of value to the text of women's mourning, the denial to it of the *culturally empowered* status of melancholia. This is certainly borne out by one editor of Isabella di Morra's poem, Giulio Ferroni, who makes a double-edged remark: "La fama della poesia della Morra (che nel nostro secolo è stata riscoperta dal Croce) è tutta legata a questa drammatica vicenda biografica; e nei suoi pochi versi si possono ben scorgere le tracce del suo isolamento scolastico, col faticoso tentativo di mettere insieme un linguaggio scolastico, certamente inadatto ad esprimere la tragicità di una condizione senza speranza" ("The fame of Isabella's poetry, which in this century was rediscovered by Croce, is completely tied to the drama of her biographical moment; and in her few verses we are able clearly to discern the traces of her scholastic isolation, with the *tiring attempt* to put together a scholastic language, certainly inadequate to express the tragedy of a condition without hope" [emphasis mine]).[54] The last part of Ferroni's statement is ambiguous. To whom does the "faticoso tentativo" belong? Is this the editor's tiring task, or is it Isabella's because she does not have adequate language available to her to express her isolation? Does the "faticoso tentativo" belong to the "traces of her scholastic isolation," which arise in her verse fragments? Or does this "fatigue" belong to Ferroni, whose unwieldy prose (as the syntax of the sentence would appear to imply) suggests his unwillingness to deal with a marginalized woman.

Ferroni's comment regards the "proper" form in which a dilemma may be articulated before it is or can be legitimated. And he is quick to condemn the inarticulateness of noncanonical authors. Isabella di Morra's marginalization is expressed within a language that is codified as Petrarchan but nonetheless assumes a difference from the Petrarchan register. In Petrarch, language is the means through which the poet determines the register of selfhood and of an ensuing canonization. In Isabella di Morra's *canzone* the Petrarchan register for linguistic expression does not imply for her a reality that accedes to language and culture as an exit from her socially determined position. She is damned if she does and damned if she doesn't.

Ferroni then has a moment of self-reflection when he states that language, though "inadequate," is not what is at stake here but rather the "oppressione che grava su di lei, e da cui essa non può immaginare

---

[54]See Ferroni, *Poesia italiana del Cinquecento*, pp. 249–50.

altra uscita che quella di un mitico ritorno del padre e di una restaurazione della ricchezza e della dignità nobiliare della propria famiglia" ("the oppression that weighs upon her, and from which she cannot imagine any other exit except that of the mythical return of her father and of the restoration of her family wealth and of the noble dignity of her own family").

Despite this act of critical "noblesse oblige," the implicit message becomes quite clear. The canon legitimates certain linguistic practices without ever examining *what* the conditions for linguistic legitimation are (as in, for example, the erotic dimension of Tasso's poetry in contrast to Isabella's "prosaicness"). In the end, our critic's humanist assumptions come to bear even further on Isabella's text when he says: "Il suo pover linguaggio di scolastico petrarchismo non è che l'eco penosa di una prigione sociale ancora più vasta, che sta intorno alla prigione privata in cui ella è rinchiusa: è una conferma ulteriore del fatto che nella società feudale non c'è nessuna via d'uscita" ("Her poor language of scholastic Petrarchism is only the painful echo of an even larger social prison which surrounds the private prison in which she is enclosed: it is a further confirmation of the fact that in feudal society there is no way out"). The critic thus reveals the exclusivist discourse of the canon. When the subject concerns, for example, women's experience of disempowerment, then this experience becomes just a singular event, nameless, everyone's and thus no one's. Her story becomes simply one among many possible others within "feudal" society. In this way Di Morra's experience becomes all too easily neutralized—and forgotten, a mere document for the archives. When the loss is Tasso's, it is elevated to high aesthetic status and becomes analyzed because his loss could also be the loss of other men. He becomes a symbol of the alienated and creative individual; he becomes celebrated; he and his language even become models. Furthermore, the canon, as an instance of patriarchal authority, legitimates itself through an imaginary literary historicity precisely because it does not recognize certain articulations of disempowerment. Thus, a "victim," such as Isabella di Morra, is denied a legitimate voice of pathos and mourning in literary form.

I would like to end by suggesting that Isabella's *canzone* is interesting not only because it allows us to expose the legitimating power behind melancholic texts but also because her lament offers a strategy for feminist criticism. Through Isabella's "prosaic" lament, and through her mourning, we can discern how her experience charts a different but hopeful space in which one can rethink the diversity of subject positions entailed in the experience of women in its complexity. From her position of extreme marginalization, Isabella di Morra rewrites Petrarchan language, the institutionalized poetic eros of her age. Even if in Renaissance Italy one cannot speak of a feminist movement per se, one needs to recognize that women did appropriate their own subjectivities, thereby refiguring feminine possibilities and thus resisting the structured bias of gender difference within Western patriarchy.[55] To rethink the specificity of Isabella's *canzone* and of her desire for a space in which she could be heard and seen is to rethink a place beyond the Petrarchan, a space not prefigured on lack as a metaphor for the phallic economics of fetishized self-recuperation. Rather, a feminine social space allows one a way to think of lack *not* in terms of a transcendental signifier but in terms of a consciousness of self *and* otherness—that is, in terms of subjects encountering others, in terms of a plurality of addressees and addressors, in terms of a proliferation of social and ethnic differences, all of which makes it possible to think of overturning the very basis of gender, class, and racial hierarchies.

[55]As Teresa de Lauretis has argued, "The specificity of a feminist theory may be sought in that political, theoretical, self-analyzing practice by which the relations of the subject in social reality can be rearticulated from the *historical perspective of women.*" Lauretis, *Alice doesn't: Feminism, Semiotics, Cinema* (Bloomington: Indiana University Press, 1984), p. 186; emphasis mine. I wish to thank Kris Straub and Jann Matlock for their helpful comments on a draft version of this essay.

Ann Rosalind Jones

New Songs for the Swallow:
Ovid's Philomela in
Tullia d'Aragona and Gaspara Stampa

Ovid's *Metamorphoses* provided a complex symbolic order to Renaissance poets, exemplarily to Petrarca, who himself became a source of figures for the poet and the poetic process. Throughout the *Canzoniere,* male divinities and semidivine heroes are invoked as inspirers and practitioners of the lyric: Apollo and Orpheus, Amphion and Linus. When Petrarca invokes feminine characters from Ovid, however, they are most often the objects of masculine desire and mastery: Daphne-Laura, Rome's Lucretia, Medusa.

Women poets, too, confronted the prestigious and multivalent system of figures for power, erotic encounter, and transformation supplied by Renaissance versions of Ovidian metamorphosis. But women's relationships to that system of references were problematic. In Ovid's poem mortals of both sexes are vulnerable to the whims and the punishments of the gods. But in accordance with gender relations in Greece and Rome, and probably in response to Augustus Caesar's attempts to restore what he saw as damaged patriarchal control in aristocratic families, Ovid recorded few instances of feminine challenge to divine power. Mortal women who tell stories that challenge the gods are violently punished: Niobe is petrified for being too proud of her children; Arachne is driven to suicide for her pride in her weaving. And in contrast to the stories of Orpheus and Amphion, there is no story of a woman who is a poet in the sense of a singer, an inventor in the lyric mode.

But Ovid does record two chilling tales of women *deprived* of voice and speech. The first, the wood nymph Echo, can speak only by repeating what has been said to her. This eternal belatedness is the result of a punishment by Juno, angry at having been distracted from discovering Jove's infidelities by Echo's "long conversations" ("longo sermone" [3, 364]). "Speak only when you are spoken to," Juno's curse on Echo signifies. The injunction in this case comes from a female deity, but it was also a message constantly repeated by men writing to women in early modern Europe. Orazio Lombardelli, the author of *Dell'uffizio della donna maritata* (written in Florence in 1574), advises his young wife that her duty is to speak as he speaks, to imitate and affirm his states of mind: "Sì come dunque uno specchio è cattivo che una imagine allegra fa parer mestre e una dolente dimostra baldanzosa e festevole; così non è savia quella donna, che essendo il marito mal contento, se ne passa ridente, e essendo allegro sta malincolica" ("Just as a mirror is bad if it makes a joyous image seem woeful and shows a mournful one as cheerful and festive, a woman is not good who, when her husband is unhappy, ignores him, laughing, and when he is gay, remains melancholy").[1] The mirror topos is shifted from a visual into an aural logic in a contemporary English conduct book by Robert Cleaver, *A Godly Forme of Household Government* (London, 1588): "As the echo answereth but one word for many, which are spoken to her, so a Maid's answer should be in a single word."[2] Such brevity is exemplified in Ovid's Echo, who, falling in love with Narcissus but rejected by the boy, who loves no one, wastes away to a bodiless voice able to repeat only the ends of his sentences. This transformation actually gives Echo a certain limited ability to revise Narcissus' speeches; for example, when he says, "I would die before I would give you power over me," she replies, "I would give you power over me" (3, 391–92). But this maneuver of fragmentary citation is necessitated by the male power that structures the episode, which opens with Echo's silencing as a result of Jove's infidelities and closes with the poet's account of Narcissus' final effect on her: combined erotic and enunciatory famine. Inarticulate because of Jove's loves, unloved because she is inarticulate, she is captured within a masculine language that rejects her.

This narrative must have offered an inhibiting rather than an enabling model of eloquence to women readers, in contrast to Ovid's tales of Amphion and Orpheus, which link musical and poetic power and assign them to male performers. More brutally, a second tale of enforced female silence in the *Metamorphoses* shifts Echo's verbal and

[1]Orazio Lombardelli, *Dell'uffizio della donna maritata* (Florence: Marescotti, 1585), p. 20.
[2]Robert Cleaver, *A Godly Forme of Household Government* (London: Man, 1588), p. 94.

corporeal enfeeblement into a register of cumulative physical violence. In the story of two sisters, Procne and Philomela, rape leads to infanticide and family mayhem and ends in human-to-animal transformation (6, 424–674). The episode begins when Procne marries Tereus, the king of Thrace, and persuades him to bring her sister Philomela for a visit. On their voyage back to Thrace, Tereus rapes Philomela and cuts out her tongue so that she cannot divulge his crime. But she encodes her tale into a tapestry, "skilfully weaving purple signs on a white background" (577), and a servant woman takes this text to Procne. Procne understands the message at once and designs an equally ingenious subterfuge: taking advantage of the festival of Bacchus to leave the palace with her attendants, dressed in the costumes of Bacchantes, she goes to Philomela's prison. She frees her sister and the two return to Tereus' palace, where Procne murders her son Itys and serves his flesh to Tereus at a banquet, in a confrontation that ends with the metamorphosis of all three principal actors into birds. Tereus becomes the hoopoe, whose savagery is emblematized by its fierce warrior's crest; Procne and Philomela become the swallow and the nightingale, singers whose laments signal the coming of spring.

Philomela, then, is both a victim and a survivor, a woman whose tongue is excised but whose hands elaborate a sign system which her sister immediately comprehends; and Procne, as reader-interpreter, becomes the avenger of her sister and a fellow singer who commemorates their fate. The sisters' mutual comprehension leads to the eradication of the husband and the son to whom they would ordinarily owe obedience. Not a pretty story. But more positively than Echo's subversive abridgement of Narcissus' words, this narrative affirms an oblique form of communication, the possibility of a metalinguistic feminine discourse that survives Tereus' attack on one woman's ability to speak and the other's ability to discover her sister's fate.

Whatever modes of semiotic ingenuity are represented in these episodes, their figures of tongue-tied or tongueless femininity could hardly have made the *Metamorphoses* an encouraging model, in any simple way, for women poets. Yet the Ovidian heroines were invoked and reinvoked throughout the poetry of the Renaissance. I want to suggest that Echo and Philomela were read and rewritten differently, that men and women dealt with the anxieties raised by both tales according to contrasting, gender-determined strategies. Male poets displaced the male violence and guilt and the female linguistic loss in both tales into purified pastoral settings and reworked them into occasions for rhetorical virtuosity. Women poets, less defensively, interpreted Echo and

Philomela through processes of empathetic identification, and they rewrote Ovid's tragic transformations into visions of saving feminine alliance and fantasies of freedom. My cases in point are Tullia d'Aragona and Gaspara Stampa, who appropriated the Roman poet's paradigms of feminine reticence as a condition to which a countercondition could be vividly imagined, as a limit to be defiantly transgressed. Resisting contemporary injunctions to silence and modesty, the Cinquecento women poets reworked Ovid's male-voiced ventriloquism and stories of linguistic mutilation for their own ends.

Echoing: Can Repetition Become Resistance?

Ovid's treatment of Echo includes two witty passages in which he plays Echo's short speeches off against Narcissus' longer ones. In addition to her citation of his refusal to give her power over him, which she turns into an offer of power over herself, a second example is her response to the youth's "Here let us come together": she answers, in a seductive abridgement, "Let us come. Together"[3] ("huc coeamus," ait, . . . "coeamus" rettulit Echo [3, 386–87]). The wordplay is designed to provoke amused appreciation for the poet's wit in cutting the opening phrase of the exchange short and giving erotic meaning to its abridged form. This kind of verbal game was picked up in Poliziano's eight-line exchange between Pan and Echo (1498), in which Pan leads the dialogue and Echo responds more briefly: "Che fai tu, Eco, mentr'io ti chiamo?—Amo" (What are you doing, Eco, while I call you?—Loving [another]").[4] The technique appears in an English variation in Barnabe Barnes's *Parthenophil and Parthenophe* (1593) in a question posed by the poet and answered by Echo: "What shall I do to my Nymph when I go to behold her?" "Hold her!"[5]

Another version of echo technique provides the structure for the paired *proposte-risposte* poems written throughout the Cinquecento: the poet adopts the rhyme scheme of an interlocutor to produce a sonnet

[3]The translation is John Hollander's, in *The Figure of Echo: A Mode of Illusion in Milton and After* (Berkeley: University of California Press, 1981), p. 25.

[4]Angelo Poliziano, "Pan ed Eco," in *Opere volgari,* ed. Tommaso Casini (Florence: Sansoni, 1885), p. 139.

[5]Barnabe Barnes, *Parthenophil and Parthenophe* (London, 1593), sestine 4. Quoted by Elbridge Colby, in *The Echo Device in Literature* (New York: New York Public Library, 1920), p. 24. Hollander devotes a full chapter of *The Figure of Echo* to this verbal technique: chap. 3, "Echo Schematic."

using the same end sounds as the poem that initiated the contest. One example is Benedetto Varchi's second collection of *Sonnets* (1555), in which he published a long section of *risposte* demonstrating his skill in imitating the rhymes that fellow poets had addressed to him. Tullia d'Aragona, a courtesan poet who dedicated her *Rime* (Venice, 1547) to the Medici clan, adopted the same answering technique. In her anthology of *carte* written to her by famous men, she too composed *risposte* echoing the rhyme schemes established by her interlocutors.

The figure of Echo was frequently invoked in pastoral poetry, typically as an audience or secretary for the male poet's laments. Sannazaro, for example, in Eclogue 11 of the *Arcadia,* assigns Echo the duty of recording his woes:

> E tu, che fra le selve occolta vivi,
> Eco mesta, rispondi a le parole,
> E quant'io parlo per li tronchi scrivi.
>
> [13–15]⁶

[And you, who live hidden among the forests, grieving Echo, answer to my words, and write whatever I say upon the trunks of the trees.]

Sannazaro's Echo, like Lombardelli's good wife, is represented as a sounding board for the male speaker and, in addition, as a secretary inscribing his oral poetic performance.

Women poets, however, represent Echo as alter ego rather than audience. Luciana Borsetto argues that they understood the figure as an emblem of their own obligatory imitation of Petrarch; she cites Vittoria Colonna's and Chiara Matraini's *centoni* of lines from the *Canzoniere* as cases in point.⁷ Less obediently, not so much imitating Ovid as challenging him, Gaspara Stampa demonstrates a successful process of feminine composition by elaborating an analogy between her suffering from unrequited love and Echo's. Stampa, a *virtuosa*—that is, a musical performer who made her living in the palazzi and academies of Venice during the 1540s—wrote a sonnet midway through her *Rime* (Venice, 1554, dedicated to Count Collaltino di Collalto), a poem in which, paradoxically, she claims the muted voice of Ovid's heroine in an energetic narrative of vocal loss. The poem opens by posing an appar-

---

⁶Jacopo Sannazaro, *Opere volgari,* ed. Alfredo Mauro (Bari: Laterza, 1961), p. 106.
⁷Luciana Borsetto, "Narciso ed Eco: Figura e scrittura nella lirica femminile del Cinquecento," in *Nel cerchio della luna: Figure di donna in alcuni testi del XVI secolo,* ed. Maria Zancan (Venice: Marsilio, 1983), pp. 192–94.

ently insoluble literary problem: how to speak of a love that drains the poet of the capacity to speak. Yet, as Fiora Bassanese points out, Stampa's claims to poetic inadequacy are often contradicted by their own dramatic force.[8] In the quatrains of Sonnet 152 she represents poetic despair as evidence of amorous despair:

> Io vorrei pur, ch'Amor dicesse, come
>   Debbo seguirlo, e con qual'arte, e stile
>   Possa sperar di far chi m'arde humìle,
>   O diporr'io queste amorose some.
> Io ho le forze homai sì fiacche e dome,
>   Sì paventosa son tornata e vile,
>   Che quasi ad Eco imagine simìle,
>   Di Donna serbo sol la voce e 'l nome.[9]

[I wish indeed that Love would tell me how I should follow him, and with what art and skill I might hope to make the man who sets me afire humble, or to lay down these burdens of love. My strength is so weakened and worn down, I have become so fearful and unworthy, that, an image almost identical to Echo, of woman I retain only the voice and name.]

But, like her opening concern with "art and style," the disembodiment Stampa attributes to her metamorphosed self still leaves her with the two attributes of a poet: a voice and a name, discursive power and literary reknown. And the pathos of her final tercet coexists with two formulas that call further attention to her powers as a poet: her claim to outdo Ovid's Echo and her placement of *favella,* a term rich in overtones of narrative, fable, fluent speech, the fascination of storytelling, as the last word of the poem:

> Né perché le vestigia del mio Sole,
>   Io segua sempre, come fece anch'ella,
>   E risponda a l'estreme sue parole,

---

[8]Fiora Bassanese, "Gaspara Stampa's Poetics of Negativity," *Italica* 61 (Autumn 1984): 336. For the debate over whether Stampa was a courtesan or a musician, see Bassanese's *Gaspara Stampa* (Boston: Twayne, 1982), pp. 26–31.

[9]Gaspara Stampa, *Rime* (Venice: Plinio Pietrasanta, 1554), p. 81. A modern version of Stampa's text, accessible and thoughtfully introduced though flawed by its adoption of Abdelkader Salza's reordering of the poems, is Maria Bellonci's edition of the *Rime* (Milan: Rizzoli, 1976).

> Posso indur la mia fiera, e dura stella
>   Ad'oprar sì, ch'ei crudo, come suole,
>   S'arresti al suon di mia stanca favella.

[Nor, even though I constantly follow the footprints of my Sun, as she did, too, and answer to his final words, can I induce my haughty and harsh star to make him, cruel as always, stop at the sound of my exhausted speech.]

In contrast to her failure to move her beloved, this speaker-poet does "arrest" the attention of a larger audience, whose sympathy and admiration the sonnet is constructed to win. Speaking as Echo, she reactivates the nymph's relation to language. No longer merely listening to Narcissus and abbreviating his words, Stampa's Echo becomes a speaker of her own desires and more, an eloquent accuser of the "cruelly" self-absorbed male beloved.

Philomel and Procne: How Not to Swallow Silence

Given the violent disruption of natural and familiar order carried out in Tereus' rape and silencing of Philomela, Ovid's narrative might seem likely to resist adaptation to amorous and pastoral convention. In fact, however, in male-authored poetry the sexual violation dwelt on in the Roman's version of the tale was condensed into a conventional topos, a periphrasis for the coming of spring: the "sad sisters" announce the new season, usually a season of melancholy for the lover-poet. Petrarca wrote two sonnets on the theme, 310 and 311 of the *Canzoniere*. The first of these poems typifies minimalist allusion to the Ovidian heroines: they appear in a single line (3) and are immediately incorporated into a joyful landscape evoked in order to emphasize the contrasting misery of the speaker.

> Zephiro torna, e 'l bel tempo rimena,
> e i fiori et l'erbe, sua dolce famiglia,
> e garrir Progne et pianger Philomena,
> et primavera candida et vermiglia.
>
> Ridono i prati, e 'l ciel si rasserena;
> Giove s'allegra di mirar sua figlia;
> l'aria e l'acqua et la terra è d'amor piena;
> ogni animal d'amar si riconsiglia.

> Ma per me, lasso, tornano i più gravi
> sospiri, che del cor profondo tragge
> quella ch'al ciel se ne portò le chiavi;
>
> et cantar augelletti, e fiorir piagge,
> e 'n belle donne honeste atti soavi
> sono un deserto, et fere aspre et selvagge.[10]

[The zephyr returns and brings back good weather, and the flowers and the grasses, his sweet family, and the complaints of Procne and the weeping of Philomela, and spring, pure white and crimson. The meadows laugh and the sky clears; Jove rejoices at the sight of his daughter; air, water and earth are full of love; every creature puts its mind again to loving. But to me, unhappy man, return the heaviest sighs, drawn up from the depths of my heart by the woman who took the keys of heaven away with her; and the singing of birds and the flowering of meadows, and gentle acts in lovely, honorable women, are a desert to me, and wild and savage beasts.]

Petrarca's references to the happy amorousness of animals in this landscape (8) and to "the gentle acts of lovely, honorable women" (13) demonstrate his lack of sustained interest in the Ovidian myth. The poem effaces Philomela's rape and Procne's revenge, purifying both into the simpler "cantar" of unspecified "augelletti." In Sonnet 311, on the nightingale, it is even clearer that Petrarca has broken Ovid's link between Philomela's grief and the plangency of the nightingale's song. Petrarch's "rosignuol" is masculine, even a paterfamilias, apparently only temporarily separated from domestic bliss: "che sì soave piagne / forse suoi figli, o sua cara consorte" ("who laments so sweetly, perhaps for his children, perhaps for his beloved mate").

Sannazaro, too, suppresses the horror of the Ovidian tale. After the invocation of Echo in his eleventh eclogue, he resilences Philomela and Procne. He shifts his emphasis from Philomela's "antichi guai" to her "soavi accenti" and represents Procne as an exemplarily repentant figure, regretting her former misdeed: "del tuo fallo ancor ti lagni e penti" ("even now you lament and regret your fault" [51]). Not only does this characterization suppress Tereus' role as rapist and provoker of later events (in the kind of maneuver analyzed elsewhere in this volume by Barbara Spackman, whereby a crime *against* a woman is

---

[10]Francesco Petrarca, *Canzoniere,* ed. Gianfranco Contini (Turin: Einaudi, 1964), p. 384.

turned into a crime *by* a woman). Sannazaro goes on to dismiss the bird sisters as poetic rivals who threaten to drown out his own performance:

> lasciate, prego, i vostri gridi intensi,
> e fin che io nel mio dir diventi roco,
> nessuna del suo mal ragioni o pensi.
>
> [52–54]

[Leave off, I pray, your wild cries, and until I myself become hoarse from speaking, let neither of you females tell or think of her misfortune.]

In Sannazaro's Arcadia there seems to be air space for only one singer at a time.

In this mythological-textual context, Gaspara Stampa's sonnet to the swallow and the nightingale can be read as a direct counterreply to Petrarca's self-isolation from the natural scene and to Sannazaro's competitive lyric. In her Sonnet 173 she establishes a relationship of willed empathy with the mythological heroines. Rather than banish them from the scene of her performance, she invites them into a chorus of lament. Allying herself with both victims of masculine cruelty, she defends Procne's revenge as a justified response to Tereus' outrage; and she establishes a criminal analogy between the king's attack on Philomela and her count's abandonment of her:

> Cantate meco Progne, e Filomena,
>   Anzi piangete il mio grave martire;
>   Hor, che la Primavera, e'l suo fiorire,
>   I miei lamenti, e voi tornando mena.
> A voi rinova la memoria, e pena
>   De l'onta di Tereo, e le giust'ire,
>   E me l'acerbo, et crudo dipartire
>   Del mio Signore morte empia rimena.

[Sing along with me, Procne and Philomel; rather, weep together over my deep suffering, now that spring and her flowering, returning, brings back my laments and you. In you, she renews the memory and the pain of Tereus' shameful act, and your just anger; in me, the sudden and cruel departure of my Lord brings back savage death.]

In the conclusion to the poem, Stampa's reproach to the men is refocused into a promise of poetic support for the women. Her apostrophe suggests that the figures worthy of trust and capable of a collaborative exchange are the Ovidian heroine-victims, to whom she vows an elegy in return. As in her sonnet on Echo, Stampa ends by modulating into a vocabulary of poetic power, into the high style and skill she promises in a confident future tense:

> Dunque essendo più fresco il mio dolore,
>   Aitatemi amiche à disfogarlo,
>   Ch'io per me non ho tanto entro vigore.
> E, se piace ad Amor mai di scemarlo,
>   Io piangerò 'l vostro à tutte le ore,
>   Con quanto stile, et arte potrò farlo.

[So, because my grief is newer, help me, friends, to release it, for I do not have enough strength within me. And if Love should ever free me of my woe, I will weep for yours at every hour, with all the skill and art I can.]

In effect, the sonnet represents its speaker as less isolated than the departure of her beloved suggests she must be. By breaking down the historical and cultural distance between herself and the mythological figures she addresses, Stampa revitalizes the myth: in the woman's poem Procne and Philomela are rewritten not into an ornamental shorthand for the coming of spring but as a fable of troubled feminine identity, eased through woman-to-woman solidarity. In both poems, this and the sonnet on Echo, Stampa turns myth into drama. She appropriates it to illustrate her own situation in the present and to manipulate a double audience: the count (how can he read such laments and remain a Narcissus?) and those Venetian readers who recognize her revision of the egotistic melancholy of pastoral and her refusal of the quasi-silence of an Echo unable to construct a discourse of erotic and poetic self-affirmation.

Tullia d'Aragona wrote a sonnet in which she, too, identified herself with Philomela. But Tullia's Philomela is represented at the moment of her escape from Tereus' prison. This fantasy of freedom is the first stage in a poem that moves its heroine through a complex series of rhetorical positions related to Tullia's profession. As a courtesan, she was constantly on view, the target of many men's gazes, and the self-consciousness in her reworking of Ovidian material corresponds to the visibility and the skill in flattery required by her career. Tullia equates Philomela's prison with the psychic prison of love and perhaps with the demands of sexual commerce: to be free of love is to resemble Philomela as airborne bird, liberated from earthly constraints. But Tullia's

Philomela escapes only temporarily. The sonnet tells a tale of recovery from one love followed immediately by entrapment in another:

> Qual vaga Philomena, che fuggita
> E da la odiata gabbia, et in superba
> Vista sen'va tra gli arboscelli, et l'herba
> Tornata in libertate, e in lieta vita;
> Er'io da gli amorosi lacci uscita
> Schernendo ogni martire, et pena acerba
> De l'incredibil duol, ch'in se riserba
> Qual ha per troppo amar l'alma smarrita.
> Ben havev'io ritolte (ahi Stella fera)
> Dal tempio di Ciprigna le mie spoglie,
> Et di lor pregio me n'andava altera;
> Quand'a me Amor, "Le tue ritrose voglie
> Muterò," disse, e femmi prigionera
> Di tua virtù, per rinovar mie doglie.[11]

[Like the longing Philomela, who has escaped from her hated prison and, proudly visible high in the sky, is flying away among trees and grasses, returned to freedom and to a life of joy, so was I freed from the bonds of love and, scornful of all suffering and pain, from the incredible grief reserved for whoever has lost her soul through loving too much. Confidently I had taken my trophies (oh, cruel star!) from the temple of Venus and, proud of their value, I was leaving it behind—when Love said to me, "I will change your stubborn will," and he made me a prisoner of your valor, to renew my suffering.]

Georgina Masson praises this poem as one in which Tullia, atypically, "wrote from her heart."[12] Certainly its first lines celebrate an exhilarating loosening of bonds, and the story is narrated to a general audience rather than to the specific men Tullia usually names as addressees in her poems.

Yet the sonnet also remains implicated in the discursive requirements of Tullia's courtesanship. Even her opening image of freedom is ambiguous. While it seems reasonable to interpret "la odiata gabbia" as a

---

[11]Tullia d'Aragona, *Rime della Signora Tulla d'Aragona; et di diversi a lei* (Venice: Giolito de Ferrari, 1547), p. 10. A modern edition, in which the poems have been reordered and occasionally prefaced with names of addressees not present in the original, is Enrico Celani, *Le rime di Tullia d'Aragona, cortigiana del secolo XVI* (Bologna: Forni, 1968), reprint of Gaetano Romagnoli's edition (Bologna, 1891).

[12]Georgina Masson, *Courtesans of the Italian Renaissance* (New York: St. Martin's, 1975), p. 118.

symbol for the sexual demands and legal dangers that the courtesan imagines eluding, the poet also fixes her heroine in a position of public desirability. Philomela's flight is described in visual terms ("in superba vista" [2–3]) which imply that she is still the focus of many eyes.

Tullia's use of "l'alma smarrita" (8) may mark her awareness of another audience, as well. "Smarrita," in its Dantesque overtones, implies repentance, or at least a recognition of the spiritual consequences of passion; thus Tullia hints at the conversion she claimed throughout her collection of poems, in an attempt to win the support of her royal patrons, the Medici. Even so, a compliment to lesser clients remains a necessity for the courtesan-poet. Tullia sets up a sliding signifier that potentially flatters all men: the vagueness of her allusion to her two lovers strategically leaves their identity unfixed. By naming neither man, she leaves open the honor of having been her first or second beloved to any man reading the poem. Then, too, Tullia's Amor acts as a go-between, a procurer for the man; his command forces the woman to comply with the desires of the new beloved whose interests he serves. By assigning such power to Amor, Tullia encourages the male reader to imagine the pleasures of her obedience. Her adoption of the figure of Eros guarantees the intensity of her passion for a beloved who she invites her reader to imagine might be himself. Tullia's sonnet, then, is significantly shaped by the multiple audiences she woos throughout her *Rime*. Nonetheless, its opening permits a glimpse of a transformed speaker, a free bird-woman singing a melody as yet unheard in the cities and courts of the Cinquecento.

I want to end my analysis of women poets' metamorphoses of Ovid with a startling and challenging poem by Gaspara Stampa. She, too, performs for a multiple audience in her Sonnet 174. But this is a counter*blason,* a list of the male beloved's misdeeds that extends the accusation in the preceding sonnet into a full-scale denunciation of masculine cruelty:

> Una inaudita e nova crudeltate,
>> un esser al fuggir pronto e leggiero,
>> un andar troppo di sue doti altero,
>> un tôrre ad altri la sua libertate,
> Un vedermi penar senza pietate,
>> un aver sempre a' miei danni il pensiero,
>> un ridir di mia morte quando pèro,
>> un aver voglie ognor fredde e gelate,

Un eterno timor di lontananza,
   un verno eterno senza primavera,
   un non dar mai cibo a la speranza. . . .

[An unheard of, extraordinary cruelty, a prompt and fickle readiness for flight, a carriage too proud of inborn graces, a habit of stealing others' freedom away, the ability to watch me suffer without pity, thoughts constantly wishing me harm, laughter at my death as I lie perishing, desires always as cold as ice, an endless fear of separation, an endless winter without any spring, a refusal ever to give food to hope. . . .]

The vehicle for this turn from pastoral melancholy to satiric attack is Stampa's self-transformation, her representation of herself as another female creature from Ovid: here she is no longer a long-suffering victim of masculine betrayal but a figure of terror, the Chimera. In the *Metamorphoses,* Ovid alludes briefly to this monster (6, 339), a fire-breathing composite of animal parts including the bust of a lion, the body of a goat, and the hindquarters of a dragon. The Chimera laid waste the province of Lycia until she was finally slain by Bellerophon. The aspect of the creature emphasized by Stampa, however, is not her defeat by the hero but her miraculous nature, which the poet intensifies by associating herself with a tumultuous sea, the "abyss" or lethal whirlpool into which Scylla, another victim of love, was transformed:

m'han fatto divenir una Chimera,
   uno abisso confuso, un mar, ch'avanza
   d'onde et tempeste una marina vera.

[All these have turned me into a Chimera, a confused abyss, a sea that exceeds in breakers and tempests any actual seacoast.]

Rather than modeling herself on the gentle Philomela, Stampa claims the Chimera's power to strike awe into men's hearts. Like the Sphinx or Medusa, she aims for an effect of fearful wonder, of epic *meraviglia* rather than Arcadian pathos. The poem is directed not at the male beloved as an appeal for pity but to a larger audience invited to marvel at the change in the speaker and to admire the drama of her sonnet: its reversal of laudatory convention, its relentless parallel structure, its unexpected ending. Stampa selects and recombines Ovid's female models to construct a powerfully accusatory figure who denounces masculine indifference and refuses feminine passivity. In spite of the poem's apparent dependence on the Roman poet and its fixation on the Venetian count, the woman lover as woman poet is the active figure in Stampa's *blason*. This is imitation with a vengeance.

Modern Readers: The Feminist Critic as Procne

Three modern critical texts, written by Christiane Makward, Caren Greenberg, and Jane Marcus, suggests that the figures of Echo and Philomela have retained their power to disturb—but that when the readers are women, they may welcome the disturbance of gender and lyric norms. Makward frames her essay, a study of Marguerite Duras and Hélène Cixous, with a discussion of Echo and Philomela as figures for feminine silence and delirium. But she interprets both modes of discourse as deliberately destabilizing choices on the part of contemporary women writers. If male critics cannot comprehend these new languages, Makward suggests, the feminist theoretician of language can. She traces a movement from hysterical regression in Duras's refusal of masculine assertion (a resistant silence) to paranoid power in Cixous's celebratory interweaving of schizophrenic discourses (a positive wildness in language). Makward concludes by defining this progression as a transformation of the entrapped woman into the woman with wings, a "Narcissea" entering "the age of glory."[13]

In a reinterpretation of the Echo myth that shifts the emphasis from woman as writer to woman as reader, Caren Greenberg explores Ovid's text as an allegory of feminine critical revision replacing narcissistic masculine declaration. Reading the figure of Echo as a woman approaching male speech according to her own desires, Greenberg suggests that the violent aggressivity in two versions of the myth (Ovid's stress on Echo's gradual disembodiment, Longus' narration of Pan's dismembering and scattering of the nymph's body) are symptoms of male anxiety, raised by the threat to male authorship implicit in Echo's revisions of Narcissus' words: "Like a printed text, Echo's body provides a new location for his words, and Echo's voice provides a new reading of his text. At this point Echo's body stands instead of Narcissus' body as a point of origin for his speech, but her body is at the same time a locus of her own sexual desires."[14] Hence, in the men's

---

[13]Christiane Makward, "Structures du silence / du délire: Marguerite Duras / Hélène Cixous," *Poétique* 35 (September 1978): 324.

[14]Caren Greenberg, "Reading Reading: Echo's Abduction of Language," in *Women*

texts the wasting away and chopping up of that menacing body as a force of counterreading. Greenberg's conclusion resonates strikingly with my sense of the liberating processes at work in Cinquecento women's rereading and rewriting of Ovid. As Greenberg suggests, such revisions of a presumably fixed text and tradition transform masculine literary affiliation and critical practice into new and more flexible processes of writing and reading: "Repetition by a different-sex speaker is a creative act of reading involving a new locus of desire." Similarly: "The acceptance of the critical act as creative rather than destructive and the creative act as something of a reading (of self, of texts, of the reader, for example) permits Echo to read Echo and Echo to write Echo" (pp. 307–8).

A similar link between writing and reading is drawn by Jane Marcus, arguing for a materialist-feminist criticism. She opens her politically motivated reassessment of the Philomela myth by referring to Virginia Woolf's retelling of the story in *Between the Acts* as "an appropriate metaphor for the silencing of the female, for rape and male violence against women."[15] But, like Greenberg, she then explores the positive potential of feminist criticism as a mode of identificatory and transformative reading. Marcus interprets the two figures of the myth as follows: "The voice of the nightingale, the voice of the shuttle weaving its story of oppression, is the voice which cries for freedom. . . . The voice of the swallow, . . . Procne's voice, is the voice of the reader, the translator, the . . . feminist speaking for her sisters; . . . the voice which . . . demands justice" (p. 79).

Is it anachronistic to suggest that Italian women poets of the Cinquecento were Procnes, too—critical readers of the Ovidian tradition, translators of their own Philomelas and Echos, reweavers of the mythological threads they drew out of a masculine fabric of representations? And in what relations to those bird-women do we, today's readers, stand, listening for a new song in Renaissance figurations of women by women?

---

and Language in Literature and Society, ed. Sally McConnell-Ginet, Ruth Borker, and Nelly Furman (New York: Praeger, 1980), p. 305.

[15]Jane Marcus, "Still Practice, A/Wrested Alphabet: Toward a Feminist Aesthetic," *Tulsa Studies in Women's Literature* 3 (Spring–Fall 1984): 79. For another powerful feminist rereading, see Patricia Klindienst Joplin's critique of the original Greek myth as a displacement of male dynastic and political violence onto women and her suggestion that feminist critics can read it as an example of resistance instead, as an alternative model of peace-establishing communication among women; "The Voice of the Shuttle Is Ours," *Stanford Literature Review* 1 (Spring 1984): 25–53.

CONTRIBUTORS

STANLEY CHOJNACKI is Professor of History at Michigan State University. He has written essays on the public and private experience of Venetian patricians in the late Middle Ages and Renaissance. Currently he is completing a synthesis of Venetian patrician society.

ELENA CILETTI, Associate Professor and Chair of the Department of Art at Hobart and William Smith Colleges, is currently working on a book on Anna Maria Luisa de' Medici and eighteenth-century patronage. She has published in *Mitteilungen des Kunsthistorischen Institutes in Florenz, Paragone, Burlington Magazine,* and *Women's Art Journal.*

ELIZABETH S. COHEN teaches history and humanities at York University. She has published on gender relations in Renaissance Europe in *Histoire Sociale / Social History* and *Continuity and Change.* Together with Thomas Cohen, she is completing a book manuscript tentatively entitled "Words and Deeds in Renaissance Rome."

CARLA FRECCERO, Associate Professor of French at Dartmouth College, has written a book on François Rabelais's narrative structures and has published numerous articles, including feminist analyses of Rabelais, a biographical essay on the poet-activist June Jordan, an analysis of the feminist "sex wars" in the United States, and a study of rape in the tenth novella of Marguerite de Navarre's *Heptameron.* She is currently completing a book on the interrelation of history and literature in the *Heptameron* and an essay about the politics of Madonna's music videos.

STEPHANIE H JED, Associate Professor of Italian and Comparative Literature at the University of California at San Diego, is author of *Chaste*

Thinking: The Rape of Lucretia and the Birth of Humanism (1989). Her current research deals with issues of literacy, power, gender, and interethnic contacts in sixteenth-century Italy.

ANN ROSALIND JONES is Professor of Comparative Literature at Smith College. She has published works on feminist literary theory and on Renaissance texts of various kinds: the novel (Thomas Nashe), drama (Webster), and lyric (Scève and Sidney). Her study of women's love lyric in the Renaissance, *The Currency of Eros,* was published in 1990.

CLAUDIA LAZZARO, Associate Professor of the History of Art at Cornell University, is author of *The Italian Renaissance Garden: From the Conventions of Planting, Design, and Ornament to the Grand Gardens of Sixteenth-Century Central Italy* (1990) and several articles on Renaissance villas and gardens. She is currently studying allegories of love and lust in Renaissance painting and prints.

MARILYN MIGIEL, Associate Professor of Italian and Director of Medieval Studies at Cornell University, has published essays in *Italica, Quaderni d'italianistica, Stanford Italian Review,* and *diacritics.* She is currently working on a study of gender and medieval and Renaissance Italian literature.

JULIANA SCHIESARI, Assistant Professor of Italian at the University of California at Davis, has published essays on Tasso, Ariosto, Alfieri, and the genealogy of gender morals in Renaissance Italy. She has recently completed a book on gender and melancholia.

BARBARA SPACKMAN, Associate Professor of Italian and Comparative Literature at the University of California at Irvine, is author of *Decadent Genealogies: The Rhetoric of Sickness from Baudelaire to D'Annunzio* (1989). She has written on Machiavelli, Marinetti, and D'Annunzio and is currently working on a study of the rhetoric of fascism.

SHARON T. STROCCHIA, Assistant Professor of History at Emory University, has completed a book manuscript entitled "Death and Ritual in Renaissance Florence." She is now studying the social history of Benedictine convents in Renaissance Florence.

INDEX

Library of Congress Cataloging-in-Publication Data

Refiguring woman : perspectives on gender and the Italian Renaissance / edited with an
introduction by Marilyn Migiel and Juliana Schiesari.
    p.   cm.
  Includes bibliographical references and index.
  ISBN 0-8014-2538-7 (alk. paper). — ISBN 0-8014-9771-X (pbk. : alk. paper)
    1. Sex role—Italy—History—Congresses.   2. Women—Italy—History—Renaissance,
1450–1600—Congresses.   3. Patriarchy—Italy—History—Congresses.   4. Italian
literature—16th century—History and criticism—Congresses.   I. Migiel, Marilyn,
1954–   .   II. Schiesari, Juliana.
HQ1075.5.I8R44 1991
305.3'0945—dc20   90-55736